Close-Up

Volume 1: America

International Film Stars
Series Editor: Homer B. Pettey and R. Barton Palmer

This series is devoted to the artistic and commercial influence of performers who shaped major genres and movements in international film history. Books in the series will:

- Reveal performative features that defined signature cinematic styles
- Demonstrate how the global market relied upon performers' generic contributions
- Analyse specific film productions as case studies that transformed cinema acting
- Construct models for redefining international star studies that emphasise materialist approaches
- Provide accounts of stars' influences in the international cinema marketplace

Titles available:

Close-Up: Great Cinematic Performances Volume 1: America
edited by Murray Pomerance and Kyle Stevens

Close-Up: Great Cinematic Performances Volume 2: International
edited by Murray Pomerance and Kyle Stevens

www.euppublishing.com/series/ifs

Close-Up

Great Cinematic Performances

Volume 1: America

Edited by Murray Pomerance
and Kyle Stevens

EDINBURGH
University Press

Edinburgh University Press is one of the leading university presses in the UK. We publish academic books and journals in our selected subject areas across the humanities and social sciences, combining cutting-edge scholarship with high editorial and production values to produce academic works of lasting importance. For more information visit our website: edinburghuniversitypress.com

© editorial matter and organization Murray Pomerance and Kyle Stevens, 2018, 2019
© the chapters their several authors, 2018, 2019

Edinburgh University Press Ltd
The Tun—Holyrood Road
12 (2f) Jackson's Entry
Edinburgh EH8 8PJ

First published in hardback by Edinburgh University Press 2018

Typeset in 12/14 Arno and Myriad by
IDSUK (Dataconnection) Ltd, and
printed and bound by CPI Group (UK) Ltd, Croydon, CR0 4YY

A CIP record for this book is available from the British Library

ISBN 978 1 4744 1700 6 (hardback)
ISBN 978 1 4744 3179 8 (paperback)
ISBN 978 1 4744 1701 3 (webready PDF)
ISBN 978 1 4744 1702 0 (epub)

The right of the contributors to be identified as authors of this work has been asserted in accordance with the Copyright, Designs and Patents Act 1988 and the Copyright and Related Rights Regulations 2003 (SI No. 2498).

Images (all digital frame enlargements)
Ethel Waters in *The Member of the Wedding* (Fred Zinnemann, Stanley Kramer Productions, 1952)
Irene Dunne in *The Awful Truth* (Leo McCarey, Columbia, 1937)
Cary Grant in *His Girl Friday* (Howard Hawks, Columbia, 1940)
Janet Gaynor in *Sunrise: A Song of Two Humans* (F. W. Murnau, Fox, 1927)
Katharine Hepburn in *The Lion in Winter* (Anthony Harvey, AVCO Embassy, 1968)
Bette Davis in *Dangerous* (Alfred E. Green, Warner Bros., 1935)
James Stewart in *Vertigo* (Alfred Hitchcock, Paramount, 1958)
Carole Lombard in *To Be or Not to Be* (Ernst Lubitsch, Romaine Film Corporation, 1942)
James Mason in *Lolita* (Stanley Kubrick, MGM, 1962)
Montgomery Clift in *A Place in the Sun* (George Stevens, Paramount, 1951)
Tony Curtis in *Sweet Smell of Success* (Alexander Mackendrick, Hecht-Hill-Lancaster, 1957)
Peter Sellers in *The Pink Panther* (Blake Edwards, Mirisch, 1963)
Richard Burton in *The Spy Who Came In from the Cold* (Martin Ritt, Salem, 1965)
Jerry Lewis in *The King of Comedy* (Martin Scorsese, Embassy/Twentieth Century Fox, 1982)
Sidney Poitier in *In the Heat of the Night* (Norman Jewison, Mirisch, 1967)
Gene Hackman in *The Conversation* (Francis Ford Coppola, American Zoetrope, 1974)
Gena Rowlands in *Gloria* (John Cassavetes, Columbia, 1980)
Jack Nicholson in *The Passenger (Professione: Reporter)* (Michelangelo Antonioni, MGM, 1975)
Dustin Hoffman in *Rain Man* (Barry Levinson, United Artists, 1988)
Elliott Gould in *The Long Goodbye* (Robert Altman, Lion's Gate, 1973)
Al Pacino in *Donnie Brasco* (Mike Newell, Mandalay, 1997)
Whoopi Goldberg in *The Color Purple* (Steven Spielberg, Amblin, 1985)
Cate Blanchett in *Blue Jasmine* (Woody Allen, Gravier/Perdido, 2013)
Oscar Isaac in *A Most Violent Year* (J. C. Chandor, Washington Square, 2014)
Kristen Stewart in *Clouds of Sils Maria* (Olivier Assayas, CG Cinéma, 2014)

Contents

Acknowledgments — vii

Close-up: great American performances — 1
Kyle Stevens and Murray Pomerance

1. Ethel Waters in *The Member of the Wedding* — 13
   Anna Everett
2. Irene Dunne in *The Awful Truth* — 25
   Steven Rybin
3. Cary Grant in *His Girl Friday* — 36
   Adrienne L. McLean
4. Janet Gaynor in *Sunrise: A Song of Two Humans* — 47
   Janet Bergstrom
5. Katharine Hepburn in *The Lion in Winter* — 56
   Homer B. Pettey
6. Bette Davis in *Dangerous* — 67
   Lucy Fischer
7. James Stewart in *Vertigo* — 79
   William Rothman
8. Carole Lombard in *To Be or Not to Be* — 91
   Alex Clayton
9. James Mason in *Lolita* — 100
   Rebecca Bell-Metereau
10. Montgomery Clift in *A Place in the Sun* — 111
    George Toles
11. Tony Curtis in *Sweet Smell of Success* — 124
    John Bruns

12	Peter Sellers in *The Pink Panther* Daniel Varndell	135
13	Richard Burton in *The Spy Who Came in from the Cold* R. Barton Palmer	147
14	Jerry Lewis in *The King of Comedy* Murray Pomerance	158
15	Sidney Poitier in *In the Heat of the Night* Frances Gateward	169
16	Gene Hackman in *The Conversation* Brenda Austin-Smith	178
17	Gena Rowlands in *Gloria* David Greven	188
18	Jack Nicholson in *The Passenger* Rick Warner	199
19	Dustin Hoffman in *Rain Man* Jason Jacobs	212
20	Elliott Gould in *The Long Goodbye* Douglas McFarland	223
21	Al Pacino in *Donnie Brasco* Timotheus Vermeulen	234
22	Whoopi Goldberg in *The Color Purple* Lester D. Friedman	243
23	Cate Blanchett in *Blue Jasmine* Shonni Enelow	253
24	Oscar Isaac in *A Most Violent Year* Charles Ramírez Berg	263
25	Kristen Stewart in *Clouds of Sils Maria* Elliott Logan	274

The cast	286
The contributors	288
Index	294

Acknowledgments

We wish to express gratitude to our friends and collaborators at Edinburgh University Press—Eddie Clark, Gillian Leslie, Rebecca Mackenzie, Emma Rees, and Richard Strachan—as well as to Barton Palmer and Homer Pettey for welcoming this volume into their series, "International Film Stars"; also to Sarah Burnett for copy-editing and Steve Flemming for cover design.

Further assistance along the way has come from Matt Bell, Başak Candar, Alex Clayton, Nick Davis, Mark Kermode, Chris Meade, David Orvis, Bob Rubin, Jonathan Soja, Rick Warner, and Evan Williams.

Our families have sheltered us in the storms of production, such as any endeavor involving the art of performance inevitably endures. We dedicate these volumes to James Pearson, Nellie Perret, and Ariel Pomerance.

To be natural is such a very difficult pose to keep up.
(Oscar Wilde)

An actor relaxes in front of the camera by concentrating.
(Michael Caine)

Close-up: great American performances

Kyle Stevens and Murray Pomerance

The twentieth century may one day be known as the era of performance in American culture. The thought, "All the world's a stage,/And all the men and women merely players" comes from Shakespeare's *Twelfth Night* (1602). But, at the broadest level, thinking of the widespread nature of performance, and of the manifold ramification of performances in organized life, involves a movement away from the shared belief, if not assumption, that an all-powerful god authored and continually re-authors the world. We feel inspired now to consider the nature of action and agency, to wonder what is behind the visible act and what it implies. In crime fiction and popular culture, since the 1940s certainly, authors have figured what Ian Sansom, in a review of Dorothy B. Hughes's *In a Lonely Place* (1947), called the "illusion of the 'normal'" (15). In academic circles, starting in the 1950s, Erving Goffman's dramaturgical analysis expanded the field of sociology by elucidating the performative aspects of self-presentation in everyday life. Following him, and Elizabeth Burns's work on theatricality, Judith Butler helped propel massive social change by arguing for the extent to which sex and gender can be conceptualized as performative in ways that are inherently culturally conditioned. Goffman's and Butler's work, in turn helped give rise to the field of Performance Studies, the case for which was made largely by Richard Schechner. In philosophy, Ludwig Wittgenstein, J. L. Austin, and Stanley Cavell effected a change in thinking about language and truth by expanding the purview of thinking from what is said to how it is said, that is, to the theatricality of language use. In the realm of expressive culture, of course, cinema as a performance-driven art burst forth at least from the late 1910s to dominate the popular ethos. Now that screen fictions are a presence in our daily, if not hourly, lives, aesthetic performances shape our perceptions of others as never before: what types of people we detect, what gestures we attend to, what assumptions we make about them, and so forth. So it makes good sense to study screen performances.

This collection treats seriously film performance as a meaningful, and even poetic, aspect of film style. Doing so does not necessitate giving actors power or authority over our experiences as audience members, nor does it perpetuate intentional fallacies of authorship. Rather, contributors to this volume consider the results of actors' work as a hermeneutic. The twenty-five chapters that follow all aim to demonstrate the richness of the conversations we can have when we attend carefully, even lovingly, to *precisely* the sights and sounds of the onscreen figures who so captivate us. What are the extents to which screen acting can proceed? How do screen performances play upon our sensitivities as we watch the screen?

The underestimation of screen performance

The present book, dedicated to what we are terming American cinema, is the first of a two-volume set. "American cinema" is, of course, a fraught term. One might choose, for example, a foreign-born performer headlining an important Hollywood film helmed by a major American director, and call the work an American performance. Some few of the actors written about here are not citizens of the United States, but their work figured in works produced by American personnel predominantly for an American audience, and it is therefore work that addressed American sensibility first and foremost. Their screen work in the films discussed by these contributors constitutes a kind of American moment. Volume 2 will consider the international scene. Our authors emerge from variant academic backgrounds and biographical experiences, and bring a wide-ranging and stimulating set of approaches to the question of what actors do in their "great" moments.

Both volumes of this collection investigate and illuminate single performances. This approach may seem to be common-sensical, as indeed it is, but it is an approach that has rarely been taken within the history of film theory and criticism. A few words are necessary in order to account for the novelty of our strategy. Generally, the dearth of scholarship on the art of screen performance is often bemoaned. James Naremore observed in 2006 that

> most of the serious books on directors or individual films virtually ignore the theatrical dimensions of the medium and the essential artistic contributions of performers. The aesthetics and ideology of cinema tend to be discussed in quasi-literary terms, or almost exclusively in terms of the cinema-specific aspects of narrative, editing, and directorial mise-en-scène. (62)

This critical skittishness presumably stems not only from a literary-based and deeply entrenched preference for story construction but from the notion that performance connotes a distressing degree of presence, and thereby disinters an affinity with the art of theatre that cinema studies has tried, pointlessly, we think, to bury since its inception. As the study of film grew into an academic discipline in the 1970s, scholars fervently wanted to look outside a film itself—to semiotics, to psychoanalysis, to the science of Althusserian Marxism—to understand the medium. Yet breaking down each signifier of a face as it unfolds its expressions over time is often too complex a task, and, even if one tried it, the result would not be scientific since others might disagree about when one emotional display shaded into the next, or about what vocabulary could best be attributed to each expression. And, indeed, a performance onscreen is about more than expression.

Another reason that acting *per se* has been historically neglected within Film Studies is "because of its seeming dominance within popular discourse on the movies," a dominance that was certainly notable, with critics and reviewers early on having had little or no knowledge about the mechanics of production and the history of filmmaking and thus finding themselves forced to talk about actors alone, and doing so in an opinionated but not especially curious manner (Wojcik 1). So, the implication goes, screen acting is not sufficiently academic a topic. Further, in part audiences pay attention to actors because they most obviously *appear* to author the motion picture, to be associated with it—this indubitably a result of actor presence being touted in advertising. Actors' doings are what the audience sees done, directly in film or indirectly as performers visit popular mass cultural venues such as *Entertainment Tonight* to give interviews about their current work. This plain-sightedness underpins the common impulse to refer to movie characters by the names of the actors, as when people talk of "a Julia Roberts movie," or, reflecting on one they have just seen, comment on how "Julia Roberts does this," or "Julia does that," with no reference to the fact that she was working to embody a character. Film theorists have folded this phenomenon of actor-identification into discussions of the cinematic medium's special ability to capture reality: the actor's presence *as self* destabilizes fictional constructions. Besides, this verbal slippage between actor and character need not impede one's ability to reflect on portrayal and talent. We know that when we talk to our friends about how moved we were by what Judy Garland did, singing about rainbows with her little doggie, we are really reflecting on having been affected by *this* Judy Garland, giving *this* performance (not as Judy but as Dorothy), in this present *Wizard of Oz* (1939). And even if the medium encourages us to focus on the being who was once alive during the space and time recorded and projected before us—Garland, say, in the summer of 1939—our experience of the power of specific film performances, and our desire to talk about them with others, is surely also a testament to their nature as art.

Furthermore, at least implicitly, critics have dwelled on elements of editing and cinematography with the understanding that audiences simply already care about the actors—which, following the Brechtian 1970s poststructuralist revolution, was understood to be a symptom of a problematic attachment to the pleasures of narrative, a distraction from more formal elements deemed worthy of notice. But although actors may benefit from being obvious narrative agents, and from the fact that the human face is a perceptually privileged object, it does not follow that audiences are thinking carefully about performance as form, or, indeed, as accomplishment. So the supposedly organic impulse to talk about performance actually hinders its discussion, for we become blind to the complexity of the simultaneous choices before us. In some sense, it is easier to dwell upon what directors do, why, for instance, Stanley Kubrick chose red for the color of his pool table in *Eyes Wide Shut* (1999) or that astonishing angle which allows us to see planets in eclipse at the opening of *2001: A Space Odyssey* (1968), than it is to think about why, dancing in his clothes in front of his mirror in Jude Law's bedroom in *The Talented Mr. Ripley* (1999), Matt Damon chose to make those particular smiling expressions.

Film Studies' antipathy has placed a large burden on screen performance scholarship to provide the tools necessary to understand the history of performance, and to defend its legitimacy as a topic from those critics and scholars who denigrate the labor of performers as theatrical (or worse, who believe that the true cinephile is so visually oriented as to care only about seeing "bodies in space"). Thus, extant texts seek to generalize and to theorize, to illuminate broad patterns. This is important and valuable work, drawn upon in chapters of the current volume, yet it rarely aims to understand the accomplishments of individual actors or to shed light on particular cases. It doesn't look closely, deeply, or movingly enough.

Andrew Klevan notes that there are two ways cinematic performance has generally been discussed. The first is "a field of film commentary that examines performers as 'stars' and assesses their significance from a range of contexts and cultures" (i). The other field "places emphasis on 'acting,' exploring, for example, the influence of the Melodramatic, Vaudeville (or Music Hall), Continental Cabaret, Stanislavsky or Method techniques," and so forth (i). The former perspective, star analysis, gained traction in the 1980s due to Richard Dyer's groundbreaking work, which precipitated attention to the phenomenon of stardom, what stars' personae signify, and how this signification embodies ideological tensions at given historical moments. As Pamela Robertson Wojcik writes, "Since performance and persona are seen as inseparable, descriptions of acting in film tend to be descriptions of an actor's persona across a body of work, or an analysis of a type, rather than close descriptions of individual performances" (2). The last section of Naremore's *Acting in the Cinema* and essays in Lesley Stern and George Kouvaros's *Falling for You: Essays on Cinema and Performance* attend to specific actors, but first through the lens of stardom, as does Charles Affron's *Cinema and Sentiment*. Attending to the labor of stars may provide an entrée into the machinations of the Hollywood studio system and be a means of describing behind-the-scenes techniques, or of justifying the recounting of entertaining anecdotes. However, by isolating individual performances this volume does not seek "to extract particular mannerisms or gestures that are repeated across a body of films as a feature of the star's persona" (Wojcik 7). Partly for this reason we do not include here performances by many highly regarded actors who have already received quite sophisticated attention, such as Marlon Brando, Charlie Chaplin, James Dean, Greta Garbo, Marilyn Monroe, and Meryl Streep.

The second perspective that Klevan isolates (the turn to considering actorly training) is found in works aside from Naremore's book, including Cynthia Baron and Sharon Marie Carnicke's *More Than A Method: Trends and Traditions in Contemporary Film Performance*, Roberta Pearson's *Eloquent Gestures*, Murray Pomerance's *Moment of Action: Riddles of Cinematic Performance*, and Kyle Stevens's *Mike Nichols: Sex, Language, and the Reinvention of Psychological Realism*. Somewhat surprisingly, even these discussions of pedagogical methods have historically focused on stars. Most famously, discussions of The Actors Studio, centering on Lee Strasberg's and Stella Adler's versions of Stanislavksy's famed Method, revolve around stars like Brando, Faye Dunaway, Robert De Niro, and Dustin Hoffman. Moreover, we must be careful to temper the explanatory force of the knowledge of actors' training. Do we really perceive similarities between James Dean's in *Giant* (1956) and Jane Fonda's in *Barefoot in the Park* (1957) because they both studied under Strasberg?

We might recognize something like an ethical turn in terms of the politics of representation that dovetails with discussions of performance in recent decades. Critics nowadays question whether the body of a figure onscreen is good or bad for cultural progress toward civil equality (often phrased in terms of stereotypy and inclusion). This extends to concern for the politics of industrial labor, about what sort of people have access to what sort of work, a concern that crystallizes around casting choices. Yet these discussions, like the emphasis on stardom, tend to be about the body of the actor as cultural marker, and not about the creation of character or affect as an occupational accomplishment.

Representation and expression

All of these approaches are predicated upon a notion of cinema that involves faith in its power to index reality, to *represent* bodies and identities in the everyday world. Such "journalistic" representation, of course, raises identity issues about such categories as race, class, age, and gender. But far beyond merely pointing to who their characters are in terms of these classifications (sociologically, politically, psychologically), performers can lead us to examine and wonder about how they express and model behavior—ways to flirt, giggle, or wither with a look. Holding fast to the idea that cinema is fundamentally a medium of representation—a window on the world—reinforces the need to see stars or actors rather than fictional characters, presence rather than imagination. This attachment to the logic that good performances are either a function of filmic technology or of the actor's mere physical presence, and concomitant resistance to conceptualizing screen acting as an expressive art, extend back to the early days of narrative feature-length films. In his classic essay, "The Work of Art in the Age of Mechanical Reproduction," for example, Walter Benjamin laid out a system of thinking about film actors, the tenor of which has proven remarkably durable. He first compared the screen actor to the stage actor, noting that while "[t]he stage actor identifies himself with the character of his role" we cannot say the same of the screen actor, due to the fragmentary nature of film editing and the many performances given over the course of shooting. He found that "the performance of the actor is subjected to a series of optical tests" (122). Writing in 1936, he persists in thinking of film acting as silent film acting, leading to his even more damning suggestion, by describing actors as mere puppets, that actors' labor was not even worthy of the name of craft, much less art:

> Let us assume that an actor is supposed to be startled by a knock at the door. If his reaction is not satisfactory, the director can resort to an expedient: when the actor happens to be at the studio again he has a shot fired behind him without his being forewarned of it. The frightened reaction can be shot now and be cut into the screen version. Nothing more strikingly shows that art has left the realm of the "beautiful semblance" which, so far, had been taken to be the only sphere where art could thrive. (123)

Although Benjamin is right that since the ancient Greeks mimetic action has been the marker of poetry, of art, nevertheless by removing semblance as a necessary condition for a successful screen performance he removes it from the realm of the aesthetic. But performance must always be alive in the realm of the aesthetic.

Similar statements abound in the history of film and writing about film. In his famous essay "Magnification," Jean Epstein writes that "The close-up is the soul of cinema," attributing his reveries to the technology, to the proximity of camera to human gesture, not mentioning the actor at all (234). Similarly, Béla Balázs extolls the technological ability to "penetrate to a strange new dimension of the soul," rather than an actor's ability to present a soul for penetration (65). This is not to mention Lev Kuleshov's famed experiment that supposedly proved that facial expression can be a function of editing. In all these views, good acting was attributed to the magic of the medium, not to the force or quality of the actor.

Neorealist lineages and Method orthodoxies share this Benjaminian line of thought by preserving the myth that actors are simply "playing themselves." This implies, of course, that the actors aren't *acting*. They are not *creating* something that refers to the world. They are simply allowing themselves to be captured while being. However, not all depictions of self-expression—just as not all self-expressions—are aesthetically valuable. As Susanne Langer writes, "The laws of emotional catharsis are natural laws, not artistic" (216). There is thus something more than being affected that makes a performance successful. We want to get at *that* in this book.

In order to appreciate the importance of the actor's art to cinematic language, we must do more than pay lip service to the so often glibly adduced duality inherent in screen performance—that the actor is not the character. We must be able to conceptualize the "I" from which we might say that an actor speaks, in the way that a poet, director, or novelist does. We know that this voice is not identical to the voice of the person, although at the cinema it is often folded immediately into the appearance of the actor, an impression that is heightened when that actor is a star, since the actor uses his or her own body and voice to create a fictive voice to create a character. The conflation of actor and fictive voice is an easy one to make, but we must make that distinction, for without a sense of that poetic voice, we cannot have a sense of acting as a mode of fictional representation. The chapters in this book help us to do so by carefully describing the precise intricacies of particular performances.

Description

Etymologically, "to perform" denotes to act, to finish, to carry out, to execute. It is natural for us, in our own day-to-day existences, to call any action that is completed "performed." Hence, to study performance is something of a self-conscious act. In a way, even to think about it is also to do it, so it is organic that many of the following chapters involve moments that reflect upon the activities of both writing and movie-going. But this is not to say that description and analysis of performance are simply subjective, or of merely diaristic significance. Our collection thus aims to demonstrate the value of the thick description of performances and our experiences of them—an aim that often requires authors to acknowledge their own role in shaping what they are relaying having seen and heard. Girish Shambu argues in *The New Cinephilia* that we live in an age that is skeptical of the value of description, a mindset that extends back to the advent of the discipline. He quotes Stern and Kouvaros: "One could argue that—in Anglo-Saxon scholarship at least—post-1970s theory entailed a decided rejection of the descriptive (conceived of as always duplicitous, subjective, rhetorical, misleadingly mimetic) in favor of a turn towards a more scientific or technical language" (12). So, in part, subtending the following chapters are the questions: What sort of descriptive work has the field historically avoided? What has the scientific or technical turn taken us away from, and toward? Why has description been abandoned? What are we afraid of knowing about movies if we emphasize the claims that performed human actions make upon us?

We do not attempt to pinpoint the answers to such questions with scientific precision, partly since the very impulse to pinpoint objective claims with scientific precision may be part of the problem. We do not need to posit a hypothetical, idealized spectator in order to talk about our responses, and how we might view them in relation to the text we agree is before us. We start where we are as both audience members and writers, nor can a richly feelingful and deeply sensitive reading of performance be possible in any other way; but one must take care—every private view is not necessarily shared, yet to some extent private views may be, and part of our challenge in looking at screen acting is to try to determine that extent. Disavowing one's subjectivity and specificity can be as narcissistic a gesture as proclaiming them, whereas offering up one's own experience to the world to see if others can entertain it—question it, engage with it—is a gesture of conversation.

In his *Moment of Action*, Pomerance writes: "Not knowing the personality of the actor it is virtually impossible to discern the boundaries of the performance with accuracy" (4). One may never know to what extent the actor was "really" feeling something while the camera was rolling—even the actor may never know. And because so little attention was typically given to preserving records of soundstage interactions, we are blocked from all but surmising what impact on a performative moment came from the director, the producer, the cinematographer, or an actor's comrades on set. But this should not bother us. Conscious intention at every level need not be a criterion for effective art. Pomerance continues: "When we consider performances that have touched and provoked us, we call up biography, memory, desire, feeling, and orientation—in short, the self. Since cultural studies began to exert its hegemony over intellectual life it has seemed unfashionable, even futile, to enunciate the self" (16). So, while writers of the following chapters do not pretend to look and listen from an objective standpoint, imagining themselves as an Everyviewer, the aim is to elucidate the performances. And finally as we make the commitment to it, every act of elucidation is a springing from, a revelation of, the elucidating self. What I see in a performance onscreen is, minimally, what I have been equipped by my culture and my personal history of experience, to recognize and to value.

One boundary we established in choosing performances for inclusion in this volume was that they be to some degree already acknowledged as culturally visible, that the films to which they contribute remain in circulation, and that they operate in a mode ordinarily valued in film discourse. That is, the performances under analysis can be called realist in that they aim to be convincing in their displays of characters' thoughts, feelings, and desires. We thus exclude experimental work that may be excellent but opens up too large a set of discussions to adequately address, such as Maya Deren's balletic mime in her *Meshes of the Afternoon* (1943) or Divine's camp in *Pink Flamingos* (1972). This may appear to assume too much shared belief about American cinematic style, but it is no more than is routinely found in movie reviews or trailers that tout award-worthy turns as "Oscar bait," which measure merit in terms of realism, and realism in terms of convincingness.

Even a realist performance can be an essay. An actor may weave a thesis of sorts into the task of filling out a story. For example, in *Some Like It Hot* (1959), Marilyn Monroe indicates Sugar Kane's bright intelligence while professing to be stupid—thus making this appearance of stupidity in fact appear to be a performance of femininity, a performance that Sugar believes the world requires of her, in particular the men to whom she delivers it. It is this very sheen of metaperformance that Monroe brings to the work, and we might well doubt whether the entire film would work without it. Without it, would we root for Sugar to end up coupled with Joe (Tony Curtis), who himself performs masculinity as Junior (with intertextual reference to Cary Grant, with whom Monroe starred a few years prior in Howard Hawks's 1952 *Monkey Business*). We wager not. It is a consequence of Monroe's choices that we are satisfied with their coupling, as both thus seem to be camping up their gender, and so, to be a match.

The I of the actor

When we speak of convincing or realistic performances, we usually delimit ourselves to an idea of realism we expect to share with fellow audience members. We expect onscreen bodies to exhibit thoughts, feelings, and desires in ways that we find comprehensible and engaging. What we really mean by realist, then, is psychological realism, a term neglected in film criticism (for more on the history of this term and its evolution, see

Stevens's *Mike Nichols*). Many of the most intoxicating performances call our attention to psychological realism, the style in which the film indexes not just bodies but also how those bodies index minds, encouraging us to delve into characters' psyches by showing us that their minds are consciously calibrating the actions of their bodies, veiling and unveiling for other characters and for us (and often in different registers). Because such acting effects a diegetic doubling that echoes the formal doubling of actor and role (both of which echo the doubling of conscious lived experience, where, as Sartre has it, we experience the I and the not-I at once), James Naremore dubs it "metaperformance." Metaperformance emerges as a thread throughout this volume. Given the dominance of cinema for defining standards of realist performance over the past 100 years, and the influence of realist performance on cultural opinion about how people do or should behave, onscreen expressivity shapes expressivity in everyday life, too. Hence, we organized the collection chronologically by actors' birth dates in order to surface similarities and differences that yield insights into the evolution of cinematic human expression. We selected performers notable enough to appeal to readers across the world, not because they are stars but because they are artists of expression whose work is valuable. We hoped that choosing well-known turns would prove accessible to a range of readers, who can then apply the skills exhibited to their own favorites.

Our intention is not to instantiate a canon of the absolute *best* performances, although we believe that the performances under discussion are all highly estimable and reward deep consideration. Rather, our primary ambition is to demonstrate why particular stretches of acting are powerful, meaningful. This surely, in turn, makes the case that the acting under consideration is of superior quality, but we do not begin there, or merely assert such evaluative claims. As editors and authors we selected the performances you will find here because with each of them we felt there was a conversation to be started.

Works cited

Affron, Charles. *Cinema and Sentiment*. Chicago: University of Chicago Press, 1982.
Balázs, Béla. *Theory of Film*. London: Denis Dobson, 1952.
Baron, Cynthia, Diane Carson, and Frank Tomasulo, eds. *More Than a Method: Trends and Traditions in Contemporary Film Performance*. Detroit: Wayne State University Press, 2004.

Baron, Cynthia, and Sharon Marie Carnicke. *Reframing Screen Performance*. Ann Arbor: University of Michigan Press, 2008.
Benjamin, Walter. *The Work of Art in the Age of Mechanical Reproduction*. Trans. J. A. Underwood. Scottsdale: Prism Key Press, 2010.
Burns, Elizabeth. *Theatricality: A Study of Convention in the Theatre and in Social Life*. New York: Harper & Row, 1973.
Dyer, Richard. *Heavenly Bodies*. New York: Routledge, 2003.
Goffman, Erving. *The Presentation of Self in Everyday Life*. Garden City, NY: Anchor Books, 1959.
Klevan, Andrew. *Film Performance: From Achievement to Appreciation*. London: Wallflower Press, 2005.
Langer, Susanne. *Philosophy in a New Key: A Study in the Symbolism of Reason, Rite, and Art*. Cambridge, MA: Harvard University Press, 1979.
Naremore, James. *Acting in the Cinema*. Berkeley: University of California Press, 1988.
Naremore, James. "Acting in the Cinema: Commentary by Authors and Critics," *Cineaste* 31: 4 (Fall 2006), 60–3.
Pearson, Roberta. *Eloquent Gestures*. Berkeley: University of California Press, 1992.
Pomerance, Murray. *The Eyes Have It: Cinema and the Reality Effect*. New Brunswick, NJ: Rutgers University Press, 2013.
Pomerance, Murray. *Moment of Action: Riddles of Cinematic Performance*. New Brunswick, NJ: Rutgers University Press, 2016.
Sansom, Ian. "Only Death Is Consistent," *Times Literary Supplement* 5928 (11 November 2016), 14–15.
Sartre, Jean-Paul. *Being and Nothingness*. New York: Washington Square Press, 1993.
Springer, Claudia, and Julie Levinson. *Acting*. New Brunswick, NJ: Rutgers University Press, 2015.
Stern, Lesley, and George Kouvaros, eds. *Falling for You: Essays on Cinema and Performance*. Urbana: University of Illinois Press, 1999.
Stevens, Kyle. *Mike Nichols: Sex, Language, and the Reinvention of Psychological Realism*. New York: Oxford University Press, 2015.
Taylor, Aaron. *Theorizing Film Acting*. New York: Routledge, 2012.
Taylor, Diana. *Performance*. Trans. Abigail Levine. Durham, NC: Duke University Press, 2016.
Wojcik, Pamela Robertson, ed. *Movie Acting: The Film Reader*. New York: Routledge, 2004.

Chapter 1
Ethel Waters in *The Member of the Wedding*

Anna Everett

When Ethel Waters reprises her award-winning performance as Bernice Sadie Brown in the 1952 film adaptation of the 1950 Broadway theatrical production *The Member of the Wedding*, several aspects emerge that are worthy of comment. Bernice is introduced early in the film as the camera cuts to a medium two-shot framing her and John Henry (Brandon De Wilde, her seven-year-old charge). From the moment she appears, Waters's powerful and commanding onscreen presence is undeniable. A woman of large stature in both height and weight, Waters as Bernice is foregrounded significantly in many of her scenes—an A-list co-star rounding out this celebrated ensemble cast. Bernice is introduced wearing a black skull-cap that reveals a shock of nearly all-grey hair, a large black patch over her right eye, and a substantial white apron with pockets. She is situated in the kitchen at the sink. Strategic to her character's sphere of influence, Bernice is positioned intentionally in the kitchen and centered between twelve-year-old Frankie (Julie Harris, the tomboy and central character) and John Henry (Frankie's cousin and next-door neighbor).

Of course, this setting is consistent with Bernice's status as a domestic worker in the Addams household. But more importantly, Waters portrays Bernice as an unusual type of black woman domestic in the South of the contemporaneous pre-Civil Rights Movement era.

At this historical juncture, it is certainly unusual to see a celluloid black domestic worker who at once evokes Hollywood's ubiquitous mammy archetype while simultaneously subverting a number of its most derisive and two-dimensional features. In fact, Waters's characterization of Bernice as a sort of anti-mammy mammy-like figure suggests symbiosis between Carson McCullers's progressive black character design and Waters's own dignified interpretation of the role. In any case, the instant that Waters appears onscreen, she delivers a flawless depiction that bespeaks a comfortable familiarity with all aspects of this complex character as well as an affective intensity of feelings demanded by the story.

Transformative performance and the mammy-like anti-mammy

One of the pleasures of watching Ethel Waters performing Bernice onscreen, besides appreciating her incredible talents as an actor and singer/vocalist, comes in deciphering her unique reinscription of the maid against the familiar grain of previous representations of Hollywood's demeaning mammy stereotype. It is not for nothing that in 1950 Waters won the New York Drama Critics' Circle Award for her portrayal of this character on the Broadway stage. That was a fitting corrective to Waters being denied the Best Supporting Actress Academy Award in 1949 for her stellar portrayal of Dicey, the illiterate laundress, in Elia Kazan's *Pinky*. If Hollywood's vehement racism resulted in the refusal to recognize Waters's brilliant acting a year earlier, fortunately, the prestigious Drama Critics' Circle Award testified to her towering talent that would, or shall we say could, no longer be denied.

Portraying similar character types in *Pinky* and *Wedding*, Waters's cinematic acting is particularly noteworthy because it instantiates the notion of developing essentially an anti-mammy mammy figure. This creation presents a devastating rebuke to and recoding of Hollywood's reprehensible go-to representation of black womanhood in circulation from cinema's inception on through the release of this film. Unlike traditional mammy roles, that relegated black women actors to comic relief or bit parts signifying racial otherness and abjection, romantic unattractiveness, and asexuality in the text, Bernice, by contrast, ruptures this hegemonic signifying chain. Signifying against representational economies that in juxtaposing black maids primarily against their white female employers function to reify America's racial hierarchies and privileges, that elevate white female characters in binary opposition to their black counterparts, Waters's larger-than-life rendering of Bernice sets Hollywood's abject stereotypes of black womanhood on their heads. It is crucial for Waters to negate the usual stock signifiers of black mammyhood: for example, the bulging eyes; the handkerchief head covering; the atrocious imitations of black vernacular speech remarkable for their indecipherable white-Southern-inflected dialects and malapropisms; and the self-sacrificing, two-dimensional character throwbacks to race relations of the antebellum slavocracy, to borrow scholar Ed Guerrero's term.

As a New Negro artist and contributor to the Harlem Renaissance cultural movement of the 1920s and 1930s, Waters was having none of Hollywood's denigrations of her blackness. Thus, none of the discursive markers of the simple-minded, infantilized mammy is present in Waters's interpretation of Bernice. Rather, Waters imbues her anti-mammy mammy figuration with her own sense of artistic integrity and womanly sensuousness that most likely hews closely to McCullers's literary imagination. Nothing conveys this recoding of the black woman, a substitute mother-figure for Frankie, more than the famous scene in which Bernice lovingly disabuses the delusional young girl of her dangerous fixation on being a member of her brother's upcoming wedding. The two have an intense heart-to-to heart talk, as the ever-present and perplexed John Henry (largely off-camera), looks on.

The key tête-à-tête begins when Frankie asks Bernice about the death of Ludie Maxwell Freeman, Bernice's one true love and soul mate. In this potent scene, that showcases her emotive range, Waters as Bernice replies to Frankie's question about whether or not she thinks often of Ludie. Framing an initial establishing shot in the kitchen, zooming in and alternating between individual shots of Frankie and Bernice, the camera pans to a medium close-up on Waters only so that audiences gain an intimate knowledge of Bernice as a sensual, sexual woman. And Waters delivers her highly emotional lines while continuing to sweep the kitchen floor. In a thoughtful, melancholy, and reflective tone, Bernice responds in the affirmative: "I do . . . Sometimes I wish I didn't know Ludie at all. Makes you too lonesome afterwards. You go home from work at night and a terrible lonesome cringe comes over you—take up with too many sorry men to try and get over that feelin'.'" Then, she makes it clear that she does not include her current lover T.T. in the category of "sorry men," informing Frankie, and the audience, exactly why T.T. is special to her. In a carefully framed two-shot, Bernice's face lights up with an easy smile and warm vocal tone. "Oh," she says, "I wasn't referring to T.T., he is a fine, upstanding gentleman that's walked in the state of grace all his life." This is not a throwaway line. It functions importantly as an index of black celluloid respectability.

Still, Bernice informs Frankie that marrying T.T. is not in her plans. Not only does Waters's Bernice share with Frankie the different emotional registers distinguishing her love of Ludie and her immense respect for T.T., but she does an impeccable job of conveying those disparate sentiments through her uniquely expressive facial gestures. Toggling between a range of feelings from immense, deep-seated pain to reflections of fleeting joy, Waters convincingly communicates them all, especially with the help of director Fred Zinnemann's extreme close-up shot on Waters's glistening face (she is sweating in the summer heat and with mild exertion from her chores). Waters's ability to reveal the deepest interiority of Bernice's feelings of pain and profound loss and their ongoing impact is doubly articulated by her expression and the camera close-up.

As Bernice asks God for the strength to endure Ludie's death, it is Waters's solemn face and her tearful eyes looking up to the heavens that deliver the impact of her inconsolable pain. This scene is capable of eliciting empathy from all who witness this celebrated instance of Waters's virtuoso performance. Here, Waters is able to summon tears as she concludes her poignant soliloquy with Frankie looking on in recognition of their mutual senses of loss. When we cut from a medium close-up of Frankie looking at Bernice, the counter-shot is a significant close-up of Waters who utters Bernice's personal truth:

> Don't you see what I was doing? I loved Ludie. He was the first man I ever loved. Therefore, I had to go and copy myself forever after. And what I did was to marry off these little pieces of Ludie wherever I come across them. That was my misfortune. They all turned out to be the wrong pieces. But *my intention was to repeat me and Ludie.* Now don't you see? ... If you fall in love with some unheard thing as this, what is ever going to happen to you? Will you be tryin' to break into weddings the rest of your days? [Emphasis added]

Without question, here Bernice and Waters demolish the asexual, black mammy construct with this masterful retelling of Bernice's complex romantic past, even as it gestures toward the fact of Bernice's current love life with her boyfriend, T.T.

In an equally powerful scene that captures Waters's performative brilliance, Frankie dismisses the notion that she will fall prey to some unreasonable and impossibly captivating thrall that will doom her to loving weddings in the same way that Bernice was in the thrall of loving Ludie. As Bernice goes along with Frankie's conversational dodge, we see how Waters's demeanor turns on a dime, when Bernice recalls a bad experience with one of her "sorry" husbands. In recounting his bad acts of larceny and psychological abuse, Bernice regales young John Henry and Frankie, and the audience by extension, by laughing uproariously at her own folly for allowing herself to be taken in by that miscreant. Just as she gets to a crucial plot point in her recollection, Bernice stops abruptly, realizing how age-inappropriate her reminiscence is for the consumption of her young charges.

Of course, here Waters is at her actorly best, displaying the full range of conflicting emotions: wanting on the one hand to share details of this sad but funny experience and thereby spare Frankie a similar fate; and recognizing her adult responsibilities to these young children whom she clearly loves and needs to protect. And throughout this film text, Waters's acting integrity connotes what could be considered an anti-mammy performativity vis-à-vis her role as the maid Bernice. In this way, Waters upends and contests the enduring markers of the black mammy stereotype rather effectively. In addition to her resplendent performance of Bernice discussed above, two other performative moments are particularly relevant and deserve brief commentary.

In perhaps one of the film's most poignant scenes, Bernice, Frankie, and John Henry are cuddled together and framed in a touching medium-shot in which John Henry spontaneously breaks out into the familiar spiritual song "His Eye Is on the Sparrow." Reflexive of her own successful career as a singer (and her hit recording of this very song), the scene highlights Waters's shift into her charismatic songstress mode. Waters then imbues Bernice with musical heft as she joins John Henry and Frankie to sing the crucial musical number that forms this scene's powerful crescendo. At this point, the camera zooms in to an extreme close-up of Waters. As she sings the favorite song, gleefully revealing her famous gap teeth, the veteran actor's countenance demonstrating steadfastness and spiritual resolve fills the entire film frame. Slowly the camera cuts to a three-shot showing Frankie, Bernice, and John Henry snuggled up together and singing in unison, with Waters warmly ensconced in her familiar center spot between the children. At the song's conclusion, the scene fades to black, satisfactorily. It is important to note that the particular song lyrics, "I sing because I'm happy, I sing because I'm free, for His eye is on the sparrow and I know He watches me," are featured not merely because of their familiar choral refrain but because they function as a critical subtext underscoring Bernice's role as protective mother figure to these vulnerable white children entrusted to her capable and ample arms, and her heartfelt care, a trust depicted effectively and lovingly onscreen. On one hand, this imagery could be interpreted as an exemplary instance of Waters's redeployment of the essential black mammy role and its racial discursive function. On the other, the character can be viewed from a more nuanced perspective.

Taking into consideration the entire film, we can see the extent to which Waters's Bernice does break with the conventional mammy stereotype to challenge some of its most potent racist attributes. That said, Bernice's narrative function in *Wedding* echoes several of those attributes as well. For example, mapping the black mammy/maid discursive lineage from *The Birth of a Nation* (1915), *Imitation of Life* (1934), *The Little Colonel* (1935), to *Gone with the Wind* (1939), *Belle Starr* (1941), *Mildred Pierce* (1945), and *Duel in the Sun* (1946), among others, Bernice checks out as a black domestic worker and cook, employed as a loyal and trusted maid, working in the household of a white family in racially segregated America, and assuming maternal responsibilities there. In fact, nothing distills down both Bernice's adherence to and departure from the quintessential mammy than the scene where Ludie's death is discussed. However, it is Waters's incomparably charismatic and captivating performance, especially in this vital scene, that rescues the role of Bernice from the stock characterization.

Speaking candidly of the mammy performative lineage, except for the white male actor donning blackface to portray Mammy in *The Birth of a Nation*, one must acknowledge that Hattie McDaniel, Louise Beavers, and Butterfly McQueen each have left an individual imprimatur on this staple of Hollywood's maternal melodrama films. Furthermore, one could even presume that because other roles were foreclosed to these talented black female entertainers, ironically their powerful and fierce mammy performances could be partly responsible for the persistence of this damaging Hollywood construct.[1] Be that as it may, any serious consideration of Ethel Waters's masterful screen performance as Bernice reveals key instances in her subversion of the celluloid mammy, and her instantiation of the anti-mammy mammy figuration.

Four signifiers

As Waters's Bernice inspires this notion of the anti-mammy mammy figuration, the fact that *Wedding* is set in the postwar 1950s suggests alternatively the idea of a neo-mammy heuristic. Given that as an exceptional transmedia text Carson McCullers's *Wedding* features a somewhat more progressive imagining of the mammy-like black maid protagonist; and given Waters's respect, influence, and acting bona fides in the entertainment community, the Waters and McCullers joint creation of Bernice on the Broadway stage and in the Hollywood film represents something new. Since McCullers's backdrop was the beginning of the modern Civil Rights Movement, to craft Bernice in the mode of a plantation mammy would have been anachronistic. And considering McCullers's transgressive approach to her teenage girl coming-of-age text, replete with its aspects of gender fluidity, it is likely that developing Bernice according to traditional Southern mammy norms would be anathema to McCullers as well. Taking the entirety of the *Wedding* film text into view, Bernice can be seen going far beyond a mere temporal recalibration of the mammy role outside the originating antebellum frame. Rather, she transgresses the mammy construct in four fundamental and consequential ways, so that a neo-mammy signifier is rendered untenable, especially with Waters's A-list star turn added to the mix.

First and foremost, what disqualifies Bernice from any neo-mammy contention is the narrative centrality of this beloved black maid to this essentially Southern gothic coming-of-age tale focused on a motherless teenage white girl. No mere bit player that Bernice; she's not even the script's minor comic relief. In a noteworthy departure, the maid Bernice becomes an anti-mammy signifier because her narrative function is not relegated to the margins of the story. Instead, she occupies a pivotal position in the soul of this novel-to-stage-to-screen transmedia narrative ecology. In the film, Bernice is the second most important character propelling the melodramatic action forward. And for her part as Bernice, Waters enjoys a phenomenal amount of screen time, including a necessary range of prolonged extreme close-up, medium close-up, medium and wide camera shots. Hollywood mammies and maids never command such profound screen presence and narrative story time.

A second anti-mammy signification is Bernice's consequential backstory, which the narrative accommodates by providing ample time for unfolding Bernice's past life. Exemplary here and discussed above is the scene wherein Bernice recalls the death of her true love, Ludie. This prolonged segment in the film encompasses Waters's most virtuoso performance in the entire film, and it provides a fitting lead-in to our discussion of the film's and Waters's third and quite potent anti-mammy signification.

Arguably, the most transgressive reshaping of the traditional black mammy-cum-black maid archetype is screenwriters Edward and Edna Anhalt's fleshing out of Bernice's character arc to include, and even foreground, her active sexuality as a normative component of her womanhood. This anti-mammy attribute represents a seismic shift in the representational economy of the celluloid mammy. As a deliberate choice, in the effort to advance a more three-dimensional character design of Bernice, this normalization of Bernice's unoppressive sexuality and desirable womanhood reworks the discursive trajectory of the mammy icon significantly, and thus warrants more elaboration (see hooks).

That we most frequently encounter the black mammy figure in the maternal melodrama genre is no revelation, given that mothering and caring for white children and families are her primary narrative raison d'être. And despite being forced to increase the Southern slave population, the black female's gender status in the slave economy was never in doubt. But, in America's cult of ideal womanhood, the black female's status as belonging to that valued and protected category was summarily denied. In 1851, Abolitionist Sojourner Truth famously asked at the Women's Rights Convention, and on behalf of America's black sisterhood, a burning question that clearly resonated with the whole of the black community for decades: "Ain't I a woman?" That the question needed to be asked in the first place points up the unique status of real black women, a status replaced by what their problematic reel simulacra represents and perpetuates. From its cinematic inception, the de rigueur black mammy is figured as maternal, but rarely as a fully articulated woman; hence the pertinence of Bernice and her ability to problematize and disrupt Hollywood's discourse of the asexual maternal mammy. When Bernice recounts how Ludie stirred her womanly passions in her youth, by comparison she indicates how her current boyfriend T.T. fails on that score. So, McCullers's audacity in humanizing Bernice as a desiring and desirable woman highlights how untraditional this anti-mammy mammy signifies.

The fourth and final signifier of Bernice's innovative design and Waters's transformative portrayal is Bernice's discursive function as a full-fledged member of the Addams family. At first glance, it may seem a statement of the obvious to acknowledge that the black mammy and/or maid is a primordial feature of America's middle- and upper-class Southern white families, particularly as expressed in Southern literature, cultural lore, and national mythology. And, once incorporated into the potent visual culture of film and television, this overdetermined and romanticized Southern construct easily became the dominant signifier of black womanhood as a whole in the American celluloid imaginary since 1915 and through generations thereafter. However, upon closer inspection we see that Bernice breaks through that abject construct of dim-witted servitude and unquestioning loyalty. Unlike the traditional scenario whereby the black mammy's close association with white children functions to infantilize her, *Wedding* makes clear that Bernice is the capable and trusted adult figure who cares genuinely, and responsibly, for Frankie and John Henry. In the pre-Civil Rights milieu of 1950s America, the film crafts a notably realistic and complex relationship between Bernice and her young charges. The relationship is characterized not by a racial hierarchy but by instances of mutual affection and appropriate parent-child interactions and activities such as taking meals together, baking cookies, justly meted-out discipline, and the sharing of deeply personal stories and experiences.

Throughout their relationship, Bernice remains the adult in charge, and Frankie and John Henry clearly rely on her maternal wisdom, guidance, and love. Most importantly, though, is the deeply intimate mother-daughter conversations and experiences that define Frankie and Bernice's relationship. It is these and other activities and scenarios that delineate Bernice's anti-mammy mammy function and present an effective counter-narrative to the usual demeaning and subservient mammy discourse of Southern lore.

Enlivening Bernice through Ethel Waters's powerful star discourse

Without question, one of the key factors in the phenomenal successes of *Member of the Wedding* as both theatrical and cinematic texts is the unparalleled star turn of Ethel Waters in the headlining role. Another aspect driving the popularity of the 1952 film adaptation was the tight and well-coordinated performances of the theatrical ensemble cast members as they reprised their individual roles: Waters, of course, as Bernice, Julie Harris as Frankie, and Brandon De Wilde as John Henry. Holding this eccentric cast of characters together is the towering talent of consummate stage and screen entertainer Ethel Waters, whose performing background extends back to her public introduction in the 1920s as a blues singer on the black vaudeville circuit, the nightclub scene including the Cotton Club in Harlem, on through her stints in radio and in such all-black race films as *Cabin in the Sky* (1943) and the racially integrated social problem film *Pinky* (which led to her Academy Award nomination portraying Pinky's grandmother) and up to her starring role on the TV show "Beulah" (1950–1) (see Samuels; Waters).

In many ways, Waters's headlining role on TV and in *Wedding*'s racially integrated film cast signaled a new order of representational opportunities for black women performers in Hollywood. From her groundbreaking role as the first-ever African American star of a US television series to her starring role in Hollywood's mainstream film production of *Wedding*, this veteran entertainer's career certainly was phenomenal in Jim Crow America of the 1950s. Particularly noteworthy in this regard is the fact that Ethel Waters's name appears in the opening credits above the film's title.

As an A-list Hollywood film, *Member of the Wedding* has much to recommend it as one of the era's more powerful works of cinematic art. Waters's brilliant performance is chief among this film's many creative flourishes. No stranger to the added actorly benefits of perfecting a theatrical role on the stage before translating it to film, Waters's reprisal of her role as Bernice is nothing short of perfection. And beyond Waters's own abundance of charisma, film audiences are able to witness a performance for the ages and across generations in ways impossible for, and unavailable to, those who were fortunate enough to catch her performance on the Broadway stage. For one thing, film spectators were able to enjoy all the nuances and exuberances of Waters's award-winning performance whether or not they could meet the expense of a good theater seat. Moreover, because film director Fred Zinnemann opted to capture a large portion of Waters's performance in medium to close-up shots, there is no such thing as bad seating for film fans of Ethel Waters, as the fulcrum of her acting brilliance is on full cinematic view.

To highlight Waters's ability to infuse Bernice with the full force of her own undeniable charisma and star quality, two final scenes are particularly revealing. The first shows Waters's complete grasp of Bernice's intense emotional ties to the Addams family, especially her ties to Frankie and John Henry, and to her own tenuous family ties represented by her boyfriend T.T. and Honey Camden Brown, her non-relative godson.

Bernice describes Honey as the only family she's got left (following the death and loss of her first husband and true love, Ludie). Waters is capable of displaying the full panoply of emotions involved with a character's recollection of a painful memory (her failed romantic relationships after Ludie's death) as she tries desperately to prevent Frankie from making a similar error of judgment regarding the unreasonable expectations about her brother's wedding. Bernice rightly equates the girl's wedding obsession with her own desire to recapture her love for Ludie in a series of subsequent loveless marriages. When Waters shifts so effortlessly between shedding actual tears and expressing warm, spontaneous smiles we recognize her acting chops and expressive skills hewn over decades of performing dramatic and comedic roles. As the camera zooms in on Bernice, Waters is able to convey the heartfelt feelings of frustration and strained compassion.

At the film's conclusion, Waters turns in one of the story's most emotionally demanding performances. Here she confronts her own unwarranted feelings of complicity in the tragic and untimely death of the child, John Henry. Exhibited with a sad countenance and disquieted demeanor, Bernice's subtle yet powerful emotions of self-flagellation for not taking John Henry's assertions of feeling sick and failing to recognize the seriousness of the boy's condition are palpable. Here, Waters expresses very precisely the gamut of incredibly complex feelings one expects from a beloved character in the throes of trying to process such life-changing events. Compounding matters is Bernice's doubly overwhelmed emotional state as she must reckon with Frankie's imminent departure from her life forever. And these are affective emotions which Waters communicates superbly and with the methodical precision the film's denouement necessitates. In terms of Waters's storied performative precision, it remains unclear whether or not she was an adherent of or influenced by the Method acting approach which was all the rage in Hollywood in the 1950s. Nevertheless, one thing is clear: Waters so enlivens her performance that audiences need not call on their willing suspension of disbelief in order to accept Waters and Bernice as one and the same essence.

Finally, we need to take notice of Bernice's costuming at the film's end. She is clad in a fur-trimmed, black, iconic Sunday outfit and quintessential African-American church-lady's black hat. Never dressed in Hollywood's usual French-maid-style costuming, perhaps due to the Addams's unpretentious middle-class status, Bernice wears everyday house dresses denoting her working-class standing. And it is only her near-ubiquitous oversized white apron that marks her maid function. In this final scene, Bernice's strikingly tailored and apparently funereal attire codifies very effectively her profound loss (for both John Henry and now Frankie as the Addams family's relocation to another city is occurring in real time onscreen). Significantly, Bernice's striking and elegant black costuming bespeaks the termination of her maid function, and is powerfully evocative of Ethel Waters's own irrepressible, lifelong glamour, and bravura star persona.

All told, if we reflect attentively on the foregoing discussion, we can grasp quite clearly and unequivocally an essential parallel meaning of this modern Southern story: Bernice's narrative centrality in *Wedding* was not merely the social advance her anti-mammy mammy character represents. Her crucial character development turns on the fact that the film, rather than merely commenting upon it, subtly enacts Bernice's essential positioning as a true member of this household, and thereby her deep and true belonging in our newly evolving post-Jim Crow American family.

Note

1. I discuss in a different context the complex dynamic at work between black women actors who are often condemned for accepting and portraying the mammy roles and the same black audiences who celebrate their performances. See my analysis of Louise Beavers in *Imitation of Life*, in *Returning the Gaze*.

Works cited

Everett, Anna. *Returning the Gaze: A Genealogy of Black Film Criticism, 1909–1949.* Durham, NC: Duke University Press, 2001.
Guerrero, Ed. *Framing Blackness: The African American Image in Film.* Philadelphia: Temple University Press, 1993.
hooks, bell. *Ain't I a Woman: Black Women and Feminism.* Boston: South End Press, 1999.
Samuels, Charles T. *His Eye on the Sparrow: An Autobiography.* New York: Doubleday, 1951.
Waters, Ethel. *To Me, It's Wonderful.* New York: Harper & Row, 1972.

Chapter 2

Irene Dunne in *The Awful Truth*

Steven Rybin

> But a run of laughs, within life; finding occasions in the way we are together. (Stanley Cavell)

In *The Awful Truth* (1937), Irene Dunne delights in the exhilaration of the everyday, wringing ardent humor from passing minutes in ways that distinguish her from other heroines in screwball comedy. This chapter lingers on a handful of Dunne's moments in this film, and on the performative joy she and her character take in the fun and largesse of life.

Thoughtfully going wild

Critical commentary on Irene Dunne in *The Awful Truth* tends to focus on her thoughtful and ironic approach to screwball comedy. "Unlike the genre's stereotypical leading lady," biographer Wes D. Gehring writes, "who exhibits bonkers behavior continuously, à la Carole Lombard in *My Man Godfrey* (1936), or Katharine Hepburn in . . . *Bringing Up Baby* (1938), Dunne's screwball heroine chooses when she 'goes wild'" (71). James Harvey notes that, "Dunne shows us what such human qualities as complication and essential reserve, native tact and intelligence are capable of—what flights and surprises and even transformations" (243). Maria DiBattista, meanwhile, ranks Dunne as the most "self-sufficing" and "ironic" of all the fast-talking screwball dames, "above or beyond capitulating to an overmastering feeling or irresistible impulse" (210). The knowing edge to Dunne's performances is what leads no less philosophical a person than Stanley Cavell to report about how he loses himself entirely in Dunne's screen presence. "My sense of *The Awful Truth*," Cavell declares, "is that if one is not willing to yield to Irene Dunne's temperament, her talents, her reactions, following their detail almost to the loss of one's own identity, one will not know, and will not care, what the film is about" (233).

Taking this cue from Cavell, this chapter suggests ways a viewer might be mesmerized by Dunne while viewing *The Awful Truth*, when the watching eye yields to her "temperament, her talents, her reactions." When we turn our eyes to performance in this way, we are following what Murray Pomerance calls "the transcendent performance," the screen turn that "stuns watchers by virtue of a seemingly sharp originality, a spontaneous burst of attitude and feeling that, springing out of—and away from—the narrative moment, brings a quality of intensity, novelty, and purity" (23). In *The Awful Truth*, Dunne's "sharp originality" may be, at least initially, easy to miss, given that in screwball comedy we are usually primed to look for sudden bouts of physical glee or playful wordplay as verifications of character spontaneity. Although Dunne's performances are not bereft of these elements, she offers us a more self-contained and everyday pleasure. Dunne's transcendence in *The Awful Truth* is indeed so thoughtful that she almost always brings into her trajectory some aspect of the everyday world (an object, a costume, another player) as she rises above routine expectations of what a film comedy might achieve. In contrast to the equally delightful but very different performances of a Lombard or a Hepburn in the genre, Dunne does not have her characters manically plunge ahead: instead she has them thoughtfully linger, circling around a moment with patient attention to see what good humor it might offer. Her Lucy Warriner in *The Awful Truth*, one half of a couple planning to divorce but that might, should they rediscover a connection, remarry, is a constant guide to the viewer, showing a way of thoughtfully *being*. Finally, her way of thoughtfully *being* onscreen is what brings the couple back together.

"It Happened One Orange"

It would initially appear that Jerry Warriner (Cary Grant) is the one with the intellectual scheme. As her soon-to-be former husband, he has concocted a performance to maintain the marriage, inventing a completely fictional two-week vacation in Florida; the viewer meets him as he bathes under a lamp to acquire the right sort of Florida tan he'll need to pull off this fib. Further, he'll arrange for a group of friends to greet Lucy in a surprise party at their home to corroborate his lie, a strategy complemented by a basket of Florida oranges meant to verify his falsehood. He is staging—and performing—fidelity.

Dunne's Lucy, by contrast, has no situation to concoct. We join her in the middle of pleasure: an evening out with handsome Armand Duvalle (Alexander D'Arcy), still underway as she bounces in wearing a delightfully ostentatious white fur and glowing silver gown. Her appearance here is one of ironic innocence. DiBattista has described her as "a figure of light who enters the film as a vision in resplendent white" (220). As soon as Lucy sees Jerry she begins to inhabit that dress differently and hers becomes a knowing put-on, done with a lightness of touch that matches the luminosity of the glittering dress (and that in its effortless elegance outdoes Jerry's comparatively goofy scheme with the oranges). "How brown you are!" Dunne declares to him, admiring the fake tan and wrapping him in a hug of white fur just as he detects Armand arriving behind her, with a smirk, in the foyer. Lucy knew Armand would lag, of course, and so already began to respond to a situation that had not even happened yet, with this luxurious hug and her cooing admiration of Jerry's tanned skin. As she describes her evening to Jerry, and how she has happened to arrive on the arms of this Continental gentleman, she steps over to the couch, but her breathy, giggly delivery of the details is, in contrast to Jerry's careful orchestration of the scene, almost perfunctory. She's less interested in keeping her little lies together and much more delighted by the appearance of Mr. Smith, the couple's pet wire fox terrier (played by the inimitable Skippy, of *The Thin Man* (1934) and *Bringing Up Baby* (1938)). Shortly thereafter, her canine pal joins her on the couch, a squeaky toy for them to play with clutched between his sharp little teeth.

In contrast to the way director Leo McCarey initially stages Grant's movements as a means to prepare the way for the arrival of key co-players, Dunne's movements around the scene are the work of an actor who responds, with comic jazz, to the playing of her co-stars. There is the delightful moment when Lucy discovers Jerry's "Florida" fruit: it is actually a basket of California oranges, revealed as such in a stamp on the peel of a single orange she holds in her hands. This potentially playful object is directly paralleled to the little squeaky toy Mr. Smith brings her earlier in the scene, and as with the dog, Dunne has Lucy throw the orange to Grant in a bid for play. (Unlike Mr. Smith, though, Jerry hasn't yet learned how to catch.) Dunne's expressions and gestures here are emblematic of her character's responses to the situation. Rather than merely becoming upset at the stamp as visual proof of Jerry's feint, Dunne's Lucy takes pleasure in the little orange, this expressed through a knowing smile and a quick, playful throw of the "ball" to Grant. All of this is punctuated by a little gesture that completes the moment: beaming with a toothy smile, Dunne holds her right hand to the skin of her neck, as if she were holding back just a little glee, a delight she's waiting to release if Grant will only play ball and throw back the orange. Here Dunne conveys the pleasure that her character takes in the situation; even as this marriage is about to fall apart, Lucy tries to preserve it through play. The oranges thus serve the same final purpose for both characters—to keep them together. But unlike Jerry, who has placed the oranges here as an inert stage piece, intended only to statically express ongoing belief in married fidelity as social performance, Lucy finds in the orange a dynamic purpose, a way to keep things moving, differently than before but with a renewed sense of the possible pleasures of married life.

In a sense, both characters want to keep things the same, in order for their marriage to continue. But unlike Grant's Jerry, Dunne's Lucy already realizes that to keep things the same in a satisfying way, those tokens, even prosaic ones like oranges, must be given a sense of life that moves them out of their inertness. This is perhaps why she has been gallivanting with Armand. He is a variation on the sophistication that Jerry possessed but had perhaps let lapse into routine. As Grant walks over to Dunne, now sharing the frame with her, she darts her eyes back and forth from his eyes to the orange he holds, all the while continuing to clutch at the basket of fruit with both hands. It is almost as if she's fully prepared to throw him another one. But Grant, rather than throwing the orange back, circles it around in his hands as the two characters discuss faith and trust. He has still not learned to play.

"Bringing Up Doggy"

Screwball heroines are distinctively cinematic women; their breathless movements from one setting to the next give the genre an endearing goofiness (think of Katharine Hepburn bounding across a golf course in *Bringing Up Baby*, or Carole Lombard bouncing gleefully across the frame of *My Man Godfrey*). Dunne's work in *The Awful Truth*, although somewhat more physically contained than other screwball performances, is no less cinematic. In the narrative, Dunne's thoughtfulness often has a way of changing the space, of finding in everyday haunts new kinds of liveliness.

In at least a few scenes Dunne's most important co-star is not Grant but Skippy. As suggested earlier, the dog indicates his suitability as a co-star for Dunne in his first appearance, greeting her on the couch with a squeaky toy. Skippy will next appear in the courtroom sequence, which near its end involves the question of who will enjoy custody of Mr. Smith. The judge, as is only sensible, invites the dog back into the courtroom (the pooch was thrown out earlier for disrupting the proceedings) so that he may choose which of his caretakers to return to. Cavell remarks that the dog in *The Awful Truth* functions as "the muse of the marriage" (Lucy and Jerry met in a pet shop where the canine was purchased) but he is also proof that "McCarey's farce is made not for the stage but for film" (245), given that the dog's presence in the film's choreography involves complex bits of animal direction and staging that could not be achieved on the stage. Dunne and McCarey declare again their affinity for this sort of cinematic fun in the courtroom scene, in the way Lucy wins Mr. Smith over: in a close-up of Lucy's hand, she slips the little squeaky toy out of her coat sleeve, a mischievous little cheat that attracts the dog's attention but goes unseen by the other characters (as it would go unseen to a stage audience).

Lucy and the dog are thus closely bonded through their shared and smart sense of play. Mr. Smith, indeed, is in many ways the man at the center of her life. Both being creatures of cinema, each can, in his or her way, intelligently and mischievously intervene in situations away from the glimpse of other eyes. The way Dunne has Lucy play with Mr. Smith throughout the film is reflective of this smartness. After Jerry has embarrassed himself by crashing one of Lucy's recitals, Lucy and Mr. Smith perform a clever game of hide-and-seek. Like Lucy in the courtroom, Mr. Smith is smart enough to cheat a bit when there is pleasure to be had: his head buried in his paws as Lucy hides the toy, he looks up to spy the hiding spot just when he thinks she isn't looking. Although we see Jerry play with Mr. Smith at certain points in the film, their interactions have a rough-and-tumble quality, as when Jerry interrupts Lucy's meeting with a new paramour by obnoxiously prompting the dog to accompany his piano playing with barking, before wrestling with him on the ground. By contrast, Dunne and Skippy tend towards smarter fun. Mr. Smith is so smart that he is able to prompt Lucy to reveal things she might otherwise not, giving Dunne the opportunity to convey Lucy's occasional quality of circumspection, or reserve. These are aspects of her personality that distinguish her from more thoroughly manic and unreserved screwball heroines and that continue to reveal her as the perfect partner for Jerry.

Later in the hide-and-seek scene, after Armand has arrived to talk with Lucy about their intent to explain to her husband the innocence of their night together, Jerry arrives unexpectedly, prompting Lucy to hide Armand in an adjoining room. Jerry has brought a hat with him and Aunt Patsy (Cecil Cunningham), who has been socializing with Lucy, must now do something with a second hat Armand has left on the table—so she tosses it to Lucy. This dull hat becomes, for Dunne, the key object in the scene, obviously indicative of Lucy's desire to delay her honest explanation of what she was doing with Armand but more expressively suggestive of the playful uses to which such an object might be put. Dunne clutches the hat behind her back, and adjusts her position as Grant circles around her. Skippy has run over to the other side of the room and once again is burying his head in his paws, intermittently stealing quick looks at Lucy as she contemplates what to do with the hat. Her solution is not clever enough to trick Mr. Smith, who has seen her plop it behind a curtain. The dog now returns to the rear side of the couch on which Dunne and Grant are sitting. While Jerry apologizes for his suspicions about Armand Lucy secretly wrestles with Mr. Smith, who now refuses to return the hat. There is something different about Dunne's play with the dog here. It's more roughhouse than her earlier hide-and-seek trick, a touch more aggressive, as if Mr. Smith were intentionally trying to coax Lucy into one of those spontaneous bursts of physical glee that Dunne's self-reserve keeps in check. McCarey cuts to a reverse-angle shot of Dunne and Grant on the couch. Jerry notices something odd in the aggressive play that Lucy is working to hide, as Dunne crosses her legs back and forth, adjusts her hair, and edges into the corner of the couch in an effort to mask the tussle with Mr. Smith over the hat that is continuing out of our, and Grant's, view. Lucy has won this little battle with Mr. Smith, but only temporarily. He scampers over to the other side of the room, again burying his head in his paws, beckoning for the play to continue.

Skippy has created an opening here for Dunne to convey a hesitant reserve and a momentary uncertainty about how to combine her desire for play in her marriage (expressed in her first appearance in the film, in the scene with the oranges) with the truth of why Armand has a presence in her life. After she has retrieved the hat from Mr. Smith, Lucy encourages Jerry to play a little with the dog, which gives her just enough time, with him distracted, to try to find a hiding place for Armand's hat. In essence, she is directing the scene. Dunne points to where Grant should hide the ball while she goes over to the other side of the room to hide the hat behind a mirror. This neatly inverts the way in which Jerry "staged" the social gathering in the early sequence with the oranges, revealing Dunne's character to be equally adept, at least for a moment, at orchestrating an event to hide the revelation of a truth. As with Grant's placement of the oranges, Dunne is trying to turn this object—which Skippy has made playful—back into an inert thing, a thing that will rest silently, for if it moves about and gets into Jerry's hands it will reveal Armand's presence.

Dunne's positioning and movements with the hat convey a desire for rest. She needs to think a little more about what the next bit of business will be, how exactly she will word what she has to say about her night with Armand. So after she has hidden the hat behind the mirror, Dunne has Lucy lean against the side of a chair, a position that figures her in an in-between moment, restful but ready to respond. As Grant sits down to continue his confession, Dunne remains where she is, poised but hesitant. Mr. Smith's function in the scene is to disrupt this hesitancy, to remind Lucy that play must continue throughout the everyday life of a marriage. So he brings the mirror crashing down in his retrieval of the hat. And when Grant puts the hat on, he looks as silly as he did at an earlier moment when he crashed Lucy's recital. Dunne has Lucy take pleasure in that earlier silly moment: at the beginning of this present scene, as she plays with Mr. Smith, she delights in telling Aunt Patsy of how beautifully ridiculous Jerry looked. And as he looks so ridiculous here, with this oversized hat on his head, Lucy again cannot help but reveal her pleasure, as Dunne lets escape a quiet, breathy laugh. Dunne's thoughtful playfulness has finally led to a little moment of pleasure. Her self-reserved containment has found its momentary reward.

"His Girl Lucy"

Like many films of the 1930s, *The Awful Truth* uses diegetic newspaper headlines to reveal key plot points. On the eve of his divorce from Lucy, Jerry consorts with Barbara Vance (Molly Lamont), known in the newspapers as "debutante and heiress." These newspapers tell the viewer all the ostensibly fun things Jerry and Barbara are doing: vacationing at Bar Harbor, Maine; racing speedboats; attending polo matches; taking in horse races; watching a college football game; dancing in a club. All of this fun, which would seem a transcendence of the everyday, is enough to clinch Jerry and Barbara a line in the society pages, which confirms their impending engagement.

However, in the montage in which we see Jerry's new "romance" unspool, McCarey gives a few clues that it is not very romantic and not much fun. First, there is no actual lovemaking going on: not so much as a kiss. Second, Jerry does not appear to be enjoying himself: in the shot at the horse track, he's even frowning. Third, and following from the first two points, all of this "fun" is reduced to mere information—discourse—that is reported, in the newspaper, rather than experienced or conveyed as fun (either by the actors or by us). Most importantly, though, no transcendence of any meaningful sort has been experienced by Jerry and Barbara: although activities such as horse racing and speed boating are ones in which only the very wealthy might participate, this is not largesse. It is routine: the things the wealthy are expected to do.

As Irene Dunne will remind us when *The Awful Truth* draws to its close, some degree of material comfort is a necessary requirement for genuine pleasure, but it is not a sufficient one. Further, there is nothing particularly interesting cinematically in what Jerry and Barbara are doing in their escapade: all of their outings are expensive activities but also utterly conventional ones; they may be easily undertaken offscreen by any viewer of *The Awful Truth* who can afford to pay for them. What Dunne gives to her viewer, by contrast, is a gift not so easily possessed, located entirely and fully in the cinematic moment that she and only she can give to us in quite this way. In his essay on the pleasures that are to be found in the experience of largesse in cinema, George Toles, working against theories that are suspicious of visual plenitude, makes exactly this point. Largesse, he writes,

> implies magnanimous giving, a plentiful outpour ... each potential viewer as the beneficiary of a potentially equal footing. The things that the camera registers and transmits, shot by shot, are not available somewhere offscreen in an equivalent form; they do not correspond to a possessable, material reality that matches up to it and can be 'had' on decisively different terms. (10)

There is an interesting and implicit notion here that the author of any given moment of a movie is the one who is, at that moment, giving the most pleasure to us; in this sense, Dunne's generosity is something that, alongside Jerry, we cannot help but come to recognize and appreciate as *The Awful Truth* reaches its conclusion.

The most generous of her moments in *The Awful Truth* is her song-and-dance routine near the end, when she visits the Vance home in order to shatter decorum. Offering to do a nightclub routine for the horrified Vances, Lucy chooses a phonograph of Dixie Bell's "My Dreams Are Gone with the Wind." As Cavell acknowledges, Lucy's performance involves the manufacture of a kind of past: she poses as Jerry's fictional sister, Lola, claiming knowledge of him that goes back their entire lives. This aspect of Lucy's diegetic performance is entirely farcical (or, at least, it exaggerates marital knowledge as something that might go back a lifetime), and it is not entirely her own: Jerry has made up the sister on an earlier telephone call, and Lucy is casting herself as this phantom sibling now. But in at least two elements of the dance Dunne makes vivid claims on the performative authoring of the moment. First, what we see here is a film moment enacted and sung by Irene Dunne, herself a talented singer in real life and in other films; our knowledge of this fact as viewers furthers our enjoyment of Dunne's transcendence of the everyday, which is accomplished in part through song. But further, and important for Jerry and the Vances, the performance is obliquely inspired by something Lucy does not invent but rather saw (along with us, and Jerry) earlier in the film: a song-and-dance, to the very same song, performed by Jerry's casual date, the working-class nightclub singer Dixie Belle Lee (Joyce Compton). Lucy's authoring of the moment is felt to the extent that we forget almost entirely about Compton's earlier turn as Dunne here takes over the number.

Where Compton was presented to us as part of a glittering spectacle in a nightclub, Dunne is entirely her own spectacle. Rather than remaining fixed in one spot as Compton was, Dunne takes the Vance sitting room as her stage (with Jerry, sitting among the Vances, as one of her viewers), its backdrop (polite lamp and end table, innocuous and flower-patterned curtains and chair) offering no distraction from her singular charms. And rather than merely re-perform something she performs every night, to predetermined beats as Compton in the nightclub does, Dunne (in improvisatory fashion, as encouraged by McCarey's approach to comedy) makes up this one-time show, in its little details, as she goes along. The dance is her reminder to Jerry that what she is giving him here can't be purchased anywhere else (in the Compton song-and-dance routine, which may be viewed by buying a drink, or with Barbara Vance, who is utterly incapable of even Compton's level of invention). Rather than go fully through with the gesture of lifting up her dress (in a way that would only echo Compton's own earlier rendition of the jig), Dunne hilariously points to the dress and in so doing appeals to our (and Jerry's) memory of the earlier version of the routine we have seen. "Get it?" she asks Jerry, and by implication, us. If we are attuned to Dunne's screwy thoughtfulness, we certainly do.

"The number has some wind effects in it," Lucy tells us at the top, "but you'll just have to use your imagination about them." The point of the routine, of course, is that Dunne is the one using her imagination, conjuring the romance lyricized in the song through the delightful silliness of her own improvisatory movements and gestures. "There's bound to be stormy weather," Dunne sings in a warble we recognize as a comic variation of the voice heard in *Roberta* (1935) and *Show Boat* (1936), among other films. Just as important to the comedy here, though, is the way Dunne finds ways to harmonize the silliness of her voice with the uninhibited movements of her body, gyrating back and forth and slapping herself on the sides. In so doing, she finds a physical, embodied equivalent for the amorous storms she sings about. This play with physicality stops just short of eroticism—her main work here is to disrupt the bourgeois propriety of the Vances, even as the silliness of her movements retains a kind of ironic self-propriety. But the promise of a future reconciliation with her lover is nevertheless a goal of the dance. As she bounces screen right, her partner, Cary Grant, is there now to catch her, having removed himself from the audience of Vances to become part of the show.

This is the moment as analyzed, or as an example of words that might evoke the pleasures Dunne gives us, and the pleasure we take in Lucy as she dances her way to a reunion with her man; on the page here I hope to have captured part of what makes her work so delightful. But the moment soars in ways that are not finally possessable, by criticism or any other method of life. The fact that Dunne's performance, like all great, transcendent performances, finally darts away from us, does not make writing on film acting irrelevant. We need some effort of words to know how performances affect each of us. But we also need to know when to acknowledge the inexhaustibility of a great performance. This song-and-dance, and indeed everything Dunne does in this film, is eternally re-viewable, its generosity offering every viewer the opportunity and ground to giggle anew. Discovering how to giggle again is part of what brings Lucy and Jerry back together. Our own giggling again and again alongside *The Awful Truth* reminds us that what the performer gives us in cinema, when it is well and truly bountiful, cannot be purchased or possessed; knowing this, indeed, is part of the delight.

Works cited

Cavell, Stanley. *Pursuits of Happiness: The Hollywood Comedy of Remarriage*. Cambridge, MA: Harvard University Press, 1981.
DiBattista, Maria. *Fast Talking Dames*. New Haven, CT: Yale University Press, 2001.
Gehring, Wes D. *Irene Dunne: First Lady of Hollywood*. Lanham, MD: Scarecrow Press, 2006.
Harvey, James. *Romantic Comedy in Hollywood from Lubitsch to Sturges*. New York: Alfred A. Knopf, 1987.
Pomerance, Murray. *Moment of Action: Riddles of Cinematic Performance*. New Brunswick, NJ: Rutgers University Press, 2016.
Toles, George. "Luxury and Largesse in Film," in *Movie: A Journal of Film Criticism* 4 (2013), 7–19.

Chapter 3

Cary Grant in *His Girl Friday*

Adrienne L. McLean

"Excuse me, Madame, are you referring to *me*?"

So inquires Cary Grant, as Walter Burns, in the screwball "newspaper" comedy *His Girl Friday* (1940). I don't know whether the line is from Ben Hecht and Charles MacArthur's play *The Front Page* (from which this and a 1931 film version were adapted), or from Charles Lederer's screenplay, Morrie Riskind's uncredited dialogue additions, or the ad libbing that director Howard Hawks encouraged among his fast-talking performers on the set. And I frankly don't care where it came from. Because what makes it hilarious is how Grant delivers it. I have tried it myself over the years, substituting "Sir" for "Madame" as the occasion demands, and it was always a thrill to get any part of it "right"—the way Grant leans forward and pushes the words out through a sneer, head cocked just a little under his black flat-top fedora, shoulders turned toward the camera in a sort of gangster contrapposto as he points his right hand like a gun at Alma Kruger's Mrs. Baldwin—"Mother"—who is identifying him as her kidnapper and, on his punched "me," jabbing his thumb into his tattersalled double-breasted chest. There is no outrage in his attitude, only contempt, and his extended pronunciation of "excuse" is just about perfect: he draws out the "yeeewwwwse" of the second syllable against the tightness of his lips, and subsequently sucks his teeth and flicks his narrowed eyes—just once—in disdain down and then up the body of the flustered woman. Again pointing at her and claiming he's never seen her before in his life, he accuses her in declamatory tone and gesture of framing *him*, and of "joyriding, plastered," which sends her into further sputtering paroxysms. Grant is so funny that one almost forgets he's lying, and that "Mother" has been abused in all sorts of ways, none of them pleasant, at the behest, if not the literal hands, of Walter Burns.

The exchange is thus also a performance of a performance, indicated by a perfect split-second of discombobulation that flashes across Grant's face just before he looks behind him in a fake "Who, me?" bit that he uses to gather himself to respond to Kruger. *His Girl Friday* is loaded with moments of comic genius, primarily carried by Grant as Burns, a character who continually exhibits feelings to us that he is hiding from others in the room for various strategic purposes or else, as in the scene with Mrs. Baldwin, who must fib convincingly in order to protect himself from the consequences of actions he has taken earlier. Dissembling as such is a relatively common trope of the screwball comedy, especially in the "comedy of remarriage," in Stanley Cavell's classic phrase, which *His Girl Friday* of course is. *Morning Post* editor Walter Burns cannot reveal his abiding but heretofore careless love for his paper's best journalist and his ex-wife, Hildy (Rosalind Russell), in order to make her realize for herself that retirement and impending marriage with the boring but good Bruce Baldwin (Ralph Bellamy) is a wrong choice. In large part because Hildy had been written as a male character in the stage version of *The Front Page* and performed as such in the earlier film version, more than most other screwball movies—if not more than all, in fact—the nature of the primary couple as near-equals in their professional realm makes *His Girl Friday* what Gerald Mast calls "a curious and complex romantic comedy in which love is expressed through work and work is expressed as love" (209). Ironically, despite Hildy's gender change and especially Russell's full participation in the film's famous rapid-fire overlapping dialogue—the actors speak their lines at almost double Hollywood cinema's "average speaking rate" (McCarthy 283)—it is only Burns who dissembles in order to accomplish his twin goals of making her return to him and to his newspaper.

The fact that he is simply given so much to *do*, so many layers to perform in so many comedic ways, adds to the feeling that, despite the fine performances by everyone else, especially Russell, *His Girl Friday* truly belongs to Cary Grant. And our delight in him is at once because and in spite of the fact that, well before Hitchcock almost made Grant's character a duplicitous murderer in *Suspicion* (1941), Walter Burns is one of the most disgusting protagonists of any screwball comedy, arguably of any classical narrative film that is not overtly about evil. As Pauline Kael writes in her profile of Grant, "The Man from Dream City," his performance is one of "monomaniac egotism" in which "callousness and unscrupulousness" are expressed in "all-out, unsubtle farce" and mugging is "raised to a joyful art." Grant "hits [his] lines with a smack," "snorts and whoops," his Walter Burns a "strong-arm performance, defiantly self-centered and funny" (56). The antinomies these words set into play, and how Grant's performance negotiates them and to what effect, is the topic of this chapter.

Director Hawks turns out to have been the source of some of Grant's odd noises; in the face of Grant's boredom with standard ways of representing anger, he gave him a "better way" through passing along an anecdote about a man who "would whinny like a horse—*whoo, whoo, whoo*—just like that" when he got mad ("Well, that's fine, I'll do that," Grant told Hawks) (in McBride 71). Conversely, whinnying aside (it's really more like a high-pitched hum when Grant does it), Sarah Kaufman, who uses Grant to epitomize "the art of grace" in her book on the topic, not only lauds the "Mozartian mystery of Grant's performances" (xix) and his "dark beauty, cultured diction, and gift for comedy" generally (4) but credits Hawks with "unleashing Grant's full-body expressiveness" (6). Yet Hawks factors not at all in Kaufman's lengthy exploration of a moment in *His Girl Friday*'s lunch-table scene, in which Walter begins the process of undermining Hildy's relationship with Bruce Baldwin:

> [Grant has] drawn our eye to his shoulders, squeezing them together slightly, not relaxing them until now, this instant, when that little action that starts in his neck and trickles across the top of his suit jacket shouts out loud and clear that Hildy is making a stupid mistake. It's not flamboyant, there's nothing self-indulgent in that gesture, and it's over in a wink. But it reveals the calculating

> trickiness as well as the feelings of his character. That liquid, nearly imperceptible roll of a muscle hangs there like an echo, a ripple in the airwaves, a shiver in the emotional current that encircles Grant and Russell and us. (5)

While I frankly can't identify the precise moment that Kaufman is referring to here, such detailed descriptions of Grant's "nuanced physical maneuvering" (5) are helpful in reminding us that material bodies are the site of acting and/as performance, and I build on this further below. But while director Stanley Donen—who worked with Grant in his later, more suave older-man-of-the-world phase—also appreciates Grant's "unique" abilities as a "fearless" performer, he calls his Walter Burns one of the "greatest performances ever given by an actor," not because of his "dark beauty" and other "gifts" (indeed, Donen remarks that Grant's art was *not* "a gift from God") but because the performance exemplifies the "enormous amounts of work" behind his "remarkable" acting (in Nelson 120–1).

Yet by the time of *His Girl Friday* (his twenty-ninth film), Cary Grant was more than a hard-working actor; he was a star. His appeal at that point was as a "comedian-hero," in Kael's words, the "hero" coming not only from his wondrous, nearly obscene handsomeness but the exotic roles he played in his effective forays into drama and action-adventure such as one of the other of his five films with Hawks, *Only Angels Have Wings*, or George Stevens's *Gunga Din*, both in 1939. Screwball, a mode that combines physical and other forms of "low" comedy with drawing-room wit and farce, was perfect for Grant; Kael describes the "audience's pleasure" in watching a "muscular, full-bodied man making a fool of himself" (45), as he had in Norman Z. McLeod's *Topper* and Leo McCarey's *The Awful Truth* in 1937 and Hawks's *Bringing Up Baby* and George Cukor's *Holiday* in 1938 (and as he would again in Garson Kanin's *My Favorite Wife* and Cukor's *The Philadelphia Story* later in 1940, the latter two also comedies of remarriage). *His Girl Friday* is apart from the other comedies, though, through the utter disregard Walter Burns appears to have for the world. He makes everyone *else* the fool, even, in the end, Hildy. More than any of his other comedies, then, *His Girl Friday* is a signal text in showing how important Grant could be to films that might, upon reflection, be more than usually abhorrent in their gender, class, and racial politics while remaining "joyful" entertainment.

Of course, Hawks's presumed authorship of *His Girl Friday* has perforce made Grant's role in it the subject of many academic studies. Hawks, in his own words, thought Grant a "personality rather than an actor" and liked working with him because, as Hawks put it, "I know what he's gonna do" (in Mast 53). The designation "personality" suggests that Hawks expected and was happy to make use of the pre-existing identities that Grant brought with him to any film as well as the easy relationship they quickly developed on the set, which could be disconcerting to someone, like Russell, who had never worked with the taciturn director before (see McCarthy 283; Russell and Chase 85–7). Donen, in contrast, is adamant that Grant's "fantastic" acting and the "ease and comfort" he projected on the screen were the result of attention to the "minute detail of it all;" he recounts how Grant's "scripts were full of little notes to himself" and the like (in Nelson 121). These characterizations are not necessarily antithetical, yet the doubled discourse—Grant is a gifted natural, Grant is great because he works hard—marks the critical analysis of *His Girl Friday* more than Hawks's other comedies. Frank Nugent in the *New York Times*, for example, thought Grant "splendid, except when he is being consciously cute" (12 November 1940). James Naremore goes so far as to suggest that Grant is "slightly miscast" as Walter Burns (218) but never says precisely why, only briefly mentioning Grant's "international" accent (though Adolphe Menjou, who played Burns in the 1931 film version, also had one). In sum, these comments suggest that Grant's performance in *His Girl Friday* is extraordinarily virtuosic and very, very funny, and that he also gives the film a number of incoherences that, in the estimation of many, make it not so much a complex text as a fractured and ideologically dissatisfying one.

Andrew Britton, in his study of Grant, comedy, and male desire, for example, argues that Grant's persona "is profoundly incompatible with industry, and this is, of course, an essential aspect of its attractiveness. Yet it also raises ideological problems, which appear in the fact that each class type can merge into the confidence trickster." Britton remarks on the "loathsomeness" of the Walter Burns character and argues that *His Girl Friday*, despite its "astonishing brilliance," in the end hardly shows the triumph of love or even the value of professional labor and its communities but instead "traces the process by which Hildy is worn down into submission" (n.p.). For Robin Wood, despite "many small touches of comic invention through gesture and expression that give the film its surface aliveness," its "chief virtue—its brilliant dialogue—becomes almost a vice" because its "dazzle masks an essential heartlessness which the film seems at times to be judging but which is never, in fact, adequately 'placed'" (67). He wants, therefore, to differentiate between "the disturbance that results from a fully realised, fully organised work of art, and the uneasiness produced by unresolved or unbalanced elements in a flawed work," of which Grant is arguably the main element (71). Richard Schickel calls Grant in *His Girl Friday* "all brass and brashness, fast and loud as he almost never was. His charm is all in his speed, his irresistible energy and single-mindedness," the film itself "a *tour de force* for both Grant and Hawks, a test of their limits." Hawks is able to "quick-march a comedy so fast that no one stopped to think about the stench of the sinkholes we were being hustled past" and Grant keeps "his frenzy concentrated," never letting it "deteriorate into something we might understand as unattractive desperation . . . In a way," Schickel concludes, *His Girl Friday* was Grant's "ultimate test: could he make even charmlessness charming? Yes, he could" (99).

Or could he? Is Grant miscast in *His Girl Friday*, and what—beyond accents—might that claim mean? To me there is no question that Grant remains charming in *His Girl Friday* even as Walter Burns does not—even as I, like Robin Wood, want nothing for Hildy but to "walk out on *both* men" at the end, the boring one and the psychopathic manipulator (in Britton n.p.). When Hildy calls Burns "wonderful in a loathsome sort of way" we understand the "loathsome" doesn't apply to Grant; but when she remarks on Walter's dimple, wherever on his body it is located (neither he nor she seem to be referring to "that ridiculous hole in [his] chin" as Myrna Loy's character does in *Mr. Blandings Builds His Dream House* in 1948), it is only Walter's because it is Grant's. Such questions are of course raised by consideration of all star acting, but with *His Girl Friday* what I find fascinating is, on the one hand, why Grant's body in this film, its appearance and stances and gestures and voice, have alone commanded so much of my attention over the years, no matter what his co-stars are doing nor how well they are doing it. And concomitantly, how Grant's offscreen and onscreen generosity towards his co-stars in mechanical and formal as well as practical ways—a generosity that is an extraordinarily significant part of his appeal in this film, especially—is at once displayed and subverted through Hawks's representation of a visual and aural equality. Without Hildy as played by Rosalind Russell—who incidentally thought, *pace* Hawks, that Grant was *not* "just a personality" but a "true comic, in the sense that comedy is in the mind, the brain, the cortex" as well as an actor who could "immediately . . . become any character that was called for" (Russell and Chase 87)—*His Girl Friday* might have succeeded in making Grant's Walter *only* loathsome; as written he is completely horrid. And yet the very strength of the other performances in the film—there really isn't a bad one—serves ultimately and somewhat paradoxically to reinforce Grant's status as cynosure, even though we never see him in a scene by himself, never watch him except in the company of others (even when he's alone in a shot he's talking to someone). Well before this chapter was a gleam in a volume editor's eye, in other words, I was fast-forwarding through *His Girl Friday* to get to the scenes with Grant.

In the remainder of this chapter I consider Grant's face and costumed body and all that he does with both to make Walter Burns loathsome and duplicitous as well as hilarious and attractive. Hawks may indeed make Hildy the "equal" of Walter in many important ways, through what Gerald Mast calls "perfectly balanced symmetrical compositions, implying the essential harmony and complementarity of the two regardless of their verbal warfare" (45), as well as the compatible rhythms of their rapid-fire speech, which in turn "accompanies the rhythm and pace of their loping walk" (214) and conveys the "energetic harmony of their collaboration" (230). And Russell is certainly as fine an actor as Grant. But because she is not *shown* to be duplicitous (though there are small hints that she has been in the past), her visual and aural equivalence only accentuates how Walter's ability to perform sincerity where he feels none is going to make their implied remarriage again a living hell for her. Indeed, Grant's essential genius, in this film and others, may lie in how "defiantly self-centered" all of his performances are, with *His Girl Friday* only foregrounding that aspect of his persona more forcefully than his other vehicles, even Hitchcock's *Notorious* (1946).

Although Grant's status as a visual dreamboat of the "tall-dark-and-handsome" variety, in Kael's words, had not quite overtaken him at the time of *His Girl Friday*, we can start by acknowledging simply how good he looks here, to my mind better than in any other of his black and white vehicles (*Notorious* is a close second). He never appears in any of the ridiculous get-ups or circumstances of the other screwballs—for example having his coat ripped up the back or having to wear a woman's feathery bathrobe or chasing a leopard in *Bringing Up Baby*. He has really only one costume in *His Girl Friday*, a light and perfectly cut double-breasted tattersall wool suit with which he wears a crisp white long-sleeved shirt and a dark tie, and in it he is completely at ease with his body, hands in pockets or out. He adds a carnation to the lapel in his first scene with Hildy, where it remains whenever he's wearing the jacket. Except for the scene following his examination for a life insurance policy, when we get a glimpse of Grant's sunken but muscular chest as he buttons his shirt and reties his tie, the jacket stays on; and whenever he leaves his office, which means all of the climactic final third or so of the film, he also wears the black fedora. The length of the jacket sheaths him in tweed authority, the light tone and faint plaid checks making him stand out against the darker suits of the other men in the film while linking him to Bruce's similarly colored but bulky and unbecoming raincoat (in the lunch-table scene, Bruce's dark suit blends in completely with the set). Even Hildy, in two severe but fussy, geometrically patterned dark suits and those outré hats (designed by Kalloch), can't draw our eye as much as Walter does.

It also helps that he's lit throughout with high-key three-point "glamour lighting": he's hardly ever in the dark, literally or figuratively, though other characters are, including Hildy. Kael refers a couple of times to what she calls Grant's "huge neck" in her story on the "slapstick Prince Charming" (48) and while she implies that the thickness of his neck, along with bowlegs, kept him from early stardom on Broadway and in films, it was attractive by 1940 and remains so. (I can't claim that Grant made thick necks fashionable, but one reason he still inspires raptures is probably that handsome men are now supposed to have them, as a sign of buff masculinity.) In other films, the "rolling shuffle of his slightly bow-legged walk" (Eliot 2) is more obvious than it is here, because most of his shots are close-ups or Hawks's favored medium long shots, especially for the two- and three-shots with which this film is replete. Grant's broad hips—which gave him the stability he needed as a music-hall acrobat in his youth—are less obvious here as well, and his stride under the long jacket is confident and swinging whenever he does cover space, as in the famous tracking shots from right to left and back again, with and without Hildy, through the newsroom in early scenes. And conversely when we don't see the source of his locomotion in tighter shots he seems almost to glide from place to place, sometimes menacingly so, as when his forward lean drives Hildy around the press room at the courthouse in a back and forth serpentine as he seeks to keep her from going to Bruce, or his advance towards poor Mrs. Baldwin in the scene I discussed above. Add physical control and sartorial splendor to Grant's glossy but not excessively styled dark hair, the "crystalline dazzle of his smile," and those "unforgettably piercing topsoil-brown eyes [rendered here as blackest black]" (along with "that irresistible cleft in his chin"), in biographer Marc Eliot's words (2), and it's no wonder that we can't take our eyes off him.

Hildy does, though—in fact, she's forced to. When Walter realizes that she's getting married the next day ("Tomorrow, as soon as that?"), for example, and that he doesn't have much time to keep her from leaving both him and his paper, he turns away from her to face the camera and she is left to address her lines to his back. We read his slightly opened mouth, unfocused concentration, and furrowed brow, and the stroking and finger-tapping of his lapel as he handles the carnation—he finger-taps the phone on his desk, too—as signs of conniving thought, signs that she can't see. When he turns towards her, the plan made, his smile snaps into place, the manipulation begins, and she's lost though she doesn't know it. By the end of the complicated lunch-table scene (they all order roast beef sandwiches, but the food that's delivered certainly isn't sandwiches), with Bruce the leaden but good-hearted stooge in Walter's and Hildy's sexually inflected cross-talk, we have seen the small crinkle-eyed glances of desire—Kael calls them Grant's "delighted stares"—he flashes towards Hildy that we know mean that she is worth pursuing. And we've heard his crowing maniacal laughter and some whinnying and watched him pound his knee as he recalls amusing events from their shared past to show Bruce how little he knows his bride-to-be, and now realize how easy it is for Walter to lie to anyone—"anytime, anyplace, anywhere."

The remaining comic set pieces in *His Girl Friday* all turn, therefore, on Walter's dreadfully self-centered actions in keeping Hildy away from Bruce and writing for his paper, culminating in the perfectly timed courthouse fugue of Walter, Bruce, and Hildy talking over each other: Bruce trying to get Hildy to leave with him, Hildy gabbing and typing away at the story Walter is waiting for, the one for which he is rebuilding the front page of his paper by phone ("No no, leave the rooster story alone, that's human interest"), and finally Hildy's realization that Bruce is gone, Walter telling her to forget him. Then another perfectly timed fugue involving Walter and Hildy competing to be heard on separate phones, and the arrival of the other reporters and the beleaguered Mrs. Baldwin, at which point Walter's lying becomes at once funnier but more baroque, his voice louder, his gestures more highly stylized. One misstep in the comedy is surely when Walter pounds three times on the rolltop desk for emphasis as he calls Mrs. Baldwin a "cock-eyed liar!" The three knocks are the signal for the poor fugitive being hidden inside to reveal himself, and Grant's expression says it all—not only that Walter, who has just been exhibiting the highest level of his skill at dissembling and obfuscation, would never do such a stupid thing, but that Cary Grant wouldn't either.

Kael claims that the "slight stylization of his comic technique—the deadpan primed to react, the fencer's awareness of the camera, all the self-protective skills he'd acquired—worked against him when he needed to be expressive. Cary Grant acts from the outside; he's the wrong kind of actor to play a disharmonious character" (62). I used to think *His Girl Friday* supported this assertion perfectly, but over the years I have come to think that the problem with Grant as Walter Burns is that there is little complexity there narratively at all. He's an entertaining monster, not really interested in truth but in being right, who wants Hildy to work for him and will do anything, including marrying her again, to put her back on the job. As many have pointed out, the quick resolution of the ending, following a charmingly loose and unfrantic scene in which he and Hildy are handcuffed together but prevail against the mayor and his minions (the two really do seem fond of each other as they stand completely at ease, finishing each other's sentences, though signally it takes handcuffs to make them so harmonious a couple), is a return to the status quo ante. There are equivocal signs of gender "equality" because Hildy is carrying the suitcase and will keep her job at the paper after she and Walter remarry, but Walter is more a monomaniac than ever. How many more divorces, how many more Bruce Baldwins, will there be down the line?

Despite *His Girl Friday*'s brilliance, its "many small touches of comic invention and expression" (Wood 67), its winking in-jokes (referring to Bruce Baldwin as looking like "that fellow in the movies, Ralph Bellamy," or Grant ad-libbing his original name, Archie Leach, in another exchange), and of course the beautiful face and precise physical control and the "sheer authority," in David Thomson's words, that they give him (in Schickel 97), I do think that Cary Grant makes *His Girl Friday* something of a mess as a film. But it still is and always will be compulsively watchable, because while he may be miscast as Walter Burns, he is perfectly cast as Cary Grant.

Works cited

Britton, Andrew. *Cary Grant: Comedy and Male Desire*. Tyneside-by-the-Sea: Tyneside Cinema, 1983.
Cavell, Stanley. *Pursuits of Happiness: The Hollywood Comedy of Remarriage*. Cambridge, MA: Harvard University Press, 1981.
Eliot, Marc. *Cary Grant*. New York: Harmony Books, 2004.
Kael, Pauline. "The Man from Dream City," *New Yorker* (14 July 1975), 40–68.

Kaufman, Sarah L. *The Art of Grace: On Moving Well Through Life*. New York: Norton, 2015.
Mast, Gerald. *Howard Hawks, Storyteller*. New York: Oxford University Press, 1982.
McBride, Joseph. *Hawks on Hawks*. Berkeley: University of California Press, 1982.
McCarthy, Todd. *Howard Hawks: The Grey Fox of Hollywood*. New York: Grove Press, 1997.
Naremore, James. *Acting in the Cinema*. Berkeley: University of California Press, 1988.
Nelson, Nancy, ed. *Evenings with Cary Grant: Recollections in His Own Words and by Those Who Knew Him Best*. Milwaukee, WI: Applause, 2012.
Russell, Rosalind, and Chris Chase. *Life Is a Banquet*. New York: Random House, 1977.
Schickel, Richard. *Cary Grant: A Celebration*. Boston: Little, Brown and Company, 1983.
Wood, Robin. *Howard Hawks*, 2nd edn. Detroit, MI: Wayne State University Press, 2006.

Chapter 4

Janet Gaynor in *Sunrise: A Song of Two Humans*

Janet Bergstrom

In May 1927 Janet Gaynor became a star overnight when Frank Borzage's *7th Heaven* began its tremendously successful run in New York City and then everywhere. Critics assumed that the skills she learned while making that film carried over to her heartfelt, subtle performance in F. W. Murnau's *Sunrise: A Song of Two Humans*, which premiered on Broadway later that year at the beginning of the fall season. But *7th Heaven* and *Sunrise*, both made for William Fox's studio, were shot in the reverse order of their release: in fact, *7th Heaven*'s start date was delayed until after *Sunrise* was finished. Gaynor credited Murnau for teaching her how to act during the six long months they spent creating that demanding film (Gaynor 7). When the first Academy Awards were announced on 18 February 1929 to honor achievements for the 1927/1928 season, Janet Gaynor won the Award of Merit (as the awards were then called) for best actress for her combined performances in *Sunrise, 7th Heaven,* and *Street*

Angel.[1] The second two were directed by Borzage. All three were produced by William Fox, won other awards, and became classics.

Of these films, *Sunrise* must have presented the most difficult challenges for this young actress, new to roles of dramatic complexity. Janet Gaynor had started her acting career in about 1925, in western and comedy short films. She got the lead role, with George O'Brien, in *The Johnstown Flood* and in John Ford's *The Shamrock Handicap* (both 1926), but was considered a newcomer when it came to demanding dramatic roles and public recognition. How was she able to project the thoughts and emotions of her character in *Sunrise* with such understated, intelligent expressiveness given a story that could have come across, with a different director, actors, technical team, and studio resources, as clichéd? This was Murnau's first American film. William Fox had famously given him carte blanche to make a masterpiece for his studio—no constraints of any kind, the run of his facilities and personnel. Murnau's contract stipulated that Carl Mayer, his favorite writer, would handle the script, and gave Murnau approval over it. The plot was simple, as Murnau preferred. He had worked it out with Mayer during pre-production in Berlin so that he could orchestrate an integrated composition deploying technical virtuosity in the service of a drama with clear lines and great emotional involvement with a minimum of inter-titles, a visual story that required each actor to bring a character to life convincingly.

The press had circulated rumors that Lillian Gish would play the wife in *Sunrise*, but when Murnau arrived in Los Angeles in 1926, he had still not cast this part. According to Gaynor, after she had already been chosen to play Diane, the lead female role in *7th Heaven*, the West Coast studio head, Winfield Sheehan, wanted her to play the wife in *Sunrise*.

> Mr. Sheehan said that of course Mr. Murnau could have anything he wanted. He was the great director of that period … Mr. Sheehan wanted him to use me, and of course he'd never heard of me. So Murnau said, all right, he would make a test. I had to get dressed in these drab clothes and put on a blonde wig so that I really looked like a German woman, with a big braid on the back of my head, and I took a test. This, too, was a very dramatic part. After the test he said, "Yes." I was accepted, and I was to do his picture. (Gaynor 6)

Of an extraordinarily strong cast, large and small parts alike, Janet Gaynor had the difficult task of embodying a character who has no "big scenes," whose screen presence must captivate the audience without detracting from the film's overall movement, using the smallest gesture or her entire body to increase her character's depth.

A farmer (George O'Brien) leaves his young wife (Gaynor) and child every night, seduced by a vacationing woman from the city (Margaret Livingston). His wife, with hope in her eyes, agrees to take a trip with him across the lake to the city in their small boat; midway there, under the sway of the city woman, he comes close to murdering her but he can't go through with it. His wife is terrified. As they touch land, she flees to a streetcar emerging from the forest. He climbs on, begging her not to be afraid of him. In the city, during a wedding they chance to enter, she believes and accepts his tormented repentance: they are reborn as a couple. They share the pleasures of the metropolis as if newly in love: playing in colossal fairgrounds, performing an impromptu "peasant dance" in a nightclub, sharing wine in an elegant restaurant. They start home across moonlit waters. A powerful storm arises and capsizes their boat. The husband, thrown to the rocky shoreline, calls out his wife's name. He searches for her with the village men, but the lanterns in their boats find only reeds he had wrapped around her to keep her afloat in the storm. Certain that she had drowned, the man is strangling the city woman when he hears that his wife lives. He appears at her bedside: her eyes slowly open to look at him with relief, trust, and happiness. The sun begins to rise over the village, the city woman leaves.

From the moment that Janet Gaynor, as the wife, walks toward the boat that will carry her and her husband to the city until, returning, the boat disappears under high waves, she will be an important presence in every scene. Not that these scenes will necessarily represent the husband or the wife's point of view. Part of Murnau's brilliant design in *Sunrise* is to move in and out of subjective story positions, for instance moving the camera—the film became famous for its camera movement—in and out of a character's possible field of vision and beginning certain large sections of the film, such as the fairground scenes, apart from any particular character at all.

Before the couple begin their trip, the woman from the city dominates. She is the first of the three principal characters we see, as she finishes dressing in her rented room in a modest village house. Visually she is the opposite of the wholesome, country-dressed wife that Gaynor plays with her blonde hair pulled back plainly. The city woman has a curly black bob, makeup, sexy lingerie, cigarette smoke curling around her, a short black satiny dress and high heels as if she is ready for a night on the town, not for meeting her lover in a swamp. On her way out, she motions to the wife of the couple she's renting from to shine her high heels, making her get up from dinner with her husband.

The city woman walks along the path toward her lover's window where she whistles for him to come out. Now we see the husband for the first time, sitting at his dinner table in his small home, turning to that sound. We see her whistle again, until he stands up. Only now do we see his wife as she brings dishes to the table. Perhaps he is undecided, but after another whistle, from the city woman's viewpoint outside, we see his silhouette behind the curtain. He gestures to the right and she departs in that direction.

When his wife returns to the table with their dinner, he is gone. She realizes that she is alone. We understand from the way she sits, expressionless, her body dejected, that this is not the first time. Murnau then gives us a contrasting image of the man and his wife in a strange flashback as their housekeeper (whom we have not yet seen) tells another woman: "They used to be like children, carefree … always happy and laughing …." That title gives way to a pastoral scene outdoors during the day (the housekeeper seems to conjure up this vision or memory): the wife, her entire body radiating vitality and happiness, sits under a tree holding her small baby near the field her husband is tilling, driving a team of oxen. He stops next to her and takes the baby she holds up for him with joyous, playful energy: they are in harmony. He runs back to resume plowing. A second title within the flashback tells the difference between that time and the present: "Now he ruins himself for that woman from the city—Money-lenders strip the farm—and his wife sits alone." Night shots, lit by a lantern, show him watching his oxen being led away.

The lovers' meeting in the swamp, and all the husband's scenes after that until he backs away from the murder, are "big performance scenes" for both of them, supported by all the considerable cinematic means at Murnau's disposal: the sexual spell the city woman casts over the farmer, her strength in pulling him away from the values and the life he had lived before, conjuring up the magical power of the city through images that take over the screen, and her own magnetism: the fabulous city montage in the swamp ends in her wild dance facing the man kneeling at her feet, until he throws his arms around her thighs and buries his head there.

The sexual tension becomes increasingly violent—the sex-drive that the woman arouses in him is only a step away from murder, that is, murdering her. We see this twice, first in his visceral reaction to her whispered idea that his wife could "get drowned," and again near the end, after he thinks his wife is dead, when she comes to him thinking he carried out her plan:

both times, he begins strangling her. In the first part of the story, her sexuality overpowers him: she is stronger than he is, as we see when the camera follows their footprints leading out of the mud that is so wet her high heels leave deep imprints, along with the man's large boots, until it catches up with their feet walking ahead, then moves to show the woman picking reeds that she tells him to tie around himself to avoid drowning in the accident he will fake to get rid of his wife and be free to sell his farm and "come to the city!" A little later when he sits on his bed, perhaps still uncertain, he seems to be tormented by superimposed images of her seductive head that encircle his own, coming and coming until he does what she wants. Her hold over him is not broken until he cannot bring himself to kill his wife.

In the midst of so much high drama, with both lovers fascinating throughout the deepening entrapment of the haunted-looking husband, Janet Gaynor was able to hold her character's screen presence in cutaway shots to her at home with her small child, sobbing, or the next morning, after she is dressed, coming to her husband who has fallen into his bed during the night and tenderly pulling a blanket over him, or when he approaches her about the trip and we see her expression slowly changing in close-up shots, at first showing guarded affection, then some hope as she tries to smile, wanting to believe him about this vacation yet still protecting herself, then suddenly in the next room whirling around happily with her child, telling her housekeeper that she is taking a trip across the lake and she may be gone for a long time. Later in the city before the couple has been reconciled, we see subtle changes in her eyes and face, ending in crushing sorrow, her body collapsing.

As the husband pushes the boat off their landing to begin the trip to the city, we see their dog barking wildly. Does he want to come with them? Is this a warning to the wife? He breaks his chain, swims to the boat and the wife pulls him on board as her husband scowls, already turning the boat to take the dog back to land. This is an important scene for Gaynor, demonstrating an extraordinary range of small movements that express feelings that could not be described in words, some of them simple (her love for her dog: she holds it close and strokes it affectionately, happy for its unambiguous loyalty, despite getting water all over her dress), some of them conflicted. Her eyes betray uncertainty about leaving with her husband, who is not showing any signs of affection or even attention to her, his head down, his eyes elsewhere. At one point, looking worried, she begins to get out of the boat, but then sits back down and smiles, trying to believe that their trip is a good sign for their future as a couple.

As they progress into the broad lake, she looks off in one direction to see a flock of birds, some of them taking off in flight; her expression somber, she then turns in the other direction to see more birds. She seems to be on her own in her end of the small boat, not really with her husband, rowing furiously, not looking like himself, so dark is his expression, his eyes sleepless, his face unshaven for days. While George O'Brien's performance is intense and darkly purposeful toward a specific goal that we know, Janet Gaynor's performance is highly nuanced, uncertain, strongly yet softly projecting herself in a body so fragile in the middle of a seemingly vast expanse of water. When her husband stands, his shoulders hunched over, and slowly steps toward her, she takes fright, shrinking back into her corner of the boat. When his arms reach toward her, sudden terror distorts her face. Leaning back toward the water, she holds up her hands in prayer. This—or something inside him—breaks the city woman's hold and he sits down, rowing fast as they near the shore. This is the first turning point in the film: O'Brien and Gaynor have opposite performance requirements and styles, befitting each of the characters they portray in that crisis.

O'Brien, brilliantly out of character from the popular roles he was known for as well as from his own sport-loving personality, acts in a particular direction, withdrawing more and more inside himself as he moves from sex to murder; then, throwing off that weight, he will move toward winning his wife's trust again and returning to the lives they had known before. Gaynor, on the other hand, has many directions in which to go, none very clear except when she realizes her husband is going to try to kill her and she almost seems to lose herself in fear. Her body language is as conflicted as her facial expressiveness, even in fleeing from her husband once she is ashore.

Yet she still conveys, somehow, that she loves him with absolute purity. When he breaks down during the wedding in the city, sobbing and begging her forgiveness, she holds his head tenderly in her lap, stroking it not unlike her simple, unqualified expression of love for her child or for her loyal dog. Her subtlety takes on new dimensions after this second movement of the story and they can be together again in harmony, as seen so beautifully when they leave the church steps and walk into the midst of the huge city plaza, soon transformed for them into their own private meadow before the reality of the city intrudes and they realize they are at the center of a traffic jam. Now they can begin to regain the playfulness of their lives that we glimpsed in the flashback scene. The wife teases her husband whom she knows (again) so well and he responds to her as we must imagine he would have done before, such as when she entices him to get a shave in the barbershop or their shared reaction to the photograph they had taken of themselves, not realizing the photographer would choose to print the moment when they kissed before his backdrop that replicates the dream-like meadow they had stepped into after their renewal of vows in the church.

Janet Gaynor recalled vividly how she learned to act in this way:

> I had six months with Mr. Murnau, and I must say it was a most gratifying experience. Trying!! He was unbelievably trying. But he was wonderful, too, and he was a great director. I worked for him and I learned so much, it was like training. Working with him was the equivalent to a year of dramatic school. Of course, this was all pantomime, and the slowness, and the thought behind it! If you were eating a piece of cake [in a restaurant when first in the city, as her husband tries to convince her not to be afraid of him]—all the thought, all the process that would go on in your mind while you were lifting up the piece of cake, because my husband in the film was trying to kill me. Really, it was the image in the mind. I've not only never forgotten it, I'm sure that I have used it always, these things that he taught me. (Gaynor 7)

First, there were rehearsals:

> Although we had scripts to follow, the director would take you through a rehearsal of a scene like this. Supposing you were to enter a door, walk to the center of the room, wonder where your husband was, feel tragic because you knew he was with another woman—I'm just making this up—the director would take you through this. Then maybe you'd walk over to the fire, go to warm yourself, because just the thought could make you cold, or you would seek something for comfort. The director would take you that far in rehearsal. (Gaynor 8)

Then they would shoot the scene—with Murnau, as many as thirty times:

> So, the cameras would turn. You would come in and do it, go over to the fire, and be warming yourself, and because there was no sound, [Murnau's] voice would come over and say, "And now, maybe there's hope! You hear something! Maybe that's his footsteps!" And you would react to this kind of direction, spontaneously. For the actress, at least for me, it was very exciting, because it would sort of come in to your mind and flow out again through your body. It was a very exciting sort of experience. Murnau was all mind, really. He directed in that way. It was a mental picture that he gave. (Gaynor 8–9)

O'Brien recounted that Murnau

> wanted to get the cast and all of us together, and this resulted in us practically being a family. Janet Gaynor, Margaret Livingston, the cameramen and myself. I don't think we spent a nickel for food on the whole picture. We were always eating at his house. He insisted, you know? We'd go to lunch, we'd talk, but all the time he was judging you. We knew each other so well. (O'Brien)

According to O'Brien, they shot in continuity, to keep the characters' moods. He used to go home exhausted every night and fall into bed, living his character throughout filming.

Not only did they have strong and conflicting emotions to convey, but many of the sets were constructed in false perspective, with floors slanted downward toward the camera to make the spaces seem larger or take on some other quality planned in advance. This affected the performances, for the actors had to learn how to walk on slanted surfaces while giving the impression that they were flat. Janet Gaynor remembered the scene when she and her husband are asked to do a "peasant dance" (named as such on a music cue card placed on a horn in the dance band):

> In "Sunrise" they built what they called "the city." It was a city street—not one, many city streets—and it had an elevated [railway], beautiful buildings, a real street-car that ran. Then when he would shoot it, he had children dressed up as grown-ups way in the back, to force the perspective. In some of our other sets, the floors would be slanted, and the whole thing was done to bring about this terrific perspective. I don't think anyone else has ever done that. I know in "Sunrise" George O'Brien and I had to do a dance, and we certainly weren't professional dancers—anyway, it was supposed to be a folk-dance—but even so, to try to do it on that slanted floor was something. We had to whirl, and we'd usually whirl and whirl and end up in the camera. (Gaynor 10)

From scenes of quiet suffering to the joyous, vigorous dance with her husband, an enactment of complementarity regained, to her bruising physical pain and fear of being lost in the crushing waters of the storm, to her beatific revival at the end of *Sunrise*, Janet Gaynor more than met the challenges of a consistently superior embodiment of naturalness and inner life projected outward. Murnau appreciated her performance so much that he chose her to be his female lead in his next film, *4 Devils*, which, to our sorrow, is today considered lost.[2]

Notes

1. The "year" at that time followed the model of the theatrical season, not the calendar year. The ceremony was held later, on 16 May.
2. See Janet Bergstrom, *Murnau's 4 Devils: Traces of a Lost Film* (Twentieth Century Fox, 2003), a documentary found on all DVD and BluRay versions of *Sunrise*.

Works cited

Gaynor, Janet. "The Reminiscences of Janet Gaynor" (1958), Oral History Collection, Columbia University, New York.
Martin, Dave. George O'Brien Oral History, 8 January 1961. Unpublished. Collection Robert Birchard.

Chapter 5

Katharine Hepburn in *The Lion in Winter*

Homer B. Pettey

> She must have been tough as nails to have lived to 82 years old and full of beans. Both she and Henry II were big-time operators who played for whole countries. I like big-time operators. (Katharine Hepburn (in Edwards 351))

A major conceit of *The Lion in Winter* (1968) is the game of political and emotional chess, in which King and Queen (Peter O'Toole, Katharine Hepburn) vie for power through a series of subterfuges, sacrifices, and exchanges. To portray Eleanor of Aquitaine, Katharine Hepburn must weave multiple performances of sexual, familial, and political manipulations, while still creating a comic, romantic, and tragic figure. The late 1950s and early 1960s saw Hepburn performing four of Shakespeare's more complex, transgressive female roles for the fledgling American Shakespeare Theatre, Portia in *The Merchant of Venice* (1957), Beatrice in *Much Ado About Nothing* (1957), Viola in *Twelfth Night* (1960), and Cleopatra in *Antony and Cleopatra* (1960). She also played the enigmatic, obsessive mother-wife,

Mary Tyrone, in Sidney Lumet's screen adaptation of O'Neill's *Long Day's Journey into Night* (1962). To the role of Eleanor, then, Hepburn combines physical realism with Shakespearean dynamic wit, naturalistic emotions with classical disdain. Hepburn's Eleanor understands the necessity of playing shifting roles and donning several masks to regain what she has lost. For Hepburn, Eleanor's physical, emotional, and verbal reactions to the unfolding plots-within-plots paradoxically must be as histrionic as they are realistic. In the medieval world of political intrigue, Eleanor's performances are not merely a game, but her only strategy for survival.

The screen transformation

Filmmaker Anthony Harvey and his cast rehearsed *The Lion in Winter* as though it were a stage production, which accounts for much of Hepburn's measured performance. Harvey's choice to spend two weeks this way, at London's Theatre Royal Haymarket, allowed for a fast fourteen-week production schedule, because "65 per cent of the film was made in sequence" ("Prior-Rehearsed, 'Lion in Winter' Thereby Speeded," *Variety*, 30 October 1968, 12). One avenue into Hepburn's choice would be those scenes from the play that retain the stage directions and its original language: these would make it possible for us to see and appreciate how she builds upon what is already given, to bring a character, moment by moment, to startling life. It would be erroneous, however, to assume that the film is merely a stage production, since Hepburn especially recognizes the camera's—not a theatre audience's—role in construction as it limits her mobility within the frame. That consciousness of her body within the frame makes her gestures, movements, and especially her close-ups all the more evocative. Hepburn takes from the play's directions the crucial introduction to Eleanor: "She is a truly handsome woman of great temperament, authority, and presence ... Finally, she is that most unusual thing: a genuinely feminine woman thoroughly capable of holding her own in a man's world" (Goldman 11). Hepburn adds subtlety, irony, and emotional discharges that are calculated to keep her audience, Henry, Alais (Jane Merrow), and her sons Richard (Anthony Hopkins), Geoffrey (John Castle), and John (Nigel Terry) guessing both her motivations and her next move. In short, Hepburn's Eleanor is that unusual thing, indeed, an actress fully aware of the pretenses of her acting, as though for her—at these critical moments in her life—performance, appearance, and reality are all the same.

The pattern of Eleanor's machinations, calculated and explosive mood swings, and wry and piercingly sardonic comments can be found in Hepburn's understanding of the character *qua* political theater. Her presence is structured dramatically, both in the play and in the film. In James Goldman's play, as in the film (the script of which he wrote), Eleanor does not appear until after a scene in the king's young lover Alais' bed chamber with Henry II arguing over the girl's conflicted roles as mistress, potential bride to his son John, and jealous antagonist to Eleanor. The emotional context is set, therefore, when she makes her entrance. In the film we begin with Henry and young John sparring with broadswords, then move to this argument between Henry and Alais in the open air before scenes identify the other sons, Richard and Geoffrey. In the play, Eleanor remains absent from a somewhat later scene (I: 6) in Philip Capet's (the King of France) bedchamber, where Henry verbally jousts with Philip about rightful lands and exposes Richard's homosexuality (Goldman 55–66): a display of political strategies. A third scene in the play (II: 2) repeats the setting and character arrangement of the opener, with Henry disclosing to Alais that he has locked up his unruly and potentially dangerous sons in the cellar of Chinon palace. Crucial to the play, we might note, is not Eleanor's separation from these three scenes but her *presence* there, both implied and explicit, that she is invoked and implied in all of the central political and amorous conversations. Eleanor, not Henry, is the key to the play, as Hepburn, more than Peter O'Toole, is the focal point for the plot, characterization, and emotional content of the film. The Hepburn performance is the crux around which the complex familial and state action spins. O'Toole recognized Hepburn's tenacity in capturing Eleanor; her role seemed to spill out onto the set. O'Toole, twenty-five years younger than Hepburn, claimed that she reduced him "to a shadow of my former gay-dog self ... She is terrifying. It is sheer masochism working with her. She has been sent by some dark fate to nag and torment me" (Edwards 352).

Several key scenes with Eleanor shape the film's narrative arc. Eleanor's arrival at Chinon and her alternation there between sweetly affectionate and viciously spiteful responses to Henry. Eleanor's tense re-acquaintance with her beloved son Richard, who calls her Medea. Henry and Eleanor quarreling over his possible marriage to Alais and their own sexual histories, concluding with a performance for Eleanor's benefit of Henry and Alais kissing. The exceptional mirror scene with Eleanor (examined closely below). Henry's announcement that the Pope will annul his marriage to Eleanor and her scathing retaliation that she slept with his father. Eleanor descending into the Chinon cellar to provide her three sons with the weapons to kill their father. Each of these moments in the film adaptation requires Hepburn's skill to create performances within a performance; that is, Hepburn must simultaneously indicate and conceal: indicate as she conceals Eleanor's true feelings, for to reveal too much is to be trapped by her husband and adversary. Eleanor's ostentatious arrival and departure by medieval boat both find Hepburn taking on the pose of a grand queen with an air of almost light-hearted triumph. Of course, this posture is mere pretense, too, a performance solely for Henry's benefit. Hepburn's laughter at the film's conclusion must be interpreted as genuine appreciation of the sport of jousting with Henry over their known worlds.

The reality of Eleanor of Aquitaine, so far as the chroniclers attested, was that of a complex person, as Gervase of Canterbury depicted, "an exceedingly shrewd woman, sprung from noble stock, but fickle" (120). Amy Kelly's famous biography, *Eleanor of Aquitaine and the Four Kings*, describes the central characteristics of this remarkable woman:

> She came as her own mistress, the most sophisticated of women, equipped with plans to establish her own assize, to inaugurate a regime dedicated neither to Mars nor to the Pope, nor to any king, but to Minerva, Venus, and the Virgin. She was resolved to escape from secondary roles, to assert her independent sovereignty in her own citadel, to dispense her own justice, her own patronage, and when at leisure, like the Empress of Byzantium, a vast decorum in her precincts. (158)

Shrewd, independent, sophisticated, yet fickle—these traits, no matter how seemingly contradictory at times, inform Hepburn's perception of how to play Eleanor. An early *Variety* review of *The Lion in Winter* captured her expansive and multi-layered performance, which would prove to be the source for much of its huge box office:

> Miss Hepburn's performance is amazing. Whether coldly scheming some political coup, sincerely or insincerely remorseful over a failed marriage, or—at one dramatic highlight—crying out that people, not abstract causes and martial things, are the breeders of war and tumult, she is terrific. Her lightning-bolt flashes of irony show the Queen as a woman totally aware. ("The Lion in Winter British—Panavision—Color," *Variety*, 23 October 1968, 6)

A concurring review in *The Independent Film Journal* praised the actress's remarkable shifts of guises:

> Whether she is joyously recalling the glory of her Crusades-cavorting heyday when she was dazzling the troops with her beauty, or whether she is offering her son her talons for motherly support, or acknowledging the role that sex has played in history, the actress is always remarkable. Perhaps her most splendid moment occurs in the dressing table scene as she takes inventory of her jewels and of the passing years. ("The Lion in Winter," Independent Film Journal, 29 October, 1968, 892)

Brenda Davis in *Sight and Sound* credited director Anthony Harvey with drawing out Hepburn's performance as Eleanor, whose "malice has been so long polished and refined that she seems to glow with it, like burnished bronze" (44).

Crucial to these astute observations of Hepburn's performance are the actress's choices according to her cinematic strengths, her peculiar, utterly characteristic method of Affect, Articulation, and Action. The Hepburn character feels to the fullest depths and expresses emotion, ebullient, angry, frightened, ashamed—whatever—to the very fullest extent of what the voice and body will allow. Hepburn's affect draws upon her early films, such as *Alice Adams* (1935) and *Morning Glory* (1933) in which she acts out the pretentious alter egos of her characters. Affect, as we look at Hepburn's use of it, and unlike the rather confused *in-between-ness* and *beside-ness* doctrines of Affect Theory, applies not to some vague sense of the body, but to that form of acting that displays both real and calculated passions in order to influence the emotions of other characters. In this sense, affect is a type of performative domination over others. Hepburn assumes this position through carefully guided hand gestures, deliberate postures, and mercurial expressions of someone who has taken on an affected personality. It is meticulously mannered. Hepburn's physical choices in *The Lion in Winter* often deliberately show contrivance, not just in Eleanor's acting out her various guises, but also in Hepburn's choice of those guises. Take, for example, Eleanor's arrival at Chinon at the beginning of the film, an appearance for appearance's sake. She swans in with sweeping gestures, calling attention to herself, and immediately dominates the scene by recounting her political status, role as mother, and sexuality to her estranged sons: "Good, good Louis; if I'd managed sons for him instead of all of those little girls, I'd still be stuck with being Queen of France and we should not have known each other. Such, my angels, is the role of sex in history."

Hepburn's vocal articulation—she was born and raised in the upper-class northeast—is breathy, stagey, flamboyantly precise. Her familiar verbal adroitness can be observed in her screwball and romantic comedies, especially *Bringing Up Baby* (1938), *Adam's Rib* (1949), and *Desk Set* (1957). Throughout her film career, Hepburn was known for her specific verbal enunciation, the quick rhythm of her speech, and the fluency that she brought to verbal encounters, especially gender-based arguments. In short, she was an articulate actress, and nowhere shows this more than in *Lion in Winter*. So much of Eleanor's presence in the film depends upon Hepburn's ability to use language as her only defense, to articulate her political force through shifting verbal expressions, and to betray, often when the situation best suits her, raw emotional tirades. She can also be humorous as she delivers biting commentary, such as her assurance to Alais that she cares not a whit about Henry's infidelities: "Henry's bed is Henry's *province*: he can people it with *sheep* for all I care.—(*Hepburn pauses for effect.*) Which, on *occasion*, he has *done*." Hepburn's exchanges with O'Toole belong as much to a kind of verbal jousting as they do to the world of sinister diplomacy.

As much as Eleanor's character calculates affect and employs strategic articulation, she also exercises determined action. Her proud, even sculpted body moves sharply and definitively. She becomes a force. Hepburn's physicality separated her performances from those of other Hollywood stars; particularly revealing are the demanding scenes (shot in Uganda) in *The African Queen* (1951) and the displays of her athletic abilities in *Pat and Mike* (1952). Here, Hepburn realizes the significance of this aspect of Eleanor's performances, and ties posture to word to deed. Her awareness of the physical nature of Eleanor's relationships, particularly with Henry, transforms scenes of verbal jousting into poignant moments of recognition, love, and jealousy.

With Richard, Eleanor's beloved son who now rules her precious Aquitaine, she must forge an alliance, but Richard demurs any alignment of power as they walk along the parapet. Richard clearly sees through his mother's pretenses when she tries to gain his trust as an ally against Henry: "Don't play a scene with *me*." Hepburn shifts her approach to Hopkins in their most intimate scene in the film, choosing for Eleanor to seduce Richard with words, again recounting her sexual history. Hepburn cozies up to Hopkins in a two-shot, making sure that her head remains above his as she looks for his reaction with a desirous leer: "Men *coveted* this talon once. Henry was eighteen when we met and *I* was Queen of France. He came down from the North with a mind like *Aristotle's* and a form like *mortal sin.—*We shattered the Commandments on the *spot.*"

Hepburn's emphasis on "mortal sin" telegraphs that she is awaiting a response. Richard rejects her, so a new attack is required. Hepburn become more physical with Hopkins, moving closer to him as Eleanor offers Richard everything she owns in a will. But, as Richard notes: "Paper burns." When this political approach fails Eleanor, Hepburn takes on her most excessive moment of physical self-deprecation. Grabbing Hopkins's hands, Hepburn pulls them to her breast: "We were always hand in hand." Richard rejects his mother with, "As coarse and hot as that." Hurt, infuriated, and desperate describe the quick emotional range that Hepburn now enacts, as she pulls up both sleeves, takes out a long pin from beneath her cloak, and, in a close-up of her forearm, carves a blood line into her skin. Richard cries, "Mother!" and collapses into Eleanor's arms. Now, Hepburn looks into Hopkins's teary eyes, using the moment for Eleanor's dominating, Oedipal seduction: "See? You do remember. I taught you dancing, too, and languages and all the music that I knew and how to love what's beautiful. The sun was warmer then and we were every day together." The overhead shot concludes the scene with the two embraced.

When she finds herself not winning the political game with Henry, Eleanor often resorts to seductive and sexually aggressive language. Henry seduces her as well—not with sexuality but with what Eleanor desires most. If she resigns Aquitaine to John, Henry's favorite, then she can have her freedom—as simple as her signature. The contractual marriage would be complete, so long as John obtains Aquitaine. Hepburn gives Eleanor an affected smiling presence as she hears the word "freedom," although trying not to let any notice be given to the wringing of her hands:

> HENRY: I thought it might appeal to you. You always fancied traveling.
> ELEANOR: Yes, I did. I even made poor Louis take me on Crusade. How's that for blasphemy? I dressed my maids as Amazons and rode bare-breasted halfway to Damascus. Louis had a seizure and I damn near died of windburn but the troops were dazzled. Henry, I'm against the wall.

As the situation requires, Eleanor shifts from sexual adventurer to pitiable, tearful old woman. Almost weeping, she confesses her impotent position in the final lines of her "dazzling troops" moment. This shift, too, is another of Eleanor's ploys, which she uses to catch Henry off-guard. She claims that she will sign, if the marrying off of Alais occurs right at that moment. She elicits Henry's sympathy in order to attack him with her sexuality, even if it is her past escapade. Previously, she has laughingly lied—then admitted the lie—that she slept with Thomas Becket. Words effect Eleanor's retaliation as a kind of verbal *lex talionis*, tongue lash for tongue lash. Even with her political advantage of recovering Aquitaine, Eleanor, as Hepburn plays her, cannot let the moment pass without injuring Henry. She carefully articulates each word, pausing in a syncopated pattern that emphasizes her hatred for him, all the while broadening her grin: "I wonder, do you ever *wonder* if I slept with your father?"

This shifting from political weakness to sexual aggressor also occurs later in the film, when Henry claims that he will have his marriage to Eleanor annulled. Henry wishes to bypass patrilineal descent to Richard, John, and Geoffrey by marrying young Alais and producing a new crop of sons. When Eleanor claims that she will raise another of her civil wars against him, this time with the able assistance of his three sons and Philip of France, Henry laughingly informs her that she has misplayed the game: "You should have lied to me." As he has done with her in the past, he will now imprison his three sons until he returns from Rome with the Pope's annulment.

Sensing a great loss at hand, Eleanor strikes out in a series of escalating confessions about Henry's father, Geoffrey Plantagenet, Count of Anjou. Hepburn uses his bed and her body to simulate their sexual acts: "Did your father sleep with me, or didn't he?"

A close-up of the two actors has Hepburn taking on her most vicious and hateful facial expression, as she nearly spits in O'Toole's face: "About my *fornication* with your father—." She scoots onto the four-poster, regal bed, watching Henry with a malicious grin. Then, she falls back upon the pillows, placing her hands above her head and writhing in sexual abandon as she delivers her next verbal blow: "I've never touched you without thinking, 'Geoffrey, Geoffrey!'" When Henry fails to react as she wishes, she rears up and hisses at him, "I've put more horns on you than Louis ever wore." Returning to that paternal fornication, Hepburn uses her fingers in the air above Henry's shoulder as a combination of seduction and predatory clawing: "I *loved* your father's body. He was beautiful!" She falls back upon the bed once more in order to act out the lovemaking for Henry: "I can see his body now. Shall I describe it?" In an overhead shot, the camera captures Hepburn's entire body on the bed as she begins rubbing her hands over her arms, as though she were in the act of sex with Henry's father. "His arms were rough, with scars here—" she continues rubbing the arms and shouting in ecstasy, "I can feel his arms! I feel them!"

Sickened by her descriptions, Henry screams and runs from the room as she follows after, collapsing in the doorway. Then, Hepburn shifts from being prostrate upon the cobbled floor, pushes herself up, and looks directly into the camera, not, as the play contends, "*in desolation*," but rather in resigned mockery: "Well, what family doesn't have its ups and downs?"

Mirror

Hepburn's most famous scene occurs in her bedchamber as she confronts her mirror. *The Monthly Film Bulletin* provided a two-page photographic collage spread of Hepburn onstage and in her corresponding film portrayal ("Hepburn in Rehearsal" 132–3). The photographs indicate clear distinctions between the two types of performances. In the stage rehearsal, Hepburn's arm movements appear broad, sweeping, and somewhat histrionic, while in the film, she is aware of the close-ups and maintains a more subdued approach to the famous mirror scene. Obviously, between pre-rehearsal and camera setup, Hepburn had made decisions about her physical movements in order to translate stage performance to the screen.

Eleanor sits "feverishly covering herself with precious things" (Goldman 49), as though here in her solitude, she can assume a role now forever lost. In the previous scene, Eleanor dared Henry to demonstrate his devotion to Alais, which she believed he would not do because it is merely a ploy. That scene concluded with Henry declaring his love for Alais and then passionately kissing, as the camera focuses upon Hepburn's expression of distress, anger, and despair. Within her room, Eleanor fancies another time, another life, in the film's only monologue. (In parentheses and italics are my descriptions of Hepburn's performance.)

> ELEANOR: (*Through gritted teeth.*) How beautiful you make me. (*Smiles, laughs, and then sumptuously lets down her hair.*) What might Solomon have sung had he seen this? (*Deftly picks up a hand mirror.*) I can't, I'd turn to salt. (*Waves the mirror in the air, dreamily, hypnotically.*) I've lost again. I'm done, for now. (*She holds her head between her hands in close-up, scowling grimly, then becomes almost tearful before she pauses with a half-smile. Her eyes close briefly in resignation, then open. She rests her chin upon her folded arms.*) Well—there'll be other Christmases. (*Picks up an elaborate necklace whose ends she clasps daintily, between thumbs and forefingers. Her*

gown nearly exposes her left breast.) I'd hang you from the nipples but you'd shock the children. (*Camera shoots directly into the large mirror as she muses.*) They kissed sweetly, didn't they? I'll have him next time. I can wait. (*Seeing the jewel box, she reaches in and picks up a crown.*) Ah, there you are, my comfort and my company. We're locked in for another year: four seasons more. Oh, what a desolation, what a life's work. (*Puts on the crown as* GEOFFREY *enters*) Is it too much? Be sure to squint as you approach. You may be blinded by my beauty. (*She laughs through tears flooding up.*)

This scene with her boys arguing over the transition and interruptions of power at Henry's court concludes with Eleanor alone and grabbing the arabesque-shaped hand mirror again, as the camera shoots her reflected face: "My, what a lovely girl! How could her king have left her?" (*Hepburn speaks with vicious sarcasm, smiles knowingly and to no one in particular. Then her face shifts to sadness and despair as she puts down the mirror, which has caught and held, perhaps, her true inner self.*)

In New York, the film opened at Lincoln Arts on a reserved-seat basis and brought in $10,000 on each of the first Saturday and Sunday, which was enough for the production company to secure a $300,000 advance for more reserved seating at the theater ("'Lion' a Roaring $300,000 Advance," *Variety*, 6 November 1968, 27). For Avco Embassy, *The Lion in Winter* was an international box-office success. In Italy alone during the first month, the film "set all-time house records," as it did in Portugal ("'Lion in Winter' Big B.O. in Rome & Lisbon," *Variety*, 5 November 1969, 28). In Chicago, the film had thirty-three "record breaking weeks at the Esquire Theatre" before a first-week "fantastic" box office at the Evergreen and Old Orchard Theatres ("*The Lion In Winter*" Advertisement, *Independent Film Journal*, 5 August 1969, 9). Addison Verrill's review attributed much of the film's success to Hepburn's marvelous performance "at the pinnacle of a long and vigorous career," but even more because "Katharine Hepburn is the last of the veteran Hollywood superstars who has not seen fit to make cameo appearances, do a television anthology or make Grand Guignol excursions into high camp" (Addison Verrill, "The Lion in Winter," *Boxoffice*, 28 October 1968, 13.) In early November 1969, *Variety* reported that the film "landed on the cover" of the *Saturday Review* and that Arthur Knight claimed in that magazine that Hepburn's performance was "perhaps the finest characterization of her career . . . it is difficult to image another actress who could bring to the role an equal range and intensity" ("Manhattan Critics Nearly Unanimous on 'Lion in Winter' and Hepburn," *Variety*, 6 November 1969, 12.)

Not all critics expressed delight at this film, as evidenced by Harry M. Geduld in the *Humanist*: "these films are not historical but antihistorical, since their effect is not to explain the past in terms of human values and the evolution of social forms but to reduce it to domestic quarrels and bed-hopping, to patterns of intrigue in which people are reduced to pawns in trivial games, or to fancy-dress variations on the public images of the actors themselves" (Geduld 26). Of course, Geduld remained a minority voice about *The Lion in Winter* and he misses the intricate and layered performance of Katharine Hepburn, whose acting was anything but "trivial."

Works cited

Davis, Brenda. "The Lion in Winter," *Sight and Sound* 38: 1 (Winter 1968), 44.

Edwards, Anne. *A Remarkable Woman: A Biography of Katharine Hepburn*. New York: William Morrow and Company, 1985.

Geduld, Harry M. "Last Leap of the Old Lion," *Humanist* 29: 3 (1 May 1969), 26.

Goldman, James. *The Lion in Winter*. New York: Random House, 2004.

"Hepburn in Rehearsal/*Lion in Winter*," *Monthly Film Bulletin* (Summer 1968) 132–3.

Kelly, Amy. *Eleanor of Aquitaine and the Four Kings*. Cambridge, MA: Harvard University Press, 1950.

Warren, W. L. *Henry II*. Berkeley: University of California Press, 1973.

Chapter 6
Bette Davis in *Dangerous*
Lucy Fischer

At a very early age I fell in love with my profession. (Bette Davis)

Introduction

When one thinks of Bette Davis in the 1930s, it is her association with Warner Bros. that one recalls, the studio at which she remained until 1950. In this sense, Davis was a quintessential actress of the "studio system" and, although she protested loudly about its attendant constraints (and often felt like an "assembly line" worker (Davis 157)), it seems clear that she also benefitted from them. As Thomas Schatz has observed, "Davis seemed to sense that despite her struggles with the studio powers—or in some ways because of them—her personality and the Warners' style were inexorably bound together, fused in that peculiar symbiosis of star and studio style" (27). Davis herself agrees. As she notes, "Under the contract system, month after month we were allowed to make films. And we learned something from even the dreadful ones, so we had a great chance to improve ourselves. Working all the time is the only way" (McBride 114).

Dangerous (1935) was her twenty-first film for Warner Bros. It came at a time when her acting ability had been broadly recognized in Hollywood. She had been nominated for an Academy Award in 1935 for her role in *Of Human Bondage* (1934)—an RKO film—though she did not win. *Dangerous* was the next vehicle to give her the opportunity for a distinguished performance, and it garnered some of the biggest raves of her career to date. The *New York Times* called hers "a strikingly sensitive performance" and noted that "this Davis girl is rapidly becoming one of the most interesting of our screen actresses" ("At the Rivoli," 27 December 1935, 3). The *Los Angeles Times* commented that Davis "seems actual flesh and blood" in the film: "That's how penetratingly alive she is and how electric, [and] varied as to mood" (Grace Kingsley, "Bette Davis Hit in Film," *Los Angeles Times*, 26 December 1935, 11). Finally, E. Arnot Robertson of *Picture Post*, reacting to Davis's onscreen force, remarked, "I think Bette Davis would probably have been burned as a witch if she had lived two or three hundred years ago. She gives the curious feeling of being *charged with power* which can find no ordinary outlet" (Ringgold 65, my emphasis).

Davis was again nominated for an Academy Award for *Dangerous,* and this time she prevailed (with her Oscar delivered on 5 March 1936 by D.W. Griffith). Typical of how Davis was perceived in Hollywood (as a plain Jane), the dress that she wore to the event was deemed "dowdy" and described as a "dotted house dress" (Leaming 114, Moser 39). Many saw her award as a mere consolation prize for not having triumphed the year before. Charles Affron subscribes to this theory and calls *Dangerous* a "dreadful film" (223). Similarly, Laura Moser finds Davis's acting "by no means explosive" (38). I beg to differ. Both the movie and Davis's performance stand up on their own and constitute a perfect text through which to understand the actress's broader style and skill.

But analyzing screen acting—translating performance into a series of coherent gestures, strategies, and aesthetic maneuvers—is one of the most challenging aspects of comprehending stardom. (Even Davis herself states that "There's no way of explaining what you do" (McBride 107)). Commenting on this, Affron has observed, "An almost total absence of analytical approaches to screen acting [in film scholarship] reflects the belief that [it] is nothing more than the beautiful projection of a filmic self, an arrangement of features and body, the disposition of superficial elements" (Affron 92–3). Yet surely film acting is based on craftsmanship as much as on inspiration, and is subject to rational inquiry.

Davis once noted how the scenario formed the foundation of screen performance. As she stated: "Without scripts none of us can work. It's the beginning of the work" (McBride 107). In *Dangerous* (said to be based on the life of Jeanne Eagels (Stine and Davis 70)), Davis plays the role of Joyce Heath, a once-famous stage actress now on the skids, largely because people believe that she jinxes all productions and persons with whom she comes in contact. Joyce is discovered one night in a seedy bar by Don Bellows (Franchot Tone), an up-and-coming architect who feels he owes his career choice to her: he once saw Joyce play Shakespeare's Juliet and was so inspired that, henceforth, he dedicated himself to creative work. When Joyce becomes inebriated and passes out, he takes her to his country home and, despite her antagonistic behavior, convinces her to stay a week to rest and revive. When he returns from a sojourn to the city, where he works and visits his fiancée, socialite Gail Armitage (Margaret Lindsay), Joyce is less agitated and aggressive, and the two share a pleasant evening together in which she reads to him from a play that she says she took from his library. When he learns that she has invented the drama (with details that suspiciously parallel their situation), he storms out into the rain. She follows and they end up in an embrace. The next day, the romance deepens and eventually he breaks off his engagement with Gail. He convinces Joyce to appear on Broadway again (despite her fears of a jinx) and she begins rehearsing a new play. When Don pressures her to marry him, she demurs and delays, and we learn that, unbeknownst to him, she is already wed to another man. Since her husband will not divorce her, she decides to kill him in a car crash (in which she risks her own life as the driver). Both Joyce and her husband are hurt in the ensuing accident (he more seriously than she), and her Broadway return is aborted. When Don learns of her deception, he ends their relationship. (Davis herself once remarked "To be involved with an actress is an awkward position for a man. It's almost impossible" (McBride 112).) Joyce eventually comes to acknowledge responsibility for her husband's injuries and vows to support him. She convinces the play's director to relaunch the drama with her in the starring role—a surefire hit. As the film ends, Joyce is seen approaching the hospital, flowers in hand, ready to tend to her ailing spouse. Here, the film conforms to the requirements of Hollywood film of the era, to reform or punish errant characters, whether the audience believes in their transformation or not.

When Davis first saw the script for *Dangerous*, she was not impressed: "It was maudlin and mawkish with a pretense at quality which in scripts ... is often worse than junk. But it had just enough material in it to build into something if I approached it properly ... I worked like ten men on that film" (Davis 184).

Character and storyline

There are numerous ways in which the screenplay for *Dangerous* presents a rich acting palette for Davis, and is decidedly in her "wheel house." One reason is the type of character that Joyce Heath represents: a proud, capable (but flawed) woman who is as tough as nails. Here, we recall that Schatz refers to Davis as "a female Jimmy Cagney" (27) and Howard Mandelbaum calls her personae "headstrong heroines." Finally, Richard Schickel claims that, even when she played distressed or tormented females (as she does in *Dangerous*), "she ... never ... openly acknowledge[d] her victim's status ... The women she played would be ... the authors of their own misery" (24). Kathy Klaprat finds Davis's portrayal in fan magazines consonant with her bold image: "*Modern Screen* avowed that Davis was fiery, independent, and definitely not domesticated. *Motion Picture Classic* portrayed her as hard-boiled and ruthless, determined to get what she wants (all traits which motivate many of Davis' actions in her ... films)" (363). Of course, some critics find Davis's dominant female portrayals bordering on perniciousness. Klaprat refers to them as "vamps" and Schatz deems them "bitches" and "emasculating shrews" (27). (In *Dangerous*, Joyce even calls herself a "shrew.")

Klaprat also notes that, in many Davis pictures, "characterization *precedes* narrative actions." As she explains, "Before Davis even appears on the screen ... the audience is informed that her character is contrary, hard to handle, and restless" (370–1). In *Dangerous*, as a group of men drink in a club they discuss Joyce, whom one man has just seen on the street. The words used to describe her include "vitally tempestuous," "brilliant," and "startling." She is also likened to a comet. It is a full twelve minutes before we view a bona fide scene with Joyce, who previously has been glimpsed only in passing. Nonetheless, we already know a lot about her.

It should be clear how Joyce Heath conforms to the brand of strong, self-reliant film heroine that Davis often embodied. We learn that Joyce was once a successful and renowned actress, though we never see her as such. Instead, we meet her when she is depressed and bitter, and, as one of the men puts it, "dowdy and down and out." But it is not simply a singular type of role that offers performance prospects for Davis, it is the shape of the narrative which involves continual metamorphoses of her character—a chance for tour de force transformations and varied postures. Of course, Davis was becoming known for the breadth of her acting talent. As *Time* magazine put it in 1938, Davis had "as wide a dramatic range as any cinemactress in the business" ("Popeye the Magnificent," *Time*, 28 March 1938, 33).

But specifically how is Joyce's character translated into Davis's acting technique?

Performance style

1. Appearance

In many ways Davis did not fit the model of the dazzling movie star: her self-deprecating nickname for herself was "the little brown wren" (Davis 125). Perhaps her more pedestrian appearance and her lack of vanity facilitated her taking roles in which she was actively deglamorized, and these were often the ones for which she won critical acclaim. *Dangerous* is no exception. Since she plays an alcoholic, washed-up actress, as the film opens her outfits include a shabby suit, Don's shirt and pants, and the housekeeper's oversized bathrobe (giving costumer Orry-Kelly second thoughts about his job) (Stine and Davis 70). Only toward the end of the drama does she have occasion to don two smart garments. Similarly, in early scenes, cameraman Ernest Haller photographed Davis without recourse to the kind of flattering lighting usually used for prominent actresses. This sense of realism contributed to the authentic feel of her performance.

2. Speech

In early scenes, before Joyce has succumbed to Don's charms and his desire to save her, her dialogue delivery is constantly harsh, acerbic, and sarcastic. For example, when he greets her in the bar as Joyce Heath, she shoots back (as though to challenge him), "*What* did you say?" Similarly, when she wakes up in his house the next morning and the maid, Mrs. Williams (Alison Skipworth), asks how she is doing, Joyce snarls back: "You won't be surprised to be told I feel poorly." Later, she barks at the woman, "Leave me alone!" and orders her to "Get me a drink!" When Don brings up the previous night, Joyce fires back: "Oh, you must be quite proud of your conquest!"

Of course, this hard-hitting and brittle verbal delivery is what Davis came to be known for. Richard Schickel speaks of the "brash way she clipped her words" as well as the "singular pauses she often made between syllables"; likewise he admires how she "took command of the language . . . bending it to her rhythms rather than submitting to its tyranny" (20). Martin Shingler describes her voice as "firm and steady, sustaining a deep throaty resonance" ("Fasten Your Seatbelts and Prick Up Your Ears: The Dramatic Human Voice in Film," online at www.Nottingham.ac.uk/scope/documents/2006/june-2006/shingler.pdf). More archly, Howard Mandelbaum foregrounds "the catapulting of consonants from her lips with invisible hyphens placed between syllables; [the] volcanic outbursts accompanied by fire breathing and smoke swallowing; that throaty, defiant laugh." Finally, *Time* speaks of her having "diamond dust in her voice" ("Popeye the Magnificent," 28 March 1938, 33).

3. Bette Davis eyes

When Joyce is distanced, sullen, or evasive, her eyes are usually cast downward, withholding her gaze from the persons she encounters. We find this in the scene in which Don first approaches her in the bar, as well as in her stance the morning after as she leans, contemptuously, against a window in his dining room.

As Joyce begins to spend time with Don, however, she starts (at least in moments of candor) to look directly at him, for example, when he rouses her from his barn upon his return to the country a week after he has left her there. Similarly, as they spend time together and her feelings for him warm, she regularly looks and smiles at Don attentively. But, throughout the narrative, she swings back and forth between those poles of withdrawal and attentiveness.

Joyce's direct gaze may not only signify affection but also indicate shock, as in the scene in which Don first mentions marriage to her (a subject she has reason to avoid). In response, she stares fixedly at him—an effect augmented by the length of the shot. Furthermore, her gaze can mean confrontation and rage. When, the morning after Joyce and Don have kissed, he apologizes (regretful for his behavior), she is incensed at his rejection and stares at him—this, after she has come downstairs all sweetness and light. Similarly, when Joyce's husband Gordon (John Eldredge) fails to agree to a divorce, she looks at him belligerently, teeth clenched.

Finally, her eyes can also signal deviousness. During their first evening together Joyce and Don sit on his sofa and, while he looks elsewhere, she steals a glance at him and adjusts her hair, clearly wishing to appear attractive. Her smirk and sideways look indicate her capacity for underhandedness.

4. Theatricality

Both Joyce's gaze and her bodily stance are important at moments in the film when Davis employs what James Naremore calls "metaperformance" or "acting within the diegesis" (72, 75). He notes that, "Any film becomes a good showcase for professional acting skill if it provides moments when the characters are clearly shown to be wearing masks. In such moments the player demonstrates virtuosity by sending out dual signs" (76). On the morning when Don apologizes for having kissed Joyce, he remarks that he fears he has hurt her. She immediately begins to laugh, repeating incredulously, "*Hurt* me? *Hurt* me?" But when he leaves, her hysterical laughter turns to sobs and we realize that she was crushed by his rebuff and is only giving a show of confidence. Then, in a later scene when Don raises the subject of marriage, Joyce registers shock and then moves to the couch, her back towards him. She gives excuses for her lack of enthusiasm (which we later learn are falsehoods): "Isn't it too soon?" she inquires, duplicitously. In reality she would love to have accepted his proposal, but couldn't.

Much later, after Don has learned the truth about Joyce and abandoned her, she encounters him again and claims that she never loved him but only used him to revive her career. As she says this (an outright lie), she turns her back to him; but when he leaves, she collapses against the door through which he has exited, softly murmuring, "Darling."

Similarly, after her husband refuses to divorce her, we watch her begin to hatch a plan. She turns away from him and places her hand on her head as though thinking. Next, she looks at him and, with soft upturned eyes, concocts a trip they will take to the country to reconnect. The audience knows that she is dissembling, but her husband falls for the ruse.

At other times, Joyce's theatricality is directly scripted into the narrative since she is an actress. When Don first meets her in the bar and mentions having seen her play Juliet, she immediately rises (as though in a trance) and begins to recite her lines. And much later, when Don has bankrolled a play for her, we find her rehearsing on stage.

There is one instance, however, when her scripted theatricality is also a lie. On one of their first evenings together in the country, Joyce claims to have spotted a copy of the drama "Forever Ends at Dawn" on Don's bookshelf. He fails to recognize the title but asks her to read a scene from it. She sits on a chair and begins her recitation. Later, when he looks more closely at the book, he realizes that it is an edition of *The Green Pastures*. Thus, she has invented the play, and the lines of dialogue which mirror the couple's awkward situation (engaged man spending an evening with another woman as their affection grows.) He recognizes her cunning and is outraged, storming out the front door. In response, Joyce leans against a wall and smirks, proud of having generated such a strong (albeit negative) emotion in him.

5. Facial expression

The previous example makes clear that Davis is a master of nuanced facial expression. This is apparent in the scene in which she awakens in Don's house hungover after he has brought her there the previous night. She gets up and is alarmed at not finding herself in her own bed. She looks around, and her face and head movement imply confusion. Moreover, to show how ill she feels, she grabs her head, eyes cast downward, her face grimacing in discomfort.

In the later scene in which Don apologizes to her for being intimate, he departs for the city but returns when he learns that a bridge is out. Walking past the bedroom that Joyce occupies, he hears her crying. When he opens the door and approaches her, instead of acting superior and distant (as she had earlier that morning), she tearfully confesses that she hoped he would come back. Her face registers both vulnerability and supplication.

In another scene, rendering an entirely different mood, we find Joyce in Don's convertible after the two have declared their love and are driving back to the city to begin work on a play. She sits by his side, wind blowing through her hair, with an expression of consummate joy on her face.

Playfully, she urges him to drive faster and faster (foreshadowing the crash near the end of the story). After that accident, we find her in the hospital, distraught because Don has terminated their relationship; tears stream down her face and her expression is all sadness and regret.

Moments after Don leaves her room, she stares with intensity and determination at the pills on her nightstand and grabs a pair of scissors. Her glance, gesture, and expression lead us to believe that she is contemplating suicide. In the next shot, however, she drops the scissors and turns away, and we sense that she has changed her mind. Here, in her play with a prop, we think of something that Davis once said: "While the process of acting is basically the same [on stage and screen], the screen is a fantastic medium for the reality of little things" (McBride 106).

Near the very end of the film, Joyce sits in a taxicab riding through the city on her way to see her husband in the hospital, after she herself has been released. After reading an announcement of Don and Gail's nuptials, she gazes out the window and witnesses crowds emerging onto the street from their wedding venue (a scene echoed in the later *Stella Dallas* (1937)). At first Joyce looks upset, but then grabs some flowers (meant for her husband) and smiles. In so doing, her face moves through numerous micro-positions.

This play of emotion continues as she arrives at the hospital. When we first see her leave the car she appears somber, but then her facial expression passes through expectation to happiness—all without a line of dialogue spoken.

6. Body language

Davis is also a master at using her hands and arms for dramatic effect. Schickel mentions "the abrupt gestures that accompanied her speeches" as well as "the impatient twitch of her shoulders" (20). Mandelbaum mentions Davis's "jerky movements suggesting carburetor trouble," and also likens her walk to that of "a caged lioness." Davis spoke of her recourse to gesture, a skill that may be linked to her early training in dance with Martha Graham (Leaming 50). She also tied it to the manner in which she was photographed: "I probably had less close-ups as a star than any other actress. I believed that there were emotions too great not to use [my] full body . . . One's back can describe an emotion" (Davis 195).

We have already mentioned Joyce's play with cigarettes, her gripping her head to indicate a hangover, and her touching her forehead to signal thinking. But there are other significant gestural instances as well. Early on, when she becomes angry with Mrs. Williams for censuring her drinking, she grabs her hostilely by the shoulders and pushes her out of the room. Similarly, when Joyce irately tells Don to leave his own house (on her first morning there), she points imperiously to the front door.

Finally, Davis can act not only with her hands and arms but with her entire body. When, after a week in the country, Don finds her asleep in the barn, she is stretched out languorously on a bale of hay, her hand dangling down. Her posture clearly connotes rest and relaxation, a radical change from her earlier demeanor. Davis is also required to collapse several times in the drama and she does so quite subtly. The first instance occurs when, drunk in the bar, she is overcome by dizziness and sinks into a chair. The next morning, having awakened with a hangover, she nearly duplicates the action in Don's guest room. But Joyce's collapses are as emotional as they are physical. Following Don's visit to the hospital and the end of their liaison, Joyce buries her face in a pillow, heartbroken.

As Davis claimed, she could act with her back. The last shot of the film depicts Joyce (seen from the rear) resolutely climbing the steps of the hospital to visit her husband. Her stance and pace signal that she has faced up to her marriage and responsibility to her spouse.

7. Excess

In closing, no discussion of Bette Davis's acting style can avoid confronting the charge of "excess." Mandelbaum, for instance, deems her a "histrionic performer" with an "overeagerness to externalize" and a "tendency to underline extreme emotions." Schickel asserts that "no actress more boldly flaunted her mannerisms" (20). Clearly, here critics are foregrounding the ostensibly visible effort in Davis's acting mode, one that is "ostentatious" and defies more naturalistic approaches (Naremore 22). Davis herself makes no apologies for this. As she remarks, "I've always felt that you could be as full emotionally for the camera as for the theater. I've been criticized many times for that . . .: everybody says you shouldn't do as much for the camera, but I don't believe that" (McBride 108).

Certainly, some of her performances have been hyperbolic, for instance, in *Beyond the Forest* (1949) where her portrayal of Rosa Moline is over the top and without gradation from beginning to end. Affron, however, sees Davis as generally having "control over her own excesses of energy and vitality" (99) and in the case of *Dangerous,* she certainly does. Such restraint is especially difficult in a film in which an actress plays an actress, a role that practically solicits exaggeration. Unfortunately, Davis succumbs to hyperbole in a later film about a performer, *The Star* (1952), but manages to avoid the trap in perhaps the most successful film of her career, *All About Eve* (1950).

Conclusion

As an analysis of *Dangerous* indicates, Bette Davis was an actress who used all the tools available to a screen performer in the sound era. Her voice was unmistakable for (what Roland Barthes would deem) its "grain"—known for harshness but capable of mellowness as well (Barthes 18). In a sense, to understand Davis's technique, it is best to divide her body into several "zones." She learned to use her eyes to communicate a wide variety of emotions and stances, signaled by whether she looked up or down, at someone or away. Similarly, her face could portray a wide variety of affects, especially when rendered in close-up: disdain, subservience, hauteur, love, cunning, or joy. Likewise, her body language (posture and arm position) was a tool in her performance arsenal.

For Davis, acting was not about the famous Method through which one delved into one's consciousness to find antecedents of the feelings on the script page. As she once commented, "The present trend of the actor to personalize all tragedy . . . is sad to me." Rather, for her, the actor was to go "*out* of himself not *in*" and pretend "to be this other human being." Thus, performance had "nothing to do with self-involvement but rather [with] radiation" (Davis 57–8). She concluded that, unless one transcended oneself, there was a troubling "sameness" to one's film appearances. As she noted, actors "are all so busy revealing their own insides that, like all X-ray plates, one looks pretty much like the other" (Davis 58).

One could never say that about Bette Davis or her work. As a movie star, she was as unique as her performances from one film to another. As D. W. Griffith said before awarding her that Oscar, Davis is "a woman of uncommon originality and distinction, who, throughout a bold career, dared to be different—in fact insisted on it" (Stine and Davis 187).[1]

Note

1. Small sections of this paper were taken from one of my earlier essays. See Fischer.

Works cited

Affron, Charles. "Generous Stars," in Jeremy Butler, ed., *Star Texts: Image and Performance in Film and Television*, Detroit: Wayne State University Press, 1991, 90–101.
Barthes, Roland. *Image, Music, Text*. Trans. Stephen Heath. New York: Hill and Wang, 1977.
Davis, Bette. *The Lonely Life: An Autobiography*. New York: G. P. Putnam's Sons, 1962.
Fischer, Lucy. "Bette Davis," in Adrienne L. McLean, ed., *Glamour in a Golden Age: Movie Stars of the 1930s*, New Brunswick, NJ: Rutgers University Press, 2011, 84–107.
Leaming, Barbara. *Bette Davis: A Biography*. New York, Cooper Square Press, 2003.
Klaprat, Kathy. "The Stars as Market Strategy: Bette Davis in Another Light," in Tino Balio, ed., *The American Film Industry*, Madison, WI: University of Wisconsin Press, 1985, 351–76.
Mandelbaum, Howard. "Happy Birthday, Bette Davis (Apr. 5, 1908–Oct. 6, 1989): A Talent for Hysteria," *Bright Lights Film Journal* (5 April 2013), http://brightlightsfilm.com/bette-davis-talent-hysteria/#.V9Fv-032bIU.
McBride, Joseph. "The Actress: Bette Davis," in *Filmmakers on Filmmaking: The American Film Institute Seminars on Motion Pictures and Television*, vol. 2, Los Angeles: J. P. Tarcher, 1983, 101–14.
Moser, Laura. *Davis*. London: Haus Publishing, 2004.
Naremore, James. *Acting in the Cinema*. Berkeley, University of California Press, 1988.
Ringgold, Gene. *The Complete Films of Bette Davis*. New York: Citadel, 1990.
Schatz, Thomas. *The Genius of the System: Hollywood Filmmaking in the Studio Era*. New York: Pantheon Books, 1988.
Schickel, Richard. "Bette," *Film Comment* 25: 2 (1989), 20–4.
Stine, Whitney, and Bette Davis. *Mother Goddam: The Story of the Career of Bette Davis*. New York: Hawthorn Books, 1974.

Chapter 7

James Stewart in *Vertigo*

William Rothman

Like Cary Grant, that other Hitchcock stalwart, James Stewart is the kind of screen performer about whom it is said that he always plays himself, or even that he always *is* himself on camera. Andrew Sarris called Stewart "the most complete actor-personality in the American cinema" (99)—not *better* than Grant (no one could be) but more "complete" in the sense that he starred in films in a wider range of genres that required him to express a wider range of emotions. Stewart's performance in *Vertigo* isn't *better* than his other performances. But it is more complete. Scottie runs the full gamut of human emotions, and Stewart expresses, with unfailing precision and at times startling intensity, a diversity of moods that range from amusement, excited anticipation, unbounded joy, ecstatic love, and passionate desire to all-consuming hatred, darkest despair, murderous rage, and blood-curdling horror—and many shades in between.

Like any screen performer, Stewart has to act on camera in a way that we can believe is precisely expressive of the mood of his character within the film's world. But Stewart is the kind of screen performer who goes beyond this. His challenge is to act in character not only for the character he is *playing*, but also for the person he *is*—to act in a way that would be in character for Stewart, were he to find himself, in just Scottie's mood, in just the situation in which the narrative places Scottie. And this requires that Stewart transform every posture, every gesture, and every line of dialogue the screenplay assigns to Scottie into a manifestation of his own character, an expression of his—Stewart's, hence Scottie's—temperament.

I pointedly use the words "character" and "temperament" rather than Sarris's "personality." What I think of as Stewart's "personality" is that boyish, wryly humorous, slightly stuttering, "Aw, shucks" manner of speaking, brightened by a twinkle in his eye, that impressionists have long found irresistible. In this sense, Stewart's "personality" is in evidence in *Vertigo* only when Scottie is feeling comfortable enough in his own skin to relish indulging in what my mother would have called "putting himself out." Scottie is in such an outgoing mood in his exchange with Judy just before the fatal moment she asks him to help her put on the telltale necklace:

JUDY: Like me?
SCOTTIE: Uh huh.
JUDY: Is that the best you can do?
SCOTTIE: C'mere.
JUDY: Oh no, you'll muss me.
SCOTTIE: That's what I had in mind. C'mere!

When he is "putting himself out," Scottie could not be more affable. And we don't doubt that this persona is a true expression of Scottie's—Stewart's—temperament; it reveals an aspect of who this man really is. But when Scottie recognizes Judy's necklace and the camera gives us to see his face turn into an expressionless mask as a coldness abruptly alters his manner, we also believe this instant as revealing an aspect of who this man is, a true expression of his temperament. Stewart doesn't act as if Scottie were one person when he is amused and amusing and another person when he is not. No matter his mood, Scottie, like Stewart himself, acts in ways that express the particularities of his temperament. In all of his moods, Scottie is positively the same guy. And that guy is

Stewart, albeit Stewart transformed by the medium of film. Stewart doesn't simply *play* Scottie; he *is* Scottie. And Stewart, onscreen and off, is more than a persona; he has a "self"—*is* a "self"—with a multitude of aspects.

We cannot say that Kim Novak *is* Judy, the character she plays, if only because we don't know who Judy is. The woman Scottie knows as "Madeleine," whose temperament so strikingly contrasts with Judy's, is a character Judy plays. It is tempting to say that Judy *impersonates* Madeleine, but that word suggests that Judy had been made over into a carbon copy of Gavin Elster's wife, the way Scottie makes her over into a veritable image of the Madeleine he loved and loves. Within the world of *Vertigo*, Madeleine has no existence apart from Judy's performance. Judy doesn't impersonate Scottie's Madeleine, her performance *creates* her. Then again, *Judy* has no real existence apart from *Novak's* performance. And Novak no more impersonates Judy than Judy impersonates Madeleine; Novak's performance *creates* Judy—and Madeleine as well.

Further complicating matters, Madeleine at times behaves as if she were Carlotta Valdes, not herself. Scottie believes that when Madeleine behaves this way, she isn't acting; the spirit of Carlotta really *possesses* her. But Scottie also believes that the Carlotta who possesses Madeleine is a projection: of her own psyche. Therefore Madeleine needs a cure, not an exorcism. Blessed or cursed as he is with Stewart's capacity for wishing with all his heart, Scottie believes, because he so fervently wishes to believe, that his love for Madeleine gives him the power to save her. When Judy's voiceover lets us—but not Scottie—know the truth, this revelation doesn't prove that when Judy is in character as Madeleine she was always only acting. In truth, we do not know whether it is Judy-acting-as-Madeleine, Judy-acting-as-Madeleine-possessed-by-Carlotta, or Carlotta-speaking-through-Madeleine who speaks the words in the redwoods, "Here I was born . . . and here I died." Nor do we know, when the woman in Scottie's arms pulls away from their passionate kiss at San Juan Bautista, tells him there is something she must do, and implores him to believe, no matter what, that she loves him, whether this is Judy-acting-as-Madeleine, or Judy speaking for herself yet in Madeleine's voice. We don't even know, at the end of the film, *whose* eyes see the shadow of a nun as Death comes to claim her.

Judy is emblematic of a mystery inherent in human identity that Hitchcock continued to explore in *Psycho*. Her performance, which is also Novak's performance of Judy's performance, invites us to ponder what it might mean to have more than one temperament, more than one "self." And also to ponder what it might mean to have *no* "self," *no* temperament to call one's own. Scottie, too, is emblematic of a mystery inherent in human identity, but not the same mystery. If in *Vertigo* Novak speaks in a Babel of voices, none of them hers, Stewart speaks in one voice: his. That Scottie has a "self" (Stewart's), a temperament particular to him (Stewart's), is not in doubt. The mystery Stewart's performance evokes is how one "self" can have so many aspects, some incompatible with others. How can "positively the same guy" wish so desperately to save the woman he knows as "Madeleine" and be so unfeeling ("It can't matter to *you!*") when he bullies Judy into letting him change her into the semblance of his lost love? How can this good man with Jimmy Stewart's endearing personality force Judy up the stairs of the bell tower in such a murderous rage that we believe it would be in character for him to break her neck and throw her from the top of the tower?

In pondering Stewart's performance in *Vertigo*, it is natural to think first of the bravura passages, such as that climactic sequence in which Scottie overcomes his vertigo and drags Judy the last few steps to the top of the tower and the confrontation that ensues. In this sequence Scottie speaks every line with frightening emotional intensity. But Stewart's voice and expression register a crescendo of scorn, from "You were a very apt pupil; you were a very apt pupil!" to "Why did you pick on me? Why me?" to "Oh Judy, with all of his wife's money and all that freedom and that power, and he ditched you. What a shame!" Scottie's mood changes only when he asks, "Did he give you anything?" and she answers, "Some money." "And the necklace. Carlotta's necklace. There was where you made your mistake, Judy. You shouldn't keep souvenirs of a killing. You shouldn't have been . . ." For a moment, Scottie is too overwhelmed with emotion—desire, not hate—to go on. Then: "You shouldn't have been that *sentimental.*" Scottie knows that it is he who can't stop himself from being too sentimental. Overcome with the pain of loss, he cries out, "I loved you so, Madeleine!" He knows that Judy is Madeleine, and Madeleine is Judy. And that he cannot help but to love this woman.

But Stewart's performance is equally great in the quiet sequences in which he is behind the wheel of his Desoto following Madeleine's Jaguar through the streets of San Francisco. Or in the heartbreaking passage in which a catatonic Scottie sits motionless in a sanitarium easy chair and passively endures Midge's visit, his frozen expression betraying the agony of his struggle to keep from expressing his feelings.

And Stewart's performance is no less great when Scottie manifests what I have been calling Stewart's "personality." I will conclude this chapter by looking closely at one such passage: the first conversation, early in the film, between Scottie and Midge, old college friends, both unmarried, who aren't lovers, although she wishes they were. The seeming ordinariness of the passage enables it to illustrate all the better the greatness of Stewart's performance, ably complemented by Barbara Bel Geddes and aided and abetted, as always, by Hitchcock's camera.

In the studio

This passage follows almost word for word the screenplay draft dated 12 September 1957. Scottie's attempt to reach for his drink makes him knock over his walking stick, which he tries to catch, but in so doing he twists his body and lets out an "Ouch!" Stewart plays the moment in a way that resonates suggestively with the film's central theme of *falling*. Scottie is trying to balance his walking stick on one outstretched hand. It is his futile effort to keep it from falling that causes him to wrench his body.

Stewart voices Scottie's "Ouch!" as an expression of pain, but pain hardly serious enough to render inappropriate Midge's offscreen response: "I thought you said no more aches and pains." "It's this darned corset; it binds," Scottie replies. He wants to be *free*.

Hitchcock cuts to Midge at her drawing table. "No three-way stretch? Very un-chic," says she ironically, without pausing in her work on the easel in front of her. Hitchcock cuts to her drawing: a sketch, evidently for a magazine ad, of a strapless brassiere worn by a model otherwise naked from the waist up. Scottie responds in kind in the film: "Yeah, well . . . You know those police department doctors—no sense of style," adding the "Yeah, well . . ." to give his delivery that familiar Jimmy Stewart-esque slight stutter; he pronounces "well" as if it rhymed with "shall." With the same effect, Stewart turns Scottie's next line ("Ah, tomorrow!") into "Well, anyway," drawing out the word "well" and again making it almost rhyme with "shall"—"tomorrow will be the day."

Without pausing in her drawing, Midge asks, "Why? What's tomorrow?" "Tomorrow?!" Stewart says, his voice ironically registering shock, as if to say, "How can you not know what 'tomorrow' means to me!?" Stewart's "personality" is in full flower, so his shocked voice is comically exaggerated to indicate that he is teasing her, not really putting her down. In the screenplay, Scottie answers Midge's question by saying, "Tomorrow . . . the corset comes off. This thing goes out the window," he adds, waving his walking stick. "I shall be a free man. I shall wiggle my behind . . . free and unconfined."

In the film, Stewart forgoes the un-Jimmy Stewart-like "shall" to align his words more closely with his "personality." "I'll be able to scratch myself like anybody else tomorrow," he says, turning his gaze away from Midge to look at his hand, with which he is comically scratching—or miming scratching—himself. "I'll throw this miserable thing out the window," he says, theatrically glaring at the offending cane. As he adds, "I'll be a free . . .," Scottie sustains his comic performance by miming throwing the cane out the window, but this sudden movement makes him wince, so it is again with a semi-stutter that he completes the sentence—"I'm a free man"—in a voice now more muted, and with a soberer facial expression.

Scottie's mood, as Stewart portrays him, is at odds with the mood the screenplay assigns him ("He raises his eyebrows with a surprised and gratified smile"). Stewart's Scottie is troubled here, as if he has a premonition that the freedom he is wishing for will have unwelcome consequences. Hitchcock forgoes the cut to Midge requisite for registering the grimace the screenplay attributes to her. In film as in screenplay, what Scottie says next—"Midge, do you suppose many men wear corsets?"—is a deliberate non sequitur. The screenplay's implication is that Midge's grimace provokes Scottie to ask this question. But the way Stewart and Hitchcock collaborate on this moment, the implication is that Scottie, troubled by a cloud that has just darkened his thoughts, relies on this non sequitur to lighten his own mood.

Humoring Scottie, Midge replies, "Mmm. More than you think." "Really?" Leaning back in his chair, putting his foot up on the table in front of him, and not looking at Midge, Scottie asks in a mischievously deadpan manner, "Well, do you know that from personal experience?" "Please!" she replies. That there could be a trace of defensiveness in her response is suggested, perhaps, when she asks, "What happens after tomorrow?" The screenplay characterizes Midge's delivery of this line as "impersonal." But "impersonal" is too impersonal a word to register the trace of sternness that adds an edge to her question. By continuing to attend to her drawing, she may be trying not to reveal how much it matters to her how he copes with his crisis. Her tone is a signal to Scottie that she won't let him off the hook with an answer that's evasive or comical in the Jimmy Stewart-esque way that is surely as familiar to her as it is to us.

With the camera still on Midge, Scottie asks, "What do you mean?" He voices this question in a lower register and with no trace of irony. He is asking her a question, but Stewart's voice ends the line not by rising, but by falling, as befits a declarative statement. It's as if he's heard Midge's "What happens after tomorrow?" as a provocation. He responds by provoking *her*—provoking her to *say* what she's really thinking. Midge replies, "Well, what *are* you going to do, since you've quit the police force?"

At last, Hitchcock cuts back to Scottie, who sits straighter so he can turn to face Midge more directly, leans forward, and rests his hands and chin on top of his walking stick. Instead of answering her question, though, he says, "You sound so disapproving, Midge." The screenplay specifies that he says this "gently." But *she* is the one being careful not to give offense. Stewart's Scottie isn't being gentle to Midge at this moment. Surprised by her tone of voice, he genuinely wants her to say what she is thinking. The camera is still on Scottie as she demurs, "No I'm not. It's your life." There is a cut to Midge, who adds, "You were the bright young lawyer who decided he's going to be Chief of Police some day." Her voice is tinged with sarcasm, which makes clear that she does disapprove of Scottie's decision to quit the police.

In the middle of Midge's sentence, Hitchcock cuts back to Scottie, the camera now framing him more closely, initiating a more emotional phase in the shot/reverse shot sequence. The new setup affords us a more intimate view of Scottie's reaction to Midge's words, which cause him so much pain that he averts his gaze.

At this point, the screenplay has Scottie say, "I had to quit, Midge." And again the screenwriter uses the word "gently" to characterize the way he speaks, suggesting that he uses the same tone of voice—which Stewart does not. Earlier, his Scottie wanted Midge to tell him what she was thinking. Now he is confessing his own thoughts. Stewart leaves out the "Midge" and says only "I *had* to quit," all without looking at her. "I *had* to quit" is something he feels he *has* to say—to himself as much as to Midge.

Hitchcock cuts back to Midge, framed in a closer setup that matches the preceding shot of Scottie. "Why?," she asks, as if she were his psychotherapist (a mode of questioning Scottie himself will assume in trying to "cure" Madeleine). Midge's pencil has stopped moving, but her eyes are still directed at her drawing, as if to avoid making him too self-conscious to give a truthful answer.

Scottie explains that it's because of his fear of heights. Punctuating Scottie's words with Jimmy Stewart-esque hand gestures, and again using his cane as an expressive extension of his body, Stewart conveys that Scottie is reliving, not simply recollecting, the nightmarish event as he says, with anguish increasing until he can no longer go on, "I wake up at night seeing that man fall from the roof and I try to reach out to him and I . . . I just . . ."

At last looking at Scottie, Midge says, "It wasn't your fault." Momentarily meeting her gaze, Scottie replies, "I know." He has regained his composure. As he adds, "That's what everybody tells me," he looks contemplatively at his cane, which he is holding up, with both hands, horizontally, in front of him. This isn't a comical bit of mime; it is as if he is envisioning this object as a stand-in for the railing he was desperately clinging to when he watched that man fall to his death. We hear Midge's offscreen voice say, "Johnny, the doctors explained to you . . ." Pulling his gaze away from the cane, Scottie uses it to help him rise, and begins pacing around the room, the camera reframing with him—the first camera movement in the sequence—as he says, increasingly heatedly, "I know. I know. I have acrophobia, which gives me vertigo. And I get dizzy."

With the camera pausing with him, Scottie stops pacing and, leaning on his cane, says directly to Midge, "Boy, what a moment to find out I had it!" She replies, "Well, you've got it and there's no losing it." There is a cut to Midge—the shot reprises the less intimate setup of the shots of her in the first phase of the shot/reverse shot sequence—as she adds, "And there's no one to blame." Pressing her point, she concludes, "So why quit?" Then a cut back to Scottie. "You mean, and sit behind a desk? *Chairborne?*"

Scottie's use of this word uncannily foreshadows the devastating image of him in the sanitarium after his breakdown, quite literally "chairborne." He is leveling an indictment: if Midge believes him to be a man who could ever be satisfied being "chairborne," she simply doesn't know him. (His aversion to being "chairborne" is a real connection between Scottie and the character Stewart played in *Rear Window* (1954).)

"Where you belong," Midge replies provocatively. Scottie refrains from taking the bait. Instead, he reverts to his Jimmy Stewart-esque humorous mode. His "personality" surfacing, he says, "What about my acrophobia? Suppose I'm, suppose I'm sitting in this chair behind the desk." Using his cane as a stand-in for the desk, he adds, "Here's the desk," and begins comically miming the action he is describing, the camera reframing as necessary with his movements. "And a pencil falls from the desk down to the floor. And I reach down to pick up the pencil . . ."

Midge laughs.

". . . and bingo! My acrophobia is back."

Laughing again, Midge says, with warmth and affection, "Oh Johnny-O! Well, what *do* you do?"

"Well, I'm not going to do anything for a while," Scottie replies, refraining from emulating the affection in her voice. He begins pacing again, momentarily turning away from Midge before turning back to her to say, "Now don't forget, I'm a man of independent means, as the saying goes. Fairly independent."

"And? Why don't you go away for a while?"

Scottie is resting the tip of his cane against the wall as he answers, "You mean, to forget? Now now, Midge. Don't be so *motherly*." Midge at last looks directly at Scottie, her gaze wordlessly posing the question: Are you starting to crack up? Removing his cane from the wall, he pats it in his hand and, resuming pacing, answers her questioning look. "I'm not going to crack up." He evidently sensed in Midge's question the fear that he was headed for a crack-up—just as he turns out to be. If he were immune to this fear, he wouldn't have lashed out at Midge. In turn, she wouldn't feel so wounded by Scottie's words if they hadn't hit home. When she visits him in the sanitarium, after all, she will say to the utterly unresponsive Scottie, as if this weren't the last thing he would want to hear her say, "Mother's here."

Undeterred, Midge persists. "Have you had any dizzy spells this week?"

"I'm, I'm having one right now."

There is a quick cut to Midge, who looks concerned, but Scottie's remark is actually his way of defusing the tension by pivoting to his "personality" mode. Pointing his cane at the phonograph, he explains, "That . . . the music . . . Don't you think it's sort of, uh . . . ?"

"Oh." As Midge gets up to turn off the music, the camera reframes with her. The camera's movement, combined with hers, brings Scottie and Midge into the same frame, the first time in the sequence since its opening. They remain in the frame throughout the exchange that begins with Scottie, pointing with his cane at a large pink object on Midge's desk, and asking, in Jimmy Stewart's "Aw, shucks" manner, "What's this doohickey?"

"A brassiere. You know about those things. You're a big boy now."

"Yeah, but I've never run across one like that."

"It's brand new. Revolutionary uplift. No shoulder straps, no back straps. Does everything a brassiere should do. Works on the principle of the cantilever bridge."

"It does?" Scottie asks with comically exaggerated surprise.

"An aircraft engineer down on the peninsula designed it. Worked it out in his spare time."

"Kind of a hobby," Scottie says, musing but with a naughty grin. As he adds, with an even naughtier grin, "Do it yourself type thing," he begins walking back toward the sofa. Pausing with his back to Midge, he asks, in a voice that is anything but comical, "How's your love life, Midge?" She answers cleverly but with a trace of annoyance, "That's following a train of thought."

Scottie says simply, "Well?" Just as Midge hadn't wanted to let him off the hook, he is now demanding an answer. "Normal," she answers emphatically, without making clear what she means by this word. (Does she mean that her love life is a "do it yourself kind of thing"?) With the camera still on Midge, Scottie keeps pressing: "Aren't you ever going to get married?" "You know," says she, "there's only one man in the world for me, Johnny-O"—as if she were joking, but we can tell she means it. So can Scottie. He answers, teasingly but meaningfully, "You mean me." Pointing his cane at Midge he adds, in an oddly jocular voice, "We were engaged once, though, weren't we?"

In the middle of Scottie's line, Hitchcock cuts from Scottie to an uncomfortably intimate close-up of Midge—this is one of *Vertigo*'s greatest moments—the camera looking down on her from such proximity that we are all too painfully aware of the discomfort his words cause her. Momentarily looking up at him, then looking back down at her drawing, she replies, with a bitter smile, "Three whole weeks." When Hitchcock cuts back to Scottie, the camera reprises the relatively impersonal setup of the shot that preceded the painfully intimate close-up of Midge. The effect is to underscore both the camera's attunement to Midge's pain and Scottie's apparent obliviousness or indifference to her feelings.

Without looking at her he muses, "Yeah, good old college days." Again he points his cane at Midge and addresses her directly in that strangely jocular tone, "But you were the one who called off the engagement. Remember?"

Hitchcock cuts back to the close-up of Midge, whose face is now an impassive mask as she suffers his words in silence. Of course Midge remembers what happened between them. Hitchcock's camera has just made it clear to us that she has been holding the torch for Scottie all these years. Surely, she had called off their engagement because she recognized that their marriage wouldn't work; he was never going to love her the way she loved him, but if they went back to being platonic friends he could still be part of her life. Scottie cannot simply fail to know what he means to Midge, and is intentionally—if perhaps not consciously—getting back at her for bringing into the open his own fear that he was headed for a crack-up.

Scottie adds, "I'm still available." Tapping his cane on the floor, he muses, again more to himself than to Midge, "Available Ferguson." Scottie is not "available" to Midge the way she is to him, although she thinks she knows that he will continue to return to her as long as there is a void in his life, a void he will never let her fill. In turn, Scottie thinks he knows that she will suffer whatever slings and arrows he aims at her without breaking off their platonic relationship. Thus, when Scottie lightens the heavy mood by asking whether Midge remembers a "fellow in college by the name of Gavin Elster," he knows that their conversation will go on, as presumably it always has, as if nothing untoward had happened between them. As he is about to leave, Scottie invites Midge to go out for a beer. Breaking off their evening together just as she had once broken off their engagement, she declines, citing work, allowing him to believe—or pretend to believe—that she is the one who has always imposed a limit to their relationship.

In this passage, Stewart expresses Scottie's moods with absolute precision and overwhelming conviction, as he does throughout *Vertigo*. But our understanding of the moods Stewart's performance reveals is inflected by the two close-ups that reveal Midge's state of mind, not Scottie's. The camera's sympathetic acknowledgment of Midge's subjectivity foreshadows Hitchcock's later strategy, crucial to the film as a whole, of granting Judy a voiceover that clues us in: not only to the fact that the Madeleine Scottie loved was only a character played by her but also to the fact, which from that moment on we can no longer doubt, that Judy was, and is, in love with Scottie.

In both cases, the effect is to make us mindful of a darkness, a capacity for cruelty, that Stewart's performance brilliantly and disturbingly reveals in Scottie, a character we care about so deeply because he *is* James Stewart.

Work cited

Sarris, Andrew, *The American Cinema: Directors and Directions 1929–1968*. New York: Dutton, 1968.

Chapter 8
Carole Lombard in *To Be or Not to Be*

Alex Clayton

For what turned out, tragically, to be her last screen role, in Ernst Lubistch's *To Be or Not to Be* (1942), Carole Lombard was billed above her co-star Jack Benny, an ironic reversal of the diegetic theatrical production in which their characters, husband and wife thespians Joseph and Maria Tura, co-star. That Lombard's name was put above the title is unsurprising. By the early 1940s she was one of the most famed and highest-paid stars in Hollywood. Yet it is surprising to learn, given the centrality of her contribution to the film's theme and tone, that in this ensemble production Lombard appears onscreen for little more than half an hour. She does an awful lot with those thirty or so minutes. In his short book on *To Be or Not to Be*, Peter Barnes remarks, almost as an aside, that Carole Lombard "packs more into a line, or between [lines], than any film actress before or since" (26). This essay seeks to develop that claim by "unpacking" Lombard's delivery of a handful of lines and moments from the film. It is testament to her talent that a satisfying close account of her performance is difficult to produce. Her performance embodies a mercurial quality where transfers between moods, motivations, and personae are rendered fluidly and in quick succession.

You faker!

A good instance of this mercurial quality is an early backstage exchange between husband and wife during an interval of *Hamlet*. The screenplay reads as follows:

> JOSEPH: Audience is a little cool tonight.
> MARIA: Not to me.
> JOSEPH: Oh, I know I'm giving a rotten performance, I always do when we quarrel. Say something nice.
> MARIA: You faker. I watched your scene with Polonius from the wings and you were never better. I'd give you a kiss right now but I'm afraid I might ruin my make up.
> JOSEPH: Oh honey. You were right this morning. I felt so rotten after the rehearsal I went to Dovac and told him when he advertizes the new play to put your name first.
> MARIA: Did you darling? Oh, that's sweet of you, but I really don't care.
> JOSEPH: That's what Dovac said, so we left it as it was.
> MARIA: Oh.

The exchange is filmed in a single take with a camera matched to Lombard's movement: tracking back with her as she walks, pausing when she pauses, finally panning to take in her exit from the corridor to the dressing room. Keeping her in view for the whole of this thirty-second shot presents her various and drastic shifts of manner as a continuous unfolding sequence. At first she appears cold and high-handed, almost imperious in Gertrude's regal costume, as she paces, chin-high, past her husband. We see that she is interested in acting out a sulk for him as an extension of their previous dispute about who is the biggest scene-stealer. When Joseph appears in shot, the camera's movement conspires to sideline him, incorporating his figure but keeping him second fiddle to Maria. In an attempt to break the ice, he makes the remark about the audience being "cool tonight." "Not to me," she tosses back, without breaking her stride. The quickfire reply suggests that Maria has somehow anticipated the complaint (husbands can be *so* predictable), and seems to release a glimmer of satisfaction in her. A little smile and cocked eyebrow are momentarily available to us, but not to him. In the interval between him hearing the reply and scurrying to catch up, we are able to witness "behind the scenes" how she brings this expression under control. By the time she turns to face him, full cold shoulder has been resumed. It's an instance of how Lombard's expressive detail gives another layer to the scene, the sense that this pair of thespians deliberately hold back from a full and mutual disclosure in order to remain one another's audience.

Maria's coldness to her husband lasts only an instant. As Joseph attributes his bad performance to his preoccupation with their quarrel, her face, in profile, softens, her gaze becoming tender. He cues her next line: "Say something nice." Anticipating screwball mode, we might expect her response to be inflected with a teasing sarcasm, or else intoned woodenly (à la *Johnny Guitar* (1954): "All these years I've waited"), i.e. to imply, "You asked me to say it, not to mean it." But instead Lombard speaks with a disarming openness ("You faker . . . you were never better"), without any residue of bitterness, and lets only the contrivance of the line itself ("I'd give you a kiss right now but I'm afraid I might ruin my make up") sow doubt about whether she means what she says. She calls him a faker so lovingly we can overlook the backhanded compliment. Does she really think him a triumph onstage, or is she putting him exactly where she wants him? Lombard is testing our capacity to tell the difference between genuine and affected sentiment.

The gesture she performs after praising Joseph's stagework—closing her eyes and smiling as she leans into him—conveys something like the relief of reconciliation. She accepts his arm around her and lets him set the pace of their walking. All this seems to indicate an end to their bickering one-upmanship over who should take the limelight, perhaps even that she has ceded, after all, to the position of supporting player. It's within this mood of a truce that Joseph appears to offer her the olive branch of top billing in their next production, to which Maria responds: "Did you darling? Oh, that's sweet of you, but I really don't care." Lombard renders this single line—nothing much on paper—with several remarkable twists of implication. "Did you darling?" is rendered with a sudden turn to face him: she clasps her hands around her husband's waist in excitement. The gesture might also read as "grabbing at the opportunity," and, perhaps because of this, she immediately checks herself, mid-line. The clasp around the waist transforms into a little pat on his side, such as one might give a loyal dog, to make "that's sweet of you" more patronizing than effusive. Then, still in the same fluid movement, she turns away, slightly scrunching her nose and flinging her hand demonstratively on "I really don't care" to downplay her gratitude. She doesn't want to grant him too much glory. But the delivery of the line unwittingly betrays her pleasure at the news. She gives the word "really" an almost tipsy articulation, as if she were drunk on flattery (we know from William Wellman's *Nothing Sacred* (1937) that Lombard does a terrific drunk act). Then she finishes the movement by grasping the hem of her gown in each hand, girlishly, with a dreamy look that suggests she might be picturing herself on the red carpet. That makes Joseph's abrupt retraction of the offer ("we left it as it was") into a rude awakening. Her head snaps back into profile to face him as she recognizes she's been played. "Oh" she mutters, and stalks off.

All of these changes of demeanour, from sulky to conceited to affectionate to grateful to resentful to flattered to cross—the continuous shifts between hard and soft, warm and cold—take place across a single thirty-second shot and with no visible effortfulness or reaching for position on the part of the actress. We are constantly playing catch-up with Carole Lombard. She keeps us on our toes. This is due not just to the density of activity in her performance (how much she "packs into a line," as Barnes puts it), but also to the volatility of access she grants to her character's feelings and motivations. Solid, effective movie acting typically aims for a constant and consistent legibility, using voice and body to "translate" interior states into external signs using the array of available conventions. But some movie performances call to a greater degree on our capacity for imagination by granting only sporadic access to thought and motive. (This is related to what Stanley Cavell calls the great stars' "power of privacy" (128)). One source of the interest and humor generated by Lombard's playing, in particular, is that she perpetually veers between transparent and opaque.

Just for a minute

In more conventional moments, Maria's feelings and intentions are perfectly visible to us while remaining undetected or misinterpreted by those around her. When, in the next scene in her dressing room, Maria effusively denies knowledge of who has been persistently sending her flowers—"Joseph, *sweet*heart, I *swear* I don't know who it is!"—the demonstrative cadence of Lombard's delivery, stepping up the emphasis on "Joseph ... *sweet*heart ... *swear* ... !," does the work of undermining the claim for us while at the same time winning the conviction of her husband. We can hear she is overbaking it, but the reason is not yet given. Moments later, we find out (and on subsequent viewings are reminded) why. Maria is reading a letter from a young aviator, dispatcher of the flowers, and dwelling on the prospect of a fling. Only her dressing room attendant Anna (Maud Eburne) is present as a sounding board:

> MARIA: He's dying to see me, even if it's just for a minute. Of course I won't, definitely not; and yet I don't like to be rude to him. I think it's a mistake to ignore people who admire one and who after all buy the tickets...

Lombard voices this near-soliloquy in the dreamiest of tones. She inflects "even if it's just for a minute" with the sensuous gesture of running her fingers along the fold in the aviator's letter, arching her eyebrows as she conjures this picture of devotion. Rather than breaking off from this mood to re-assert her wifely duty, Lombard introduces a brilliant comic touch by running the line directly into "Of course I won't, definitely not," with the words spoken in an amorous tone that entirely reverses its meaning ("Of course I won't, definitely not" comes to imply, "Of course I will, ab-so-lutely"). The shift occurs only afterward with a slight stiffening of the neck, a tokenistic pang of conscience, and a quickening of pace on the line, "And yet I don't like to be rude to him," hastily reframing her desire as a kind of civic obligation. The adjustment is made more delicious by the way Lombard starts to punctuate her reasoning with more formal hand and neck movements to evoke the idiom of public oration: a speech in defense of the little people "who after all buy the tickets." The appeal is to notions of decency, a canny reframing indeed. Having sampled the delectable taste of prohibition ("only if it's just for a minute"), she now savors the erotic resonance of duty ("I owe it to my public").

If this is Maria at her most transparent—Anna sees right through her self-justifications, as we do—we are still left guessing how far she is prepared to go with this relationship. Does she seek a full-blown *affaire* or just the flattery of this young man's attention? Painting her nails and musing on the aviator's good looks, she breaks off to protest to Anna that she mustn't be misunderstood, that she loves her husband "*dearly.*" The word is delivered with an overwrought emphasis that recalls Maria's earlier claim of innocence ("Joseph, *sweet*heart") and is matched by an overly theatrical thrust of both hands. But lest we be too ready to write off their marriage, consider the inflection she gives to the following line (in reference to her husband): "He's wonderful." A different actress might have given it short shrift, or made it a more obviously disingenuous pronouncement. Lombard wrongfoots us by rendering it in a tone of genuine affection, almost an aside to herself (not a show for others), an impression aided by the way she times it to the moment she resumes painting her nails, a task more typically associated with private reverie and romantic rumination. One might wonder if Maria's flirtation with infidelity is just an act to cover the scandal of a happy marriage.

Wonderful notices

Role playing accumulates when war breaks out. Maria must conceal her links to the Polish underground when she is approached by unctuous Gestapo informant Professor Siletsky (Stanley Ridges) and invited to serve as a Nazi agent. To our surprise, perhaps, given her transparency on previous occasions, Maria's performance as the ready-to-please ingénue gives nothing away. "Oh, you want me to be a spy!," she giggles coquettishly, with an entirely convincing expression of wide-eyed delight. Lombard here resists the temptation of what James Naremore calls "expressive incoherence" (76) which would expose her character's true feelings to the audience whilst keeping them hidden to present diegetic company. Instead, we have greater purchase on her real motivations than Siletsky only because of our superior epistemic status, not because of any coded aside on the part of the actress. In the next line Lombard takes this a step further and leaves us unable to unpeel role from reality. "You know I once played a spy," she tells him, hastening to add: "It was a great success, I had wonderful notices." Lombard's delivery conveys the narcissism of false modesty through the way, on each clause, she lifts her eyebrows and closes her eyes ("great success" ... "wonderful notices"), as if humbly to accept the warmth of this remembered adulation. The phrasing of this line as a kind of "by-the-way" aside supports the impression of it as a boastful supplement that Maria just couldn't resist. On the other hand, it is equally plausible as an improvised tactic. The character flaw of "thespian's vanity" provides the perfect cover for a swift acceptance of this strategically valuable position. Lombard's delivery leaves us guessing whether the disclosure of vanity was unconscious or contrived.

Maria's role playing comes under its most significant pressure in the film's antepenultimate scene when she is being quizzed by the Gestapo.

Here, by virtue of Lombard's performance, the film's matchless blend of farce and suspense comes to a head. That combination is embodied by the two military officers who have arrived to conduct the interview, the ridiculous Colonel Erhardt (Sig Ruman) and the menacing Captain Schultz (Henry Victor). A complicated series of events have suggested to them that the man whom we met as "Siletsky" may have been an imposter wearing a false beard, and this leads them to suspect the actress associate to whom he has been romantically linked:

> SCHULTZ: It struck me as rather peculiar why anybody like you could be, shall we say, attracted to Professor Siletsky.
> MARIA: Well, Captain, you never can tell about those things. For instance, I think you're rather attractive yourself. Perhaps my taste is a little peculiar.
> SCHULTZ: But I haven't Professor Siletsky's distinguished beard. That's probably what fascinated you so much.
> MARIA: Yes it did intrigue me, it brought out the child in me. I always felt like pulling his beard but thank heavens I didn't.
> SCHULTZ: What do you mean by that?
> MARIA: It was a false beard, gentlemen, you know that. He fooled me and he certainly fooled you, Colonel.

This dialogue is played out in a static medium three-shot with the overbearing shoulder and profile of Captain Schultz placed frame right, Colonel Erhardt in the center, and Maria boxed into the lower left-hand side of the frame. A backlight serves to line out the contours of Lombard's fur hat and shoulders and makes Maria appear pinned in place by the fixed eyelines of the two onscreen interrogators. There is nowhere for her to hide. This arrangement, whilst perfectly defining the character's situation, presents a challenge for Lombard since she must enact Maria's evasions with severe limitations on physical movement. Lombard's typically energetic movement is further subdued by the wraparound of a fur-lined coat (the getaway is imminent so Maria is dressed for a swift exit). The attention is squarely on Maria's face, which we study for signs of unwanted disclosure. As Captain Schultz barks his inquiries, we become peripherally aware of her unsteady breathing and twisting hands, at the base of the frame, as Maria tries to suppress a telltale anxiety. Most striking of all, her wide eyes, fearfully fixed on Schultz's face but scanning very slightly from side to side, convey the restlessness of a search for escape. As Schultz finishes formulating his suspicion, we witness on her face the dawning of an avoidance strategy and the resumption of a virtual mask. At the end of the question about her attraction to Professor Siletsky, Maria's lips curl upward into a smile and she turns her large eyes coyly downward, as if Schultz had somehow delivered a compliment rather than a charge of duplicity. Looking down allows Maria a second or two to forestall and discharge her nervous energy into the impression of bashful shuffling. Then her face snaps into a fixed position on "For instance": an idea striking her. Maria locks on the charmless Schultz's face for the purposes of disarming flattery: "I think you're rather attractive yourself." Immediately sensing her misjudgment (we might notice, as she does, a twitch of indignation rather than any pleasure in Schultz's reaction), she disguises the retreat by resuming her downward look. At this point we observe a slight tightening of her features that suggests she regrets the tactical error. By way of a counter-punch, she transforms the compliment into an insult: "Perhaps my taste is a little peculiar."

Schultz fires back the remark about Siletsky's beard, trying to entrap Maria by getting her to admit, or to struggle to deny, incriminating knowledge of the man's disguise. Recognizing the strategy, intuiting that even a pause could be damaging, Maria takes the initiative, bouncing back an instant affirmative ("Yes, it did intrigue me") with a fluency that dramatically repels the attempt to tie her in knots. This necessitates an abrupt adjustment in persona, from infatuated schoolgirl to seasoned hostess. Lombard enacts this change by shifting her formerly fidgeting hands so that one rests confidently on top of the other, almost like the pose of carrying a handbag, before using them to confidently punctuate her speech. Turning to the bemused Colonel Erhardt, her demeanor now suggests the spirited regaling of an anecdote to fellow dinner guests ("It brought out the child in me, I always felt like pulling his beard but thank heavens I didn't"). Having thus taken the initiative, Maria is empowered when Schultz tries to resume the interrogation—"What do you mean by that?"—to offer her answer in the form of a punchline and with the implication they can all now enjoy their worldly knowledge of Professor Siletsky's eccentric secret. Lombard caps the line, "He certainly fooled you, Colonel," with a goofy giggle that betrays Maria's nervousness but also suggests an effort to turn the knife on wounded pride: Erhardt's not a man who likes to be "fooled" or laughed at. The Colonel turns to glare at Schultz, his scapegoat in all matters. The interrogation has been redirected and the interview derailed.

This account of select moments of Lombard's performance has tried to give voice to the impressions and implications that would, I think, be apprehended "automatically" by any attentive viewer. In this I follow the late V. F. Perkins in his conviction that "a prime task of interpretation is to articulate in the medium of prose some aspects of what artists have made perfectly and precisely clear in the medium of film" (4). As Perkins observes, the "validity and usefulness" of an interpretation is thereby to be assessed by "the degree to which we can internalize it and use it to enrich our contact with the film" (6). That ideal of enriched contact is the end goal of a form of description that tries to pay heed to moments as they unfold, and invites readers to measure the fittingness of a word or phrase against the material it seeks to evoke and explain. The purpose of urging focus on such ostensibly minute details as Lombard's momentary turns and gestures, on the way she deploys and directs her eyes, on her fluid pivots between personae, is to make what could seem like effortless effervescence more appreciable, more shareable, as achievement, as a gift.

Works cited

Barnes, Peter. *To Be or Not to Be*. London: BFI, 2002.
Cavell, Stanley. *Contesting Tears: The Hollywood Melodrama of the Unknown Woman*. Chicago: University of Chicago Press, 1997.
Perkins, V. F. "Must We Say What They Mean? Film Criticism and Interpretation," *MOVIE* 34 (1990).
Naremore, James. *Acting in the Cinema*. Berkeley: University of California Press, 1988.

Chapter 9

James Mason in *Lolita*

Rebecca Bell-Metereau

Konstantin Stanislavski advised actors to "Bring yourself to the point of taking hold of a new role concretely, as if it were your own life" (Vol. VI, 12). In contemplating this feat, we tend to think of actors as having an ineffable talent—an innate ability to change their bodies, channel emotions, virtually inhabit identities, and effortlessly convince audiences that they *are* the characters they play. A contemporary bias in favor of realist criteria—including plausibility, coherence, and consistency—means that acting is generally considered good if the actor's body fits the role, if the actor's personality is already similar to that of the character, and if the actor subsumes his or her individual personality traits to the demands of the role. Anything that reminds the viewer that this is, indeed, a performance is seen as a mistake, a violation of the unwritten contract between player and audience. It is somewhat ironic that this results in a demand for the invisibility of acting, and yet people may also criticize actors for simply playing themselves, particularly if they are typecast in roles similar to their perceived personal identities. The case of James Mason enacting the part of Vladimir Nabokov's mercurial child-molesting Humbert Humbert represents a different sort of irony. Mason's usual "type" could hardly be considered a child molester or dirty old man. If, to the contrary, his British urbanity and coolness placed him sometimes in the role of villain, his was not usually a sexualized personality.

In *Lolita*, Mason plays someone who is quite self-consciously performing a role in everyday life—that of mild-mannered professor—which conforms with his tony British accent well enough but which is also difficult to pull off without coming across as insincere, fake, or just plain dull. Add to this challenge the difficulty of working with one of the most notoriously flamboyant actors of his era, Peter Sellers, and one of the most demanding directors, Stanley Kubrick, and we set the stage for Mason's performance dilemma, one that cleverly mimicked the situation of Humbert himself. As with his Brutus in *Julius Caesar* (1953)—cast in opposition to the flamboyant and expressive Marlon Brando—Mason plays another concentrated, conflicted, and constipated character hiding a really big secret. The person playing a duplicitous and potentially alienating figure such as a child molester faces a challenge familiar to most actors: how does one *act* as if one's character is acting or faking an emotion or identity? The narrative situation may make this deception evident to some extent, but the actor must also behave in a way that conveys a degree of nervousness, concealment, and calculating detachment viewers can perceive as essential elements of lying or covering up one's motives and intentions. In playing Humbert, Mason embodies a character who covers his secret passion by camouflaging himself as rather dull and dry, uninteresting to a fault.

James Mason couldn't pull off this feat on his own, for a good actor doesn't arrive at a brilliant performance in isolation. The director creates an emotional dynamic between himself and each member of his cast, that elicits a distinct performance from each actor. When Mason accepted the role of Humbert, the actor took on a thankless task of appearing variously constrained, melodramatic, anxious, wooden, repressed, and sentimental—a challenging mix of emotions but hardly a recipe for Academy Awards or accolades on great acting. Mason was Kubrick's first choice for the role, but the actor originally turned it down because of a Broadway engagement, with Kubrick considering other sophisticated European types, including Laurence Olivier, Errol Flynn, Peter Ustinov, and David Niven, until Mason agreed to the part. Apparently Mason was not happy in the work, and legend has it that he "occasionally stormed off the set, upset by his inability to match Sellers' talent" (http://flavorwire.com/521766/20-things-you-didnt-know-about-stanley-kubricks-lolita). Although in his lifetime Mason was nominated for an Oscar for best actor in *A Star Is Born* (1954) and *Georgy Girl* (1966) and best supporting actor in *The Verdict* (1982), his performance in *Lolita* did not receive universal praise from critics. However, Mason was able to capture an array of contrasting psychological tenors, which fit his role perfectly, delivering a master performance of a character who is also "acting" practically the whole time, occasionally descending into a parody of himself, and arriving finally at a climactic scene that renders his figure at once both sublimely ridiculous and pathetically absurd.

Embodiment is essential to great acting, as David Thomson notes in focusing on Mason's voice, a physical attribute that is key to his brilliance:

> Mason's voice—aristocratic, but full of connoisseurship ... allowed the actor to become his true self just once, as the voice of Humbert Humbert in the film of *Lolita* ... He is a very bad man (if you like, or if you don't like), but he may be the purest-spoken scoundrel in all the movies. For he has to deliver Nabokovian prose as if to say it was the most normal and sensible way of speaking the English language yet invented. ("Every Word a Poison Dart," *The Guardian*, 14 May 2009)

This assessment of Mason's lovely elocution is couched in terms that focus on elements of social class and erudition, but it hints at a deeper resonance, the notion that Mason became "his true self just once" in the role of Humbert. Critics like Kellie Dawson ignore Mason's early typecasting as a villain after *The Man in Grey* (1943), and see his performance as "playing against type, ... usually cast as a desirable and debonair man of worldly sophistication" but in *Lolita* portraying a "tragically befuddled and sophomoric puppy-lover" (61). These extreme descriptions all capture a sliver of Mason's take on Nabokov's character. Disassembling his performance requires moment-by-moment and scene-by-scene analysis of modulations in tone and mood that convey a vast landscape of traits. As we dissect, we find evidence of the results, but little on the combined methods of actor, director, and other contributors that achieved this nuanced and complicated performance.

A great performance represents a complex interaction among the actor, director, script, and other actors, aided, of course by the myriad efforts of editors, makeup artists, set designers, and musicians, to name but a few collaborators. In Mason's portrayal of Humbert, this web of relationships among director and fellow actors was particularly crucial and challenging.

Mason was working among a collection of potential scene-stealers—the hilariously outlandish Peter Sellers playing several outrageous characters, Shelley Winters portraying the annoying yet pitiable "cow" mother to Lolita, and Sue Lyon inhabiting the role of seductive nymphet teenager so effectively that paeans devoted to her charms still pepper Internet porn sites. Mason occupies the space reserved for audience identification, and he must seduce the viewer into seeing these other figures from Humbert's idiosyncratic, disturbing point of view. Not a likable figure, Humbert nevertheless has traits that make him appealing, and they fit the talents Mason developed performing a variety of earlier roles, from Brutus to Vandamm in Hitchcock's *North by Northwest* (1959).

From head to toe

From the opening credits, which feature Mason's (or perhaps a stand-in's) hands holding a lovely foot and painting toenails over the sound of a lush piano score, to the opening scene in which Mason pulls a pair of gloves onto his hands, the actor's body speaks volumes. Using his resonant slightly nasal voice, Mason enacts the edge of nerves and cold calm of a man determined to kill Quilty (Sellers), for reasons that become clear by the end of the film. Abruptly flashing back to four years previously, shots of a plane and then a car accompany perky music and the mellifluous voice of Mason explaining in his elegant British accent what brings Humbert, scholar and professor, to quiet Ramsdale. Looking at potential lodging, he plays straight man to the desperately flirtatious and pretentious Mrs. Charlotte Haze (Winter), mother of the eponymous Lolita. In this brief scene, Mason conveys a series of shifts in attitude, with very few dialogue cues, demonstrating his initial interest in the lodging and his gradual misgivings as the desperate Charlotte's neediness becomes apparent. Trying to impress him, she points to reproductions of paintings, a portrait of her dead husband, and his ashes, while Mason increasingly constrains his movements to signal his character's disdain for her attempts at sophistication and his disinterest in her advances. This stiff manner bespeaks his desire to escape, hidden beneath a veneer of polite restraint and rendered comical by the exaggerated gestures of Winters, who flourishes her cigarette in its long holder as she prattles on. Once Humbert sees Lolita, she instantly becomes the object of his desire, and the actor slightly modifies his stilted manner to convey the mildest hint of surprise and delight, as he becomes the object of Lyon's seductive and challenging gaze. When Charlotte asks him what won him over to her place, he replies, with the barest hint of a chuckle, "Well, I think it was your cherry pies." This suggestive line would be easy to overplay, but Mason maintains a light, almost neutral tone, allowing Lyon's knowing look to convey her character's certainty that she's the cherry pie Humbert has in mind, a line that closes the scene.

In a comic cut to scary music and a close-up of an old movie monster, Kubrick suggests that Humbert is, indeed, a sort of monster. Then in another abrupt cut, the audience sees movie-watcher Humbert at a drive-in, sandwiched in the front seat of a car between Lolita and Charlotte. Lyon and Winters each grab one of Mason's knees. He removes Winter's hand, covers Lyon's with his own, which Winters then covers, until the three characters all have their hands stacked awkwardly on top of Mason's knee, as if in imitation of the layered performances Mason delivers in his multiple roles. The slow removal of hands to scratch noses and grasp the steering wheel occurs as Mason's face reflects a flickering combination of embarrassment, bemusement, and satisfaction. This gratified look is replaced by one of boredom in the next montage, suggesting the passage of time, as Humbert plays chess with Charlotte. When Lolita enters in her nightgown and plants a lingering goodnight kiss on his cheek, the lowering of his eyelids conveys an ever-so-slight hint of desire. In the next scene, a close-up of Mason's face captures an almost pained look of restrained lust as he peeps over the top of his book to gaze at Lyon, counting off her pelvic gyrations while a hula hoop rotates around her slim waist. As he watches, he has his exposed lower leg crossed over the other beneath a shiny robe, in a stereotypically feminine pose that underscores his peculiarly coded sexuality. When Winters sneaks up and flashes a picture, he winces as if struck, and she comments, "See how relaxed you're getting!" His demeanor throughout the scene conveys anything but relaxation.

Mason enacts the push and pull of erotic attraction, while females invade his character's personal space in scene after scene. As both mother and daughter become more flirtatious, Humbert's behavior grows more complicated. At a high school dance, Mason's face expresses both jealousy and admiration as he watches Lyon's Lolita dancing with a boy, but his body language shifts to nervous evasiveness and forced wholesomeness as Charlotte and her "swinging" female friend make suggestive comments and move in to embrace his arms and lean into his body. The next morning, as Lyon dangles a fried egg over his upturned face, Mason first appears to resist the aggressive move but then suddenly grabs her wrist and forces the egg into his mouth. Another rapid shift in mood occurs as Humbert learns that Lolita will be leaving for summer camp, with the actor's face crumpling for a moment and then returning to composure. Before she takes off, Lolita runs up to hug Humbert goodbye and then races out of the house, at a narrative turning point in which Mason's performance conveys the mixed emotions of a man utterly taken aback with yearning and loss. Entering Lolita's bedroom, Mason makes Humbert's body seem to shrink when he sits on her bed, slumping to nestle his face in her pillow. A photograph of Humbert's grinning nemesis Quilty rests next to Mason's vulnerable-looking form.

Piano and orchestra underscore Humbert's wild despair, but as the maid enters to deliver a letter from Charlotte, he sniffs and quickly collects himself. When he reads aloud the mother's confession of love, his sobs turn to nearly hysterical laughter as he gradually begins to envision a solution to his dilemma. Mason handles this scene deftly, alternately sniffling and chuckling, extending his tongue, and imitating the exaggerated dramatic tone of the letter writer by turns. This performance transforms a potentially sentimental moment into hilarious mockery, which draws at least certain viewers unwillingly—yet inexorably—into the character's perspective, creating psychological co-conspirators in Humbert's coldly calculating plan to gain lifelong access to the object of his desire. The scene ends with Mason's full-bellied laughter at the absurdity of the situation, as he reclines face up on the bed next to Quilty's portrait, concluding the first major turning point in the narrative.

Mason's chipper voiceover recounts Charlotte and Humbert's marriage and honeymoon.

Once the couple returns home, he enacts the cheerful lustfulness of his character, who looks at a bedside picture of Lolita while he is mounting Charlotte. Here, another twist foils Humbert's plans, as his wife tells him about her decision to send Lolita away to boarding school, directly after summer camp. At this moment Mason's expression takes on a menacing desperation. He rolls over, huddling with his back turned to her. His face is a pained immobile mask as he stares at the foregrounded gun that, moments earlier, Charlotte was playfully brandishing. When she asks if she is on his train of thought, viewers know from the darkness of his look and the flatness of his voice saying "Yes" that the character has foul play in mind. Mason does his version of Kubrick's signature menacing eyes, as his character's intentions darken. Lolita telephones at that moment, and when Charlotte chides Humbert for sending the girl candy, he explodes in anger. This is Mason's opportunity to show his character unleashing a flood of bitterness over his "lapdog" status, shuffling his fingers like a scurrying animal. Once Charlotte exits, Mason's voiceover reveals Humbert's thoughts as he sees the bullets in the gun chamber and contemplates using the loaded weapon to stage a supposedly accidental shooting. Pacing toward the bathroom where Charlotte is running a bath, he seems prepared to murder her, but the tone of Humbert's voiceover thoughts shifts from wonderment at this clever solution to bemusement at the stab of conscience that prevents him from carrying out a murder.

Mason demonstrates a remarkable nimbleness in tone as Humbert becomes the placating, obsequious husband discovering Charlotte reading from his diary entries (that reveal his loathing of her). Yelling from the kitchen as he prepares a drink, he becomes the brilliant authorial improviser, concocting an explanation for how what she read was a fictional account of an author who makes up "funny situations." Meanwhile, offscreen, Charlotte runs outside where she is struck in the street by a passing vehicle. In a scene of superbly dark humor, Mason enacts one after another emotional state, from excuse-making to puzzlement to stunned disbelief at Charlotte being run over. The subsequent cut to a shot of Mason soaking in the tub, Lolita's yaya musical motif playing in the background, pictures him in side angle with a drink balanced on his furry chest. He's attempting to tip his Scotch into his mouth without using his hands. In one of the most hilarious scenes of the film, Mason enacts Humbert's feigned controlled grief, covering all the while his delight at the serendipitous accident that delivered his newfound freedom and the prospects of a life with Lolita, unencumbered by a hovering Charlotte. In this tour de force, Mason captures a character who is busy covering his emotions, enjoying the irony of having everyone around him completely misinterpret his emotional state. In an almost vaudevillian "milk it and top it" closing for the scene, Mason's Humbert talks with exaggerated reasonableness to the father of the young man who ran Charlotte over, telling him he has "no quarrel" with him or his son. When the father says he was considering paying funeral expenses, Mason shakes his head, as if about to refuse his offer, and then swiftly says, "Thank you very much," much to the father's disappointment.

Mason uses his bushy eyebrows, tight smile, and subtle facial cues to great comic effect throughout the film, to glower in anger or concentration, to register shock or surprise, or to underscore layers of dramatic irony. In the scene when Humbert and Lolita, traveling together, must settle for the last remaining single room at a hotel, the clerk explains that the hotel is packed because they're hosting the state police convention. Mason, busy signing Humbert's name, pauses ever so slightly, tilts his face up to look at the clerk, raising his eyebrows and closing his eyes in a gesture halfway between a blink and a twitch, grins a nervous smile, tilts his head and sighs ever so slightly as he returns to his task of signing in. Once in the room, Mason renders his face the very model of solicitous fatherly concern, bringing the full force of his correctly urbane accent as he declares his feelings of "tenderness" and explains to Lolita why they "shall be thrown a good deal together."

Although Mason was not known as a Method actor, Kubrick forced him into this technique by exploiting the discomfort of the actor in scenes that mirror the uneasiness of the character he plays. In one of the most famous interactions of the film, Peter Sellers impersonates a policeman and rants about having a "lovely little pretty small daughter" as Mason fidgets in the background, trapped, both in his role as Humbert and in his position as an actor forced to respond to Sellers's famous scene-stealing, line improvisations, and gestures. One gets an almost palpable sense of a desire to exercise greater control, as Sellers stomps over Mason's lines and forces the actor to stammer through the scene, in which Sellers's character dominates the conversation and repeatedly refers to what "normal" guys the two of them are.

Mason then performs Chaplinesque comedy as he tosses and turns in a cot next to the large double bed where Lolita sleeps comfortably. The following morning, she hovers over Humbert's head, placing him in the awkward position of looking upside down from beneath her. When Lyon whispers in his ear, Mason's voice is hesitant, soft, and husky as she slides beside him and the shot fades to black. This bland seduction scene meets the demands of contemporary censorship (the Code was still enforced in 1962), constrains the actor, and minimizes the sexual charge, reducing it to a child's game. Then, as the couple drives along the next morning, Mason dispassionately delivers the line, "Your mother is dead," and the shot again fades to black, cutting to a scene of Lolita sobbing uncontrollably in their next hotel room. Trying to comfort her, stroking her head awkwardly, he speaks as if she were the child that she actually is. When she asks him to promise he will never leave her, he repeats the line, "Cross my heart and hope to die," first as if he were talking to a child, next somewhat ritualistically, and finally with a poignant depth and a look of sincere emotion as he contemplates what the words mean. In this moment, the actor conveys a depth and earnestness of feeling that is new to his character.

The following segment poses the greatest challenge for Mason, as Humbert's character exhibits more extreme mood swings and erratic behavior. The actor expands the range of his performance in depicting Humbert's new life with Lolita in Ohio, moving from mundane to certifiably insane. His transitional voiceover at first sounds upbeat and reasonable, but in later scenes Humbert's exchanges with Lolita sound like an amalgam of impatient father and jealous abuser. Mason's tenor changes to a pleading lover as Humbert tries to convince Lolita that he gives her everything, that they do, indeed, "have fun." Mason finds himself again forced into the uncomfortable role of straight man, floundering alongside Sellers, this time as another flamboyant version of Quilty, a "school psychologist" pursuing the couple. Feeling himself bested yet once again, as both character and actor, Mason embodies Humbert's paranoid and frustrated submission, defeated and agreeing to allow Lolita to star in the school play.

In the climactic moment, when Humbert learns she has been deceiving him about where she was when she missed her piano lessons, the actor transforms rapidly from enraged lover to groveling appeaser. Humbert hatches another scheme to start a new life for the couple and extricate himself from an untenable situation. When Lolita screams that she hates Humbert, Mason grabs Lyon's wrists and manhandles her with apparent fury, a stretch from the actor's usual range. After a knock on the door, Humbert quickly shifts to mild-mannered gentleman, nervously apologizing to a neighbor lady who has heard their screaming. As they finally leave Ohio for life on the road, Mason must appear both cannily suspicious of every male he sees and yet still the gullible Humbert, eager to believe Lolita's empty promises. While Lolita mugs and tries to distract him on the long car ride, Humbert's anxiety over being followed grows with each passing mile, and Mason's face looks more and more haggard.

Mason performs these frequent flashes of anger with pressure-cooker intensity, eventually exhibiting signs of a heart attack, severe cold, and possible pneumonia. The elegant control of Mason's voice and posh accent are belied by his haunted physical appearance, several days' beard growth, and the sagging expression of a lifeless, beaten man. Once Humbert discovers that Lolita has left the hospital with her "uncle"—that is, Quilty—Mason's performance shifts gears from an almost credible father figure to a convincing babbling psychotic, exhibiting violent outbursts. When Humbert explodes with desperate fury, the hospital staff pins Mason's frail-looking body to the floor. Humbert realizes he is on the verge of being involuntarily committed for psychosis and reverts to his reasonable persona, assuring everyone he is fine, asking, as he walks out, if Lolita left any word for him.

In the denouement, we see an insert shot of a plea for money being typewritten by Lolita, explaining that she's married and pregnant. Kubrick cuts to a carefully groomed shot of Mason, dressed in an elegant overcoat, knocking on the door of a modest flat. Mason's face falls as he looks at the woman who answers the door—Lyon, wearing a frumpy pregnancy smock and sporting large black glasses and a ponytail. At this point in the narrative, Lolita confesses to Humbert that when they left Ohio, Quilty, the only true love of her life, was following them, but the relationship eventually failed. Astonished but undeterred, Humbert begs her to leave her husband (who knows nothing of their history together) and run away with him. When Mason speaks the lines, "Live with me and die with me and everything with me," claiming, "I could wait for the rest of my life, if necessary," he conveys the constancy and humility of his love. Unable to convince Lolita to run off with him, Humbert hands over the remainder of his money to her. During this scene Mason sobs into his hands and finally rushes out of the house, to Bob Harris's lush "Lolita" theme, which underscores Humbert's aching longing, hopeless sacrifice, and total loss. According to Kubrick, this final scene was intended to reveal for the first time Nabokov's withheld secret, that Humbert actually did love Lolita, that he was not simply a pervert obsessed only with the nymphet qualities of her adolescent body. Considering the incredible range of emotions and personalities Mason had to convey while maintaining the same character identity, critics may want to rethink the actor's chameleon-like embodiment of a staggering number of emotional states and personality traits. The lack of critical attention to this transformation ironically serves as testimony to the efficacy of Mason's performance as practically invisible and organic to Humbert's character.

The final question to consider is how this feat was accomplished. Was Kubrick responsible, as the recognized genius capable of inspiring such a performance through his clever coaxing and direction? Was Mason an unrecognized genius able to shape-shift himself to an impossibly mercurial and ambiguous character? Or, was the actor simply so perfectly typecast for a role that it required him only to display all of his natural quirks and physical attributes to achieve a believable Humbert? Or was the chemistry of this particular collection of actors the ideal Petri dish for the growth of Mason's naturalistic method of impersonation, couched among a bevy of more exaggerated bravura performances in an unrecognized and perfectly camouflaged embodiment worthy of the meme, "James Mason *is* Humbert Humbert"? The answer may well be yes to all of the above, for the emotional chemistry of Kubrick and his carefully chosen cast constituted the laboratory that incubated Mason's greatest performance.

Works cited

Dawson, Kellie. "As Hollywood Teaches: Tracing the Cultural Impact of *Lolita* and its Adaptations to Film," in Rebecca Housel, ed., *From Camera Lens to Critical Lens: A Collection of Best Essays on Film Adaptation*, New York: Cambridge Scholars Publishing, 2009, 59–72.

Stanislavski, Konstantin. *An Actor's Handbook, An Actor Prepares*. Vol. VI. Ed. Elizabeth Reynolds Hapgood. New York: Taylor & Francis, 2004.

Chapter 10

Montgomery Clift in *A Place in the Sun*

George Toles

"Are they watching?"

All great screen actors who achieve stardom have a split persona, and Montgomery Clift's is especially rich in paradox. He projects vulnerability and empathetic awareness so powerfully that he frequently appears totally exposed under the camera's gaze, and yet he embodies hiddenness to nearly the same degree. No actor is better at conveying stillness and internal balance, but he was, by all accounts, always on the brink of chaos and loss of control in his offscreen life. His commanding poise is usually offset by a stricken helplessness in his eyes. Actor Robert Ryan, commenting on Clift's charged manner of looking, noted further unresolved conflict between his eyebrows and his eyes: "[His eyebrows] seemed to dominate his face, and they would have been too fierce if it had not been for the hypnotic quality in his large dark eyes." Ryan further noted that though Clift laughed readily in conversation, his laugh was never far removed from a "disturbing cackle" (Bosworth 181).

George Eastman, doomed protagonist of George Stevens's *A Place in the Sun* (1951)—a film adapted from Theodore Dreiser's magisterial novel *An American Tragedy*—is in so many respects the ideal gathering place for Clift's singular strengths as a film actor. George spends the majority of his narrative life deceiving everyone with whom he comes in contact, in addition to being self-deceived. But in his scenes with Elizabeth Taylor's Angela he also seems almost mystically attuned to a vision of romantic truth that extends beyond the domain of her personal qualities. George is an unformed child-man seeking to find a story of himself that he and others can validate. And Angela becomes a sphere of rebirth for him, dwelling in proximity to the highest imaginative possibilities—a place in the sun for him, very close yet also just beyond reach. Unlike Clyde Griffiths, the prototype of his character in the Dreiser novel, Clift's George Eastman is not merely an unreflecting cog in a social system that uses him in much the same fashion that he uses its mechanisms to get ahead. While undeniably a guilty collaborator in his own tragedy, Clift's George also seems to internalize, without much conscious understanding, the forces of light and darkness that abide at the very heart of American striving. Clift seems on a quest for not only betterment but transcendence.

Much of Clift's George and the camera's relation to him throughout the film is established in the canonical opening credits sequence. We first observe Clift from behind and at a distance as he hitchhikes (leaving behind what he considers a shameful past) without success on a busy stretch of flatland highway. In addition to having his back to us in what begins as a long-shot composition, Clift is further obscured behind the film's superimposed title credits. Unusual emphasis is placed on the initial withholding of the young man's (and film star's) identity, and on the related suggestion of his being someone with a stake in concealment. Clift's leather jacket and jeans might initially be interpreted as the uniform of the rebel wanderer, the alienated outsider.

As we shall soon be informed, the man on the highway is a poor relation of the powerful and prosperous Eastman family. He has a clear destination for his hitchhiking—the city of Carthage, where his uncle's factory is located. George has been invited to seek out this uncle for some chance of employment, and has, at the outset, no aspiration higher than securing whatever job he can. He cherishes, no doubt, a fantasy of advancing swiftly within the system by respecting all the rules of the company-and-society "game." Raised in a shabby mission, George is someone desperate to achieve outward success, and to become an insider. Thus, his affiliation in the film's opening shots with the rebel stance does not give us an accurate impression of his eagerness to defer, or his anxious conformity to the standards of those with money and clout. The overall structure of his story depicts a young man seizing every opportunity to get inside the glittering kingdom but failing to secure the place that magically materializes for him. Circumstances dictate that his climb to eminence is only possible if he makes none of the blunders typical for "one of his kind." Will the markers of his lowly upbringing and the forces that have molded him (without really *forming* a person) not fatally reassert themselves, whatever help and good fortune come his way? George's increasing acceptance by the inside world of security and elite privilege will ultimately only exacerbate his fall back to outsideness when his day of reckoning comes. In *A Place in the Sun*, there is something weirdly accursed in George's natural desire to rise, to efface his shabby past like a good American, to hold immoderate hopes. How firmly all the doors will close against him when some inherent wrongness—a "crookedness" in his makeup that contaminates his "good name"—is eventually brought to light.

George Stevens organizes the lengthy opening shot as a slow progression of Clift toward the camera, achieved by having Clift moving backwards until he reaches it. The camera does not so much close in on its subject, insisting on the star's magnitude and emotional force, as lie in wait for him. So when Clift's leather-jacketed back looms large in front of it, the camera is in effect apprehending him. From the outset then there is the suggestion that he is already somehow under arrest. Throughout the film, Stevens repeatedly offers us views of Clift from a long-shot distance, or with his back turned, or half-shrouded in darkness. The handling of his form and image is designed to offset the incredible magnetic power of Clift's face, presenting vantage points that remind us of how he might be lost from sight, ignored, returned to a shameful, deracinated obscurity. George is meant to be lost and found recurrently, in relation to his inchoate aspirations to be "someone out of the ordinary," an exception to the "dreary mass." In time, he will lose completely his formerly scorned anonymity, be visible suddenly to every eye; but his status has become an irreparable disgrace. He is illuminated by his association with a murderous deed that fixes him in the public mind as a horrible dissembler and conscienceless killer, one severed from every civilizing norm and value. His search for a place in the sun yields ultimately an imprisonment in the dehumanizing glare of infamy. George commences his narrative by making every effort to attract notice, and thus build a plausible social self that others (those who know what deserves sanction) will validate. At a certain point, however, all notice turns accusatory, and he finds refuge from it only in his prison cell on death row. Even there, his priest and mother search his words and face for conclusive evidence of guilt, in "God's eyes."

When in his hitchhiker's entry to the narrative Clift at last turns to face the camera, Stevens grants him a monumental close-up, in which a near godlike beauty is startlingly unfurled, but only to the camera and the spectator who shares its private witnessing. The face seems introspectively alive and yearning, and at first we are encouraged to believe it is in contact with some unbounded, possibly incommunicable vision. The camera tracks closer and closer to that face, probing its secret, briefly licensing its capacity for Emersonian wonder. At this precise "assumption" pivot point, we are given a deflating reverse-shot view of a glossy advertising billboard. It promptly reduces the scope of what Clift's face knows; imagines; is in touch with. We have not yet been informed that the character name is "Eastman," but the exclamatory force of the billboard inscription "It's an Eastman!" proclaims that this name is both a (widely) known quantity and an ineffable quality worth aspiring to. The entire three-word catchphrase, we will shortly discover, identifies the hoped-for identity of the man who contemplates it. His back is once again turned to us as he surveys the ad, with his hitchhiking thumb still absentmindedly raised. The name "Eastman" also attaches to the bathing suit product that the Eastman company manufactures, as the sign attests, "in the heart of America."

Hidden in the straightforward "sexual consumer" ad image is the riddle of George's eventual fate: he will meet a woman named Alice (Shelley Winters) who boxes swimsuits in the lower level of the Eastman factory where he is also employed, a woman who avoids beaches herself because she can't swim. He will one day lead her into the water (an excursion in an excruciatingly hemmed-in rowboat) as the culmination of their romance and there she will be drowned, an outcome that is a tangled mix of intention and accident. The smiling woman on the billboard—who somewhat resembles his future love, Angela Vickers—will allow George to project the possible shape of days to come in only the vaguest, daydream terms. Like George, the viewer can detect no shadows in the billboard "come on," no sense of foreboding. At most, we may be disappointed in George's facile enchantment with billboard artifice. He seems to be uncritically drinking in the huckster's sales pitch. What draws his attention back to the road is the taunting four-note call of a car horn, an abstract announcement of casual, careless privilege, of "owning the road." The driver, we will figure out later, is indeed the eventual figure of romantic veneration, Angela. She will gradually reveal herself as the unattainable fairytale princess in the tower, the glittering maiden of the advertisement turning real and immediate. Clift's and our first impressions of her have to do with distance and oblivious speeding away. Clift no sooner catches sight of her in her white Cadillac (there is no medium or establishing shot; she is in effect a magical blur attached to her luxurious, immaculate vehicle) than she is whisked away into the enchanted country ahead. In relation to such a presence, Clift's George is defined—naturally—as one left behind. He remains invisible to this driver, whose present has instantly formed auspicious ties with a future that George is striving to imagine. She is effortlessly headed toward that destination where whatever money and class can secure for a person has already been secured.

While George is watching the apparitional convertible vanish ahead of him, his attention is re-directed a third time, to a junk truck that has mysteriously, soundlessly drawn up next to him and whose owner inaudibly offers him a lift. George covers his nose and mouth with a handkerchief before entering, and with this gesture adds a foul odor to the truck's aggressive unsightliness. The truck is imbued with the force of everything shameful and coarse in the life George is fleeing—a projection of the past's oppressive burdens. It quietly reclaims the man who imagines he has placed a meaningful distance, in his present footloose state, between himself and his past. One senses that the driver's kindly acknowledgment of this wayfarer erases George's fantasy of progress. Kinship and belonging are reinforced once George is inside the cab and in motion.

In mid-journey, Clift displays George more at his ease than we will ever see him again, laughing with the driver and appearing confident that no critical assessment of him is being made. I see in this concluding strand of the film's opening a portrait of George's passivity, a vital key to his character and to Clift's entire subsequent performance. While he is aggressive in pushing into Alice Tripp's room to initiate their sexual relationship, and, later, exploding feelingfully toward her during their rowboat excursion on

Loon Lake, generally, as Clift conceives him, George Eastman approaches situations reactively. He allows others to take the lead and set the tone. He reflects their expectations back to them as an instinctive, compulsive form of protection for his barely coherent sense of self. By force of garb, circumstance, and image, Clift is connected to Jack Kerouac's life-altering road trips, J. D. Salinger's Holden Caulfield—searching for an "authentic" place that will sustain a core innocence—and Albert Camus' alienated stranger and confused rebel. The complex fusion that Clift achieves onscreen maintains the aura of the baffled, fugitive outsider—a kind of teenager—undone by malignant social circumstances beyond his understanding and control, while also exhibiting the ambitious climber, whose highest dream is to get all the way inside the system of arrangements ordained by wealth and power, and be accepted there.

Clift by no means avoids the manipulative, darkly dissembling dimensions of George Eastman, but they do not dominate his performance, or establish its final sense. His presence onscreen, his manner of observing, holding silence, attempting to explain and (partially) reveal himself, his hunched physicality, so often moving in bewilderment around the periphery of the spaces that captivate him: all of these components of Clift's expressiveness create a counter-story of stricken lostness, of being inherently a "wrong fit" for the realm he attempts to belong to. His gaze feels incurably drawn to an elsewhere allied with yearning or inexpressible pain. Clift has a rare capacity to shift in an instant from an absent look to one charged with presence. The camera ratifies his estranged outsider condition whenever it ventures close to his face (long intervals separate these intimate views of him) or studies the tense, stationary speech of his physical attitudes, in which melancholy withdrawal and an unreasoning strife are steadily discernible.

Clift's performance, as we experience it, does not seem reduced by the character's passivity. There is a tremendous latent energy in his perfectly focused facial tumult, as well as in the depth of his surrender to the dream that Angela Vickers embodies for him (in which lover and surrogate mother mysteriously coalesce), and perhaps chiefly in his desperate need to present a story about himself that he can stand behind and that others will accept and approve. Clift's power, when he repeatedly tells versions of his story and reimagines it while doing so, is the power that comes from letting the camera completely inside, giving himself to it with the same riveting fullness that he gives to his current "testimony," as though the camera, in the face of such rapt exposure, will cleanse him, undo the damage, make him into a new being, a whole person. He seems so often, under the camera's heightened scrutiny, on the verge of attaining his unattainable self. Clift's George appears to become someone in the act of explaining who he is and shaping his emotional ground in relation to others' concerns about him. He is obliged to tell a portion of his story many times in the course of the narrative, culminating with his confession on the witness stand during his trial for Alice's murder and his subsequent death row interpretation of his guilty heart at the behest of his priest and mother. George never tells the "whole truth" about himself in any of his storytelling sessions (an impossible task, of course, even for one less disposed to hide things), but his telling never has an air of wilful lying. He strives to make himself worthy of his listeners' expectations. He over-identifies with all those who preserve and regulate the established order. He attributes depth and rightness to their perspective, and sees his own as ungrounded, shallow, perhaps illusory. If others can find sense in the story he serves up, with a childlike faith, he will gain permission to embrace it himself and become more real in his own eyes.

George seeks to be worthy of the Eastman name he carries. He holds it more or less by accident; it does not automatically confer the dignity of an essence. "It's an Eastman!" How can he be sure that he's the authentic name brand ("one of us," in the obsessively recurring club-membership phrase of Conrad's novel *Lord Jim*) as opposed to a cheap imitation? Prior to the discovery of Alice's death and George's connection to her, his storytelling efforts are greeted with respect or bemused encouragement. The Eastman and Vickers patriarchs are inclined to believe that he might be "one of us," not only in spite of his squalid background but because of it. If the material is right, the mill of harsh circumstance can form a firm character. George's romantic conception of the ethereal moneyed sphere is one where he might, if chosen, perform "valorous deeds." Once Alice's drowning has come to light, however, and George is apprehended, he not only ceases to be a bona fide Eastman but is generally perceived as one set far below the common run of humanity. He is not only a murderer, but a man without a shred of honor, a coward who cannot live up to the modest obligations that even those of 'low" upbringing ordinarily fulfill. Clift's deference, sensitivity, and beauty are transformed from a passkey to privilege ("An Eastman isn't in the same boat with anyone") to a frighteningly sinister impersonation. Appearance and a pleasing manner become a ruse designed to undermine the foundations of the class system. See what comes of allowing those whose status is a patchwork, a set of unanswerable questions, to slip through the gate? George becomes the hidden plague spot in a realm of readable, presentable surfaces.

Clift's performance then is about telling stories in shifting contexts—stories in which his appearance at first proves an expert facilitator, a supremely effective calling card, and then becomes more troubling, not only to those interrogating him within the film's world but to the spectator, who is confronted with a steadily more fearful obscurity, an unresolvable amorphousness at the heart of his beauty. When we watch Clift presenting a smattering of facts about himself on his first visit to the Eastman home (awkward in his cheap, ill-fitting suit and dwarfed by the massive armchair in which he sits) or, much later, making a case for himself as a prospective son-in-law to Angela's father after the drowning, we're never shown a canny prevaricator attempting to mislead. Alice's death clearly weighs heavily on him at every moment leading up to his talk with Mr. Vickers, but when he is asked to represent himself as a young man sincerely mindful of his shortcomings yet passionately eager to win Angela's hand, he appears to confront his defects squarely, with no hint of inward strain, even though there is no mention of Alice in his account. Every assertion he makes is unquestionably heartfelt. He loses sight of other truths while speaking of those that bear directly on this compartment of his psyche. Phillips Holmes, who performed the same role as Clift in the 1931 adaptation of Dreiser's novel, enlists very little audience sympathy, since the smooth operator and crass, opportunist dimensions of his character are so persistently emphasized. Clift's George is not a practiced liar in any familiar sense of that pathology. There is no conscious underneathness to his revelations. Clift's George always makes it seem that his listener ultimately has the right to decide what he amounts to, a summing-up George cannot legitimately challenge, even in private.

If he manages to gain others' approval in the role he auditions for, he will live up to whatever conception of his potential they endorse.

Clift repeatedly depicts George finding his place, bit by bit, within the story he's presently telling. Making emotional connection with his own words, he manages to define a meaningful stance and a way of being that hold together. At his murder trial, George's face radiates as much trust as nervousness on the witness stand: trust that the court authorities will set reasonable conditions for accepting or rejecting his testimony. They will follow him, in his story, to the space he aspires to occupy ethically on the fateful rowboat, where he recoiled (humanely) from Alice's fear of him and from the prospect of killing her. He was balanced in his own mind before the rowboat lost *its* balance and tipped over. Clift's George has no inner resources with which to oppose the district attorney (Raymond Burr), nor does he conceive the prosecutor's aggressive questions as those of an enemy. George regards the DA's authority to judge the merits of his story as uncontestable, even if he weakly protests against it.

Clift unsentimentally projects a kind of plausible tragic innocence for George's fumbling existence among secrets large and small—an innocence akin to existential blankness. Apart from what his favorable appearance and accommodating disposition designate, there is no essence for George that precedes his attempts to say (yet again) who he is, or who he hopes to be. It is the child's overwhelming need to have his telling, whatever its distortions and omissions, affirmed somehow by those "in charge" that gives Clift the dual effect of transparency and opaqueness. He is wholly *there* in his utterances, most of the time, and his endearing, wholehearted conviction emits a glow, yet one keenly senses an unformed being behind his words.

The faculty of judgment is strangely and variously at sea in this film, both for George and for the viewer emotionally entwined with his aspirations, his innocent groping for self-definition, and his, by turns, alluring and disquieting enigma. The one solid, personally initiated event of George's narrative—his plan to drown Alice—is finally indeterminate. We shift from extreme close-ups of Clift and Winters in the rowboat (up until the moment when Alice loses her balance and falls) to the longest of long shots with the pair's simultaneous tumble into the water, the rowboat becoming a tiny white speck in the distance. Instead of Alice's cries for help in the water, the only sound we are granted is the call of a single bird. The optics of motive and action in George's climactic decision whether to save her or to flee, are removed—another instance of the narrative rear view. Similarly, when George first conceives the idea of killing Alice, it is as though the thought comes entirely pre-formed in a radio report of a local drowning he chances to hear. The lengthiest close-up of Clift in the film is his face penetrated and quietly overwhelmed by the words of the radio announcer. Once the idea has entered, he drops on his bed and covers his head with a pillow in a half-hearted effort to exorcise the unbidden thought. Once again he apparently lacks the strength to resist outside influences. It is not so much that George is warring with the thought internally, though that is undoubtedly part of what is going on. Clift plays the moment as though he were fleeing the sight of invisible, disapproving witnesses. ("Are they watching?," as Angela says to him during their major love scene, when she surprisingly turns to the camera for an instant and gazes directly at us).

When the guilty verdict is eventually reached in George's trial, we seem still to be confronted with a case that we are ill-equipped to judge. We certainly do not know precisely what to make of George's testimony on the witness stand, however affecting it has been, and George does not appear to know either. It is almost a relief for us when finally, without protest, he accepts the prison chaplain's hypothesis that there was murder in his heart after the boat overturned. But in this last encounter with a "superior," George is simply staying true to his fixed pattern from the outset. He willingly accepts the verdict of those more highly placed than he is about what his conduct signifies, and what treatment it does or doesn't entitle him to.

In his death row meeting with the chaplain (Paul Frees) and his mother, Hannah (Anne Revere), George exclaims that he "doesn't want to hide anything. I want to know." Yet never has a protagonist's performance on film been so consistently designed by its director to emphasize hiddenness. Commencing with our first view of George, the camera pursues so many strategies for denying us intimate access to him. Even when he is telling his stories or silently revealing himself in contexts where everything depends on our capacity for close facial scrutiny—for example, his attempt to show Mr. Vickers that he is a worthy suitor for Angela, his courtroom testimony, his farewell to Angela in his cell, his walk to the electric chair—Stevens repeatedly resorts to rear-view compositions and profile shots, subtly maintaining barriers to approachability. The long shots and turned-away shots of George which provide so much of our sense of him as a physical, sentient being—isolated; enclosed in bewilderment, embarrassment, or furtive shame—drastically reduce our impression of self-command. He strives to take meaningful steps forward, to carry out plans, but he seldom locates himself in his manner of performing deeds. He is right to claim, on the witness stand, "I couldn't help myself. I didn't know what I was doing." Stevens directs him to embody a kind of restless, woozy drift through the social realms of the narrative. Clift suggests vividly the entranced condition of someone who is dreaming his life rather than consciously inhabiting it. As the film progresses, we see how mindful he is of putting off the dread moment of waking. He hungrily seizes every phantom wisp of love and security. The Clift close-ups are typically reserved not so much for moments of full realization, as for surprise. He repeatedly appears to be struck by something he can neither dismiss nor adequately comprehend, his eyes shifting to wider, vulnerable receptiveness. The close-up moments are nearly always intense because Clift's George has so little ability to mask his need to be accepted. He shows the camera a beseeching expressiveness. He cannot defend himself from any demand, offer, interpretation that is being made of him. The stubborn strength that even Alice exhibits in his presence, no matter how beleaguered her own position, as a rule vastly exceeds his own. When we are permitted to move near to his face, it is frequently to see him rising to the possibility of a new, provisional self-definition. There is an excitement in his sudden, swift revisions of his sense of who others take him for, what they want him to be; and in his eagerness not to disappoint.

Unquestionably the central episode of Clift's performance is the second dance scene with Elizabeth Taylor, packed with close-ups, culminating in their joint flight to a nearby balcony where they confess their love. It is here that they briefly attain perfect emotional unity, in shots so massively intimate that they seem to overflow the banks of the screen. Clift apparently gave Taylor extensive coaching throughout their rehearsal period for the film, and Taylor has often acknowledged that Clift's example revealed to her what film acting, in its highest degree of truthfulness, might achieve. It is striking then to consider how completely Clift cedes authority to Taylor in their shared scenes, despite her extreme youth (he was more than a decade older), her eagerness to follow his lead, and the "pampered, sheltered rich girl" dimension of her character. Angela has been exposed to far less privation, struggle, and adversity than George, yet George never feels the impulse to instruct her on the hardships of his separate world. She arranges each of their meetings, and takes the initiative in making decisions about how they will spend their time together. Her lack of knowledge about what George conceals from her somehow does not lessen her emotional authority or reduce the curative powers of her assured, self-possessed presence. Angela imparts little of what she understands about George verbally, but her way of conducting herself when they are together strongly suggests an intuition of his darkness, sad lostness, and the disquieting tension he so carefully refrains from exhibiting directly.

At one point in the major love scene, Angela refers to herself as "Mama" and urges George to unveil everything that he is to her. And in a sense, he does achieve what feels like a plenitude of disclosure in the camera's rapt excavation of his face, in mammoth proximity to hers. Film once again explores the paradox of how a face brimming with secrets and withholding can surrender in its totality to another face, and be suddenly shorn of masking and deceptive effect, though no verbal admission has been made. Stevens explained how he edited the eerily matching faces of Clift and Taylor so it would appear that they were rolling toward each other in waves, becoming engulfed in oneness (Bosworth 187). The intensifying meld of faces leading up to their ecstatic embrace establishes a metaphoric equivalence with Alice's later rowboat tragedy. For a rapturous drowning is certainly accomplished on the balcony as George gives himself—to his fullest extent—into Angela's keeping. He sinks like a child, found at last, into the depths of her answering image and strength. In her face that combines a mother's early oceanic presence with that of a lover hazarding all—struck to the core by another's irresistible summons to remove all barriers—Taylor allows Clift to be credibly cleansed of sorrow and disgrace, and to be reborn.

To reduce the scene to a plot point, one could say that it merely depicts two excited, unreflecting young people in the familiar throes of passionate desire, which the immense alternating close-ups of them romanticize. *A Place in the Sun* has already supplied skeptical commentary on scenes of just this sort when Clift had his first unplanned date with Winters at a movie theater playing the romance, *Now and Forever*. We are deprived of any images from this movie, watching the spectators instead mocking its dialogue and action with squelching noises and crude imitations of kissing. The spectacle supplied to this crowd is promptly rejected by them as having no experiential validity or force. What they understand about love is not mirrored here. They are not drawn in. Stevens's own love scene, by contrast, built upon the director's elaborate hide-and-seek strategy in the presentation of Clift throughout the film, attains something far more unusual and challenging. It is first of all a feat of clemency.

In spite of George's arguably callow manner of deceiving Alice, to whom he feels tied by obligation and guilt but not love, he does not (in his declaration to Angela) appear to the viewer as someone merely blinded by fresh infatuation or calculating how to "move up" in the sphere of privilege. Nor is he shown to be heedless, as is often the case with him, and unable to think about his actions at this juncture. Clift's decision to make George a figure awakening, released from a maze and taking proper form at last, receiving an imprint from a second mother, herself hardly more than a child, who gives him a sense that he might exist in his own right, endows the love scene with a truly visionary power. Clift seems to be entering the world authentically for the first time, with a faith that he could indeed belong to it, because Angela has unequivocally seen him, lifting him to the light of her acknowledging presence. Stevens makes the two faces a landscape of regenerative possibility, as vast in its way as the vista of Texas stretching out before Elizabeth Taylor's gaze in his later film, *Giant* (1956). The misery and daunting confusion of George's Mission House childhood and his subsequent tangled search for definition are persuasively dissolved, for the transcendent time being, in the flow of reciprocal looking, the lovers' mutual sense of being found, rescued from separate hiding places, merged. Clift's George discovers something to aim for in his complete yielding that exceeds his comprehension and his grasp, but is nonetheless not false. Clift is equal to the challenge of divesting himself of all impediments to assent. His wounded child's strickenness is miraculously healed before our eyes. With "Mama" Angela he enters a lovers' space and time that is incalculably diffusive.

It is because so many spectators of the film believe in this place that Clift has found on the terrace with Angela as a source of identity and rebirth that they do not too harshly censure his future lies and betrayals, and his failed attempts to be worthy of the vision he was briefly granted. He is too inarticulate to speak the vision whenever he tries to tell his story, and he comes increasingly to doubt his right to lay claim to it. But the image of redemptive possibility (opening within an embrace) keeps returning to his memory and the havoc of his heart, even as he takes his final walk to the death chamber.

Works cited

Bosworth, Patricia. *Montgomery Clift*. New York: Bantam Books, 1979.
Merck, Mandy. *Hollywood's American Tragedies: Dreiser, Eisenstein, Sternberg, Stevens*. New York: Berg, 2007.

Chapter 11

Tony Curtis in *Sweet Smell of Success*

John Bruns

> In all the films I've done, I've never lost Sidney. And I don't want to lose him. (Tony Curtis)

"But! But, but, but, but . . . what?" The words pop out like potted meatballs, the final one hitting the ear with a good Bronx wallop. They come from Tony Curtis, who plays the smooth-talking, nail-biting, hand-wringing press agent Sidney Falco in *Sweet Smell of Success* (1957). It's a breakthrough performance, and Curtis exploits his teen-idol persona in order to delve into the dark side of charm. Up until the film was released, Curtis was known as the "duck-tailed heart-throb for teenage girls" (Naremore 31), appearing in films like *The All American* (1953), *Johnny Dark* (1954), *The Purple Mask* (1955), and *Trapeze* (1956). The latter film, starring Burt Lancaster, was a box-office hit. *Sweet Smell of Success* was produced by Lancaster's own production company, Hecht-Hill-Lancaster, and co-financed by Curtis's and his wife Janet Leigh's Curtleigh Productions, and was meant to use Ernest Lehman's successful novelette, first published in *Cosmopolitan* in 1950 under the title "Tell Me About It Tomorrow," and adapted for the screen by New York playwright Clifford Odets, to capitalize on the success of the Lancaster/Curtis combo.

Yet upon its release the film baffled audiences and critics. Curtis himself would complain he got "bum-rapped" by Hedda Hopper, an irony perhaps not lost on him given that the film depicts the slimy, snake-pit world of press agents and gossip columnists. Tony Curtis was for teens, but *Sweet Smell of Success* wasn't. An embittered core audience saw their "American Prince" behaving like an American Prick. Oddly, and perhaps tellingly, critics felt Curtis portrayed Sidney Falco as not unlikeable enough. *Variety* lamented that, although interesting, his Sidney Falco "is not quite the heel as written" (31 December 1956). A. H. Weiler, writing for the *New York Times*, wrote that Curtis "does not entirely emerge the black-hearted villain he is supposed to represent" ("The Screen: 'Sweet Smell of Success'; Film at State Dissects Power-Mad Columnist", 28 June 1957, 24).

It may be easy to dismiss these confused receptions as simply a matter of taste or, perhaps, expectations. Those teenagers who went to see *Sweet Smell of Success* anticipating throbs of the heart were likely disappointed. The one and only Louella Parsons, in her column titled "What Hollywood is Talking About," spoke of the "shock in store for Tony Curtis fans when they see what an unmitigated heel he is . . . with nary a redeeming bone in his body." Others, already familiar with the story's character portrait of Sidney as a heartless cur, were likely to see in Curtis's performance a vulnerability uncalled for by Lehman and Odets's treatment. But these differing perceptions orbit around the same gravitational force, call it "charm." In role-playing games, charisma is an attribute that determines a character's effectiveness in social interactions (a player rolls for "charisma," say), a charm cast by a character in order to bring a target under one's influence. But role playing is what *Sweet Smell of Success* is all about. Curtis's Sidney slips from cynicism to sincerity depending on when either is needed in any particular situation. His performance is not so much a departure from his teen heart-throb image as an extension of it, a full-tilt, sensorimotor display of charm's unbreakable spell.

No doubt James Wong Howe's superb cinematography contributes a great deal to the darkness of the film, its beautiful sleaziness, but so do the performances—Curtis's in particular. To return to A.H. Weiler's review of the film, recall that he expresses some mild disappointment that Curtis "does not entirely emerge the black-hearted villain he is supposed to represent." What Weiler says in full in his paragraph on Curtis is that this is exactly why Curtis gives us a "disturbing portrait." Disturbing because Curtis remains somewhat enigmatic, neither entirely villainous nor entirely likeable? Or both simultaneously? Disturbing perhaps because we can never be quite sure what Curtis is up to, whether he is sincerely counterfeiting, or counterfeiting sincerity. We can never, therefore, relax.

From the outset, we see that Curtis is an act, a twenty-four-hour variety show, all scheme and hustle. He is an ambitious little swine, a sweaty, slimy, smarmy, sexy, Broadway bastard who will stop at nothing to get what he wants (he makes the churlish Pete Campbell of *Mad Men* look like the sweetie-pie Elmo from "Sesame Street"). What he wants is to cozy up to J. J. Hunsecker (Lancaster), a character based not so loosely on the then well-known columnist Walter Winchell. Curtis is so eager that he is willing to plant false evidence (a reefer) on Steve Dallas (Martin Milner), at Hunsecker's own suggestion. Dallas is dating Hunsecker's younger sister, Susan (Susan Harrison), of whom Hunsecker is fiercely, depravedly, protective. Ruining Dallas is Curtis's ticket. Problem is, Dallas has, in Curtis's words from the film, "integrity . . . acute, like indigestion." Dallas performs, to be sure—but his performances are pure—as jazz guitarist for the Chico Hamilton Quintet.

And Curtis is rotten to the core. Indeed, one is not entirely sure there's a there there, a core to rot to, a self to loathe. Indeed, *Sweet Smell of Success* funnels all of its characters through fake moments of sincerity, revealing the performance behind all social interactions. Interestingly, *Sweet Smell of Success* was released only a year after the first publication of the widely influential book, *The Presentation of Self in Everyday Life* (published in America in 1959), in which the author, Erving Goffman, argues that performance constitutes the ground of identity, that everyday life is role playing. The business of *Sweet Smell of Success* is a kind of "information game," to use Goffman's term, "a potentially infinite cycle of concealment, discovery, false revelation and rediscovery" (8). In this game, Curtis is an absolute master.

One of the most protracted examples of this gamesmanship is a scene in the 21 Club. In dire need of a positive write-up for a client in Hunsecker's newspaper column, Sidney makes his way to a backroom where J.J. is seated at his regular table. With him are Senator Walker, a blonde singer named Linda James, and her manager Manny Davis. Sidney takes a seat just behind and to the right of Hunsecker, assuming the dubious position of right-hand man to the King, a kind of Viceroy—although more vice than royalty. Curtis intently watches the scene before him: Hunsecker will have no more bullshit from his guests, who are now shifting uncomfortably in their seats (Manny is not "managing" Miss James, but "pimping" her—and much too publicly—to the Senator). One could describe the look on Curtis's face as a sneer but this would be wrong, or only partly correct. His brow is furrowed, his head is drawn slightly toward his left shoulder, and his chin is turned to his right. He is not sneering, but making observations, studying. He senses—he *knows*—what is happening. Of course an actor knows a scene ahead of time, has memorized lines and can anticipate cues. But here, Curtis brilliantly, and without any elaboration, conveys that Sidney has witnessed this scene before, knows what's coming. His eyes are not on Hunsecker but on the guests, whom Hunsecker is now "getting" (in anticipation of Edward Albee's George from *Who's Afraid of Virginia Woolf?*).

To distract from Hunsecker's unpleasant line of inquiry, Senator Walker turns and asks, "Are you an actor, Mr. Falco?" Linda eagerly wonders the same. "*Are* you, Mr. Falco?" Hunsecker interrupts: "Well how did you guess it, Miss James?" She confesses that she finds him pretty (like her, we have not been able to take our eyes off Curtis). Hunsecker is not through, however. Turning to eye Curtis, he announces, "Mr. Falco, let it be said at once, is a man of forty faces, not one. None too pretty, and all deceptive." How, and to what, should Curtis respond? Without a doubt Hunsecker is trying to humiliate Sidney, expose him for what he is: nastier than a two-faced man, but nowhere near as talented as the one with a thousand faces. Surely a nervous smile is called for. Yet the smile Curtis now flashes is something other than nervous. It is both beguiling and beguiled. Aiming his eyes directly at Hunsecker, Curtis turns his right nostril upward somewhat; his left eyebrow follows. "See that grin?" gloats Hunsecker. We cut to a close-up of Curtis, and he seems to be beaming with a combination of contempt and unabashed admiration. "That's the uh, that's the charming street urchin face," says Hunsecker.

Pausing on this close-up of Curtis, one can't help but think of Soviet filmmaker and theorist Lev Kuleshov and his famed "third experiment," in which he and his students at the Moscow Film School juxtaposed a single shot of the famous Russian movie idol Ivan Mosjukine with three separate images. Each one—a bowl of soup, a girl, a child's coffin—retroactively assigns a different meaning to the face of Mosjukine (a man's hunger, his love, and his mourning, respectively). Proof, Kuleshov and his students concluded, that regardless of an actor's individual quality, his perceived psychological state is linked to a large degree to montage. Can one not reproduce the experiment here? While Hunsecker seems confident that he can identify Curtis's look as "the charming street urchin face," it's hard not to imagine this image circulating widely as Curtis's own publicity photo. And wouldn't this grin work just as well as "the quick dependable chap" that Curtis flashes for Hunsecker? That a psychological state cannot be determined definitively from a face is precisely what makes Curtis's performance so dangerously alluring.

When Hunsecker elaborates on the "quick dependable chap" face—the one he likes, the really cute one, the one that says "nothing it won't do for you in a pinch"—Curtis shifts in his seat, slowly, deliberately, and "the charming street urchin face" seems to change. It's not exactly a physical transformation: the right nostril is still raised along with his left eyebrow; his lips still puckered lusciously. His eyes are perhaps a bit more narrow and focused, the head no longer cocked to the right. Otherwise, it is virtually indistinguishable from the previous face, the "grin" that Hunsecker so confidently identifies. Yet something is different. Perhaps this is further proof that Kuleshov and his students got it right. What has changed is that Hunsecker is now turning on Sidney, reminding him not so subtly that he is an uninvited—even unwanted—guest. Further, Sidney has failed a test, failed to earn and keep the trust of Hunsecker, who charged him with the task of preventing his younger sister Susan from seeing Steve Dallas. When we cut back to the close-up of Curtis, on Hunsecker's biting line, "Nothing he won't do for you in a pinch . . . so he says," we can read on his face something like contempt. With a cut to a two-shot of Sidney and Hunsecker, the Falco face has disappeared altogether. Hunsecker turns, cigarette poised pointedly between the index and middle fingers of his right hand, and quietly snaps, "Match me, Sidney." Curtis pauses, lifts his head, and gives a defiant declination: "Not just this minute, J.J." Now, a small miracle, the face returns—morphed into something more like a "fuck you" face.

That Curtis can take one look and, within less than a minute of screen time, adjust it, recalibrate it, reinterpret it not just once but twice, is his brilliance. What we watch in this scene is more than Curtis's *visage*. We watch him *envisage*. Not "visualize" but something more archaic: "be in face." To be sure, Hunsecker is boasting here that he knows these Falco faces, "*all forty of them*," and has himself been duped by at least one ("the quick dependable chap"). So he is sending out a warning to his guests: beware. In this scene Curtis shows that one can never be wary enough, can never be quite as certain as Hunsecker.

Perhaps that is Hunsecker's most poignant warning, in fact: that none of us can know. After all, no one at the table knows as well as J.J. how deceptive a face can be. Small wonder that he settles on forty—forty faces, each one a thief's—linking Curtis with Ali Baba. There is self-reflexiveness in this touch as well, Tony Curtis having starred as Kashma Baba, the son of the famous Bagdad thief, in Kurt Neumann's *Son of Ali Baba* (1952). Indeed, Kashma Baba was exactly the sort of role that made Curtis a teen heart-throb. In *Sweet Smell*, Curtis takes full advantage of the trope.

Early in the film, Curtis tells his assistant Sally (Jeff Donnell), "You think I'm a hero. Well, I'm no hero. I'm nice to people where it pays me to be nice. Look, I do it enough on the outside, so don't expect me to do it in my own office." What Curtis is suggesting here is that Sidney's office functions something like a backstage. The "being nice" to people is actually "playing nice," or simply performing. So, the outside world is all performance, whereas in the sanctum of his office he shouldn't have to play nice, shouldn't have to perform. Indeed, the office is wholly a kind of backstage, the place to which he rushes just after each performance, to change clothes, plot, prepare. Goffman refers to "issues dealt with by stage craft and stage management," stating that they provide "a clear-cut dimension for sociological analysis" (15). In a section of his book devoted to regions and region behavior, Goffman tells us that social interaction is divided between front regions and back regions, the former being the space in which a performance occurs, the latter being the space "where the impression fostered by the performance is knowingly contradicted as a matter of course." The back region, or back stage, is where the performer can "relax, drop his front, forego his speaking lines, and step out of character" (112). Or as Murray Pomerance puts it, in his reading of Steven Spielberg's 2002 film *Catch Me If You Can*, backstage is where "the fictive role evaporate[s]," where we are assured that we are "in the presence of a 'real' person" (222).

Curtis is, in a word, the physiognomist's nightmare, or perhaps in fairness to physiognomy, his exemplar. Johann Caspar Lavater, one of the early proponents of this strange science, wrote, "The act of dissimulation itself, which is adduced as so insuperable an objection to the truth of physiognomy, is founded upon physiognomy. Why does the hypocrite assume the appearance of an honest man, but because that he is convinced, though not perhaps from a systematic reflection, that all eyes are acquainted with the characteristic mark of honesty?" (8–9).

Sally, having the benefit of being in the presence of the "real" Sidney, feels compassion, affection. As Curtis sits worriedly on the edge of his bed, moments after failing to reassure his client Joe Robard that Hunsecker has every intention of running a nice, big column about him, Sally watches. It is a privileged glimpse of a real man in real trouble. She worries about him: "I wish I could help in some way, Sidney" and "I hate to see you like this. If you feel nervous—." Curtis spits his reply: "So what'll you do if I feel nervous, *open your meaty sympathetic arms*?" With the last words he grits his teeth, in a cutting renunciation of Sally's genuine concern, as if the very idea of genuineness has turned his stomach. As he'll tell J.J. later in the film, what Steve Dallas has that Susie likes is "integrity. Acute. *Like indigestion.*"

Yet Curtis *is* nervous. We see him biting his nails throughout the film. It's a weakness, and one of the few physically unattractive traits Curtis gives Sidney Falco, if not the only one. Never in the cinema has such an ugly habit been given such visibility. Young, attractive actors often give their characters nervous tics such as Anthony Perkins who as Norman Bates in Hitchcock's *Psycho* (1960) nibbles obsessively and stutters. Dustin Hoffman adopted a piercing whimper in his role as Benjamin Braddock in Mike Nichols's *The Graduate* (1967). In both cases, the nervous tic elicits from the spectator sympathy (and, in the latter case, laughter). There's even some sweetness in Norman's nervous demeanor. But nail biting is unbecoming; indeed, it is when Sidney is seated on the edge of his bed, biting his nails, that Sally says she hates to see him like this. The second time we watch him bite his nails, at 21 just before he crashes J.J.'s table party, it's a full-on munch. A third time, inside the Broadway Theatre at 53rd St, Curtis perches himself on the stage and watches intently as Steve Dallas argues with J.J. over Susan. Here, Curtis plays the role of director, watching his actors rehearse, with his thumb and index finger to his mouth, wondering how the scene should, could, play out. After Steve Dallas delivers his line, "To me, Mr. Hunsecker, you're a national disgrace," Curtis claps his hands, slides off the stage and onto the floor.

Curtis's other nervous tic is wringing his hands, which he does more frequently than bite his nails. Taken together, these gestures convey a man who is scheming twenty-four hours a day. Curtis knows that for a guy like Sidney, success means getting your act together. And this is not easy. Sidney is prone to the same vulnerabilities of experience that he seeks to exploit in others. Particularly vulnerable are those who can't play the information game, can't tell what's front- and backstage. It's no wonder, then, that Sidney thinks success is not in this room or that, backstage or front, but above it all, free from everything. When Sidney says, "Hunsecker is the golden ladder to the places I wanna get!" Sally asks him, "Where do you want to go?" The camera, set at Sally's point of view, looks up at Curtis who adjusts his tie, casts his eyes upwards and replies, "Way up high, Sam, where it's always balmy." Sam? We have no idea who that is, but it's a brilliant touch that Curtis gives to the line, which he tops with the first of many hand wringings. And we may not even be sure that Sally is meant to be the respondent to this odd comment, given that Curtis utters the line softly, in a dysphonic, scratchy tone. His eyes are cast upwards, though they look back down at Sally as he begins to wring his hands. But she knows no better than we do where Sidney's head is at.

The hand wringing in fact conveys not just a habitual schemer, but a man who is not fully in control, like a director who watches a scene go off-track. Indeed, people don't always stay on script as expected, the way J.J. and Steve did in the scene at the Broadway Theatre. Consider a scene in which Sidney Falco tries to cajole his on-and-off-again (mostly off) girlfriend Rita (Barbara Nichols) to sleep with gossip columnist Otis Elwell (David White) in order to secure a nasty write-up that will embarrass J.J., with whom he's just had a falling out. One way to read this scene is that in following Rita into the bedroom and closing the door, Sidney creates a temporary back frame, a dressing room of sorts. Here Sidney, irritated metteur-en-scène of that tawdry tableau in the adjacent room, can quickly demand that Rita get her act together (to make him look good). When Rita protests against the role, she raises her voice like a frustrated actress fed up with her director. "What do you want all of a sudden, Lady Godiva? Where's my other shoe!" With a flourish that sweeps James Wong Howe's camera to his right, opening up the room, Curtis shouts, "What kind of an act is this?"

One might compare Curtis's delivery of this line to a moment of Robert Mitchum's in *River of No Return*, released three years previously. In a similar scene, Matt Calder (Mitchum) and Kay Weston (Marilyn Monroe), a former saloon singer, confront one another. "You're not such a mean person," Kay tells Matt, who during their treacherous journey has been treating her coldly, "Some other time and some other place, we might have even gotten along." Matt replies, "Now what's all this? What kind of an act is this?" Mitchum speaks the line quickly, drily, sincerely, with none of the over-the-top incredulity of Curtis's delivery. Writing of this particular scene, Matthew Solomon says *River of No Return* "mostly suggests that there is a distinct split between the singer's onstage persona and her authentic offstage personality" (114). While Kay may be a singer and dancer, by the end of the film she will give up performance altogether.

Yet Curtis's "What kind of an act is this?" is more severely mocking, its showiness calling attention to Rita's desperate—and in his eyes counterfeit—claims of sincerity. To Sidney, Rita is just putting on another act, playing the role of the wounded maiden whose virtue is at stake. Thus Curtis gives *Sweet Smell of Success* its real bite: it reminds us that, as with Monroe's *Gentlemen Prefer Blondes* (1953) and *There's No Business Like Show Business* (1954), "the self is rehearsed, staged, and acted just as much in private as in public, carefully managing these private performances to achieve specific and desired results and to particular strategic ends" (Solomon 114).

When Rita offers what seems a genuine plea, "Don't you think I have any *feelings*?" Curtis once again performs his reply. "I beg your pardon!" says he, while executing what James Naremore describes as "an elaborate courtly bow—a parody of the sort of things [he] performed in his swashbuckling films" (73). While Otis, waiting in the other room, is not audience to Sidney's courtly bow, surely he can hear. Mackendrick does not use a cross-cut, does not show Otis's response to the drama unfolding backstage, but Curtis makes us conscious of the fact that Otis is well within earshot, lowering and raising his voice selectively, strategically (and with stagey emphasis), to play up Rita's false modesty and disingenuousness in pretending not to realize that she benefits from the arrangement. All of this vocal maneuvering helps him downplay his own desperation: that much more than Rita it is *he* who benefits from this exchange. To paraphrase James Mason in Hitchcock's *North by Northwest* (1959), with his expert play-acting Curtis's Sidney makes the backstage a very theater. Indeed, what is unsettling about this sordid scene is Curtis's performed performance, which never lets us settle into the comfortable notion that there is an authentic self beneath.

The film's climax comes when Sidney goes to J.J.'s penthouse to find Susan, who has broken things off with Steve at her older brother's command. She has also learned that Steve was arrested and charged with possession of the reefer Sidney had planted on him. Behind closed doors, Susan is threatening suicide. Making his way surreptitiously into Susan's bedroom, Sidney feels secure that he is now in a backstage frame. As desperate as he may appear, the advantage, it seems, is his. This, Sidney thinks, is neutral ground. As Susan weeps real tears, Sidney can feign guiltlessness and, in doing so, reason with her to give up the attempt at suicide. Outside is the trap, a staging area for deception and betrayal, motivated by jealously and greed, the sick shenanigans of J.J. Hunsecker.

Little does Sidney know he has become trapped in a play-within-a-play. What we thought was a glimpse behind the scenes, Susan's bedroom, was Susan's own staging area. Of course, this is the danger of the backstage frame. As Goffman reminds us, in his 1974 book *Frame Analysis*, "Once you've got the staging area and the backstage you've got the whole thing and can feel secure in your frame anchorage. And the moment you feel secure, of course, is the moment you can be diddled" (475). When J.J. arrives, furious to find Susan in a distressed state, Sidney tells him she was upset by the news about Steve. But J.J. doesn't want Susan to think he had any knowledge of Steve's arrest, and so he plays ignorant: "What news?" Delicately trying to worm himself out of the corner in which he now finds himself, Sidney goes along with J.J.'s play-acting: "Oh, uh, I took it for granted that you'd heard about it around town" (J.J., who hears about everything around this town). "You're not gonna like this, but they picked him up on a marijuana rap." (He knows, of course, that J.J. will adore this.) But J.J. stands his ground and uses Sidney's compromised situation against him, as Susan simply watches. By trapping Sidney, she can take some comfort and pleasure in seeing J.J. beat him to a pulp. But now her doubts about her brother are confirmed. By the end of the scene (and the film), she will walk out on him.

Sidney has been diddled, and diddled badly (or brilliantly) by the cunning Susan. Of course we feel diddled, too. It's a difficult thing to do, to watch *Sweet Smell of Success* and not root for Sidney. Viewers of the film follow Sidney addictively, as they will Frank Abagnale in Spielberg's film made almost half a century later: not in hopes of seeing them caught but simply out of the sheer joy of watching them go. This joy, I think, is the center of the viewer's thrill at Curtis's performance. The character of Sidney Falco allows Curtis to explore, even explode, his own star persona. Curtis unleashes himself and in doing so gives us the sweet dangers of performances within performances. No doubt what upset Curtis's loyal fans was not that Sidney Falco was reprehensible, but that Curtis could *play* him, because the character undermines the assumptions about performance that allowed his fans to rest comfortably in the belief that their beloved star could never play a cad. But even now, nearly fifty years removed, we are not safe. True, there's an undeniable joy in watching Curtis perform, but what emerges at the end of it all is utterly frightening: because his Sidney can look you dead in the eye and say, "What kind of an act is this?"

Works cited

Goffman, Erving. *The Presentation of Self in Everyday Life*. New York: Doubleday, 1959.

Goffman, Erving. *Frame Analysis*. New York: Harper, 1994.

Kashner, Sam, and Jennifer MacNair. *The Bad and the Beautiful: Hollywood in the Fifties*. New York: W. W. Norton & Co., 2002.

Lavater, Johann Caspar. *Physiognomy*. London: Cowie, Low, and Co. in the Poultry, 1826.

Naremore, James. *Sweet Smell of Success*. London: BFI/Palgrave Macmillan, 2010.

Pomerance, Murray. "Nothing Sacred: Modernity and Performance in *Catch Me if You Can*," in *Cinema and Modernity*, New Brunswick, NJ: Rutgers University Press, 2006, 211–34.

Solomon, Matthew. "Reflexity and Metaperformance: Marilyn Monroe, Jayne Mansfield, and Kim Novak," in R. Barton Palmer, ed., *Larger Than Life: Movie Stars of the 1950s*, New Brunswick, NJ: Rutgers University Press, 2010, 107–29.

Chapter 12

Peter Sellers in *The Pink Panther*

Daniel Varndell

> What, on the contrary, could be more splendidly sincere than the impulse to play in real life, to rise on the rising wave of every feeling and let it burst, if it will, into the foam of exaggeration? (George Santayana, "The Comic Mask")

In 1969 Tony Palmer spent nearly nine months with Peter Sellers to film a documentary about him called *The World of Peter Sellers,* during which Sellers spoke about not being able to play himself, since "I will not know what to do. I don't know who or what I am, so I will not be able to help you. *I'm* not the real Peter Sellers. I'm just a plastic mockup . . . You see, as long as I'm inhabiting some other person, I have a freedom that I don't have as myself" (quoted in Tibbetts 137). Sellers cultivated this image of himself as a nobody outside of the characters he played. "In myself," said he, "I have nothing to offer as a personality but as soon as I can get into some character I'm away. I use the characters to protect myself, as a shield—like getting into a hut and saying 'nobody can see me'" (quoted in Starr vii). In his notoriously barbed biography of the troubled actor,[1] Roger Lewis claimed that Sellers was satisfying a need to pretend he did not exist, because he wanted "to be inscrutable, magically invisible," to "give himself thousands of faces" (xix) like an adolescent experimenting with his personality who, threatened with the fear of being a nobody or (worse) of being fatefully tied to an undeveloped personality, spends his time "assembling and assuming what will become the adult identity—a repertoire of mannerisms and inklings, a gathering of experiences, desires, anxieties and feelings, which are one way and another brought to order: our sense of self, which we will labour at keeping constant" (xix). This constancy is one's style, and once fully formed it is as inimitable as it is indelible. Yet Sellers was, writes Lewis, "a man inordinately concerned with his own lack of colour" (409), a man who was "disabled by the very talents and susceptibilities which had made his name . . . He was constant only in his pathetic rage at being Peter Sellers" (xxxiv).

Lewis's damning portrait of Sellers puts one in mind of the story Plutarch told of a man who plucked a nightingale and, finding little to eat, lamented that, "You are just a voice and nothing more" (quoted in Dolar 3). Even early reviews of Sellers's work suggested that his offscreen insecurities detracted from his onscreen personalities. Of his four performances in 1959 Kenneth J. Letner wrote that Sellers lacked corporeality, that "his characterizations appear to be interesting experimentations in styles, yet somewhat disembodied . . . not enough of the human being emerges." Letner ended his review with a note of cautious hope for this blossoming star: "In the future, let us hope that this mischievous clown Sellers will fill up his funny masks with all of the inner—not just the outer—resources at his command" (54). This essay will argue that it is in the role for which he is best known that Peter Sellers's "masks" were filled; that he not only satisfies Letner's hope that the human being would emerge but that his performance repudiates Lewis's claim that he was a "man of a thousand voices" and nothing more. It is a performance about performing, about the masks we wear and what they disclose as much as what they screen. In *The Pink Panther* (1963), Peter Sellers perfects in his Inspecteur Jacques Clouseau the look of a man whose unflinching self-belief is undercut by moments of exasperated self-awareness, whose unflappable dignity in the face of disaster registers, fleetingly, the barest flicker of consciousness at the vast absurdity of modern life.

Clouseau's performance

When Peter Ustinov quit the role of Inspector Clouseau in Blake Edwards's bedroom farce *The Pink Panther*, he left what was originally planned as a supporting role in an ensemble cast featuring David Niven as Sir Charles, a British playboy who has a secret identity as a jewel thief called the Phantom; Claudia Cardinale as Princess Dahla, whose diamond, known as the "Pink Panther," becomes the Phantom's next target; Robert Wagner as Sir Charles's nephew, George, a swindler posing as a graduate who wants to keep tapping his uncle for money; and Capucine as Clouseau's wife, Simone, who unbeknownst to him is Sir Charles's secret lover and accomplice. Clouseau was envisioned as a "fool who was shrewd around fools" (Lewis xxxii), yet with Sellers in the role he became, notes John Caps, "an inept force majeure among the suave mystery story [sic] being told" (75–6), so very much so that even with the sparkling and internationally acclaimed Niven in the star role, Sellers, unknown in the US at the time, ended up stealing the film. While Niven slinks with poise and elegance as Sir Charles, twirling his cane and tilting his champagne glass with a raised brow, Sellers transforms every inanimate object into a trip hazard. Door handles become foreign objects in Clouseau's grasp and open onto rooms he finds to be empty of the occupants he came to challenge. Burning his hand on a stove, he desperately plunges it into another officer's beer tankard to cool off, and gets it stuck there. Indeed, Clouseau's incompetence with everyday objects and tasks is matched only by his failure as a lover since he is increasingly, even maddeningly frustrated with, as Andrew Spicer puts it, "recalcitrant clothing, vindictive bedlinen and other impedimenta" (111). His wife's infidelity gives Clouseau an excuse for his failings both as a detective and as a husband, yet in Sellers's hands he nevertheless seems to go beyond the "conscientious cuckold" (Lewis 844), evoking something more complex, idiosyncratic, and interesting.

Clouseau's introduction was scripted to do little more than introduce the beleaguered detective who, having narrowly failed to capture the Phantom's female accomplice, is greeted by his wife whom we alone recognize as Sir Charles's partner in crime. In the scene, which was canonized in Stephen Hopkins's biopic *The Life and Death of Peter Sellers* (2004), Clouseau is sitting ponderously at his desk accompanied by the opening bars of "La Marseillaise," a mocking fanfare, given his recent failure. His ruminating is interrupted by the briefest of glances at someone out of shot, whereupon his "great detective" performance begins. Clouseau strides over to a large globe with his hands clasped behind his back (the camera pulling back to reveal an assistant standing silently before him, awaiting orders). With a swift flick of his arm Clouseau theatrically spins the globe and turns to face the window. Even with his back turned, his every gesture is aimed at creating an impression of competence and worldly wisdom under his assistant's watchful eye. After a dramatic pause, Clouseau turns and, wagging his index finger for emphasis, declares, "We must find that woman!" before bringing his hand down to rest on the globe which, still spinning, propels him directly to the floor.

The scene is funny not just for Clouseau's failure to act commandingly but in Sellers's disclosure of Clouseau's intention to create a commanding *impression*. In *The Presentation of Self in Everyday Life*, Erving Goffman distinguishes between expressions one "gives," which aim at presenting oneself to others in a particular light, and expressions one "gives off," which tend to be non-verbal and, whether purposefully engineered or completely unintentional, betray to an audience that the performance of the self is perhaps not entirely under control (14); betray, indeed, *that* one is performing (60). These expressions "given off" lead to what Goffman calls the "devastating exposures" of the self. What Sellers manages to convey is therefore not just what Alex Clayton calls the "deftly-executed failure" (51) typical of slapstick comedy, in which a performer mistimes each step to perfection. He also handles the way Clouseau himself shifts into a kind of performance-mode in order to forestall the threat of exposure by employing what Goffman calls "defensive practices" aimed at keeping up appearances. Clouseau *knows* he's a clutz, in other words, but even his efforts to cover his clutziness are clutzy, so he's a clutz imprisoned in clutzdom.

Sellers communicates this through very precise gesture and movement. Sam Wasson notes that his performance in this scene establishes Clouseau as a man who wishes to affect an Edwardian "sophisticated naturalism" (84), and we see this affectation engaged from the moment his eyes flicker up at the assistant, a double take that first registers the other man's presence and second recognizes in him an audience for the show. In addition to the eyes, Sellers also slightly alters the way Clouseau drums his fingers on the table, first as an absentminded fidget and second as a purposeful measure of beats counting up to the performance. One can compare the way Sellers uses his body to present Clouseau's performance with the way Niven uses his in those scenes when Sir Charles pretends to have a lame leg in order to win the sympathy of the Princess. He hobbles around on his walking stick until she leaves the room whereupon he magically transforms into Fred Astaire, twirling through the steps of a dance routine while whirling his cane through the air. Niven's show is illustrative of what Clayton calls the double exposure or unmasking, "the peeking out from behind the mask in the case of the comedic actor, alongside the threatened or actual slippage of the mask in the case of the comic character" (55–6). The threat of exposure in Sir Charles's private show is, however, not quite as deep as the threat to Clouseau's performance, since for him the performance is not simply a ruse; he truly believes in and identifies with the role he is playing. Lewis observes that "Clouseau, by the look in his eyes, appears to be registering, and reflecting upon, the strings of misadventure; and, no matter what, he believes he is fully rational and controlled" (839), or at least wishes to be. He has a mind and a sensibility which he wears in his expression. He conceals nothing. In this, he is in every way the opposite of Sir Charles who, with his very British "stiff upper lip," grimaces through an uncomfortable dinner in which he is insulted by the Princess, without showing his wounds. For all his faults, Clouseau not only wears his every passion in his facial expressions but allows that passion to burst forth in his ostentatious displays; bursting, to echo George Santayana in my epigraph, in a foam of exaggeration.

Spasms of enlightenment

George Santayana wrote that "art and happiness lie in pouring and repouring the molten metal of existence through some such tenable mould," such that "whether the visage we assume be a joyful or a sad one, in adopting and emphasizing it we define our sovereign temper" (132–3). What Santayana calls the "tragic mask" establishes what it means to be human, then, since, in contrast to the endless expressions we pull during our diurnal rhythms, we find ourselves periodically casting a moment of expressive action into a mold which, fixed in place, can be held up for reflection. It is in such moments that one engages with oneself as other, contemplating an expression used to reveal the "self" in the world. By casting such moments into a mold, one embraces the tragedy of life by charging the everyday with the knowledge of death which, wrote Santayana, "raises us to that height" (132).

Irrespective of the disasters that befall him, Clouseau gives off an impression that he is impervious to each social collapse, imperturbable in his presentation of the "great detective." Yet he does reveal self-awareness. Sam Wasson points out that Edwards never tracks Clouseau with the camera when he falls (and sometimes walks) out of shot by mistake (83–4). Instead, Edwards leaves empty the vacated space, a space that Clouseau has very carefully and deliberately constructed to frame each dramatic pose and declaration. This moment is held also by Sellers who briefly leaves Clouseau lying on the floor, stayed by his failure. It is in these moments of silence and suspension that Clouseau suggests an awareness of his own calamity. This suggestion is confirmed in a scene where, preparing to seduce his wife, he decides to take a shower. He turns the taps on to get the water flowing and up to temperature while he undresses and finishes a cigarette. However, when the water dribbles to a stop he pops his head behind the curtain to investigate and, when the shower suddenly gushes, pauses before drawing his head back into the shot, now drenched with his sodden cigarette hanging from his lips. He dries his face and glances briefly into the mirror with a shrug.

By glancing up at the mirror Clouseau is registering his own look of irritation much like Oliver Hardy, whom Roger Lewis called the master of "becalmed exasperation" (365) and whose characters always paused following one calamitous accident or another to reflect, just for a second, on the cruel divinity maligning them. Peter Sellers charges such moments of becalmed exasperation with a tragic mask, "half horror and half sublimity," in Santayana's phrase. "Such is the countenance of man when turned towards death and eternity and looking beyond all his endeavors at the Gorgon face of the truth" (133). Such expressions might not linger on Clouseau's face for long, but it is in such moments of reflection that he breaks the spell of his own self-importance, enabling viewers to appreciate that he does not merely live, but acts: gloriously, fabulously, and failingly in the moment. Unlike the slapstick "cretin" whose expressions betray very little self-awareness of the existential absurdity of his situation, Clouseau reflects on each failure. It is his failure and it belongs unquestionably to him, as with Sisyphus cursing the Gods with a shrug every time his rock rolls back down the mountain. He is a fool but he knows it, and *it is not his fault*. As Santayana wrote, "Without such playful pauses and reflective interludes our round of motions and sensations would be deprived of that intellectual dignity which relieves it and renders it morally endurable—the dignity of knowing what we are doing, even if it be foolish in itself, and with what probable issue" (132).

That he cuts such a tragic figure in such moments, and only ever for a very brief time before regaining his composure, reveals a sublimity to Clouseau that contributes part of his charm, which makes him so likeable. Consider the despair Clouseau feels when, called to action, he finds that his "Sûreté/Scotland Yard-type mackintosh" is missing, as if part of his very being had been misplaced. His affectation of style makes a bold claim to greatness, even immortality, through iconicity: one thinks (as Clouseau is surely thinking) of Holmes's deerstalker. The spirit of comedy resides in such figures who risk everything time and again, failure after failure, in straining to exceed the low expectations of others. "What tragedy could there be", wrote Santayana, "if there were no spontaneous passions to create the issue, no wild voices to be reduced to harmony?" (137) And what is comedy, he urges, if not this very drive to live and be, to invent something worth saying or doing, worth reflecting on in such tragic moments? In addition to the comic passion he displays in his affectation of greatness, Clouseau demonstrates a sublime self-awareness when he loses his balance and finds himself out of joint. These are the spasms of enlightenment that give his character such richness and depth. Unlike most of us, the urge to suppress or mollify the passions is not to be found in Clouseau. Worry is not part of his psychic makeup. He is spontaneous and careless, but always sure of his mind and proud of his office, willingly asserting himself through a deliberate presentation of his character.

In each instant of his Great Detective performance (giving off the ultimate essence of being at once not Holmes and not Poirot) this offic*eur* of the *leu* dons a "comic mask" providing so many expressions and characterizations that he becomes, finally, *possessed* and, as Mikel Dufrenne put it, "submissive to a foreign intention" such that the actor who plays him is similarly "caught up by the unreal, becomes unreal in the character he incarnates" (21). It is in such role playing, frozen in a grimace as he looks in becalmed exasperation at his reflection in the mirror, that Sellers's Clouseau is effortlessly and shamelessly original. It is perhaps little wonder that Sellers felt himself to be nothing outside of his roles. In such expressions of unbridled passion the world grows young.

Plastic power

This total absorption in the performance of a character recalls Sellers's sense of himself as a "plastic mockup," about which he elaborated in an interview for *Playboy*. "I start with the voice," he observed, "I find out how the character *sounds*. It's through the way he speaks that I find out the rest about him ... And then suddenly something strange happens. *The person takes over* ... he has begun to live in me" (quoted in Lewis 522). Nathan Abrams explains Sellers's obsessive use of impersonation using Max Horkheimer and Theodor Adorno's theory of "undisciplined mimicry" which, for them, describes the way Jews assimilated themselves in gentile neighbourhoods such that the host culture became "engraved in the living substance of the dominated and passed down by a process of unconscious imitation in infancy from generation to generation" (quoted in Abrams 23). This sense of the alien culture "engraved in the living" carries strong echoes of what Henri Bergson, describing the comic mode, called the "mechanical encrusted on the living" (quoted in Clayton 48). For Bergson, the comic performance is a kind of discourse, by turns combative and conciliatory, between an ego and an ideal ego; comedy is the release of tension arising from their disjunction.

Bergson's notion of the comic tension between the living and the mechanical puts one in mind of blooper reels which, as Murray Pomerance has observed, distinguish character from performer and the role player from the "worker striving beneath" (78). The blooper reel reminds us that the transcendent actor is, indeed, "human, all too human," as for example in those uncontrollable bodily urges which can disrupt a performance, such as sneezing during a take. Or in psychological disruptions, as when an actor "corpses" (that is, breaks character by laughing at his own joke, something Sellers was notorious for), fluffs his lines, or forgets what he's supposed to say next. What Sellers reveals about Clouseau, the meticulous performer of self in his everyday life, is the striving worker beneath, who, despite being French, belongs to a class of British characters—characters Sellers excelled at playing, identified by Andrew Spicer as "lower middle class fools" (111) who, with aspirations of social mobility, masquerade (usually unconvincingly) in an attempt to deny a low social status that cannot be sublimated. Clouseau is in a social class crisis, and an existential one to boot. Hence, while for David Niven we might imagine a blooper reel we cannot imagine his Sir Charles, already upper class, striving or working to seem what he deeply, unselfconsciously already knows himself to be. One perhaps thinks of Jonathan Swift's distinction between "good breeding" and "good manners," the difference being that "the former cannot be attained to by the best understandings, without study and labour" (37) while the latter are strategies that can easily be learned. As devious and duplicitous as Clouseau's enemies might be, they are all of good breeding, politely engaging tact in his presence to spare his blushes. He is always laboring to seem to fit.

Two observations can be made of this. First, that one can hardly imagine Clouseau surviving in brutish, let alone ill-mannered, company. Second, that as a worker striving to uphold an ideal, an ideal not matched by his abilities, he seems (magically) to put in very little effort. For instance, after his brief reflective pause on the floor when he's slipped off the globe, Clouseau stands without a shred of embarrassment and recollects himself by asking his assistant, in a somewhat rebuking tone, "What was *that*, what you *say*?" The assistant, who has of course employed superhuman tact throughout, behaves airily, as does Clouseau, as if nothing has happened at all. Given that the Inspecteur falls so consistently short of his own ideals, his shortness of memory is an incredible asset. Indeed, Clouseau employs a variety of "nothing happened" expressions, non sequiturs, and sometimes even outrageous accusations laying the blame on the very people arranged to confer status on him. It is perhaps not too much of a stretch, even, to say that his memory failure is the gift that counterbalances his accursed clumsiness.

Pomerance notes that the performance of forgetfulness is compelling and strange, insofar as a character who forgets, like Clouseau, is making a claim (one might suspect, for instance, that he is simply performing once more). The performance of an amnesiac in film relies on two persons inhabiting one body, "one who cannot remember and the other who cannot forget," the latter, of course, being the actor who cannot forget his lines (Pomerance 146–7). Once more the performance is split, but while the amnesiac's "inability to know who one was, who one is, who one will be, can be thought a deeply crippling misfortune" (147), Clouseau's forgetfulness is crucial to his survival in this social milieu. He demonstrates what Nietzsche called "plastic power," which is "the capacity to develop out of oneself in one's own way, to transform and incorporate into oneself what is past and foreign, to heal wounds, to replace what has been lost, to recreate broken moulds" (62). While some might perish from a single faux pas in high society, "like a man bleeding to death from a scratch" (one thinks of Bette Davis in *Jezebel* (1938)), Clouseau thrives, since those with "plastic power" are "so little affected by the worst and most dreadful disasters ... that they are able to feel tolerably well and be in possession of a kind of clear conscience even in the midst of them or at any rate very soon afterwards" (Nietzsche, 62). The lost memory, observes Pomerance, is not nothing but is figured as a "self" the character can no longer recognize. This loss of recognition guarantees Clouseau's survival because only the *ideal* ego remains, not the ego whose drama, to recall Lacan, precipitates "from insufficiency to anticipation" (5). Clouseau's anticipation is based on an imago which captivates him, but does not reflect his own insufficiencies.

It is perhaps wholly appropriate, then, that after apprehending and unmasking Sir Charles as the Phantom, Clouseau is framed and arrested while Sir Charles is freed. As he is led away from the courts into an awaiting police car, Clouseau is mobbed by admiring women as his custodians explain that when he is finally released from prison he will be famous. It dawns on Clouseau that he has finally achieved the notoriety—albeit on the wrong side of the law—for which he has strived, and when one of the officers asks him how he did it, Clouseau settles into a new character—the Master Criminal—and with a smug grin responds, "Well, you kneuw, it wasn't easy." Is this not an effective metaphor for the cinema itself? Pomerance argues that "a contrapuntal and contradictory force obstructs our acceptance of the forgetter fully finding himself: this is cinema's perpetual assertion that memory is beyond it. Watching film is all about forgetting" (149). What gets forgotten in such moments is precisely the fallible ordinariness of the actor detached from the role he plays, a role that is never simply an assembly of gestures and words, but one which must, says Mikel Dufrenne, "be given life, made to live in itself: the actor who creates a role through the life which he breathes into the work is justified in calling himself an artist" (21).

Sellers's plasticity as a performer is what charges such moments with the kind of electricity that led Walter Mirisch to call *The Pink Panther* "lightning in a bottle." Moments such as these are worthy of what Pomerance calls "moments of action," which he describes as the "nexus at which the intent and skill of the actor and the receptive energies of the audience collide, momentously touch, and spark" (5). Such moments do not impoverish the "real" Peter Sellers behind the performance, as Roger Lewis seems to think. They enrich him. What could be more "splendidly sincere," asked Santayana, than "the impulse to play in real life, to rise on the rising wave of every feeling and let it burst, if it will, into the foam of exaggeration? Life ... has the right to enact a pose, to assume a *panache*, and to create what prodigious allegories it will" (138). Such words might have been written for Peter Sellers in this role, for it is in such masquerades that truths are revealed, that dreams get crystallized into masks, and that one dares to betray a passion not despite but because of one's shortcomings. It is only in daring to dream that one can grow.

Note

1. In recent years, Peter Sellers has been portrayed by family, friends, and colleagues alike as having had a rather indifferent and even brutish personality offscreen, one underpinned by a chronic fear of failure and an infantile temperament.

Works cited

Abrams, Nathan. "Kubrick's Double: *Lolita's* Hidden Heart of Jewishness," *Cinema Journal* 55: 3 (Spring 2016), 17–39.
Baron, Cynthia. "Peter Sellers: A Figure of the Impasse," in Pamela Robertson Wojcik, ed., *New Constellations: Movie Stars of the 1960s*, New Brunswick, NJ: Rutgers University Press, 2012, 115–38.
Caps, John. *Henry Mancini: Reinventing Film Music*. Urbana: University of Illinois Press, 2012.
Clayton, Alex. "Play-Acting: A Theory of Comedic Performance," in Aaron Taylor, ed., *Theorizing Film Acting*, New York: Routledge, 2012, 47–61.
Dolar, Mladen. *A Voice and Nothing More*. Cambridge, MA: MIT Press, 2006.
Dufrenne, Mikel. *The Phenomenology of Aesthetic Experience*. Trans. Edward S. Casey, et al. Evanston: Northwestern University Press, 1973.
Goffman, Erving. *The Presentation of Self in Everyday Life*. London: Penguin, 1990.
Lacan, Jacques. *Écrits: A Selection*. Trans. Alan Sheridan. London: Routledge Classics, 2003.
Letner, Kenneth J. "Review: Films of Peter Sellers," *Film Quarterly* 14: 1 (Autumn, 1960), 51–4.
Lewis, Roger. *The Life and Death of Peter Sellers*. London: Arrow Books, 2004.
Mirisch, Walter. *I Thought We Were Making Movies, Not History*. Madison, WI: University of Wisconsin Press, 2008.
Nietzsche, Friedrich. "On the Uses and Disadvantages of History for Life," in Daniel Breazeale, ed., *Untimely Meditations*, Cambridge: Cambridge University Press, 2014, 57–123.
Pomerance, Murray. *Moment of Action: Riddles of Cinematic Performance*. New Brunswick, NJ: Rutgers University Press, 2016.
Santayana, George. *Soliloquies in England and Later Soliloquies*. New York: Charles Scribner's Sons, 1922.

Spicer, Andrew. *Typical Men: The Representation of Masculinity in Popular British Cinema.* London and New York: I. B. Tauris, 2001.
Starr, Michael Seth. *Peter Sellers: A Film History.* Jefferson, NC: McFarland, 2012.
Swift, Jonathan. "Treatise on Good Manners and Good Breeding," in John Gross, ed., *The Oxford Book of Essays,* Oxford: Oxford University Press, 2008, 34–8.
Tibbetts, John C. "Film Reviews: *The World of Peter Sellers,*" *Film & History* 40: 2 (Fall 2010), 136–8.
Wasson, Sam. *A Splurch in the Kisser: The Movies of Blake Edwards.* Middletown, CT: Wesleyan University Press, 2009.

Chapter 13
Richard Burton in *The Spy Who Came in from the Cold*
R. Barton Palmer

An archetypal narrative pattern, so theorists tell us, takes an adventurous protagonist on a journey out in pursuit of some goal, sometimes discovering for him a path back to his starting point. In the cinema, journey stories lend themselves naturally to the intensely varied, and thoroughly engaging, form of dilation usually termed the picaresque, with novelty and "color" discovered along the main character's outward-bound path and providing the material for dramatic encounters with the unexpected and unfamiliar. This is especially true of the international thriller genre, which, at least since Alfred Hitchcock's *The 39 Steps* (1935), has intrigued audiences with a rapid forward motion of the plot that finds its reflex in a constantly changing and vignette-filled scene. A non-stop infusion of novelty helps resolve the problem of what screenwriters aptly term the mushy middle by allowing reversals and revelations that disrupt or complicate the predictable trajectory of a through line for both character and plot. And, of course, the expansiveness of the picaresque mode allows for the broad representation of a world, itself a potent source of interest and meaning, especially when the intrigue at plot center is truly international and multi-faceted.

Flatness of character offers an advantage in the international thriller since character in the larger sense of the term is rarely if ever a focus. By flatness, I mean that characters of this type do not offer themselves to be known in any depth, are presented in fact as not worth knowing in this way. Following Stanley Cavell's provocative analysis of "unknownness" in certain classic Hollywood melodramas, Andrew Klevan admonishes that "our disposition toward narrative is not necessarily tied to our identification with character, but lies equally with appreciating the performer's capacities for revealing *and* withholding aspects of the character's sensibility" (9). This seems right, and also a useful way of recasting the familiar Forsterian distinction between flat and round characters. Such an approach to appreciating performance, however, does not take into full account that a film must excite the spectator's desire to know more than the actor reveals, must construct the absence of further revelation as an object of informed, perhaps suspense-driven, speculation.

The passage in Cavell's analysis of *Stella Dallas* (1937) that inspires Klevan's commentary focuses on a poignant and instructive example; Stella (Barbara Stanwyck) turns her back to the camera as she watches her ex-husband, to whom the care of their daughter has been consigned, depart with the girl. Stanwyck's refusal to face the camera (and King Vidor's decision not to cut to another and more revealing angle) deprives us of the opportunity to recognize and then identify with Stella through the conventional gesture of a facial close-up; the withholding image, however, fashions a compelling roundness from a spectacular lack of spectacle. If she "withholds," it is because the director has arranged for her to do so. Stanwyck's "performance" should be seen, in other words, from within the context of the film's production, including the deployment—or not—of standard industry practices. Arguably, reading this performance moment on the film's own terms, as Cavell and Klevan tend to do, is only the first of the critical gestures that an informed appreciation requires. Acknowledging that the specifics of this crucial image were produced by the actor through collaboration with the director and others on the production team offers a second pathway to measuring achievement, one that takes authorship into account as well as other relevant details of production history. Sometimes, in fact, only this contextualized reading of what appears on the screen provides a coherent explanation of the particular whatness of screen acting.

"They said I was good in it, but I don't see how I could have been"

Production context provides much useful material for an analysis of Richard Burton's acclaimed performance as British agent Alec Leamas in Martin Ritt's *The Spy Who Came in from the Cold* (1965), an international thriller in which, rarely, conventional flatness of character is a mirage and the plot turns on the revelation of a deeper self that, even when emerging to the expressive surface *in extremis*, does not reveal all its secrets. Based on the bestselling novel by John Le Carré, the film's narrative is meta-dramatic, with its plot focusing on what Klevan and Cavell see as one of the crucial features of performance—the productive opposition of revelation to withholding that, once deconstructed, makes clear that withholding, including "doing nothing," is always already a form of revelation, that it is, to switch sensorial registers, a particularly compelling form of silence.

Carlton Jackson observes that Ritt was determined for each of his projects to make "a statement about the human condition," and the director likely realized when reading Le Carré's novel in galley proofs that it would fit his intentions better than the other properties (including novels by literary heavyweights John Hersey and Saul Bellow) he was considering at the time, in the wake of his outstanding recent success in 1963 with bringing Larry McMurtry's novel *Horseman, Pass By* to the screen as *Hud* (21). With Ritt's assistance, that novel was considerably altered by screenwriters Irving Ravetch and Harriet Frank Jr. to focus on the title character to be played by Paul Newman. *Hud* allowed the matinee idol, with his enthusiastic agreement, to play against type as a ruthless and self-centered antihero, who serves as foil to the moral transformation of his nephew Lon (Brandon de Wilde). The result was one of Newman's most nuanced and acclaimed performances.

Le Carré's novel needed no such restructuring in order to offer a focus on a complex, unlikeable main character. After only a quick read, Ritt felt such confidence in the property that he bought the screen rights himself and decided to produce; this turned out to be a wise decision. The film proved to be a substantial financial success (earning more than $7.6 million), and it met with the approval of mainstream critics like Bosley Crowther, who found it "a tight and engrossing motion picture that not only is true to the book but also is so sharply staged and directed that it looks like a documentary film" ("Le Carré's Bestseller Adapted for the Screen," *New York Times*, 24 December 1965, online at nytimes.com). The industry also approved. *The Spy Who Came in from the Cold* won the BAFTA Award for Best Picture, while Burton won Best Actor; he also won the Golden Laurel award and was nominated for an Academy Award. And yet the actor expressed puzzlement that his appearance in the film had earned such accolades. Before the project took shape, he had read the novel and thought that the part of Leamas would suit him. In fact, as his biographer Melvyn Bragg reports, he had himself "tried for the rights" to the novel, while Ritt, who may have known about these efforts, was so eager to have him for the part that he pushed Paramount to pay the somewhat extortionate $750,000 that Burton's agent demanded (200).

From the perspective of its context of reception and production, the appreciation of *Spy* immediately raises a crucial question. Why was it that Burton's appearance in the film was much praised, while the actor himself, never a man given to modesty in any of its forms, confessed in conversation with Michael Munn to bewilderment about why his work for the film was singled out for considerable acclaim (see Munn 155)? How could he have been "good" when, so runs the implication of his remark, he was not allowed to "act," but in effect forced to withhold? What did critics see on the screen that Burton thought he had not put there? *Spy* does not deploy staging and editing along the lines of the Kuleshov effect to create a performance that Burton does not provide (the attentive reader should note that I did not write "give"). Instead, Ritt utilizes the actor's charismatic and intense presence to good effect, while creating interest in Leamas through the double narrative structure that comes to contain him, as well as to express and in some sense solve the moral problematic of the Cold War struggle: that, as Control (Cyril Cusack) affirms, "our methods cannot afford to be less ruthless than those of the opposition," defining the struggle as not between good and evil, despite what politicians were then proclaiming. In the novel, Le Carré problematizes Control's notion of the ends justifying the means through the moral stand that Leamas makes at the conclusion, a scene in which Burton, crucially, is provided with a rare performance moment.

Appropriately for an entrant in the genre where "undercover" is an existential condition, concealment figures as central to the presentation of Leamas "as himself." As Ritt helps fashion it, Burton's performance hints at a *mentalité*, especially a pondering of existential and ethical questions, that only rarely expresses itself in speech or in significant gestures. But that form of withholding, of the unrevealing unknownness that is a feature of his character *in se*, also figures in how Leamas performs the mission Control assigns him, which involves playing the role scripted for him as a disaffected former agent, often drunk and always angry at the world, who seems available for recruitment by enemy agents, while actually he is carrying out a mission to deceive them.

Once in character, Leamas conceals much of his true self from those he intends to help trap and destroy, and yet at the same time this role allows him to express and live out something of the disaffection and despair he is experiencing. In fact, Ritt makes it impossible to know when Leamas is in character and when he is performing as part of his mission. After establishing himself as an embittered derelict, Leamas throws a drunken tantrum in a local grocery, assaulting the grocer (Bernard Lee). But because the film provides no moment showing him getting into character, we do not know if this is a performance. Control believes it is, but he might be wrong. In any case, Leamas's attack succeeds. He goes briefly to prison, and after he is released enemy agents make a successful attempt to recruit him, convinced, or so it seems, that his self-abasement has gone so far it must be genuine and not a performance. Despite being in on the plot, we too are left wondering if this is play-acting, so intense and unclued for us is Burton's imitation of a blind, drunken rage.

And this is to say that the agent's performance in his clandestine role is authentic in the Method sense, that its particular power draws deeply on the emotional and intellectual qualities of the spy/"actor" in character, the fabricated state of being (with its "yes" and "no" to existential identity) on which performance depends for an intriguing undecidability. With apologies to Philip Sidney, we might say that the actor, like the poet, affirms nothing and therefore never lies. And the result is an unknownness of sorts. In the end, Leamas will discover that the actual mission, in which he has played the part of an unwitting tool, has been designed to ensure the safety of the East German espionage head, who, it turns out, is actually a British double agent. Violating a promise made to Leamas, Control furthers this betrayal by involving Nan (Claire Bloom), the woman he has come to love, and she is lured into joining Leamas at the East German compound where Control's complex double plot plays itself out in a dazzlingly complex series of twists and turns. In *Spy*, withholding solid revelation of Leamas's consciousness (at least for the most part) is of a piece with the unforthcoming minimalism of Ritt's approach to telling the story, which reproduces in cinematic terms the modernist difficulties of Le Carré's intention to elevate the cultural value of a conventional genre of popular narrative. Crowther felt it necessary to school his readers in how to appreciate what Ritt had accomplished: "To keep up with what is happening, you have to listen, Hard. But you also have to look" (Crowther). This is excellent advice, particularly when it comes to understanding the unusual way in which Alec Leamas takes shape onscreen through Burton's impersonation. But seeing Burton as Leamas, we are prevented by that impersonation from engaging with him. Crucially, just to take one example, Leamas's "truth," so to speak, is withheld in the scenes where he allows a romantic relationship with Nan to develop. Is this part of the plot? Or a sign that the "actor" is tiring of his belligerent solitude and for all too human reasons reaches out to someone who shows him kindness? How are we to understand Nan's taking the lead in their lovemaking, treating him as the erotic object? How many layers of performance are we meant to notice in these scenes?

It bears keeping in mind that, as Ritt recounted to Peter Bart, this characterization was made possible by "de-romanticizing" Burton's approach to acting: "We worked hard to scale down his extraordinary voice, his cocky bearing, his romantic aura" ("There are Spies and Spies," *New York Times*, 2 January 1966, 85). Munn records that Burton resented Ritt's attempts to "give him no opportunity to flex his acting muscles," with the rather predictable result that he was pushed toward "walking through the part with no interest or enthusiasm" (154). Burton may well have seen the role of Leamas quite differently from Ritt, who declared that he wanted a "grey film" in which none of the values were "black and white" (see Bragg 200; Ritt quoted in Jackson 83). The actor resisted Ritt's attempts to move him away from the more expressive and hence engaging approach that had recently worked so well for him in *The Sandpiper* (1965), where he appeared as a silver-tongued educator full of poetry. Burton found *Spy*'s dialogue "dull" by contrast, with his own speeches generally short and rhetorically unadorned, offering him few performance moments in which he could make use of his voice. But then the plot within the plot, and his performance with a performance, creates an unexpected depth through an interest-arousing vacancy. Moving through these scenes, Burton would have been unable to appreciate the effect.

He would of course have realized that others were often assigned to do the acting, as most notably perhaps in the meeting scene with Control. Leamas is invited to sit in a chair while his erstwhile boss stands upstage, there to deliver almost all of the dialogue between them, which Cusack does in his accustomed stagey dramatic manner, with a rhetorical flourish denied for the most part to Burton. What should we make of the unvoluble and motionless presence of Leamas/Burton in this scene? It seems to signify both the agent's surrender to the spymaster's demand that he assist in an elaborate sting operation and a reflection of Ritt's literal subordination of the star to the demands of the narrative, which is put into motion by another power and over which Leamas/Burton himself exercises no control? Perhaps because he was offered so little opportunity to perform in the way for which he had become famous, especially onstage, "Richard," as Munn reports, "had made no attempt to create a character but had simply made the character like him, as he was at the time . . . Rich really was weary, often drunk and bored, and this is perhaps exactly what director Martin Ritt wanted in the role" (155). Well, yes: weary, drunk, and bored are essential qualities of Leamas, although the character does in the end show a capacity for engagement. Acting in this case, Ritt seems to have thought, could be "being" rather than performing, which is how he must have persuaded the actor himself to think about this particular role.

As the production history reveals, the conspiratorial plotting that sets the narrative proper into motion is a startling *mise-en-abîme*, a repetition within the text of the performance shaping that, with no little dispute, resulted in the characterization Burton offers in the film. Control casts Leamas "as he now is" as the main character in the plot he has designed. Only a certain heightening is required from him as a performer. He is not to "act" except in a minimal sense but simply to "be" himself. Ritt did much the same with Burton, using him as he then was and requiring little in the way of "performance" in the traditional sense, an approach Burton disliked; he and Ritt almost came to blows at one point, it was reported, an episode that the director acknowledged but would not describe in detail (see Bart and Miller 172–3). That the actor had been instructed more to "occupy" the role of Leamas was obvious to the film's reviewers. Crowther observed that Ritt's "secret agent bears a striking resemblance to the familiar movie actor Richard Burton, even down to some of the actor's mannered ways" (Crowther). *Variety* concurred, opining that the film's aesthetic is a "perfectly controlled underplaying," one of whose results is that Burton "fits neatly into the role of the burnt-out British agent" (Review, *Variety* [31 December 1965], online at variety.com). And, of course, as a burnt-out spy, Leamas fits even more neatly into an impersonation of an agent so abused he is now willing to shop his former comrades and his country for money and the promise of some new life in the East.

Burton, in fact, seems to have been typecast for the role. Providing an account of his meeting with Burton during shooting, Le Carré seems to be describing Leamas: "Knowing him was impossible. There was something about him that was unapproachable . . . I had the impression it wasn't fun anymore" (quoted in Bragg 202). The hotel where the performers stayed in Dublin while interiors were shot at Ardmore Studios turned out to be a battleground. Burton and wife Elizabeth Taylor rowed constantly, and publicly, during shooting, consuming prodigious amounts of liquor. Biographer Melvyn Bragg suggests that "all of that might have been in the service of finding the character— Burton's way was always to make the part *be* him" (203). It seems clear enough that Burton "was" Leamas, but the evidence, including the actor's own testimony, indicates that the actor did not think he in any sense "made" the part of Alec Leamas. This was not a characterization he either designed or conceived. On the contrary, the film's production history suggests rather that Ritt, meeting violent opposition from Burton, simply "unmade" the star who was hardly his first choice for the part (it had been offered to Paul Newman and Burt Lancaster, both of whom bowed out. No doubt, the film would have been very different had Ritt shaped his Alec Leamas from either of them).

Spy foregrounds the central problematic of "acting," understood as a layering of selves on the same present body. Control's plot to use Leamas as doubly under cover, as a man divided between two versions of himself, only follows his astute reading of the man's almost completed passage into uselessness as a field operative. Leamas, he reasons, is still in enough control of his "presentation of self," as Goffman would term it, to fashion a more ostentatious performance of the emotional and psychological discontents that are ruining him, that is, his experience of himself as "burnt-out." That Ritt refuses to mark off Leamas's fabrication of moral and physical dissolution, his performance, from the strong sense that he is simply "being" rather than pretending, provides Burton's characterization with an engaging depth not produced by acting in the ordinary sense of that term. Further, Ritt's painstaking masking of Burton's glamor and charisma also reflected a central aspect of his approach to filmmaking, one that reflected his liberal politics and desire to fashion a "democratic cinema," as Gabriel Miller describes it.

An ordinary man

Ritt's film deploys the drab realism of the journey narrative, whose action, in accord with generic expectations, unfolds in various locations, in this case the northern European landscapes of the Cold War. *Spy* opens and closes at that most potently symbolic of the Cold War's locations, the wall dividing the eastern and western sections of Berlin (whose erection began in August 1961, just a few years before the film was made and hence a rich semiotic element of locative realism). Leamas's mission takes him from Berlin to London, then to Holland and swiftly afterward to the remote mountain country of East Germany before circling back west to the wall; this time Leamas finds himself on its other side, with escape to the American zone the only way he can now avoid death. Although some sequences were shot at Ardmore and at Shepperton Studios (London), real locations in the UK, Ireland, and Holland predominate.

Location shooting (some of the London sequences were even done guerilla-style) impart an authenticity that suits the film's deglamorizing reconfiguration of the spy thriller genre, since the upscale consumerist and macho fantasies of the James Bond franchise, at the time a literary and cinematic sensation, are here thoroughly deconstructed in favor of the colorless everydayness of ordinary life in both the "free" and communist worlds. Leamas is no hero, of interest only because of the pointless pretense he furthers; he is instead, to quote his own self-description, one of those "silly, squalid bastards . . . playing cowboys and Indians to brighten their rotten little lives." In the end, however, the film's painstaking locative realism provides the appropriate stage for a drama that is less political and more a matter of conscience. More accurately, the film closely follows the novel in demonstrating that the political is always also personal, thus Ritt does not depart from Le Carré's intense focus on Leamas. Conflicts in cultural values and the struggle for dominance between nations find their reflex, and perhaps their most potent expression, in the lived experience of an individual who finds himself as weary, divided, and disillusioned as the world of undeclared conflict in which he risks his life and calls upon others to do the same. The morality of Leamas's mission is hopelessly compromised. He comes to realize that he is the deceiver deceived, betrayed by the same kind of dirty trick he is himself playing on the man he mistakenly thought was his enemy.

After a bewildering series of revelations and betrayals, Leamas and Nan make their way from deep inside East Germany to the Berlin Wall, where the possibility of escaping into the western part of the city has ostensibly been arranged by Control and his associate George Smiley (Rupert Davies). With the possibility of a safe homecoming at hand, Leamas scales the ladder set against the wall, with Nan following close behind. But then the British operative who had guided them to the pre-arranged spot seizes a hidden rifle and shoots Nan dead; the British, so the implication runs, could not afford for her to return to Britain now that she is in possession of knowledge that could lead to the identification and death of their highly placed double agent. Nan slips from his grip as Leamas spies his colleague Smiley, who urges him to "come over to his own side." Leamas says nothing, but the expression he shows Smiley, and us, communicates a poignant and indecipherable message. He descends the ladder, returning to enemy territory where he might be captured and thus must be shot down. Leamas thus accepts a death that signifies solidarity with the victims of the largely hidden struggle in which he has served as a soldier.

The formal *telos* of Ritt's text, its death-like drive toward its own inevitable silence, thus finds a compensatory correlative in this completed portrayal of human becoming, as a self in flux achieves a proper finality in a return encounter with the energies that have launched it on a journey of inner change. Such is the power of the journey narrative that even extinction can be lent a resonant and uplifting grandeur, especially in the cinema where character is embodied and takes shape through a performance that can suitably climax in the portrayal of both resignation, forgiveness, and the refusal of anger. However, the spell of unknownness lingers over the film's final grim image of two bodies lying in the rubble-strewn space where once a house might have stood. Refusing to name his thoughts or offer words of reproach to Smiley, Leamas keeps his privacy, refusing, in a gesture that eminently suits Ritt's "common man" aesthetic, to be more than just another victim of poisonous politics.

Works cited

Bragg, Melvyn. *Richard Burton: A Life*. London: Little, Brown and Company, 1988.

Cavell, Stanley. *Contesting Tears: The Hollywood Melodrama of the Unknown Woman*. Chicago: University of Chicago Press, 1997.

Hewison, Robert. *In Anger: British Culture in the Cold War 1945–60*. New York: Oxford University Press, 1981.

Jackson, Carlton. *Picking Up the Tab: The Life and Movies of Martin Ritt*. Bowling Green: Bowling Green Popular Press, 1994.

Klevan, Andrew. *Film Performance: From Achievement to Appreciation*. London: Wallflower, 2007.

Miller, Gabriel, ed. *Martin Ritt: Interviews*. Jackson: University of Mississippi Press, 2002.

Munn, Michael. *Richard Burton: Prince of Players*. New York: Skyhorse, 2008.

Chapter 14

Jerry Lewis in *The King of Comedy*

Murray Pomerance

1

The Jerry Lewis who incarnated late-night talk-show host Jerry Langford in Martin Scorsese's scathingly parodic *The King of Comedy* (1982) was himself no stranger to late-night talk-show television. He had hosted specials: 19 January 1957 (with Jan Murray, Ernie Kovacs, Paul Lynde, and the Norman Luboff Choir), 18 February 1958 (with Hans Conried, Betty Grable, and Sophie Tucker), 21 September 1963 (with Jimmie Durante, Mort Sahl, and Sid Caesar); and his own talk show for two years commencing 12 September 1967 (with such personalities as Cher, The Osmond Brothers, and Tony Randall (who "fills in" for Jerry Langford in *King*)). He had "filled in" for Johnny Carson. But earlier, during the week of 2 July 1962, for a seemingly endless five-night run, he had "filled in" for the absent Jack Paar on what later came to be known as *The Tonight Show*.

I was one of the multitude in the television audience for that virtually indescribable spectacular. To grasp fully what the National Broadcasting Company found itself airing on those nights, it helps to have some awareness of the structure of network television in America at the time.

American culture from 1955 onward was in the throes of an intensive capital expansion, with the leisure sector, including TV entertainment, occupying an unstoppably swelling sector of the economy. TV was big business. The "big-business" aspect of the Western economy more generally, developing and solidifying under the banner of postwar consumerism, forced a pressured, anxiety-ridden working environment. Late-night television was aimed to tranquillize and gently entertain the agitated minds of those who might otherwise spend restless nights that left them unequipped to man the "factory" the following day. The talk show, pioneered to some significant degree by Paar, was designed to "invite" the watcher into a relatively sophisticated and tranquilizing, but at the same time "home-bound," soirée, where a dignified and articulate dominating presence would openly "invite" intelligent friends to sit in "comfort" and "discuss"—with genial superficiality—their work and life in general. Some of the "guests" would be present because of their talents at singing, telling jokes, or writing books, not to say acting in movies as major Hollywood stars; some would be fascinating raconteurs who could spiel engagingly on virtually any topic without preparation (Alexander King, Gore Vidal, Oscar Levant). When Carson took it over after Paar's retirement, the show became jazzier and quippier, but the fundamental premise of a relatively sedate host "having people in" continued. As to Paar, his only deviation from modesty and dignity came with his sometime emotionalism in responding to what people said to him: he could break into tears on camera.

As this mode of late-night television was being developed and promulgated in the late 1950s and early 1960s, Jerry Lewis had a dominant presence in an altogether different venue. First in nightclubs through the 1940s, then in motion pictures (in tandem with Dean Martin), he became the absolute epitome of unpredictable, zany, even spasmodic performance, all of which is evident in the Martin-and-Lewis screen vehicles from *My Friend Irma* (1949) and *Living It Up* (1954) through *Hollywood or Bust* (1956). The duo's "handsome man and his monkey" formula (see Krutnik) was addictive, with Lewis's improvisational genius lending it a pungent flavor of spontaneity and irregularity (since he would behave more through irruption than through planning). "Martin and

Lewis" had a life of precisely ten years (to the minute), terminating on the evening of 25 July 1956, after which point Lewis proceeded with a solo career in cinema, both performing (often in films directed by Norman Taurog or Frank Tashlin) and directing. His directorial efforts prior to the Paar engagement—*The Bellboy* (1960) and *The Errand Boy* (1961)—are works of consummate genius (see Pomerance).

What Lewis did on the Paar show the week he took it over was to thoroughly—yet with apparent randomness of intent—violate every accepted convention of late-night decorum on television. He refused to restrict himself to the noble "throne" of the host, leaping around the studio space like a court jester. He did not behave toward his guests—Eva Gabor, Bess Myerson, Jim Backus, Merv Griffin—with the dignified decorum that Paar modeled so exquisitely for more than 800 episodes over five emotional years. He did not treat the television camera as an invisible, curious "member of the family" but instead openly invoked it, at some points literally striding or hopping up and attempting to eat the lens. In addition to all this, he produced an unrelenting flow of the antics for which his onstage persona was strikingly known: loss of control of vocal amplitude; a kind of rhythmic complexity of physical movement, as in the declaratively disjunctive shifting between slowed and quickened gesture visible in modern dance since *Le sacre du printemps* (1912); grammatical trouble and sliding, abnormal vocal pitch; and repeated navigational challenge, as though he did not know where he was or how to make the next successful step forward. This was "The Kid," Lewis's internationally celebrated persona, but now taken to brave new extremes, since the Paar show was on *live* television and there were evidently no forces in front of or behind the camera that might shape, control, delimit, modulate, or otherwise gain ascendency over the performing clown.

On Paar, Lewis *was* a King of Comedy because with supreme dedication and skill he yielded will and personality to the force of the form: the "on" role took over, infused the lit set and its shadowy margins to such a degree that viewers sensed *no gap between the "Kid" and the man playing him*. But Scorsese's prescient film, and especially Lewis's astonishing performance in it, boldly explode this myth. If Lewis's onstage essence in television was purely organic, prerational, and precivil, the man behind it was depressed, mono-tonous, sober, ultra-rational, manipulative and even scheming, and in all of this thoroughly, and conservatively, socialized. If the performance exhibited an unsocialized or presocialized force, the performer himself was scrupulous about grammar and finesse, surely a student of the history of comedy but also a student of human behavior and organizational structure; and this canny, mature, acerbic Lewis is the man working in Scorsese's film.

We meet Jerry Langford in the film's opening, escaping the theater where his show originates and edging toward his limo through a tumultuous crowd of fans hungry to grasp him, modern maenads after a new, mediated Pentheus. As he arrives home and enters his pad—Jerry lives in the Seagram Building on East 53rd St., above the Four Seasons—a strong design (by Boris Leven), including a glaringly mirrored entryway, openly declares the locked-off personality of the inhabitant. The apartment is decorated in muted smoky grays and beige, with high picture windows opening onto a shapeless cityscape. Jerry pauses at his television set, already on, where a scene from Samuel Fuller's *Pickup on South Street* (1953) entrances him: Richard Widmark fingering a stranger's purse—a sanctum of sancta—on the subway. In a facial portrait we see the intensity of Langford's concentration, his reading of the Widmark gesture for rhythm, contour, and dexterity; of Joe MacDonald's lighting for subtle clarity. Here is Langford the devotee of visualized performance—always a student, always learning—yet also Lewis, who from the mid-1950s onward inhabited the sound stages at Paramount and cajoled the cinematographers, designers, prop masters, and editors to share their secrets (see Lewis). Langford might be the sober, meticulous Jerry Lewis who invented the video assist. But his reclusiveness is profound.

According to legion accounts, the backstage Jerry Lewis is variably amenable or withdrawn, chummy or hostile, depending on the absence or presence of provocation (on the latter see Levy 481 ff). But in our few direct views of the off-camera Langford here—mostly he figures as a co-star in the delirious projections of Rupert Pupkin (Robert De Niro), a paradigmatic *schlemiel* convinced he is talented and should have a spot on Jerry's show—he is an unrelentingly cold and defensive chap, with a "closed door" attitude and a glaringly, ungregariously sane civilian identity. For example, in the middle of the film Rupert crashes Jerry's Long Island getaway, finding there a "Jerry" for whose iciness and propriety he is entirely unprepared. From Langford's down-to-earth point of view, here is a stranger trespassing in his private home, girlfriend in hand, convicted of the preposterous idea that he's welcome. Jerry's "invitations" and "friendship" have been a rich subject of Rupert's fantasy life, and naïve Rupert doesn't grasp that in late-night television, the "host" is a host only by name, does not "invite" people to his "home" or to the viewer's, either, since the entire affair is a production. But on Long Island, rather than being gracious or understanding of Rupert's ill-informed motive, rather than playing the game of "hospitality" that his television program invokes onscreen, Langford is lofty in disregard for this "idiot" who would stroll into another person's space.

Lewis's performance in this country-house scene both declares and summates, in terms of his mastery of tone, posture, attitude, and conviction. No twitching outsider, but a master of grace, dignity, poise, and sensibility, Lewis shows Langford to be what Rupert and his autograph-craving chum Masha (Sandra Bernhard) can only think old-fashioned, stilted, un-hip, inimical, and seething (the opposite in every way of Rupert's imagined Jerry and, we must imagine, the TV audience's Jerry, too). To help Lewis find this mood, "De Niro opened their scene by hurling anti-Semitic epithets" at him, reported *People*; "the ploy worked to perfection" (Jerome). He has clothed himself in a light sweater and a pair of tennis shorts, because having been phoned by his houseboy he has rushed in from the golf course. He still clasps an iron, with a mixture of irritation and threatening ease: it is for play, but also a weapon. Jerry poses in front of his white mantelpiece. Perched behind him, and glaring into the camera over his shoulder, is the "young Jerry Langford" who lives in a framed photograph, clearly a young Jerome Levitch from Newark, who tried out a stage career goofing around in mimicry of recorded phonographs and would graduate, in July 1946, to taking apart the crooning of Dean Martin in an historic performative moment. The creature in the photograph is distrusting, inward-focused, even fearful as he glares.

2

It is convenient to presume the "on" Jerry Langford resembles a manic source in real life, a "Jerry" of consummate hyperaffability, even obnoxiousness, his energies limitless, omnipresent, and diffuse. His moments of "poise" are mere performative setups, compositions always ready for sudden destruction: poise and politeness primed for rapid degeneration into hilarity and garble. Seeing the gap between order and disorder so rapidly traversed in the comedic turn, we can experience the fairground thrill of gravitational inversion, body play. Behind the camera, however, Jerry Langford is someone else—less an embodied appearance than a smart producer of embodied appearances, a puller of strings.

In his "everyday" self—as the person manufacturing the performance—Lewis's Langford is a paragon of composedness and sobriety, a designer not a rag doll. A certain solitude attaches to this self-possession, since it is evident on the face of it that (like Lewis, surely) Langford is a genius (if uneducated), whose social analysis is sharp as a pin. But: more than personal, his solitude is built into the organizational structure of his work, his self-knowledge in part an accession to loneliness and a structural crypt, since in every way his public persona must be guarded from the multitudes who recognize, claim to love, feel they know, and wish to possess him. Such is the nature of fame in contemporary mediated culture. The caricature of Jerry Langford (both literal, the figure in his logo; and metaphorical, the persona he represents to his adoring fans) can be sold and resold only if Jerry himself is entirely unavailable for acquisition. Not only is his figura a Baudrillardian simulacrum, sprung out of and away from an authentic self; it cannot be otherwise if it is to be mass-circulated, since the only market for comedians as their "authentic" selves is media producers, perforcedly invisible.[1] The contrast between public glare and private darkness is struck in the film's very opening, between Jerry struggling to creep through the mob of ravenous autograph hounds and Jerry riding away in the silent shadows of his stretch limousine. At his apartment he is suddenly *to* himself and *by* himself, the silence almost ringing against the mirrored doors as he passes without being substantially reflected. If no clue has yet signaled Jerry's abject loneliness, the single dinner plate set out on the long dining table sharply pictures his singularity, his distance from social relations in this private cloud.

But at the film's moment of crisis, Lewis's performative gestures—often withdrawals of typical "performative gesture"—make a penetrating address to Langford's (and his own) aloneness, to the star's palpable separation from the universe of loving embrace and electric contact that his "on" character invokes. Jerry has been kidnapped by Rupert and Masha, nabbed from the sidewalk, indeed, a gun at his face. We're in Masha's East-Side brownstone—she comes from big New York money—where they command him to phone into the show's offices and announce that he is being held for ransom. The ransom is that Rupert be permitted a slot on the show tonight.

But for Jerry, phoning in is a virtual impossibility: as a highly valued component of a lucrative cultural product, he is kept "on ice" by the controllers of "The Jerry Langford Show." Because countless fakers routinely try for contact, the show must be able to deflect them, and so the presumption is *routinely* made that Jerry will never use the main phone line. Since here, at gunpoint, he is doing precisely that, he will be able to get through to the show's producer Bert Thomas (Fred DeCordova, at the time producer of "The Tonight Show with Johnny Carson") only if he goes through the proper secretarial channels and employs as distinguishing mark the code word they have agreed upon in advance (ironically, since the Jerries Lewis and Langford are widely taken to exhibit countless and ineradicable distinguishing marks, none of which, apparently, transact in the phone system). "What do we call our second cameraman?" is the riddle put his way, and Paul Zimmerman's script for the film specifies that Jerry answer, "Helen Keller." But Lewis, knowing he may be playing to an uninformed audience, improvises: "Helen Keller, because his favorite color is plaid." This setup mounts for us a Jerry radiant at the center of his own show yet without power to make a simple phone call to his producer. Indeed, he must call back more than once (on Masha's gilded telephone), raising his voice to the secretary, who has misidentified him. While the public marquee of the show puts Jerry "at the top" in bright lights, centers him as star feature and controlling force, glittering where Jerry Lewis, too, glitters, in structural reality he is but one of the producer's many employees, albeit richly paid.

As Scorsese has choreographed it, again by the two obsessive fans who have taken him hostage Jerry is denied agency, since they have prescripted his side of the phone call to Thomas (following Zimmerman's script: a scripted scripting)—"I have a gun ... at my head ..."—and he may not improvise (except that they permit a pause while he informs his listener that he is reading from cue cards). We are left to imagine what Jerry would say given freedom of expression; or even were he to burst into the sort of verbal antics for which he is famous. But instead, we hear a shrunken voice, an ordinary voice, magnified only by the telephone equipment. Jerry is now only like any caller at all, a typical man using a typical device, but the continuing vision of Jerry Lewis offers a stark oneiric accompaniment to the hyper-rationalized speech.

The call completed, it is time to tie Jerry up, but not before Masha brings out a bright red sweater she has been knitting for him, to see if it fits. Lewis/Langford is thus momentarily reduced even further, occupying the measly status of a clothing-store mannequin as she proudly estimates her work. The scene is constructed principally to show off Masha's lunatic offbeatness. But Jerry's complete silence, his postural stillness actually refashion the well-known jerky body as a model of obedient, dignified masculine poise. As Buddy Love in *Professor,* Lewis had shown swagger, attitude, snobbiness. Here he has none of these qualities. "What do you think? I think it's pretty good. Color's great, and I like to see him a little more casual for a change. This is a look I like to see on him." Rupert (perfunctorily): "Looks good, Jerry."[2] But Jerry is viciously silent. Rupert must bring her in line: "Come on! Take it off and let's go." Masha is deflated: "You want me to take it off? Why can't he wear it for awhile?"

Jerry is positioned in a gilded fauteuil and bound in a thick swaddling of white medical adhesive tape[3] that aligns him to some degree with Claude Rains's invisible man (1933) or Bogart's Vincent Parry in *Dark Passage* (1947), except that the head remains visible—the signal base of the famous caricature, the part of Jerry Langford that serves to remind us perpetually of his identity with Jerry Lewis—with the (big) mouth taped over. Here is a signal case of Guy Davenport's "head as fate":

> What's at play here is the aligning of the perspicacious man of popular culture (one who descries, and is all head and brain, the body being comic and weak) with the archaic heroic spirit. This spirit, says art, survives in our time as intelligence. The head as fate takes on new meaning, not as the ancient seat of a noble nature and a stoic rectitude of behavior, but as cunning and intellectual sharpness. (33)

To be clear: Langford as a backstage self is portrayed in the film as a "seat of a noble nature and a stoic rectitude of behavior" but his head, the Jerry Lewis head imposed on the character of Langford, is a sign of "cunning and intellectual sharpness": sharpness, his cannily reading Masha's borderline personality and refraining from provocation in offering no hint of his on-camera self (the one she knows and loves). He remains alienated from that caricature, in a self-effected bubble. Rupert having slipped off to find his way behind the cameras tonight, it is Masha who holds Jerry at bay now.

She has set a table before him, with gilded wineglasses and fancy cutlery. The apartment is filled with lit candles, like a cathedral. But Masha is anything but predictable, and a terrifying impulse now overtakes her, as she recognizes herself to be in the actual presence of the man she adores (or recognizes that it is a man she adores, not an image). In an alarming gesture she sweeps the table clean and segues into a throbbing rendition of Michael Arlen and Johnny Mercer's "Come Rain or Come Shine" to which Jerry offers no response at all, his eyes half-closed behind enormous eyeglass frames. When he does snatch a peek, his cool, evaluative gaze is the same one he used on Sam Fuller's film early on. She "has it": the nuances, the variations.

But now he urges her to take his bandages off. A cunning, conning tone. She imagines he imagines a party. Complying, trembling with anticipation in front of him, she strips to her underwear, skinny as a twig. He picks up the pistol and points it at her, discovering that the thing in his hand is nothing but a toy. He pulls the trigger, and a pop dart shoots out against her belly. He slugs her and races off, adhesive still ringing his ankles like iridescent shackles.

Jerry wound in bandages—an invisible man. Jerry silenced at gunpoint, a weak victim. Jerry the voiceless object, having the sweater held up to his chest. Jerry the material transactable *ding an sich*, a persona to be exchanged for a performance. (Rupert will actually say on camera, "You're probably wondering where Jerry is tonight. Well, he's tied up, and I tied him"—his funniest joke so far.) Manifesting all these Jerries is the performing Jerry Lewis, whose capacity for sincerity, frankness, directness, and *reduction* of expression constitute an utter rejection of the qualities he built a career by promulgating onscreen. *The King of Comedy* is thus an extended moment of self-regard for him. It is in his shaping and knowing a self onscreen that Lewis shows nobility and cunning at once, the dignity of bearing and the epitome of rational consciousness harmonized.

Nowhere in Scorsese's film is the Langford/Lewis on-camera zany shown fully blossomed, in direct narrative. We catch a fleeting snippet of conversation as Jerry strolls past a cabbie, in which with prototypical charm he chummily mocks his own flashy red-satin-lined suit; when Masha sights him and starts to pursue, he runs off in a prototypical "Jerry-Lewis-awkward" style. Our fleshed-out glimpses of performative "Jerry Langford" flow from Rupert's obsessive imagination, his addicted memory of "all moments Jerry" spun out in sharply delineated and spontaneously appearing fragments: Jerry performing an on-camera wedding for Rupert and Rita (with Victor Borge (1909–2000) playing Mendelssohn's "Wedding March" in a touching cameo); Jerry and Rupert lunching at Sardi's (on West 44th St., a haven of show business personalities), with Rupert kvetching about what a pain it will be to have to fill in for Jerry again (he explicitly refers to Lewis on Paar). In another dream, Rupert is in Jerry's brazenly mirrored office, taking feedback on the demo tape he left the comedian in the limousine. "You've got it. You've … got … IT!" Jerry bleats into Rupert's face, mock-strangling him. None of these out-of-control "Jerry" moments reflect the real Jerry who is kidnapped, taped to the chair, sung to by Masha as though her life depended on it.

If, as Robert Kolker suggests in his analysis of loneliness in American cinema of the time, *The King of Comedy* portrays a distinct lack of fit between Rupert and the everyday world, if our Rupert is a passageway into "the solipsism that constitutes celebrity" and an "onanist of entertainment" (211), how much more forcefully does it depict the isolation and exclusion of Jerry, since rather than setting himself apart through a labyrinthine structure of self-delusion, like Rupert, the famous comedian is forced into seclusion by the exigencies of his own commitment to production. He is not an outsider, he is a laborer who must pay the tax of withdrawal from sociability in order to retain the glow of distance upon which he is marketed. Jerry's isolation in fame is made explicit at the crux of the kidnapping scene, when a frustrated Rupert asks him point blank, "Why didn't you just listen to the tape when I asked you to? Is that so hard to do?" Jerry is confiding and to the point:

> I'm sure you can understand. Doing the kind of show I'm doing, it's mind boggling. There's so much stuff that comes down you can't keep your head clear ... I'm just a human being, with all of the foibles, and all of the traps. The show, the pressure, the groupies, the autograph hounds. The crew. The incompetence [*a look of genuine anger*]. Those behind the scenes you think are your friends and you're not too sure if you're going to be there tomorrow because of their incompetence. There are wonderful pressures that make every day a glowing radiant day in your life. It's terrific.

Central here, but also in the film as a whole, is the precariousness of the act Jerry performs night after night (and, by association, the precariousness of the act Jerry Lewis performs onscreen film after film). His success is entirely a matter of his appearance, both in his valuable audience's perception and as resultant from the expert labors of a production team, versed in the techniques of display. But every member of that team, every one of Jerry's "friends" behind the scenes, has a life to live and pressures to encounter, a pathway on which success and advancement are continual gambles with devastation. Structurally speaking what is true for Langford is true for the Lewis incarnating him, that any person's private anxiety or weakness of the moment could easily come to bear on the impression the star is compelled to give.

Writing in *The New Yorker* about another late-night hero's ongoing struggles to maintain his perch, Kenneth Tynan described what Jerry does here as the *salto mortale*—the high-wire acrobat's leap of death. If the talk show is a form balanced over an abyss, no other artist has managed to equal Jerry (or "Jerry") in giving it the spark of life.

Notes

1. Woody Allen's *Broadway Danny Rose* (1984) figures this relationship.
2. Jerry did look good in red. He frequently took to wearing red sweaters in public appearances (as, onstage with Scorsese, at the twenty-fifth anniversary screening of this film; or posing at home on his ninetieth birthday; my thanks to Charles Hsuen for the briefing).
3. Conjuring the hospital setting of his star vehicle *The Disorderly Orderly* (1964).

Works cited

Davenport, Guy. *Objects on a Table: Harmonious Disarray in Art and Literature*. Washington, DC: Counterpoint, 1998.
Jerome, Jim. "After Open-Heart Surgery, King of Comedy Jerry Lewis Bounces Back with a Bride-to-Be," *People* 19: 5 (7 February 1983), online at www.people.com. Accessed 10 August 2016.
Kolker, Robert. *A Cinema of Loneliness: Penn, Kubrick, Scorsese, Spielberg, Altman*. New York: Oxford University Press, 1988.
Krutnik, Frank. "Sex and Slapstick: The Martin and Lewis Phenomenon," in Murray Pomerance, ed., *Enfant Terrible! Jerry Lewis in American Film*, New York: New York University Press, 2004, 109–21.
Levy, Shawn. *The King of Comedy: The Life and Art of Jerry Lewis*. New York: St. Martin's Press, 1997.
Lewis, Jerry. *The Total Film-Maker*. New York: Random House, 1971.
Pomerance, Murray. "The Errant Boy: Morty S. Tashman and the Powers of the Tongue," in *Enfant Terrible! Jerry Lewis in American Film*, New York: New York University Press, 2004, 239–56.
Tynan, Kenneth. "Fifteen Years of the Salto Mortale," *The New Yorker* (20 February 1978), 310–54.

Chapter 15

Sidney Poitier in *In the Heat of the Night*

Frances Gateward

Sidney Poitier remains the most highly recognized African American actor in the history of American cinema.[1] His dramatic characterizations brought dignity, complexity, and humanity to African American depictions at the height of the Civil Rights Movement, one of the most tumultuous periods of social change in US history. He was the first black leading man in Hollywood to achieve superstar status, realized *not* with singing or dancing but on the strength of his dramatic talents. He entered Quigley's Top Money Maker Poll in 1967—the year he delivered, as part of his stellar performance in *In the Heat of the Night*, the "slap heard round the world." This essay examines Poitier's electrifying performance in one of his most iconic roles, as Philadelphia police detective Virgil Tibbs, in Norman Jewison's Oscar-winning police thriller.[2]

A fascinating film, *In the Heat of the Night* was both provocative and courageous for its time, attempting to address systemic racism in law enforcement and the culture of white supremacy in America. The film resonates with the talents and political proclivities of its makers; benefiting from the realist, and often documentary lighting design of Haskell Wexler, the astute editing of Hal Ashby, the humanistic vision of Norman Jewison, and the artistry of Sidney Poitier. It is a film very much organized around the stellar performances of the actors (Poitier supported by Rod Steiger, Lee Grant, Warren Oates, and Larry Gates, among others). Although the film relies heavily on Poitier's established, and in many ways problematic, star persona, the role of Tibbs did provide him with an opportunity to move beyond it.

As TreaAndrea Russworm notes, "When read in relation to the political movements of the era, Poitier's films have been lauded for disrupting old celluloid stereotypes of African Americans and also dismissed as being anachronistic by the late 1960's" (44). And as Ed Guerrero points out, "In 1967, Poitier was clearly the biggest box-office star of the year with *In the Heat of the Night, To Sir, With Love,* and *Guess Who's Coming to Dinner* in the theaters. At the height of his star power, however, Poitier's 'ebony saint' image was increasingly wearing thin" (72). By the late 1960s, in the shift from Civil Rights with its integrationist fantasies to Black Power with its separatist desires, Poitier came to be seen as a placater at best, an Uncle Tom or a Stepin Fetchit at worst. New stars, like Jim Brown and Richard Rountree, projected a more militant attitude, a rejection of the attempt to placate white society and acknowledge the seeming intractability of racism. In fact, it is clear that Poitier's stature as a box-office draw suddenly decreased in the Black Power era. The only important films in which he appeared were the handful he directed himself, beginning in 1972.[3] According to Sharon Willis, Poitier's key roles see him "permanently compelled to teach." He is a paragon of respectability whose "mission [is] to educate well-intentioned white people to understand and accept racial equality. The success of this project depended on his nonthreatening goodwill and his eager and patient pedagogical impulses" (5). The characters Poitier portrayed were, almost without exception, middle-class, highly educated, and morally superior. And because he was removed from black milieux, functioning to solve the problems of white communities, he was also without a sexuality. This "Poitier Syndrome," named in 1967 by Clifford Mason ("Why Does White America Love Sidney Poitier So?," *New York Times*, 10 September 1967, 123), was such that James Baldwin felt compelled to respond in *Look* magazine, acknowledging the difficult position Poitier was in:

> The black performer is in a rather grim bind. He knows, on the one hand, that if the reality of a black man's life were on that screen, it would destroy the fantasy totally. And on the other hand, he really has no right *not* to appear, not only because he must work, but also for all those people who need to see him. By the use of his own person, he must smuggle in the reality that he knows is not in the script. (56)

And though *In the Heat of the Night* still fits within the confines of the "syndrome," and the more recently identified "Poitier Effect," where his characters, just passing through, represent fantasies of "dreams of achieving racial reconciliation and equality without any substantive change to the 'White' world of 'white' culture, and especially to white privilege" (Willis 5), there are several moments where Baldwin's "smuggled reality" comes to the fore in the emotional truths offered by Poitier's performance.

They got a murder on their hands. They don't know what to do with it.

Jewison's film, adapted by Stirling Silliphant from the novel by John Ball, takes place in rural Sparta, Mississippi, a small town full of people with small minds. Populated by hostile and ignorant racists, the film is perhaps one of the earliest to conventionalize the tropes common in Hollywood Civil Rights films set in the deep South. Though the film's marketing campaign, central dilemma, and cinematic style purport that *In the Heat of the Night* is a whodunit, the film is more a character study of Poitier's Virgil Tibbs and his opposite, Police Chief Gillespie, powerfully played by Steiger. A rich Northern industrialist who was going to build a factory in town is found murdered. Gillespie, realizing he is out of his league, is reluctantly helped by Tibbs, whose understanding of police procedure and forensics makes him a formidable detective. Gillespie must contend with the fact that a black man from the North has more knowledge and skill than he. Their difference in class, ideology, education, and personalities are made visible in their costuming and their acting style. Tibbs, who, we learn, makes the very good salary of $162.39 a week, is middle-class, well-dressed in a tailored suit, well-groomed, and well-educated. With his crisp accent, slim body, and good posture, he is utterly contrary to Steiger's gum-chewing, paunch-bellied, boot-wearing, slouching police chief, modeled after the violent segregationist chief of Birmingham, Alabama Bull Connor. When Gillespie is gruff, Tubbs is mannered. When Gillespie is boorish, Tibbs is civil. When Gillespie is presumptuous, Tibbs is thoughtful. In classic Poitier fashion, Tibbs is the epitome of constraint, forced to be that way out of circumstance, since racial hegemony makes it difficult for him to act freely, but also because he seems the better man, civilized, cultured, perhaps even an example of racial uplift ideology. Tibbs's reaction to the town folk's behavior presents him as neither meek nor inferior. Rather it is used to his advantage. As Mark Harris details, "Silliphant and Jewison toughened their depiction of Virgil Tibbs, paring away so much of his dialogue that he became, by the final draft, someone who uses silence, withholding, and watchfulness as a weapon. In some ways, the changes were designed to tailor Tibbs to Poitier's special talent for controlled anger while allowing him to take a stride forward from *Lilies of the Field* and *A Patch of Blue* into a hipper, more contemporary persona" (179). This characterization, and Poitier's magnificent use of facial expression and body language, presented a new form of black masculinity never seen before in American cinema. It is used to especially good effect when he is introduced in the film.

Certainly *In the Heat of the Night* was intended as a star vehicle, as Poitier and Steiger are featured in the original trailer and in the posters, with their names above the title. And as with many star vehicles, we are forced to wait for the introduction of the featured player's character. Usually the anticipation helps build excitement for the audience. The introduction of Tibbs is disquieting, however. In the title sequence, abstract circles of light are slowly pulled into focus, and we realize it is an approaching train. When it reaches the station, a porter places a step by the door, and a suited black man disembarks with a suitcase. We know it is Poitier/Tibbs, as his shoes are impeccably shined and his movements are elegant, but we are not permitted to see his face. The frame cuts off just below the elbow. He opens a screen door, enters a building, and the title song, sung by Ray Charles, ends with the shutting of the door. The film then cuts away to another location, and we do not return to the first location for more than seven minutes. When we finally see Tibbs, it is from the perspective of a white policeman who orders, "On your feet, boy." Tibbs, sitting nonchalantly leafing through a magazine, doesn't comply. When the order is given again, more forcibly, he rises and reaches for his suit jacket, but stops when the policeman pulls his gun. Tibbs immediately raises his hands, and is forced to "assume the position" against the train station wall.

I mention the hands here, as a point I will discuss later. But what I want to highlight at the moment is the problematic opening. Our discomfort is heightened here by having a much beloved star insulted in what typically is a celebratory scene of recognition. It creates immediate empathy, for we know, of course, that a Poitier character would not commit murder. Jewison provides a low angle close-up of Tibbs with his hands against the wall, his face framed by the white sleeves of his shirt as he is searched. Yes, it reveals the silent anger Poitier expresses so well, but also profound humiliation and wariness, as there is no guarantee he will survive the encounter. It is just one of the many racially charged attempts of the townspeople to rid Sparta of this "nosey Nigger" who doesn't belong. Tibbs must endure a series of insults and slights, the inability to stay in a hotel in town, being chased by a car flaunting a Confederate flag (an incident added to the script based on an encounter Poitier experienced while working in the Civil Rights Movement), an attempted assault by a gang of supremacists, and the aggression of an old white plantation owner.

The slap heard round the world

As Gillespie and Tibbs investigate the murder, they are led by a clue to Eric Endicott, owner of the Endicott Cotton Company. As the two cops drive through the fields, a crane shot shows the expansive size of the property, with dozens of black people picking the cotton by hand. We are given a series of close-ups of hands tearing the fiber from the prickly branches, demonstrating the back-breaking and difficult work, and then we see Tibbs, in the passenger seat, looking pensively out the window. Gillespie, in an attempt to get under the detective's skin says, "None of that for you, huh Virgil." Tibbs turns quickly from the window to the Chief, incredulous. After a beat, his expression shifts from anger to ... it is difficult to discern. Is it a sense of shame, for letting the comment rile him, or is it class-guilt? They arrive at the big house, an oversized brick mansion with white columns in the style so beloved by Southern plantation owners. Gillespie casually taps the head of the black jockey lawn ornament prominent in the foreground as the two men approach the front door, which is opened by an older black man dressed as a servant. The use of all this racist iconography, coupled with the slave imagery of the cotton fields and insidious comments by Endicott, who compares one of his orchids to the "nigras, who need special care, feeding, and cultivating," creates a sense of tension and foreboding that demands release. Poitier, in an action not written in the original script, provides it with what was received by audiences as a celebratory act of violence. Endicott, outraged that he is considered a suspect by a black man, slaps Tibbs across the face. Tibbs reciprocates, without hesitation. As Russworm describes it, "Endicott's open-palmed slap is slow and indignant; his hand connects with an unflinching and almost expectant Tibbs. Comparatively, Tibbs's instinctual backhand slap is swift but protracted, graceful, and stylized. The blow nearly topples its unsuspecting target, as upon contact, Endicott careens off to the side" (69). This was the first time in American cinema that a black man struck a white man in a modern context without consequence. Endicott reminds Tibbs, "There was a time when I could have had you shot." As many critics have noted, the scene signified that times were changing. And it reflected changes in the Poitier persona. After 1968, Poitier's characters no longer accommodated the tepid liberalism that was so common in his earlier films.

A vulnerable heart in open hands

> Behold the hands, how they promise, conjure, appeal, menace, pray, supplicate, refuse, beckon, interrogate, admire, confess, cringe, instruct, command, mock and what not besides, with a variation and multiplication of variation which makes the tongue envious.
> (Montaigne)

Star studies by numerous scholars, including Richard Dyer and Christine Gledhill, have well reminded us that there is a difference between a great star and a great actor; one an image or constructed persona constantly manipulated by the culture industry, the other an artist of great talent, discipline, and technique—in fact, an individual who is both is quite rare in the cinema. Actors with charisma, that "certain something" that compels us to watch intently, and to empathize so easily, are relatively rare. Sidney Poitier is one of these. Though he trained in the famous Method, he transcended its techniques to emerge as a veritable presence. He did, however, retain its major principles and learn to use not only the famous sense memory of the Method but also his physical gifts. His mellifluous voice, his expressive eyes, and, especially in *Heat of the Night*, his dexterous, graceful hands. He is, of course, very much aware of the special nature of his hands. *The Measure of a Man*, his "spiritual autobiography," features a cover photo of Poitier holding his hands to the side of his face, the left hand held over the right. Another photograph, this one on an Internet biography (http://www.notablebiographies.com/Pe-Pu/Poitier-Sidney.html) shows him in a medium close-up, his left hand up by his chin, his long index finger on his face, pointing up to his eye.

Because Jewison and Silliphant dramatically reduced Tibbs's dialogue, nonverbal communication was *especially* critical, and Poitier's hands were used to great effect. In the aforementioned train station scene, Tibb's stillness when first confronted by the uniformed policeman makes his movements that much more pronounced. When he is forced to raise his hands, in that compulsory pose that too many innocent black men have been coerced to strike—now, as then—it is an affront to the dignity and humanity deserving of every person.

As in that scene, the physical vocabulary of hands is central to Poitier's performance throughout *Heat of the Night*. Tibb's willingness to meet racialized violence with retribution in the scene of the slap, the demonstration of his skills as a criminologist in close-ups, shot with a macro lens, as he examines both the corpse and the arms of another suspect, his discovery of a plant root that leads them to Endicott's plantation, and very especially in a scene of great compassion and emotional intensity, when Tibbs informs Mrs. Colbert (Grant), the wife of the murder victim, that her husband is dead, a task that none of the Sparta policemen have the courage to handle. Tibbs enters the police station in the morning, looking for the absent Chief Gillespie. When he finds out that the unknowing widow is there instead, he turns to leave. Changing his mind, he steels himself and walks purposely toward the office, charging in despite the protests of the police. Once in the room, he is immediately confronted by Colbert, demanding to know where her husband is, and if he is hurt. Tibbs rather curtly tells her, "He's dead." After registering her shock, he softens, explaining that he was killed and they do not yet know who did it. He quickly reaches out to her, but she gestures her rejection, leaving him to close his empty hands. After she crosses the room and sits, the scene continues in a single wordless long take, as she begins to break down. He holds out a hand toward the foreground, and in the moment of greatest anguish, she takes it. Colbert continues to clasp Tibbs's hand as the camera slowly dollies in, centering our attention not on the faces but on the hands. After a few moments, they unclasp hands, Tibbs exits and the camera moves in on Mrs. Colbert, who is weeping loudly. The shot goes out of focus and there is a cut to Tibbs outside the room, leaning against the door, clearly in some anguish himself.

The wordlessness of the scene from the beginning of the long take and the focus on the play of hands is not just masterful acting (improvised by these two exponents of the Method so clearly in the moment), but also another key moment in the history of African American images onscreen. Here is an image of a black man comforting a white woman, Jewison emphasizing the white hand grasping the black one, two people transcending race. Yet race is what it is all about, Poitier's blackness, his Otherness in this hostile white world a fact of life. Poitier never allows us to forget this, yet his intelligence, dignity, and essential humanity, demonstrated so well simply by reaching out his hand to comfort a grieving woman but also in a lightning-quick backhand across the face of a rabid racist, create an image of a black man so rarely seen and even less well understood. It is as if Poitier were waiting for this film to let loose, to demonstrate that he had held onto his anger, his rage, through so many movies over the years and now, now, finally, had his chance. He doesn't lose that syndrome that had so long plagued him, but at least some of what lies beneath could come to the light of day in the heat of the night.

Notes

1. Though Poitier was nominated and did not win an Oscar for his performance in *The Defiant Ones* in 1958, he did win in 1964 for his work in the film *Lilies of the Field*, becoming the first black actor to win an Academy Award in a leading role. His other accolades include eight Golden Globe nominations and three wins, two prime-time Emmy nominations as Lead Actor in a Mini Series for his portrayals of Supreme Court justice Thurgood Marshall and ANC activist and South African president Nelson Mandela, a Lifetime Achievement Award from the American Film Institute (1992), and a 2002 honorary Oscar from the Academy of Motion Picture Arts and Sciences for "his extraordinary performances and unique presence on the screen and for representing the industry with dignity, style and intelligence." Queen Elizabeth II bestowed knighthood on him in 1974 (he is by birth a British subject, native to the Bahamas). In addition, he has won a Grammy (2002), the Cecil B. DeMille Award from the Hollywood Foreign Press (1982), the Kennedy Center Honors (1995), a Lifetime Achievement Award from the Screen Actor's Guild (1998), and, in 2009, the Presidential Medal of Freedom, the highest civilian award in the United States.
2. Tibbs was such a compelling and favored character that Poitier would play him in the 1970 film *They Call Me Mr. Tibbs*. The title is taken directly from *In the Heat of the Night*, a line Poitier delivers emphatically when asked what he is called in his hometown of Philadelphia. The third, and last, time Poitier would play Tibbs was in *The Organization* (1971).

3. Poitier's success as an actor eclipsed his pioneering work as a feature film director. One of the first African American directors in Hollywood, Poitier helmed nine films, two of which are among the biggest money makers in African American cinema: *Uptown Saturday Night* (1974) and *Let's Do It Again* (1975).

Works cited

Baldwin, James. "Sidney Poitier," *Look* 32 (23 July 1968), 50–4.
Harris, Mark. *Pictures at a Revolution*. New York: Penguin, 2008.
Poitier, Sidney. *This Life*. New York: Alfred A. Knopf, 1980.
Poitier, Sidney. *The Measure of a Man*. New York: HarperCollins, 2000.
Russworm, TreaAndrea M. *Blackness is Burning: Civil Rights, Popular Culture, and the Problem of Recognition*. Detroit: Wayne State University Press, 2016.
Willis, Sharon. *The Poitier Effect*. Minneapolis: University of Minnesota Press, 2015.

Chapter 16
Gene Hackman in *The Conversation*

Brenda Austin-Smith

> The screen performer is essentially not an actor at all; he *is* the subject of study, and a study not his own. (Stanley Cavell, *The World Viewed*)
>
> All within me became narrowed to my lot. (Charlotte Brontë, *Villette*)

Gene Hackman was well into his forties when he took on the role of Harry Caul in Francis Ford Coppola's *The Conversation*. Hackman wasn't the director's first choice, Marlon Brando having turned down the part beforehand, but brought with him the buzz of a break-out performance as Buck Barrow in *Bonnie and Clyde* (1967) and an Oscar for his turn as Popeye Doyle in *The French Connection* (1971). In a podcast interview about *The Conversation*'s production, Coppola recalls that Hackman was anxious to get involved with the project after seeing the success of *The Godfather*, but also describes the actor's obvious misery as he adopted the persona of Harry Caul along with the character's translucent raincoat.

Coppola remembers Hackman as an affable man who retreated so completely into the loneliness and suspicion of the tormented wire tapper that he was difficult to be around on the set. Only when work concluded for the day would the gregarious and charming Hackman re-emerge. Coppola has said that he suspects Hackman to have been much more like Harry than Hackman himself was willing to admit, and that inhabiting the role was difficult for the actor because the character's unpleasantness was so familiar to him.

Coppola was also worried that Harry, the taciturn surveillance expert at the heart of the story, was too off-putting a protagonist to draw and hold the sympathy of viewers, no matter who played him. The part was certainly unusual given Gene Hackman's best-known roles, in which the depiction of good-natured cluelessness or the indulgence of lanky charisma kept audience interest tethered to a character. Buck Barrow was a knee-slapping good ole' boy, too unreflective to be despised for going along with his brother. Popeye Doyle is corrupt and monomaniacal, but also attractively violent in his pursuit of Fernando Rey's Charnier. If he nearly runs people over, at least he does so for the right reasons. Harry Caul is a harder sell. He is almost pathologically withdrawn, unavailable even to those who wish him well, like his assistant Stanley (John Cazale). The greatness of Hackman's portrayal of Harry is that in a thespian quest for the tiniest of moral qualms he rides the character up to the edge of viewer repulsion. To explore Harry Caul's clotted soul seems the artistic equivalent of plunging into the depths of a murky retention pond in hopes of surfacing with a small piece of not entirely corroded tin in hand. Nevertheless, Hackman's incarnation of Harry makes him an object of viewer pity through a performance that extracts layered uneasiness and belated regret from the actor's stymied physical confidence. Hackman creates an accidental protagonist from a character outflanked by those who, unlike him, intend completely the murderous results of their calculations.

We first catch sight of Hackman in the virtuoso sequence set in San Francisco's Union Square that fronts the film. As the soundtrack burbles and cracks, indicating the break-up of the aural signals received by the surveillance team operating under Harry's direction, a performing mime in the lunchtime crowd moves to position himself next to a man holding a coffee cup and standing in a short line of onlookers. The telescopic lens leans out and down, as the man we soon learn is Harry turns his head slightly to the right, realizes that his movements are being imitated by the mime, and then looks ahead again before dropping his head to look at the ground. Hackman begins to walk away from the mime, his steps at first slow, feigning nonchalance, but then gaining in purpose as he angles in front of the performer, trying to create a discouraging distance between them without drawing attention to his wish to escape the mime's attention. The mime, though, has latched onto Harry, and we see Harry's uncaring façade begin to shade into irritation as Hackman's pace increases slightly, and his facial expression becomes harder, even from this distance. As he walks, Hackman moves his head several times to look over and back at the mime in an awkward tell, the way someone might look in a rearview mirror at a tailing car, even though it betrays his unease to the ones who follow. Gene Hackman is a tall man, but the flattening effect of the telescoped shot foreshortens him, diminishing the impression of his height, and reducing the dominance of Harry as a noticeable figure in the landscape of the frame. In a few moments, as the zoom shot slowly but steadily narrows its gaze, Hackman's movements lay the foundation for a character who can't escape the wrong eyes, and who can't stop himself from checking to see if he is, indeed, being watched. With the heels of his shoes angled ever so subtly together, creating a gait that propels him slightly from side to side rather than smoothly forward, Harry's discomfort at being the center of attention somehow works to make his self-consciousness the most riveting element of the shot.

David Edelstein has described Hackman's acting in terms of "nervy greatness," documenting the actor's ability to call upon reserves of anger and histories of rejection in his performances. In another profile by Richard Meryman in *Vanity Fair*, Hackman talks specifically about seeing his father give a curt wave of the hand before driving off in a car, abandoning the family and leaving Hackman, aged thirteen, watching from the street: "It was a real adios. It was so precise. Maybe that's why I became an actor. I doubt I would have become so sensitive to human behavior if that hadn't happened to me as a child—if I hadn't realized how much one small gesture can mean" (www.vanityfair.com/news/2004/03/gene-hackman-dustin-hoffman-hollywood). Hackman's mastery of the small gesture is unmatched by anyone else in this film. He operates for much of the time on a reduced scale—from small to miniscule—to convey the touchiness, vanity, and inner bleakness that constitute Harry's emotional life, with very few moments of the explosive physicality he demonstrated in films like *The French Connection*.

Two early scenes give viewers excellent instances of Hackman's close work. The first takes place in the surveillance van to which Harry makes his way after the opening sequence of the film in Union Square. After climbing in and taking a seat opposite Stanley, Harry asks how the operation is going, and hears that while one of the directed camera mikes is picking up "better than forty percent," the second position mike is "not so good." Hackman's response to the line is to turn to look silently out of the side of the van. With his elbows on the counter, he bounces his clasped hands rapidly against his face, his thumbs pressed under his nose and up against his mouth in a sign of anxiety and impatience, as if willing the microphones to catch more of what they're after. Harry Caul is an economical figure not given to unnecessary verbal or physical demonstrations. Hackman's show of agitation is the first sign to us that this is a very important job, with high reputational as well as financial stakes. A few moments later, Stanley muses on the nature of the conversation the team is recording, speculating that their client is "the Infernal Revenue" and complaining that the tapes always put him to sleep. "Since when are you here to be entertained?" asks Harry, every inch the demanding boss. Replying to Stanley's confession that sometimes he wishes he knew what the targets were talking about, Harry replies, half to himself and half to Stanley, while still gazing into the space outside the left side of the frame, "I don't care what they're talking about. All I want is a nice, fat recording." Hackman's stress on the word "fat" gives mass and density to the immateriality of sound, as yet unconfined to the reels of tape he will play and replay in his workshop. Hackman might as well be expressing Harry's craving for a richly marbled steak, so intense and specific is the articulation of the character's sonic gluttony, his impossibly perverse desire to sink his teeth into voices.

We see a second early example of Hackman's fluency in revelatory gesture and intonation when, dressed rather formally (as he always is for work), Harry arrives in his warehouse workshop the next day, where Stanley is already waiting, passing the time by reading an issue of the trade magazine *Security World*. As Hackman crosses the space from the freight elevator to the workroom, we hear Stanley call out to him in greeting. Harry enters the room from the right side of the frame and as he removes his coat, says "Morning" to Stanley, who sits behind him. "There's an article in here about the convention that mentions your name," says Stanley, as Harry says "Oh yeah?" and finishes hanging up his coat. "You're one of the notables that's going tomorrow night. Did you know that?" In the time it takes Hackman to pivot toward John Cazale, hear the line, and cross over to the workbench, Hackman brings his left hand up to the back of his head to smooth his hair, touches the front of his neck briefly, and runs his hand down the front of his sports jacket. Several of Harry's traits, his fastidiousness, his competitiveness, and his need for a certain kind of attention, are captured at once here. He straightens out any wrinkles in his jacket that might have been caused by his raincoat, and is now ready for work. He is also preening at the sound of the word "notables," grooming himself for an appearance before an imaginary crowd of impressed peers. As he reaches the other side of the room, having responded to Cazale—"Yeah, I told them I'd be there"—Hackman touches his right shirt cuff with his left hand, straightening it out. Of course Harry already knew about the story, having provided the magazine with the material for it beforehand. He is way ahead of Stanley, and can't resist congratulating himself on his cleverness. The swift delicacy of Hackman's movements wraps satisfaction and pride up into one smooth gestural package even as he reaches for the tape machines, ready to begin his day listening.

Harry is thin-skinned in all ways it seems, easy to flatter and to insult, as we see in Hackman's bristly reaction to hearing that a self-styled rival (played by Allen Garfield) will also be visiting the much anticipated spy convention: "Since when is William P. Moran pre-eminent in the field?" He is egotistical, manipulative, and thoroughly off-putting to those around him. Making this petty character worthy of our curiosity and our empathy, is the task Hackman undertakes in the rest of the film, balancing Harry's loneliness and emerging fear for the safety of the young woman he has been hired to spy on, against his moral weakness and marrow-deep suspicion of others. In interviews, Hackman has referred to Harry Caul as "constipated," which captures the peculiar pain Hackman's face telegraphs whenever Harry is called upon to express an immediate and unregulated emotion. We see it in his mouth when he registers a microscopic flinch at finally hearing the defining line of dialogue—"He'd kill us if he got the chance"—that he has mined from the surveillance recording. So clenched has he been for so long, that even when he wants to, he cannot relax and let anything go.

Harry Caul is a lonely man, and the film's compositions often place Hackman in isolated circumstances, or distinguish him from others in ways that stress his character's loner condition. One of the most poignant sequences of the film depicts Harry on a trolley bus after his girlfriend

Amy (Teri Garr) tells him she no longer wants to see him. Hackman is the only person we see on the streetcar, and as he sits alone, looking into space, the pole of the streetcar loses its connection to the power line, and the car falls into darkness as Hackman's head drops forward and down in what could be despair, a reverie, or fatigue. It takes a few seconds for Harry to be roused from his thoughts and respond to the stall, and we can barely make Hackman's features out, so completely has he merged with his surroundings. The effacement the actor achieves in such a scene, effectively stifling his natural physical twitchiness, is a remarkable effort of curtailment. Similarly, a long shot of Hackman stepping carefully over disused train tracks on the way to the warehouse workshop conveys Harry's habitual meticulousness, as well as his status as someone who labours in urban spaces largely abandoned by others. When he returns to his apartment after the surveillance operation in Union Square, we can see and hear demolition equipment at work outside the window. In moments like these, Hackman conjures someone who occupies a figurative as well as a literal place on the outskirts of things, on the edge of what is barely structured. The next step, suggests the mise-en-scène, is at best a complete evacuation of selfhood, and at worst, disintegration and rubble.

For all the evidence of personal solitude provided by his story here, Harry Caul does experience close connections, just not with people. His saxophone, his recording equipment, and the small figure of the Virgin Mary that stands on his bookshelf, are arguably his most intimate companions, which means that Hackman is often in a shot or scene all by himself, with no other performer from whom or with whom to build rapport or calibrate a response. Steven Peacock's study of contemporary Hollywood film argues that while intimacy is "occasionally alluded to in Film Studies, it has been overlooked as a connective aspect of mise-en-scène" (5). While it is often discussed as an element of engagement between viewer and character, or as a "marker" of genre (5), intimacy emanates from the "depth of integration" of cinematic elements, including performance, he writes (9). Although the films examined by Peacock are more recent than *The Conversation*, the attention to gesture and décor he champions in his readings justifies the description of Harry Caul's relationship to certain objects in the film in terms of emotional intimacy that shades into protectiveness, and then into vindictiveness, as when he smashes the statue of the Virgin Mary near the film's conclusion in a metaphoric lashing out at Ann, the woman under surveillance (Cindy Williams). The one object never subjected to Harry's lacerating suspicion is his saxophone. That Harry would play along to pre-recorded music in the solitude of his living room at night is in keeping with the character's thoroughly anti-social tendencies. But it is the revelation of Harry's love for music, and his skill at, of all things, improvisation, that softens him. And it is when Hackman sits close to the camera, shirt open slightly, tie loosened, and eyes closed, that he makes Harry's privacy available for us to study in the intensity and pleasure registered in his face. As Hackman comes to the end of Harry's solo, he bows his head, hands resting lightly against the instrument, counting beats as he listens to the recorded applause, absorbed in the closest thing to belonging that we see Harry experience.

Hackman's portrayal of Harry's capacity for attachment to things at first emphasizes the character's professional focus. Soon after Harry returns to the surveillance van early in the film, Paul, a cop he has hired to moonlight on the job, is spotted by one of the targets. The operation is now effectively over, and Paul joins Harry in the van to turn over his tape and pick up his money. While Paul and Stan exchange jokes about the great time they all had a couple of years ago at the last trade convention, Harry says nothing. Hackman keeps his attention glued to the tape recorder handed to him; he is oblivious to the banter, concerned only with retrieving the machine and its auditory booty. When Harry begins the task of mixing the final recording from his three source tapes, he anchors his attention by pinning photographs of the two targets, Ann and Mark, to a ledge above the counter. Hackman's gaze returns to this picture over and over again as he rewinds and plays the tapes, the voices of the lovers from Union Square now drifting and echoing through the empty spaces of his loft. Soon, however, a corner of the photograph curls in on itself, conveniently obscuring the face of Ann's lover, Mark, and leaving no one in the frame for Harry to compete with as he looks at her.

The effect of all those hours listening to Ann's voice is not clear to us though, until Harry makes his first visit to the offices of the Corporation to deliver the tapes to his client, the Director (Robert Duvall). Hackman's stance and demeanour in this scene communicate Harry's visceral discomfort with situations outside of his apartment, his van, and his workshop. In his home territory, he deals with emanations of people, rather than people themselves, through telephones, earphones, and photographs. Their liveliness and unpredictability can be managed without proximity. In the presence of the Director's assistant Martin

Stett (Harrison Ford), Harry's distrust is palpable. When Stett leaves the frame momentarily, Hackman fills the space with uneasy business. Looking unnervingly like Mr. Hulot in *Play Time* (1968), Hackman picks up one of the cookies on Stett's desk and sniffs at it suspiciously. He then bends over, back to the camera, to look through a telescope aimed out of the window of the high-rise building, as if unable to pass up any instrument contrived to offer someone a view. It is not until Stett returns and casually tosses an envelope of cash on the settee, picking up the folder containing the tapes as he does so, that Harry's distrust of the exchange fully blossoms. Hackman is alertly thoughtful as he sits for a moment on the office settee, contemplating the money, radiating both Harry's discomfort at handing his tapes over to someone else and his dislike of Stett's unctuousness. Hackman stands, moves to Stett's desk, and with one hand returns an uneaten cookie to the dish of treats while with the other he returns the money and picks up the folder, using bad manners as a feint to mask taking back the tapes. We think for a moment that the move is unnecessary until Stett stands up suddenly and grabs at the folder. The struggle between the two men over the plastic file is absurd enough to be almost comic, until Stett warns Harry that the tapes are dangerous, that someone might get hurt. Hackman's tight hold on the file seems more instinctive than fully intentional in the first few seconds of their confrontation, but solidifies as he wrests the object from Ford's grip, as if besting a would-be child snatcher. As the two wordlessly contend over the folder of tape recordings, Hackman faces the camera with an expression of muted shock, overtaken immediately by barely suppressed anger, before settling into determined blankness, the expression of choice for a character terrified of giving anything away.

In a 2015 profile of Hackman in *Grantland*, Steven Hyden zeroes in on the "jocular forms of misdirection" Hackman has perfected over the years, pointing to his trademark "heh-heh," a sound that conveys the absence of the good humour it should otherwise indicate (www.grantland.com/Hollywood-prospectus/the-greatest-living-american-actor-at-85-gene-hackman-is-gone-but-still-in-charge). Hackman's characters are never less amused, less mollified or disarmed, than when they laugh, and there are plenty of tight smiles and fake laughs in *The Conversation*. But what is more intriguing is when the lava-like reserves of Harry Caul's unexpressed anger exert their forces more directly against Hackman's falsely jovial surface. Even in his portrayal of the careful, cautious Harry, there are moments toward the end of the film when Hackman taps into the emotional volatility he is known for in other work. These eruptions of anger and hostility seem to well up in Harry out of nowhere, and appear completely out of proportion to the circumstances that trigger him to rage. In these scenes Hackman's coiled-up physical energy emerges from under wraps in a convulsive wave: he hurls a garbage can across a warehouse floor, snaps a bugged ball-point in two, swears at a visitor after realizing she has filched the tapes, and after initial hesitation, brings a paperweight down again and again on the body of the small, plastic Virgin Mary before ripping it apart with his hands in his search for the microphone someone has hidden in his apartment. The fury Hackman brings to these scenes endows Harry with a reassuring immediacy and force of response, at the same time that it indicates his impending personal implosion. Even as his unleashing of it makes him recognizably human, we are horrified at the amount of venom he has harbored for so long, never showing rage at the time he felt it, continually undone at the prospect of being undone.

Looking for a through line in Hackman's work, Hyden finds that his "filmography unfolds as a treatise on how authority is established, then corrupted, then dissolved." Harry's corruption began years ago, as Moran tauntingly reminds him, when he turned in other tapes that resulted in the deaths of three people. The character dissolution traced in this film is delayed, and perhaps even deserved. That it is in some way mourned is a credit to Hackman. His ebullience muffled, his glad-handedness thwarted, the actor taps a private, perhaps even contrived, history of slights and resentments in order to animate the pocked inner life of Harry Caul.

The achievement of his performance is that Hackman gives Harry's slow emergence into the realms of feeling its conflicted due. If we believe for a moment that Harry responds, even in a stunted way, to the appeal of Ann's voice on the tape unspooling in his bleak, industrial workshop, it is because Gene Hackman creates a moving sense of the space that Harry's loneliness, rage, bitterness, and guilt could take up if those emotions were fully exercised and committed to in the name of something or someone else. Hackman shows us the distance between Harry's potential for outrage, for sabotage, even for sacrifice, and what the character is actually capable of, which is so much less than any of these. To watch Harry toss away the envelope of money he believes someone is going to die for, and then to see him pause, turn back, and grab fistfuls of it from the ground, is to witness a man who knows and despises his own cravenness, even as he enacts it. That we can, at the end of *The Conversation*, be afraid that there is still something for such a character to lose, and not want it to be taken away, is an abiding tribute to the actor who plays him.

Works cited

Cavell, Stanley. *The World Viewed: Reflections on the Ontology of Film*. Cambridge, MA: Harvard University Press, 1979.

Meryman, Richard. "Before They Were Kings," *Vanity Fair* 523 (2004), 276.

Peacock, Steven. *Hollywood and Intimacy: Style, Moments, Magnificence*. New York: Palgrave Macmillan, 2012.

Chapter 17

Gena Rowlands in *Gloria*

David Greven

Directed and written by John Cassavetes, *Gloria* (1980) stars Gena Rowlands, the wife of the director and recurring star of his films. Given that this is an essay on Rowlands's performance, I will not dwell on the film's production history or on Cassavetes's consistently indifferent public stance toward it except to say this: since he claimed he did the picture for purely commercial reasons so that he could make the kinds of films he believed in, and since he had no intention of directing his screenplay until Rowlands, for whom he'd written the title role, asked him to do so, it might seem odd that I think it's his best film. Liking *Gloria*, certainly valuing it over Cassavetes's other work, seems like anathema for several reasons, not the least of which is that such an estimation presumably capitulates to a mass-critical, mass-audience response, joining in with normative tastes to celebrate an accessible work by a difficult, unconventional filmmaker whose movies frequently alienated audiences. Then again, despite more than usual critical acclaim at the time and Rowlands's Oscar nomination for Best Actress, the film still failed to do well at the box office and remains a seeming anomaly in Cassavetes's career.

While the case for Cassavetes's filmmaking stature is still controversial, the case for *Gloria* as a lesser work in the maverick actor-director's oeuvre seems to be a decided one. David Thomson's view of the Rowlands-Cassavetes relationship encapsulates some ongoing critical tensions:

> Gena Rowlands was a virtuoso in *A Woman Under the Influence*, but the grueling domestic scenes of that movie showed how far a camera confused the director's adoration of a pressurized performance. Rowlands is a test case of the Cassavetes approach. Was she a great actress, a prisoner in her husband's films, or the chief recipient of Cassavetes's assumption that performance was the heartfelt metaphor for life? He believed in an actor's burrowing into a role as almost a behavioral credential. Gena Rowlands is so moving and pathetic in *A Woman Under the Influence*, yet I'm not sure that her part actually deserves a movie. Or is a movie. Doesn't it seem more like an endless actor's improvisation? Then consider that Cassavetes wrote and contrived such things. *Gloria* feels not like life but a deliberate remaking of an old movie in rehearsal. (117)

While I share some of Thomson's reservations, I hold the opposite view of *Gloria* and Rowlands's performance in it.

What's particularly salient for me as I write this chapter is my impression of Rowlands's work here and in relation to her other performances. I have admired and responded to her consistently fine, intelligent work in a number of cinematic and television projects. No matter how many performances of hers I see and appreciate anew, it's always her acting in *Gloria* that particularly draws me in and rivets me. Not to denigrate her other performances in the least, especially in television films such as the 1979 *Strangers: The Story of a Mother and Daughter*, in which she co-starred with Bette Davis, and *An Early Frost* (1985), in which she plays the mother of a gay man (Aidan Quinn) dying of AIDS, I consider her performance in *Gloria* the one where she accesses the fullest range of her gifts and connects most deeply with the audience—which also holds true for Cassavetes's work here.

Rowlands's unlikely heroine Gloria Swenson, modeled it is said on Gloria Swanson, is a former gun moll and showgirl now middle-aged and living in the South Bronx. She happens to knock on the door of her friend and neighbor Jeri Dawn's (Julie Carmen) apartment at an inopportune time. The Dawn family is imperiled. The hapless paterfamilias, Jack (Buck Henry), works as an accountant for the mob and has been exposed as an FBI informant, having said, aloud, and in reference to a small black account book with secret information about the mob's finances, "I have it written down somewhere." Jeri begs Gloria to take the two kids, their teenage daughter Joanie (Jessica Castillo) and their young son Phil (John Adames); reluctantly, Gloria agrees to do so, but Joanie, whimpering and running to her room, refuses to go with them. Gloria and Phil, a most unwilling rescuee, go back to Gloria's apartment, Phil constantly trying to get back home. A short time later, the gangsters assigned to the job murder the Dawn family. Missing Phil and the precious book he clutches at his father's instruction, the mob men now go on a hunt for Gloria and the boy. The next morning, a news broadcast identifies Gloria as Phil's abductor, letting the mob know her involvement, if they haven't already figured it out.

Cassavetes introduces Rowlands/Gloria in the most offhanded way imaginable, by way of the peephole the sweaty, neurotic Jack looks through when he hears a knock at his door. "It's Gloria," he says, in a tone both irritated and befuddled. We see Gloria through Jack's point of view, an unglamorous woman in a housecoat. But even here, in this unflattering distorted shot, Gloria has something about her, a distinctiveness that lies in her insolent indifference to any social niceties. Let into the apartment, she brusquely and cheerfully announces, "Ran outta coffee." When the distraught but intent Jeri begins to explain the dire situation, she responds, with hilarious understatement, "I think I came at a bad time." Phil establishes his quirkily adamant, impatient, and frequently humorous child-tyrant persona right away in response. "You did! You came at a bad time. You came at a *terrible* time!" Gloria responds only to the boy's mother: "Jeri, you know I'd do anything for you. But I don't like kids. I hate kids. Especially yours." With amazing precision and economy, all that we need to know about this odd, ill-timed neighbor's suitability for her role as Phil's protector is conveyed to us in Gloria's first scene. The somewhat frowzy woman in the tan housecoat seems like one of those tough I-mind-my-own-business-so-please-mind-yours types one associates with the curt but also easygoing working-class milieu of New York City. When Gloria takes Phil back to her apartment, she hands him her cat, implying that she's that other stock urban type, the solitary cat lady. But even this gesture and the manner in which she interacts with the cat upend the associations of the stereotype. Picking up the handsome feline, Gloria says, "That's my boy" in a manner that suggests something of the tone she might have used to palliate tough mob men in her youth. She asks Phil if he likes cats and would like to hold this one, a beast that in terms of scale seems almost as large as he is. Gloria plops the animal unceremoniously in his hands, which are not quite big enough to catch the cat, almost as if she were trying to knock the child out for a while.

Much of the strategy in both Cassavetes's and Rowlands's presentation of the character in these early scenes is to present Gloria in an unsentimental and unvarnished way and not to associate her with conventional maternal warmth or incipient maternal longing. But it doesn't take viewers long to realize that Gloria is a passionate, fiery woman who comfortably hid herself in that unassuming housecoat. The chief possessions she fusses over and packs, as she gets ready to flee her apartment with Phil after the mob assassination of his family, are her clothes, all in dry-cleaning bags. And although she wears a different outfit in every scene while outdoors, Gloria leaves the bulk of her outfits behind as she and Phil flee to Manhattan. Indeed, perhaps the most acute link between Rowlands's Gloria and the classical Hollywood women stars emulated here—especially Marlene Dietrich (with whom Rowlands is said to be fascinated) but many others as well—is her clotheshorse aplomb, a series of scintillating though always plausible outfits that exquisitely match and mirror her every mood and situation. (The costume designers for the film were Peggy Farrell and Emanuel Ungaro.) The outfits are not so much high-fashion as they are Gloria's fashion. One could imagine some viewers finding the outfits tacky or cheap, faux-elegant; but on Rowlands/Gloria they exquisitely and appositely suit her.

As Gloria, Rowlands comes across as a mixture of Barbara Stanwyck in *Stella Dallas* (1937) and Dietrich in *Destry Rides Again* (1939), with Bette Davis in *Marked Woman* (1937) another central muse. Rowlands has frequently discussed her admiration for Davis, with whom she worked in the television film *Strangers*. Although it may seem odd as a point of comparison, Rowlands's portrayal of Gloria echoes Davis's performance in *What Ever Happened to Baby Jane?* (1962). There's a certain animal primacy that expresses itself through hair, gait, makeup, and costume, however distinctly maintained and intended, that links Gloria and Baby Jane—two feral, highly particularized portrayals. And Rowlands has something else down, that richly recalls Davis: a determined, distinctive "Gloria" gait. Part of what makes her performance classic is Rowlands's remarkable ability to provide and harness a wide array of affects. First, Gloria is darkly, subtly funny in an impatient, New Yorker manner, especially when she deals with the pesky, adamant, oddly touching Phil. "You are *not* the man," she gently reprimands him, wiping off his bloody nose with her fingers, a raw, gentle, intimate gesture. Phil has just been exploding at Gloria, hurling out the words his father, on the verge of being killed, imparted to him: "*I* am the man. You, you're not the man. I am the man. I do anything I can. *I* am the man!" Part of the appealingly unsentimental aspect of the movie is just how brusquely and indifferently Gloria treats Phil much of the time while always looking out for him and frequently risking her own life to do so, as the mobsters menace and stalk them relentlessly. (Cassavetes strove with young Adames to create a child presence that would be the antithesis of the usual Hollywood sentimental one.) A great deal of attention and care is paid to the visual framing and negotiation of the adult body and the child body. Posed against a nighttime window, Gloria stands with Phil comforting her by embracing her at the waist in one scene. Rowlands keeps her body held-in, rigid, yet she allows the embrace.

In one of the several bravura sequences of the film, Gloria and Phil, leaving her friend's apartment in Manhattan (to which they first fled after the shootings in the South Bronx) are confronted there by the mobsters. This entire passage is an extended series of parries between Rowlands and Adames performing an oddball, incommensurate version of Hepburn and Tracy. Phil appears to have fled, since he ran out while Gloria was in the shower to check out the story of his family's fate in a newspaper; Gloria hears the news broadcast identifying her as Phil's abductor. The way Rowlands plays the brief scene of Gloria listening to the news is one of the small, defining touches in her interpretation: instead of looking alarmed or angry, she looks amused, if somewhat pained. Gloria steps out of the apartment to find Phil in the hallway, obviously troubled but also defiant, announcing to her, "I'm not going with you." Gloria is having none of this, saying she doesn't have the time for his histrionics, which leads to his, "You're not the man, I'm the man" tirade. The conversation moves to the stairs, Phil plopped down, still defiant but defeated, Gloria wiping blood from his nose as she reprimands him. On her line, "You are driving me crazy," the mobsters appear, knocking at the apartment door, and she immediately switches into high-alert stealth mode. Rowlands conveys all of this wordlessly, through physical movements. She eases off her signature high heels, one at a time, and grabs Phil, about to go down the next flight of stairs, only to be surprised by the ascending presence of another mobster. (The feral grace of her legs arching out to allow shoe-removal is worth an essay itself!) She turns around, holding her bag and heels in one hand and Phil in the other, and ascends the previous flight of stairs to hide behind a small corridor with Phil, as the mobsters come perilously close to discovering them. In *A Woman Under the Influence* (1974), Rowlands's first Oscar-nominated role for Cassavetes, her alcoholic, mentally ill Mabel Longhetti flailed about, too much in your face (much like Cassavetes's direction); in *Gloria*, Rowlands keeps her body astonishingly controlled, compact within the frame. As she slithers up and down stairs with Phil and her accoutrements, she maintains a corporeal economy and precision even as she conveys—effortlessly, primally—the controlled terror of the situation. So much of this terror is offhand, subtle: the mob men move lackadaisically and implacably, and when they notice her, they call out to her in pseudo-friendly, casual terms, conveying the friendly demeanor of former acquaintances even if they're about to kill the boy and her as well.

The sequence continues out into the street, with another confrontation between Gloria and Phil, but one that reverses the terms of the spat they just had. Now, she announces that she cannot take care of him anymore, that he should run back home and seek out relatives to take care of him. Adames's performance has been controversial in the eyes of many (the poor child was disgraced with a Razzie the year the film was released), but he contributes greatly to the enduring and astonishing freshness and vivacity of the film. As Gloria tells him to leave her alone and go away, a scene that evokes fairy tales and grim abandonments of children, Adames wordlessly, almost animalistically, grabs at Gloria, holding on literally for dear life. One especially interesting dimension of Rowlands's performance here is her ability to make the character's shifting thoughts lucid. Speaking to herself, into the air, Gloria remarks "What am I doing here?" In some invisible but palpable way, her thinking shifts, and she announces forthrightly, "That's *it*," her shoulders moving up and down as if locking into defiant position, and from here she attempts to lose Phil. She is still negotiating with him as he adamantly refuses to leave her side when, in an almost aleatory fashion, the mobsters drive across the street, make a U-turn, and pull up in front of them. There is no time for the woman and child to think, much less flee.

When the mobster in charge of this particular group addresses Gloria from the front seat, his tones and language bespeak a casual, if irritated, attitude toward the whole inconvenient business. Killing Phil is just business, after all, with no sadistic intent involved, a message Gloria has apparently failed to get, which must be why she's being so obstructive. "Gloria, we're not interested in you. All we want is the book and the kid. You understand? We'll take care of that kid." Gloria's response confirms how well she knows her hunters: "Hey, Frank, what are you gonna do, shoot a six-year old Puerto Rican kid on the street? He don't know nothing. He can't even speak English." (Gloria frequently says this, in humorous contrast to Phil's hyperarticulate child-speech.) Frank (Frank Belgiorno) shakes his head, then silently turns to the backseat to get a gun, most likely to shoot them both. Again without a word, but with an immediacy that conveys instinctual shifts in thinking and action, she pulls out her own gun and steadily and unflinchingly shoots at the car, most certainly killing Frank and the driver; the car flips over. This stunning sequence concludes with a moment that alerts us to the non-realistic dimensions incorporated into the film's tableaux of gritty realism. After she's done shooting and the car has flipped, Gloria moves to hail a cab, yelling out, in full tough-New-Yorker mode, "Taxi!" Bill Conti's magnificent score, attuned to every seismic shift in the action and the emotions of the characters, revs back up on this line, making the entire moment stylized, florid, dramatic—in a word, operatic. The taxi pulls up, Gloria and Phil jump in, Gloria gives directions, and the cab driver says, "That looks like some accident," to which she responds, "We're not interested in accidents." When the cab driver fails to disengage from his rubbernecking, Gloria responds, "Are you deaf?" and he immediately speeds away.

Part of what distinguishes a great performance from a very good or even a brilliant one is a level of instinctive daring that unobstructively heightens it. That certainly defines Rowlands's work here. While there are many ways in which that daring comes through—her willingness to be brusque, insensitive, or dislikable—it's the actress's willingness to allow us to see Gloria as vulnerable, aged, defeated, and simply wearied that, perhaps most impressively, conveys her commitment to the role. Gloria's displays of anger and impatience are bracing, but the moments in which she's simply confused and desperate, or conveys a weariness over her situation, are most resonant. In a brief scene, Gloria and Phil are in one of the endless series of taxis and livery cars in which they ride throughout the movie. The visual palette is dark and mournful. Phil begins talking about his sadness: "I want to go home, Gloria." This is a striking moment for him and the young actor, too, given Phil's hyperverbal intensity and relentless energy. Gloria attempts to cheer him up: "Hey, think of something funny." When he says, "I can't," she responds undeterred, "*You?* You can't think of something funny? Hey, anybody says something funny to you, you practically split your blood vessels laughing." At this line he does smile, and Gloria smiles back: one of those smiles that seem like the deepest, warmest tokens of friendship. But then she rubs her forehead. Is it because her side of this interaction with the child is a performance, a job, more work than spontaneous fun? Is it because worry, the reality of their difficulties, has suddenly hit her? Or is it because she's simply tired? However one looks at it, this moment conveys and enriches the sense of Gloria's depths.

Similarly, in a brief scene on a bus, Gloria sees an older man, whom she identifies as her uncle (though this may be a facetious remark), and goes up to him. It would appear that she's seeking advice or comfort. That he's mob-related becomes clear when he immediately begins discussing her predicament and the mob's anger toward her for killing a lot of "good people." Again, with a plangent simplicity, Rowlands simply says of Phil, "His mother was a friend of mine." To which the "uncle" responds, "You've got to be out of your mind." Rowlands plays Gloria's response simply. She smiles, sadly, and then gets up and leaves. Her sad smile acknowledges the wisdom in the older man's statements while also conveying an underlying air of disappointment in his lack of empathy. But she won't punish him for it.

There are so many moments like this, in which Rowlands conveys depths of emotion and levels of response in a manner so offhand it achieves plangency. I'm going to focus on one more scene that I think conveys the greatness of her performance (and that of the film). Gloria's involvement with the mob stemmed from a relationship she had with Tanzini (Basilio Franchina), "Tony" as she names him, an Italian, Old-World, aging gentleman and a mob official. She decides that her only option is to meet him face to face, in his elegant and capacious apartment full of mafiosi and their staff, and give him the vital account book. In a lovely moment, she calls him up and they banter as if it's old times despite the deadly situation (she chuckles and smiles, "You got fat?").

In my view, *Gloria* is significant as a subtle and devastating feminist critique of Coppola's 1970s *Godfather* films, notwithstanding their status as masterpieces. It's an exploration of the woman's (and the child's) experience of a culture of masculine violence and rigid customs that produce, and depend on, this violence. When Gloria visits the mafia headquarters to meet with Tony, everything about this environment, for all of the menace clearly embedded there, is low-key, casual, harrowingly ordinary. A courtly dark-haired handsome young Italian attendant with a moustache and Old-World manners asks with great courtesy if she would like coffee while waiting for Tony. When Tony comes in, looking a bit Carlo Ponti-esque, tan and trim and with dark glasses, what is especially significant is that the former lovers do not embrace; he doesn't even kiss her on the cheek, walking past her seated form and sitting across from her. "Where is the child?" he begins, getting down to business right away. He assures her that "those weren't murders that we did," they were simply done to set an example (obviously, killing Phil will constitute a further one). With measured calm, Gloria affirms, "I understand." When he says that she must trust him, she responds, "Trust you? Tony, I know you." Every action and word is quiet and unruffled, even though she knows that her old, perhaps still loved boyfriend will most likely kill her or have her killed, and that there is nothing he will do to spare Phil's life. When Gloria says, "I know you" to Tony, Rowlands conveys a history of a relationship in a few rueful crinklings of her eyes and a bemused smile. But then she switches gears once again, probably as a ploy, perhaps because she wants a moment of connection for herself: "Hey, you got a minute? Smoke a cigarette with me." As they share a smoke, memory's weight presses down on the atmosphere. The two re-enact a scene that most likely occurred frequently between them, usually after lovemaking. In any event, it signals their former intimacy. But very little occurs between them, really, and certainly nothing changes. "Tell you what, Mr. T.," Gloria says, rising, as she leaves the book on the table, "I'm going to get up and walk out of here now. If you want to stop me, you can." What follows is one of the most acutely wounding, and deeply offhand, moments I've experienced in a movie. Tony rises, and speaks to his colleagues: "She's leaving." He has never had any intention of letting her walk out of there alive. The same courtly, dark-haired attendant with the moustache is the most aggressive and unrelenting of the henchmen who shoot into the elevator Gloria has miraculously managed to enter, before the doors close. (In the film's final scene, set in Pittsburgh, Gloria and Phil reunite at a cemetery. It is not clear whether this final scene is actually occurring or is a fantasy/dream sequence. It works exquisitely well either way one interprets it.)

V. I. Pudovkin notes of the actor's work and its composition from disintegrated pieces:

> The film actor is deprived of a consciousness of the uninterrupted development of the action, in his work. The organic connection between the consecutive parts of his work, as a result of which the distinct whole image is created, is not for him. The whole image of the actor is only to be conceived as a future appearance on the screen, subsequent to the editing of the director; that which the actor performs in front of the lens in each given piece is only raw material, and it is necessary to be endowed with special, specific, filmic powers in order to imagine oneself the whole edited image, meticulously composed of separate pieces picked sometimes from the beginning, sometimes from the middle. It is therefore understandable why it was from the first in films that there appeared exact directorial construction of the actor's work. (109–10)

Despite the adulation of critics such as Ray Carney, who has written numerous books on Cassavetes with the intention of establishing his greatness, Cassavetes remains a filmmaker whose oeuvre has hardly reached a critical consensus in terms of its aesthetic merits. Nevertheless, with Pudovkin's insights in mind, we can establish that Rowlands provides for *Gloria* far more than raw material to be reassembled, made a feat of the "directorial construction." She shapes the movie through her acting choices, which in *Gloria*, to my mind, indicate an actress at the height of her powers. Indeed, I would argue for the reverse of Pudovkin's position: Rowlands's ownership of a role she personally championed inspired Cassavetes's most inspired and controlled filmmaking; it was the core of *Gloria*, Cassavetes's directing being reshaped by *her*. Her performance in *A Woman Under the Influence*, for all of its memorable urgency, reflected a certain formlessness that is the limitation of Cassavetes's work, for all of its power. In *Gloria*, however, the actress provides the controlled, sustained depth of characterization that inspires, indeed demands, commensurate directorial effort.

In its range of affectional states and delicacy, its bringing together such distinct versions of a character's emotional life as Gloria oscillates from stone-faced Athena-like retributive force to salty, gruff, impatient survivor to tender, smiling confidante, Rowlands's performance is one of the great achievements in American cinema acting, lifting the film up to her level and inspiring the director's most controlled and yet fluid filmmaking. When Gloria single-handedly faces off against a group of mob henchman who have abducted Phil, who mistakenly believed they were his friends, she points a gun at them and Phil asks, "Gloria, what are you doing?" "Saving your life, stupid," she replies. A sustained immersion in *Gloria* amply reveals that Rowlands certainly knows what she's doing throughout her performance.

Works cited

Pudovkin, Vsevolod Illarionovich. *Film Technique and Film Acting, the Cinema Writings of V. I. Pudovkin*. New York: Lear, 1949.

Thomson, David. *A Biographical Dictionary of Film*. London: André Deutsch, 1994.

Chapter 18
Jack Nicholson in *The Passenger*
Rick Warner

With a few notable exceptions, studies of film performance have tended to give art cinema short shrift. By "art cinema"—an unavoidably fraught designation—I refer to an eclectic, global category of feature-length narrative films made and distributed at the periphery of the mainstream. Art cinema is perhaps best defined as an institutionalized practice that both converses with and critically deviates from the conventions of more overtly commercial cinema, generally through experiments with film form that entail much greater ambiguity, that stress aesthetics as much as the plot, and that tend to embrace slower, more ruminative tempos within and between scenes.[1]

In performance studies there is often an unspoken assumption on the part of the critic that the work of an actor is more salient, more interesting, and more favorable to analysis when it occurs firmly within the parameters of mainstream narrative cinema.[2] Even when scholarly discussions attend to a wider and more varied range of dramatic systems, there is still a prevalent tendency to demote art cinema on the grounds that it insufficiently invests in character and relegates the performer to a mere component of form at the behest of a director—often an auteur—whose expressive enterprise comes first. For instance, in *Reframing Screen Performance*, Cynthia Baron and Sharon Marie Carnicke single out the art cinema of Michelangelo Antonioni as espousing a formalist method that of necessity "delimits actors' evocative gestures and expressions in order to use them as graphic elements" (38–9). According to this frequently rehearsed view, the Italian director imposes a style in which performance is pared down and all but nullified, its pathways of spectator investment blocked.

In my view, it is this ingrained critical perspective—not simply Antonioni's style of filmmaking—that tends to obscure the work of the actor in his art cinema, rendering it less legible and vital within a given film. Jack Nicholson's subtly powerful performance in Antonioni's *The Passenger [Professione: Reporter]* (1975) warrants careful examination precisely because of the delicate ways in which it denies such a weighted and convenient distinction between character-driven, actor-centered cinema on the one hand and modernist art cinema on the other. Commentators have tended to praise Nicholson's performance insofar as he makes himself a malleable substance in the hands of a visionary director and incurs a degree of risk uncommon for a major Hollywood star. My purpose in what follows is to venture a more focused and incisive appraisal of Nicholson's contribution—what he brings to the creation of a character suffering from an identity crisis, and how he nimbly embodies the film's irregular moods and contemplative rhythms.

Public remarks that Nicholson and Antonioni have both made about the nature of their rapport would seem to discourage this line of inquiry. Where the actor speaks of no "give and take" (McGilligan 282) in an aesthetic regime that perceives human figures as "moving space" (Walker 53), the director expresses a need to divest the star actor of his familiar quirks and mannerisms so as to sculpt an "imploded" performance (McGilligan 282). My argument will chiefly consider not the production history but the performative process on display in the completed work. What we are given to see, hear, and question in *The Passenger* carries out a project in which actor and auteur are in fact equally important, in a shared examination of the vagaries of selfhood. As I am going to show, the "implosion" that the film stages in its narrative of a burned-out news reporter hinges on Nicholson's versatility. His performance brings to the film a dynamic blend of curiosity, wit, humor, aimlessness, despair, and boredom that serves as a fulcrum for the film's dramatic and reflective aspirations.[3]

Unbecoming David Locke

It must be said that Nicholson's roles over the course of his career have repeatedly explored elemental questions of identity that follow from and challenge culturally constructed notions of masculinity. This is a vital part of his legacy as an actor who came to prominence during an era of American filmmaking in which the critical re-evaluation of male heroism tended to coincide with the impulse to sketch out a "post-classical" film style (Bingham 99–108; Elsaesser 225–35). Before *The Passenger*, Nicholson had already played an anti-heroic drifter in the midst of a crisis regarding his place in the world: Bobby Dupea in Bob Rafelson's *Five Easy Pieces* (1970), an aspiring concert pianist turned oil rigger who wavers between two equally enervating affiliations of class. That a gendered preoccupation with identity runs through Nicholson's oeuvre is smartly indicated in Candice Breitz's video installation *Him* (2008), which re-edits clips from a range of the actor's performances, from 1968 to 2008, on seven monitors set up in the formation of a group therapy circle. With uncanny continuity, his characters, despite their changes of age and wardrobe, are made to converse with each other on the basis of recurring anxieties, many of which stem from amorous conflicts with women. *Him* offers a minutely observed "linguistic and cinematographic concentrate" of the actor (Allen 74), surveying as it does the mental, emotional, and corporeal dimensions of his leading-man persona as it has enthralled audiences over time. In this gathering of Nicholsons, arrogance contends with frayed insecurities and teary confessions; vile misanthropy rubs shoulders with disarming tenderness and understanding; explosions of incensed hostility are offset by a charming sense of composure. We have, in short, a composite portrait not just of an individual actor's behavioral idiosyncrasies and antics but also, more generally, of a type of maleness that viewers have gravitated toward and readily identified with, its unsavory elements notwithstanding. At the same time, Breitz's installation shows that at its crux Nicholson's screen persona carries a certain disquiet concerning individuality itself. A clip from *The Passenger* appears early and incites a meditation on the fixtures of personality. "I used to be somebody else, but . . . I traded him in," admits Nicholson as David Locke, a journalist who indeed tries to become someone else.[4]

The Passenger follows Locke's impromptu odyssey away from the trappings and strictures of his middle-aged life: his occupation and colleagues, his attractive wife from whom he is already somewhat estranged, his possessions, his habitual behavior, his very name. After seeing the familiar roar of the MGM lion that starts the film, the spectator is plunged without bearings, without story details, into a rudimentary African village in the midst of a pinkish-tan desert. This arid, sweltering environment and the disorientation it induces in Locke touch off the process whereby he comes undone. And one can already discern a sense in which his unraveling corresponds to the stripping away of Nicholson's trademarks as a star. Our protagonist, upon being unable to free his Land Rover from the sand where it is stalled, falls to his knees, flails his arms, and cries out, "All right! I don't care!" The sentiment of concession pertains as much to Nicholson himself in that this brief "Jack-like" tantrum gives way to perhaps the least demonstrative role in his career.

His unstated aims apparently thwarted, Locke returns to his desert hotel and finds the fresh corpse of Robertson, an Englishman to whom, as it happens, he bears a striking resemblance. He switches the photographs in their passports, so as to fake his own death and assume this other man's identity, vocation, and travel schedule, not fully knowing at this stage that Robertson traffics arms to a resistance army in Chad. This scene stands as one of film's most impressive aesthetic achievements, from its delayed disclosure of the source of a sound recording of Locke and Robertson engaging in genial conversation, to Antonioni's roving camera and layered interplay between the past and present, between onscreen and offscreen business. Nicholson's no less remarkable feat is to execute the scene's physical and psychological demands with sinuous grace. While engrossed in the acts of switching photos and listening responsively to the taped discussion, the mood he conveys—unruffled, already committed to a decision whose basic entailments neither he nor we can know at this point—also correlates with Antonioni's formal maneuvers in the scene. More than once, the itinerant, searching camera takes cues from the direction and intensity of Locke's gaze around the room. Scarcely a Kuleshov effect that prohibits the actor's expressivity, this marked yet tenuous rapport between character and the director's style amounts to a kind of free-indirect discourse. That is to say, here and in other scenes, the film's loosened, unconventional syntax momentarily mingles the implied perspective and subjectivity of Locke with that of the auteur filmmaker, in and through a pensive and exploratory style that does not neatly denote where the one figure's inquisitive consciousness leaves off and the other's begins.

One such instance is when Locke looks up from the table and casts his eyes beyond the left border of the shot, prompting the camera to move in accordance. He nods in a way that reacts to the recording *and*, at least seemingly, gives the camera the go-ahead. In a single take, the camera slowly tracks leftward, across a bare white wall, and pans to focus on the terrace outside; after a brief silence, Robertson, as if revived from the dead, walks into the shot, soon followed by Locke, with both men now framed by the window within the composition as they stare out at the desert. Without an edit or signaled transition (except for a change in sonic tenor from the recording to their dialogue) we have in fact receded in time. The subtlety of this "glideback," as Seymour Chatman refers to it, owes in large measure to Antonioni's command of the film medium (195). But we would be remiss not to point out that this effect depends on Nicholson's ability to embody the disposition of a character who is mentally divided between multiple and intersecting timelines at once (Pomerance 206–10, 214–15), a character who is prone to flights of memory that seem to inflect his comportment whether Antonioni cuts to the past or not. If this particular scene inspires one to rewatch it looking for a concealed cut, this is doubtless because of the relaxed manner in which Locke resurfaces on the terrace, now suddenly wearing a short-sleeved plaid shirt whereas he was shirtless seconds earlier. Between the initial and latter parts of the shot, Nicholson, while out of view, has hurried around the other side of the wall and thrown on the garment, knotting it at the waist, but the character's return—his altered affect, his gentle walk—reads otherwise.

This oddly fluent, unbroken articulation of a shift in time works as it does because of the actor's craftiness. His performance suggests the movements of a mind situated both here in the now and there in the recent past, both here at the table and there on the terrace. His work thus conspires with and grounds the scene's stylistic ambiguity, its collision and confusion of temporal registers.

Behind the moustache

The Passenger revolves in a reflexive manner around the question of acting itself. Its plot loosely borrows a Hitchcockian theme of theatricality (Pomerance 208), and one way of interpreting Locke's never-explained decision to don the identity of Robertson is that he wants to become more of an agent, an actor, in the liberation struggle he can only observe in his job as reporter. Moreover, the film flirts with the premise that all identity is provisional, a matter of performance and mise-en-scène.

Nicholson's portrayal of Locke shores up this premise in some ways, but refutes it in others. While he plays a rootless, decentered man who flits between various markers of identity and belonging, none of which seem to stick (Rohdie 145), he communicates with equal force a sense of not being able to shed certain attributes of his character, his Locke-ness. This trope finds an intriguing parallel in Nicholson's against-type appearance in the film. Locke, the story insists, is English, but the ineffaceably American performer playing him makes this specification an absurd stretch. What is more, despite the film's concerted rarefaction of Nicholson's star image, he manages to smuggle in some of his recognizable tendencies as a performer.

Though commentators often associate Nicholson with the Method in one or more of its variations, his training under multiple teachers—to name a few, Jeff Corey, Martin Landau, and Lee Strasberg—was too multifarious to be attributed to a particular approach or school. He recalls that what he took from Strasberg wasn't a Stanislavskian credo rooted in the actor's incorporation of personal experiences, but the elastic principle "anything that works" (Crane and Fryer 18). If Nicholson displays extraordinary versatility within and across various genres, tones, and collaborative situations (Carnicke 47–54), one must also acknowledge his habit of weaving in gratuitous flashes of his singular charisma and personality—his star persona—regardless of his role, with a spirit of play that flies in the face of the tortured solemnity for which some Method devotees of his generation (Dustin Hoffman and Robert De Niro) became known. This habit reaches burlesque extremes in later works from *The Shining* (1980) to *The Departed* (2006), but it turns up as early as *Five Easy Pieces*.

For all its minimalist quiet, *The Passenger* is leavened by short-lived moments in which Nicholson's persona, as it had accumulated by 1975, shows through the part. It is tempting to read this as Nicholson's sly rebellion against his assignment, but a far more elaborate relationship comes into effect here between role and performer (and between auteur and actor). Peter Brunette has written that *The Passenger* stands out among other Antonioni films because of its tinges of comedy and lightness that issue directly from Nicholson's distinctive gifts as an actor (177). To be sure, if the film turns into a thriller of sorts once Locke becomes Robertson, it also indulges in erratic beats of restrained humor that serve to indicate Locke's partial and imperfect transformation.

Brunette rightly finds humor in a scene that occurs in a Rococo church in Munich. Locke, posing as Robertson, has an awkward meeting with his rebel clients, then checks the handsome payment he has received from them in an envelope and mutters to himself in surprise, "Jesus Christ!" Suddenly aware of his surroundings, he glances upward and gestures an obligatory apology, presumably to God.[5] This moment indeed tends to elicit laughter from audiences, but it only makes more palpable the comic undercurrent that is already in play. After all, the fake moustache he wears in the scene verges on absurdity, especially in its combination with Nicholson's furrowed forehead and arched eyebrows that cannot help but connote mischief. There are multiple shots in which his clients have their backs to us and his facial expressions form the centerpiece of the composition, as he improvises his way through the encounter, gauging his convincingness by their reactions. In a long-held medium shot, for instance, his eyes slink back and forth between the faces of the men on either side of him who have clearly already found his conduct a touch odd (he has missed the arranged rendezvous point). One could say he plays it cool were it not for the lack of concern in his bearing. He gives off not poise but self-amused listlessness. While he appears to enjoy courting danger, his performance as a seasoned and politicized gunrunner rings blatantly false.

Another moment of understated comedy occurs when Locke-as-Robertson phones Avis from a Munich bar to inform them of his new travel plans. "I'm going to Barcelona. That's right. For the rest of my life," he says, unmindful of that line's foreshadowing. No other scene in the film shows the protagonist in such high spirits, and Nicholson's charm is strongly manifest. Filmed from the chest up against a wall as the offscreen clinking of glasses forces him to raise his voice, Locke fidgets with his artificial moustache between lines and then spontaneously peels it off. After he hangs up the phone, he turns, discards his cigarette, and with great relish, puts the moustache on the spherical lamp next to him, rhythmically smoothing and tapping it into position on the imaginary face of the glowing orb. He then wipes off his hands and approvingly studies the little readymade he has just crafted. He spins and exits the frame on the opposite side, but not without a final flourish. Still in flowing rhythm with the previous actions, he contorts his face and, with his thumb and forefinger, wipes the glue from his upper lip.

This exquisite bit with the faux moustache has the feel of extemporaneity. At one level, it comes across as an actor's exercise in object transformation—one that Nicholson exploits for all its worth. And yet, the business he performs and the self-satisfaction that underlines it suit the dramatic purpose of the scene. Locke at this point has persuaded at least himself of his credibility as Robertson (despite the fact he has no way of getting his hands on the weapons he is meant to supply). The "disguise" of his former identity is, he thinks, no longer necessary, and the elation he embodies comes from his newfound sense of liberation. Of course, the clash of competing tones in the scene is such that his change of travel plans harbors foreboding implications. He will indeed be going to Spain for the remainder of his life, which is just a few more days. One detects this premonitory aspect more on a second viewing, but, as Chatman observes, Nicholson manages throughout the film to communicate the notion that somewhere in the recesses of his character's psyche, "liberation" and a death instinct are tightly bound (188–9). The scene therefore turns not on the sort of dramatic irony that puts the viewer a step ahead of the character, but instead on Locke's half-knowing self-destructiveness.

The motif of transparent playacting extends from the fiction to Nicholson himself, or rather, to the repeated performance traits that constitute his singularity onscreen. Even in an Antonioni film, he can only dial back his idiosyncrasies so far. Not unlike Locke, he cannot elude the substrate of his already formed personality. Later in the film, Nicholson-as-Locke sits smoking a cigarette in front of a roadside café somewhere in Spain and has a conversation with the architecture student (Maria Schneider) who soon becomes his lover and accomplice, a character identified only as "Girl" in the end credits. He takes off his aviator shades and confesses to his pretense, his flight from his old life: "Everything," he says, "except a few bad habits I couldn't get rid of." Filmed as they are in alternating singles, in soft natural light, they blithely consider alternative roles for him: a waiter in Gibraltar, a novelist in Cairo, a gunrunner. All the while one catches little flickers of the magnetism on display in Nicholson's earlier, less restrained performances. In close-ups that fall on his side of the shot/countershot exchanges, he squints against the sun and—in his nasal, unhurried, world-weary yet cocksure way of speaking—considers his predicament and attracts her interest in the process. Antonioni appears at once drawn to and circumspect of his male lead's work in this magnificently relaxed scene. When Nicholson-as-Locke responds to the Girl's approval of his arms dealer option, he grins and gently teases her in a way that his character from *Easy Rider* (1969) or Bobby Dupea (on a good day) might. For this shot, however, Antonioni cuts to a more distant view, so as to temper, yet keep in play, its seductive energy.

Suspense by other means

In the film's second half, Locke continues to follow Robertson's itinerary while evading contacts from his former life who have traveled to Spain in search of Robertson, namely his producer and Mrs. Locke, who, by this point, has caught on that her husband has switched the passport photos. Locke also has to slip the Spanish police (in a car chase), and, in the meantime, travels in tandem with the Girl, who appears, on a cynical reading, to be vaguely in cahoots with the Chadian government agents who are also on their trail. Murray Pomerance offers a different, more compelling view by persuasively arguing that she is Robertson's widow, the "Daisy" mentioned throughout the dead man's datebook (232). If a number of interpretive possibilities spiral around this character, the film manages to relentlessly suspend our capacity to know and confirm her true identity.

Antonioni's handling of these thriller elements empties them of the plot-centered, action-oriented excitement they work up in popular films, as does Nicholson's portrayal of Locke's returned malaise. Once the joy—the fantasy—of slipping his former identity wears off, severe apathy sets back in and his actions, thoughts, and motivations, if he has any, become even more opaque. Seeing that the comic touches fade, and that Nicholson's charisma as a performer grows fainter, it may seem as if Locke's submission to the death that lies in store for him stands in rough parallel to Nicholson's "implosion" for the needs of Antonioni's aesthetic system.

However, more of a negotiation between director and actor plays out in the film's expressive features. Scenes fluctuate in shot scale between wider, spacious compositions that privilege the environment over the human figure and tighter shots, relatively few of which draw nearer to the performer's face than medium close-ups. The wider shots serve not merely to displace the character from a position of significance or assert the camera's autonomy (though this does happen at times). Occasionally they bring to bear inquisitive attention on Locke's whole figure: his carriage, his movement through a given space, his way of walking into a room. While these wider shots amplify the viewer's consciousness of architecture, they also, more pointedly, stage the *interaction* of character and setting as a crucial index of Locke's improvised journey, his trial of a new life (Pallasmaa 116–23). Shots of Locke ambling through visually arresting environments hang in one's head both during and after the film—his spry descent of the concrete steps of the Brunswick Centre in London, its tiered ramparts looming overhead; his zigzagged path atop the vertiginous, Gaudí-designed Casa Milà in Barcelona.

Repeating a framing tendency from his earlier work, Antonioni films Nicholson-as-Locke from the back at several points, either up close or from afar, defining him as a spectator within the film and, thus, as our surrogate of sorts—a relationship that is more hinted at than confirmed. Nicholson's acting at these intervals bleeds together moods of desperation and boredom, curiosity and indifference. One such shot transpires late in the film as Locke, somewhere in rural Spain, must choose whether to head back to Northern Africa or press on to the hotel in Osuna, where Robertson has a mysterious appointment. In short, it is a decision whether to honor his original epiphany of assuming Robertson's name and vocation. The shot begins as Locke—shown from the back and from the waist up—strolls into the frame and inspects an anonymous passerby we see pushing a bicycle up a steep gravel path. Locke surveys the rocky terrain through his sunglasses, tucks one hand in his pants pocket, then swivels and heads languidly back to the convertible he has rented, the mobile frame tipping down to examine his feet. He walks in a circular pattern and slips offscreen for a moment, until the Girl moves over to the car, too. Sitting on the passenger side of the vehicle, he agrees, at her urging, to keep Robertson's meeting at the Hotel de la Gloria, but he does so with little sign of purpose, sparing himself the energy it would take to argue.

The circularity of his walk back to the car in this long take is subtly evocative. In graphic terms it prefigures the circular movement of the extremely long tracking shot that eventually shows Locke's dead body, lying on his hotel bed in the same supine position as Robertson's corpse in Chad. The circularity also echoes Locke's time-killing gesture of spinning his empty beer glass in a Barcelona café earlier in the film. These associated details do not reduce the actor and the character he inhabits to a purely formal scheme of lines, shapes, and surfaces. Instead, they are linked events in what must be understood as the film's restyling of suspense, which finds expression across equally balanced levels of film form and the actor's performance.[6]

In traditional thriller plots, suspense governs the spectator's affective investment through a rhythm of withholding that nonetheless augurs a future resolution. The film, it seems, knows full well where the drama is headed and how things will shake out, but, in the meantime, we are kept partly and pleasurably in the dark, with the assurance that we will be informed when the appropriate time comes. By contrast, Antonioni's "modernist variant" of suspense turns on "missing pieces" and unclear pauses that are keyed to "the hauntingly unknown" (Perez 368).

Recalcitrant uncertainty marks the film at most if not all turns, for the characters as well as for the spectator—even after multiple viewings. In Antonioni's art cinema, this kind of suspense famously involves *temps mort*, stretches of "dead time" where the pacing slows and nothing eventful seems to happen, at least not by the action-based standards of mainstream cinema. Of all the actors to dwell in Antonioni's filmic worlds, including talents such as Marcello Mastroianni, Jeanne Moreau, Richard Harris, and Monica Vitti, no one has adapted to the rhythm, feel, and temporality of the director's *temps mort* more astutely, more *resiliently*, than Nicholson. In fact, his low-key turn as Locke stands as a milestone in the history of what now goes by the name of "slow cinema," a continuing strand of post-World War II art cinema that has evolved through the innovations of such filmmakers as Antonioni, Andrei Tarkovsky, Abbas Kiarostami, Hou Hsiao-hsien, Béla Tarr, and Tsai Ming-liang.

For all its radical suspense, *The Passenger* may seem to adhere to a deterministic plot arc that inevitably concludes with Locke's demise at the Hotel de la Gloria. But the film's circularity expresses, on the contrary, a meditative recursion—a constant circling-back to the decisive moment of Locke's assumption of Robertson's identity and, thus, to its unsettled implications. Nicholson's brilliance in the film comes down to his engaging ability to keep in abeyance—to suspend—our most basic assumptions about his character's motives and choices, our sense of who this man called Locke is, our sense that he knows himself. It is a testament to the actor's skill that the film comes alive precisely where the formulaic suspense dissolves, where the thriller plot yields to stark contingency and back-to-the-beginning confusion, and where Locke's plan to escape himself runs up against the residues of his already forged temperament.

Notes

1. For an elucidating account of the definitional problems that come with the category of art cinema, see Galt and Schoonover 2010. Unfortunately, however, the authors say little about performance styles that distinguish art cinema.
2. For example, Klevan (2005), despite the broader inclusiveness suggested by his book's title, focuses exclusively on classical Hollywood films, without mention of different traditions and their merits. For an argument that does justice to the complexities of performance in art cinema, particularly in the work of Robert Bresson, see Jones 1998. For a cogent rethinking of performance in Antonioni's cinema that in some ways informs my take on *The Passenger*, see Forgacs 2011.

3. There is a practical, concrete sense in which we ought to consider Nicholson's influence *on the methods of Antonioni*, rather than vice versa. The star actor's limited availability required the director to work more quickly than usual and to adopt a more improvisatory shooting style (Antonioni 339–40).
4. Breitz's *Him* makes up one half of a diptych with *Her*, which features clips from Meryl Streep's performances in a similar format. A video version of these two installations can be viewed at the artist's website, http://www.candicebreitz.net.
5. Nicholson here deviates from the film's original script by adding both the apology and the blasphemous reaction that makes it necessary (Peploe, Wollen, and Antonioni 58–9).
6. Antonioni recalls of his approach to *The Passenger* that he needed "to reduce suspense to a minimum, even though there had to be some left—and I do think some has been left, even if it is an element of indirect, filtered suspense" (Antonioni 346).

Works cited

Allen, Jennifer. "Jack and Meryl on the Couch," in *Candice Breitz: Inner + Outer Space*, Cologne: Walther König, 2008, 68–76.
Antonioni, Michelangelo. *The Architecture of Vision: Writings and Interviews on Cinema*. Ed. Carlo di Carlo and Giorgio Tinazzi. New York: Marsilio, 1996.
Baron, Cynthia, and Sharon Marie Carnicke. *Reframing Screen Performance*. Ann Arbor: University of Michigan Press, 2008.
Bingham, Dennis. *Acting Male: Masculinities in the Films of James Stewart, Jack Nicholson, and Clint Eastwood*. New Brunswick, NJ: Rutgers University Press, 1994.
Brunette, Peter. *The Films of Michelangelo Antonioni*. Cambridge: Cambridge University Press, 1998.
Carnicke, Sharon Marie. "Screen Performance and Directors' Visions," in Cynthia Baron, Diane Carson, and Frank P. Tomasulo, eds., *More than a Method: Trends and Traditions in Contemporary Film Performance*, Detroit: Wayne State University Press, 2004, 42–67.
Chatman, Seymour. *Antonioni: or, The Surface of the World*. Berkeley: University of California Press, 1985.
Crane, Robert, and Christopher Fryer. *Jack Nicholson: The Early Years*. Lexington: University Press of Kentucky, 2012.
Elsaesser, Thomas. "The Pathos of Failure: Notes on the Unmotivated Hero," in *The Persistence of Hollywood*, New York: Routledge, 2012, 225–35.
Forgacs, David. "Face, Body, Voice, Movement: Antonioni and Actors," in Laura Rascaroli and John David Rhodes, eds., *Antonioni: Centenary Essays*, London: BFI, 2011, 167–82.
Galt, Rosalind, and Karl Schoonover. "Introduction: The Impurity of Art Cinema," in Rosalind Galt and Karl Schoonover, eds., *Global Art Cinema: New Theories and Histories*, Oxford: Oxford University Press, 2010, 3–27.
Klevan, Andrew. *Film Performance: From Achievement to Appreciation*. London: Wallflower, 2005.

Jones, Kent. "A Stranger's Posture: Notes on Bresson's Late Films," in James Quandt, ed., *Robert Bresson*, Toronto: Cinematheque Ontario, 1998, 393–401.

McGilligan, Patrick. *Jack's Life: A Biography of Jack Nicholson.* Updated and expanded. New York: W. W. Norton & Co., 2015.

Pallasmaa, Juhani. *The Architecture of Image: Existential Space in Cinema.* Helsinki: Rakennustieto, 2001.

Peploe, Mark, Peter Wollen, and Michelangelo Antonioni. *The Passenger.* New York: Grove, 1975.

Perez, Gilberto. *The Material Ghost: Films and Their Medium.* Baltimore: Johns Hopkins University Press, 1998.

Pomerance, Murray. *Michelangelo Red Antonioni Blue: Eight Reflections on Cinema.* Berkeley: University of California Press, 2011.

Rohdie, Sam. *Antonioni.* London: BFI, 1990.

Walker, Beverly. "Interview: Jack Nicholson," *Film Comment* 21: 3 (May/June 1985), 53.

Chapter 19
Dustin Hoffman in *Rain Man*
Jason Jacobs

Accompanying the end credits of Barry Levinson's *Rain Man* (1988) are sixteen black-and-white photographs that we should assume are a selection of autistic savant Raymond Babbitt's (Dustin Hoffman) snaps, taken with an Instamatic camera during his car journey from the Wallbrook mental institution in Cincinnati to Los Angeles. We see no photos of his brother, Charlie (Tom Cruise), who effectively abducted him in order to extract "his share" of the $3 million inheritance left to Wallbrook by their recently deceased father. In fact, there are no photos of any human beings at all, save for the lower half of the legs of a woman we see waiting in the doctor's reception where midway through the journey Charlie takes Raymond for a diagnosis. (In the movie we see Raymond photograph a male patient's legs as well, just at the moment Charlie explains to the nurse that his brother is "autistic" not "artistic".) The rest of Raymond's images are of various roadside structures, signs with places and numbers, parts of buildings and cars. A few are quite evocative of moments and places we glimpsed during the movie that has just finished (for example, a shot taken of the railroad crossing when they stop for the passing of a train and Raymond watches its blinking warning lights), and many are blurred or out of focus suggesting they were taken during travel in the Buick Roadmaster that is Charlie's only portion left to him by his estranged father. The two photographs with the crispest focus are the first and last—the latter a close-up of the "Dynaflow" badge from the Buick the brothers drive. Either brother could have taken that shot.

Images generated by a camera simultaneously show the objects in view and the viewpoint from which they are seen; in this sense, these final images ought to tell us something more about Raymond's thinking, since even a poor amateur snap can often tell us what the photographer was getting at or going for. However, as we find at the end of *Psycho* (1960), with the various objects that Lila Crane (Vera Miles) observes as she sneaks through Norman Bates's house, these photos do not give us any deeper insight into Raymond's mind or thoughts. And that in itself points us toward the achievement of Hoffman's performance, which is not the concealment of some interior life beyond visibility, in the way we typically reserve our approbation for great performances in terms of the actor's capacity to instill the belief that the character is living and thinking even when not onscreen. While with more certainty than for most characters we would know what Raymond is up to offscreen (in terms of the timing and content of his meals, his viewing habits and so on: pancakes with maple syrup on the table first; Italian food on Mondays; Mott's apple juice; twelve cheese puff balls eaten with toothpicks; *The People's Court, Jeopardy*; lights out promptly at 11 p.m.), Hoffman inhabits a character who is both human and apparently without a legible interior, a mindedness that most of us watching any other film would recognize in a character even if we did not share it.

This performance is, of course, motivated by realism and the considerable research Hoffman invested in working up the role. He is playing an autistic savant as accurately as he can, but even here we have to be cautious because, as with playing the role of a master magician or musician there is a vast range of capacity, ability, and individuality that describes those with this rare disorder. Thanks to the pioneering work of Lorna Wing and others, the continuum or spectrum of autism is no longer understood as "a terminal illness . . . a dead soul in a live body" (Smith 11). The research Hoffman put into the role is documented by Ronald Bergan's 1991 biography of the actor; however the success and impact of the film significantly increased the visibility of, and professional and public interest in, the condition of the autistic savant. Daniel Smith acknowledges the accuracy of Hoffman's performance:

> *Rain Main* gave the impression that autism endows people with savant-like gifts, something that's true in only a small minority of cases. But Hoffman's performance got a great deal right about the experiences and behaviours that typically come with autism: the need for sameness and routine, the sensitivity to loud noises, the awkward gait, the discomfort with physical intimacy, the literal-mindedness, the tendency to parrot back and repurpose phrases ("echolalia" is the technical term), the repetition of actions such as rocking and handflapping ("stimming"). Before 1988 [...] autism was a psychological novelty item ... After 1988 it was everywhere and portrayed in a reasonably accurate form. *Rain Man* both made autism widely recognizable and made the use of the condition in books and films an emblem of one's interest in and compassion for the disabled. (12)

This is no small achievement, but it is worth comparing that earlier notion of the condition as "a dead soul in a live body" with the way that Hoffman's other performances have been characterized. Pauline Kael argues that his eponymous role in *Tootsie* (1982) is based on "Hoffman, the perfectionist," but she admires it because it "enables him to show a purely farcical side of himself" (429, 431). Both Stanley Cavell and Manny Farber have a problem with what they see as a hollowing out of character in Hoffman's breakthrough film, *The Graduate* (1967), although Cavell is more generous than Farber, who concludes that "Hoffman and his plaguing environment of adults are indented into the screen with a diamond drill, glistening and hollow at the same time" (198). This sense of hollow-but-hard Hoffman is most eloquently captured in David Thomson's assessment, where he claims that the actor is "small and often timid, but a nucleus of hard identity never wavers, never seems fully threatened, and never floods us with animation" (452) and credits Tom Cruise for surviving Hoffman's "black-hole narcissism" in *Rain Main* (219). Such criticisms almost endorse that sense of autism as a living body without a soul, a needful thing without the inner spark that would draw us safely (*contra* a black hole) to its heart. And yet Hoffman in *Rain Man* communicates a soul—whatever that is—more effectively than anything else, since there is no conventional interiority to form the ground on which he might perform otherwise. (Anyone, whether religious or evangelically atheist, who has lived or worked with severely disabled people for a long time, knows this to be true.)

Hoffman manages this communication by using the accuracy of his rendering of this type of autism as a platform from which to stage a deep responsiveness to the world and the wondrous objects it regularly presents to our regular disinterested or disgusted eyes. Hoffman's Raymond is like a sponge, endlessly porous to the stimuli and spectacle of things around him, and particularly attracted to objects and structures that embody or demonstrate regularity, order, and movement, which is to say those things that echo and mirror him. (If we were generous, we might say this is the source of Thomson's thought about Hoffman's apparent "narcissism.") Hence our first view of Raymond is from behind, in long shot, as he instructs Charlie's girlfriend Susanna (Valeria Golino) on the distinction and specifications of the Buick, this an echo of Charlie's more emotionally charged account of it to her earlier in the film. The car has special resonance for Raymond because it is a complex machine he was allowed to control ("slowly, on the driveway"). Indeed, the privileging of cars as emblems of control, freedom, and confinement is marked throughout the film as analogous to our internal sense of how we wish to drive our appearance in the world. It is no surprise in this sense that Charlie's business, and its associated problems, concerns the importing of beautiful luxury cars (four Lamborghini Countachs), which we first see hovering between parallel cables as they are offloaded at port. While the cables evoke order and continuity, the floating cars connote wealth and freedom, the glitter of super-rich consumerism, also a kind of delirious disembodiment. But this image also resonates with his brother Raymond's attraction to both the order of structures and patterns—such as the lines of the roadside he watches as they drive, or the numbers, times, and calculations he is so incredible at handling—*and* the optical attractiveness of small, otherwise undistinctive items, such as the Las Vegas prostitute Iris's "sparkly" necklace and bracelet as well as the "twinkly" lights of that city of naked commerce.

While the film is careful to have Tom Cruise calibrate Charlie's development as a gradual loss of interest in the world of things and money in favor of his relationship to Raymond, Hoffman is equally hygienic in never suggesting development "inside" Raymond: he acquires interests after exposure to wider parts of the world (in particular dancing, and his recognition that his brother is funny as well as important: his "main man," the deliberate designation of his brother as which echoes young Charlie's mishearing "Raymond" as "Rain Man"), but at his greatest moment of panic, after setting off the smoke alarm at Charlie's Los Angeles apartment, he calls for his Wallbrook companion "V-E-R-N." Hoffman's tease—and this is a very witty as well as playful performance beside being precise—is to make us want more out of Raymond than he can give, and hence encourage us to accept—as Charlie appears to be doing in the film's concluding shot—that Raymond will never be anything but what he is. Hoffman's project in this role is to say, in effect, "That is enough." During the first days of their journey, what seemed to Charlie like Raymond's enclosure and confinement within the shell of the self ("I know there's someone in there!" he exclaims in one of many moments of frustration with Raymond) turns out to be a challenge (to Charlie and to us) to take on the responsibility for accepting people whoever and whatever they are, and *as* whatever or whoever they are. That responsibility has its costs, as well as its risks, but in Raymond's case the audience sees, well before Charlie does, what is on offer.

A key moment in our recognition occurs during the journey away from Wallbrook and out of Cincinnati, with Charlie and Susanna in the front of the Buick and Raymond in the back. The top is down (Ray needs as full a view of the world as possible, even to the extent of watching Fred Astaire and Ginger Rogers dancing in *The Barkleys of Broadway* (1949) simultaneously on his black-and-white Sony Watchman and on the color television in his Vegas hotel suite). As they drive across the Ohio River on the John A. Roebling Suspension Bridge we get several shots of Raymond admiring this fabulous work of engineering. Bridges are magnificent things, forceful emblems of humanity's capacity to overcome the obstacles of the natural world. Levinson's direction leaves the architectural symbolism and figurative gestures both legible and occasionally italicized, including, alongside those, Hoffman's face as Raymond admires the bridge "in motion" as they travel along it and beneath its blue ironwork, intersecting with and slicing through a deep blue sky. What Hoffman expresses with his open-eyed and keen face is *aesthetic feeling*, a taste for the beauty of the world, in both its overt and magnificent displays, like this bridge, as well as in its tawdry attractions (like Iris's necklace), and its unnoticed, liminal, and purely quotidian "unspecialness." As we see with Ray, these moments can jolt us unexpectedly into a mode of wonder. Ray is altogether surprising. During an airport scene he insists on flying with Qantas. We might catch him, under Charlie's frustrated remonstrations, describe Australia as having "lovely beaches." This is true. Did he read about this and is now simply parroting a guidebook or, could we say he has seen a picture, photograph, or painting that has inspired this essentially aesthetic response?

One can account for these instances by reference to the performer's accuracy in rendering autistics' attraction to "shapes, forms, light, dark, shadows, the sound of the car on the bridge—it's almost like seeing things again for the first time" (Levinson speaking in his Blu-Ray commentary). But Hoffman moves us to something deeper, something shared, even universal, in his look of wonder. To check this, compare it with Raymond's fixed vision when watching *The People's Court* or *Jeopardy*: there, he is staring directly at an object but the shining sense of "for the first time" is utterly absent. By contrast we again get a flicker of obsessive wonder when we see him watching the clothes spin in a dryer later in the movie. Hoffman makes movement seem directed and propelled, even if prompted by distraction, so that it seems beyond our usual merely fidgety, hesitant, and nervous reaction to the world. He is equally a master of photographic stillness and concentration, as here, and when he first hears the Wheel of Fortune sound during a game of blackjack at the casino.

The bridge sequence comes quite early in the movie, so we have an inkling of the lesson callow Charlie has to learn—that his brother is not "acting like a fucking retard" or like a child or a dog (we can notice how Cruise uses a rapid hand clap to corral attention in the way one might do with a recalcitrant puppy; at one point he tells Raymond to "Just stay!"), or even a ticket out of financial catastrophe—although hope of the latter, of course, does help Charlie's pace on that learning journey. The film echoes Camille Paglia's idea of America, as "a land of transients and transience, of movement *to* and *across*," with two brothers at its center, one who mirrors his autistic Other in his inability to communicate, especially romantically with Susanna, who complains on their (interrupted) journey to Palm Springs that she wants to "feel like I'm going away . . . with someone. Call me crazy" (Paglia 573). Like Raymond, Charlie has a seemingly impenetrable core that is the foundation for his unbending sense of entitlement, mendacity, and resentment. It is Charlie who makes the transition to, what we are led to assume in the final shot is, a "better person." Raymond does not change, even in those significant plot moments when he appears to: the little laugh in the motel bathroom just before Charlie realizes his brother is the "Rain Man" he thought was a mere imaginary friend; or the moment that precipitates the primal scene of three-year-old Charlie being left in a scalding bath by Raymond, the event that led to Ray's incarceration at Wallbrook; or the moment Raymond leans his head to the right to touch Charlie's, toward the end of the movie in Dr. Marston's (Barry Levinson) office. None of these things change the film's resolve to maintain Raymond as what he is when first we see him. For only one of the brothers does their journey across America prompt inner realignment, "growth" as the dime-store therapists might put it. Bergan cites this as part of the movie's failure: "Just as Raymond hardly develops as a character and lives by rituals, so the film is restricted inside conventional modes" (234). I disagree. The conventional mode is central to the movie's power.

This is why the hard nucleus that Thomson sees as the pivot of Hoffman's skill is a mistaken target. What is at core in Hoffman's best performances (this one; *Marathon Man* (1976); and the vastly under-rated *Agatha* (1979)) is self-doubt, a hesitation at depth about his right to receive and benefit from the success he has earned. The corollary of that condition is very often the projection of either a hard perfectionist ethic, or a vapid sentimentality; in these films Hoffman just avoids both, while evoking the risk of their proximity.

His performance in *Rain Man* is not well helped by Levinson's characteristic decision, throughout the film, to place Hoffman off-center, in long shot, or in the periphery of the lens in order to signal the evolving risk of Raymond wandering distractedly into danger. Thankfully, the director avoids painting Raymond as a victim of random public cruelty, except for a brief scene when Ray is stuck on the road in front of the DON'T WALK sign. (Levinson made a good decision to remove from the final cut a scene showing Ray wandering into a shop, taking and consuming his cheese puff balls and Mott's apple juice, and breaking a packet of cookies; the owner cruelly berates him before Charlie comes to the rescue.) Our emotional proximity to Raymond/Hoffman is far better achieved when we are close to his face (one that is a quarter of a century older than Cruise's), a face that demonstrates continuous activity just below the edge of blankness. The sequence where Ray is disturbed by Charlie touching objects in his room at Wallbrook captures the unity that Hoffman asserts between the rapid-yet-droning urgency of his voice and the laser-sighted notice of order disrupted that is communicated by his eyes.

The film's wider, and quite distasteful, ideological project is to condemn the inanity of consumer culture, particularly the repetitive nature of daytime television (which we notice many of the residents of Wallbrook watching) and the flashy vulgarity of consumerism. That attitude might feel virtuous and deep among one's dinner partners in

Santa Monica, but it seems too glibly elitist (a quality it shares with later films such as *Fight Club* and *American Beauty* (both 1999)), a marker of those who may pity the disabled (whether physically, mentally, culturally, or educationally) but do little beyond directing money in their general direction (a version in fact of Charlie's initial plans for his brother). Hoffman's performance largely negates this ideological project, however, because with the precision of a toothpick in a cheese puff ball he is able to imbue Ray with a sense of the sheer liveliness of existence, the constant availability of interest in the multitude and multiplied objects and sounds of the world. While he may not develop "inside," Hoffman's Ray has a body that, like the world around it, is constantly in motion, sometimes echoing itself, as in the moments he holds both hands up to his chest, almost touching the fingers of each as he repeats the Abbott and Costello routine "Who's on First," or the mantra "Never hurt Charlie Babbitt, Never hurt Charlie Babbitt." I take this gesture of the hands as a kind of prayer, its accompanying litany salving the harsh recall of trauma or present distress by gathering and holding the words close to his heart. It would be easy to over-play such moments, but with Hoffman's mercurial changes they are quickly forgotten, and the journey continues. By some lights this quality of attention to the here and now is a blessing where the past and future lose their grip on our present and allow us to see things as they are. The psychiatrist R. D. Laing put this eloquently:

> The most simple things are the most difficult things: getting through a day well is not easy, that is the most difficult thing in life, I think, is living. For me. I mean really living. A lot of the time I'm in the present and I'm thinking about the past or scheming about the future and missing every present moment, instead of actually partaking of the sacrament of every present moment. (*Did You Used To Be R. D. Laing?*)

Hoffman plays Ray as afraid of some aspects of the world—air travel, busy roads—because of their risks. But they are also means to compress time by speeding ourselves up. The slowing of the journey not only serves the plot, but also allows us and Hoffman to show an autistic savant in a variety of situations. For example, as rain confines them to the Honeymoon Haven Motel in Missouri, further delaying the journey, we see Ray writing and drawing in one of his notepads. Once his detailed, realist drawing of the façade of the Wallbrook institution ("definitely not going to see my home again") is finished, Hoffman immediately rips it from the notebook and discards it on the floor—there is no hint of a flourish, or dissatisfaction with it, and Levinson cuts to the page as if in astonishment at the investment made and value unrecognized. For the value is in the moment of making, not in the display, or recognition of achievement. Neither does Hoffman play Ray as afraid to be looked at or mocked or ignored. It was for this reason that, despite his extensive research, the actor found the role difficult:

> The challenge ... became to do what I always try to do, which is to bring it home and not try to do a character that is not myself ... I'd gone into analysis years ago, and someone told me that Freud said the problem with us is that what we feel about ourselves is based upon what we think others feel about us. We spend a lifetime trying to get to say, Fuck 'em. The question never hits autistics: what do you think of me? Am I boring this person? It doesn't exist. (Bergen 231)

What others think is a primary issue for most actors and the success of their careers, however; and one of the finer aspects of Hoffman's rendering of this apparent indifference is that we feel empowered to share Charlie's irritation with Ray, without forgoing the natural human drive to become proximate to those who are ill, wounded, or otherwise impaired (for example, Ray's repetition of the local radio station sting, "97X. BAM. The Future of Rock and Roll!" is particularly annoying). Our irritation counters the film's stronger tendency to encourage sympathy for Ray the more Charlie insults him. In part this is because the film balances its essential melodrama with comedy. Take the sequence in the Vernon Plaza Hotel, where he has been tasked by Charlie to read the phone directory because Charlie is eager to get to bed with Susanna: but it's nine minutes before "lights out at 11 p.m.," insists Raymond. Charlie flicks the room light off anyway and instantly Raymond lights his handheld torch in order to continue reading—the calm automatism of the gesture a witty retort to his brother's control and sexual frustration. This sequence ends with Susanna realizing the extent of Charlie's plan to extort Ray. She leaves them both, and we are left with Charlie observing Raymond rocking himself on his bed, looping through the "Who's on First?" routine (not very dissimilarly from the way Abbott and Costello did themselves). It is a sentimental reminder of the times we attempt to console ourselves as children when we hear our parents argue; but it leaves the marker of Cruise's troubled sense of his brother as a burden to contrast with the final shot of the film where his reaction to Ray's departure on the train is far less legible: "Yes, this is my brother, yes I will miss him, a love that cannot be mirrored, but—perhaps, who knows?" Hoffman convinces us that, in Ray's own way, such love can be reciprocated.

It is a standing realist criticism of the film that in the moment Raymond touches his head to Charlie in the scene just prior to this ending is to be found a direct contradiction to one of the central features of autism, the fact that the typical autistic savant does not want to be touched or hugged. But it is Raymond who initiates the touch, just as he mirrors and transforms Charlie's treatment of him as a kind of dog, by patting him five times on the head, and once, very briefly, on the shoulder after the devastating bathroom scene when Raymond relives the trauma that separated them. In these gestures Hoffman seems to intuit a kind of contact with the world that transcends the ambiguity of touch that Merleau-Ponty describes in *Phenomenology of Perception*:

> If I can, with my left hand, feel my right hand as it touches an object, the right hand as an object is not the right hand as it touches: the first is a system of bones, muscles and flesh brought down at a point of space, the second shoots through space like a rocket to reveal the external object in its place. In so far as it sees or touches the world, my body can therefore be neither seen nor touched. (91)

The rest of us live with the ambiguity of our contact with a world that we touch and which touches us back at the same time. It is wrong to assume that Raymond's reaction to being touched is a distaste for human contact. This is directly negated when Susanna delivers him a kiss, and when he is taught to dance by Charlie in their Vegas suite. In a later interview with Brian Linehan, Hoffman recounts meeting Temple Grandin, who told him that contrary to that belief, her experience was that autistics want to be touched and hugged as much as the rest of us. However, when it does happen they cannot take it: "It's just an unbearable feeling for whatever mysterious reason" (www.youtube.com/watch?v=1HWQLTILs8A).

Bergan claims Hoffman cites Peter Sellers in Hal Ashby's *Being There* (1979) as an inspiration for his *Rain Man* performance, and that both actors seem to require some salve, through the masking of playing a character, for their deep sense of self-doubt. Sellers never quite wears that mask, as Geoffrey Rush's outstanding performance in *The Life and Death of Peter Sellers* (2004) makes clear, and *Being There* relies too much on a credulous cynicism about American politics and public life. However, Hoffman possesses what Sellers did not, which is a compensating capacity that does not convert doubt into needy melancholia. Although he experiences discomfort and distress, Hoffman never has us believe Ray is unhappy, and has him laugh at himself, his own ritual. Sellers and Hoffman may have both lacked confidence in themselves, but I suspect the former's sense of entitlement to success was stronger. Receiving an American Film

Institute Life Achievement Award a decade after *Rain Man* was released Hoffman reflected, "There was this reel of pictures, me playing all these different roles. I had my first—and only, thank God—panic attack. What followed was depression . . . It had to do with a central core in me, which was that I never felt I deserved success." It is that core that Hoffman offers to us as Raymond in *Rain Man*, who deserves nothing but our acceptance of what he has to be.

Works cited

Bergan, Ronald. *Dustin Hoffman*. London: Virgin Books, 1991.
Cavell, Stanley. *The World Viewed*. Enlarged edn. Cambridge, MA: Harvard University Press, 1979.
Farber, Manny. *Movies*. New York: Hillstone, 1971.
Kael, Pauline. *Film Writings 1980–1983*. London: Arrow Books, 1986.
Laing, R. D. "Interview," in Tom Schandel and Kirk Tougas, *Did You Used to Be R. D. Laing?* (1989).
Merleau-Ponty, Maurice. *Phenomenology of Perception*. Trans. Colin Smith. London: Routledge and Kegan Paul, 1962.
Paglia, Camille. *Sexual Personae*. New York: Vintage Books, 1990.
Smith, Daniel. "Call a Kid a Zebra," *London Review of Books* 38: 10 (19 May 2016), 11–15.
Thompson, David. *The New Biographical Dictionary of Film*. New York: Knopf, 2010.

Chapter 20

Elliott Gould in *The Long Goodbye*

Douglas McFarland

"Mkgnao," announces Leopold Bloom's cat early in the morning, in his master's kitchen in the house on Eccles Street. This is the first we see of Bloom in *Ulysses* and his first encounter with another living creature. "Oh there you are," responds Bloom to the cat's greeting. "Milk for pussens?" (45). On the one hand this exchange seems silly, perhaps endearing, but certainly not heroic. Hovering behind the day in the life of this Dublin Jew is Ulysses, the mythic hero of *The Odyssey*, the two figures in a continuing contrapuntal relationship. As is the case with Joyce, so it is with Robert Altman and Elliott Gould in their adaptation of Raymond Chandler's *The Long Goodbye*. The iconic and the everyday are immediately set against one another. Gould's rendering of Marlowe awakens to an insistently hungry "pussens." But unlike Leopold Bloom, a host of figures necessarily shadow any re-visioning of Marlowe. Chandler's own versions of the character, in the five novels published from 1939 to 1953, are joined by the Marlowes of film played by Humphrey Bogart, Robert Montgomery, George Montgomery, Dick Powell, James Garner, and Robert Mitchum.

Any reincarnation of Marlowe, Gould's included, has hovering behind it a matrix of Marlowes drawn from novel and film. And any performance of Marlowe will be judged and assessed by its audience within that context. In the documentary accompanying the DVD release of *The Long Goodbye* (2003), Altman revealed his intention to create a Rip Van Marlowe, a detective of the 1940s who found himself awakening in 1973. The particular social and moral ethos of that earlier age would provide a device for satirizing the new ethos of the 1970s. But the film offers more than a satire of the Age of Aquarius. Gould's performance as Marlowe, a figure who navigates through a multiplicity of earlier iterations, is the subject of the film. Gould re-imagines rather than resurrects Philip Marlowe. And through this re-imagining, director and actor explore fundamental issues of human identity: the possibility for authenticity, the cost of irony, and the difficult task of discovering personal identity in an impersonal world.

"Elliott Gould as Philip Marlowe . . . Now a Major Motion Picture from United Artists"

Altman was less than enthusiastic about directing *The Long Goodbye* until Elliott Gould was mentioned for the role of Marlowe (Thompson 75). It was Altman's practice to match the persona of a particular actor to his own conception of the character he was to play (Self 135). Gould brought to the role an offscreen professional identity that had emerged in the late 1960s and early 1970s. He received an Academy Award nomination in 1969 for his part in *Bob & Carol & Ted & Alice*, Paul Mazursky's film about the new sexual mores of the 1960s, and in the following year was the subject of a *Time* cover story ("Elliott Gould: The Urban Don Quixote," 7 September 1970, 33–40). Gould was proclaimed a "Star for an Uptight Age," and compared to a whimsical and neurotic Don Quixote (apparently Gould's favorite book). Milton Glazer, better known for his poster of Bob Dylan, portrayed him on the cover with bushy hair and overflowing moustache. Some said he was the Jewish Richard Burton; others the Jewish Jimmy Stewart; or as Gould himself typically put it, the Jewish Elliott Gould (*Time*, 35). In *The Long Goodbye* he is the Jewish Philip Marlowe, a detective for an "Uptight Age," and despite Altman's assertion, hardly a figure from the 1940s. His laid-back attitude, his repetitive mantra, "It's okay with me," his disregard for convention, his flippant gait, the "cool" way he can strike a wooden match with his thumb, his vintage automobile, and his one crumpled black suit—all these and other mannerisms and accessories are suggestive more of the 1970s than the 1940s. Gould, in short, brings his own public persona as an actor to his re-imagining of Marlowe.

Thirty-nine years later Gould had not shaken this image. In an interview at the Edinburgh Film Festival in 2012, he was innocently asked, "Have you been here before?" He responded, "I know where here is, but what is here? Here is what? Here is for any one of us. Or for me, is where I am . . . So wherever I am, I'm here" (Gould). Far out.

"The First American Jazz Actor" and a real cutie-pie

Gould brought more than his personality to the role. He had a specific understanding of himself as an actor. He once referred to himself as the "first American jazz actor," adding, "I liked to let myself go and just riff, and behave with elements around me." He acknowledged Altman's granting him the freedom "to develop this jazz style" (Tomlinson 224). Foremost in the development of American jazz improvisation, as it took shape in the late forties and early fifties, was Charlie Parker. Once the melody and chord changes of a standard tune had been laid down, the soloist could push, extend, violate, tease, and/or subvert that "standard." Parker's nickname was appropriately "Bird." Jazz improvisation provided the freedom for Parker and others to sing freely and spontaneously within certain parameters. The Beat writers, especially Jack Kerouac, who prefaced *Mexico City Blues* with the assertion that he wanted to be considered a jazz poet, sought the freedom that comes with breaking through to some unattainable truth (Holmes 238). But Parker, and I would argue, Gould, sought the freedom of unmediated performance. And while Parker might riff on "My Funny Valentine," Gould riffs on Marlowe. Contributing to the richness of his improvisations are the shadows of the many Marlowes of book and film, as well as Gould's own offscreen style and identity.

The first ten minutes of the film provide an overture in which these elements are woven into Gould's performance. Before the United Artists logo has faded from the screen, that joyous celebration of the city and the industry, "Hooray for Hollywood," fills the theatre. The song was first performed onscreen by the irrepressible Johnnie Davis in Busby Berkeley's *Hollywood Hotel* (1937). Leading the Benny Goodman Band,

Davis belts out with energetic abandon and visceral delight the tune that would become an anthem for all those enraptured with the movies. The audience that has come to the theatre for a Phillip Marlowe hardboiled mystery is immediately thrown off balance. The music invokes another era, another genre, and the fictional status of film. The music also eliminates the Marlowes of the novel, but reinforces the presence of the Hollywood Marlowes. To put it differently, the audience is provided criteria for passing judgment on Gould's interpretation of Marlowe. The attention of the curious audience is not on the plot of the murder mystery, but on Gould's performance.

The camera moves slowly away from a cheap metal bas relief on which "Hollywood" has been engraved, revealing the interior of a bedroom with a body sprawled across a bed. Because it is a bedroom and because the camera does move so slowly, as if it were feeling itself about, there is a furtive quality to its voyeuristic gaze. The slow movement of the camera as it turns inside the room and moves toward the body on the bed also invites the audience to gather evidence and make judgments. For a brief moment we wonder if the body is not a corpse in what we know is a murder mystery. But then we see Gould has crossed Marlowe's legs at the ankle. This is a sleeper, not a corpse. Legs aren't splayed; they're situated comfortably. Gould's first gesture of performance. Marlowe is at rest. In his stillness, in this state of being staged, Gould has already begun to act. The camera maintains its leisurely pace, giving the audience even more time to assess the material context, the place this sleeping figure has created for itself, as though to reflect Stanley Cavell's astute observation that a film actor is not "ontologically favored over the rest of nature, in which objects are not props but natural allies (or enemies) of the human character" (37). In this instance the scene (setting and props) suggests identity: the bed is unmade; it has no headboard—there are prominent marks, some sort of scratches on the wall, where the headboard should be; the lights on a cheap pole lamp are lit; an ashtray is on the bed alongside the unconscious figure; an opened magazine lies next to the ashtray; the room has no windows. And what of the figure itself: Marlowe (surely this is Marlowe) has gone to bed (surely it's night) without disrobing, without even removing his shoes. An aura of carelessness, not passivity, informs the room and the figure within it. Even before Marlowe says a mantra he repeats throughout the film, "It's okay with me," we know that about him.

And then there is movement. A cat darts in from outside the frame onto Marlowe's chest. Place having provided the physical and psychological context for it, now perspective qualifies performance. To put it differently, the cat trainer cries "action" and the cat then Marlowe spring to life. The cat is hungry and perhaps a little miffed that Marlowe has forgotten to feed him. This is funny, or at least disorienting. I didn't know hardboiled detectives kept pets, answered to anyone, let alone a cat. The Elliott Gould of the *Time* magazine cover story, enduring the "endless comic agonies of contemporary American life," has taken over the Phillip Marlowe who, like Leopold Bloom, is enmeshed in the quotidian details of life. Instead of wondering who has been killed, what tough-looking blonde will show up in his office, and, if we have read the book, when the needy Terry Lennox will come calling, we ask where does Marlowe keep the cat box and how often does he empty it? The playfulness of Gould's Marlowe is revealed a short while later. He has used a piece of cardboard as a flap to cover the cat's entry way in and out of the apartment. In order that the cat, or anyone else for that matter, does not become confused, Marlowe has written on the cardboard, "*el porto del gato*," making it apparent that his "Latino pussens" is not bilingual. The most striking moment in the relationship between Marlowe and his cat comes in the kitchen. In a scene that is surely improvised, Gould's re-imagined detective attempts to outwit his pet by filling with his fingers an empty can of Coury brand cat food with a substitute. Improvisation, the actor's own persona, and an iconic model hovering in the background come together in the context of the un-heroic details of life.

In an earlier and subtler improvised gesture, Gould reveals a deeper aspect to Marlowe's character. After the cat has made his will known, Gould rises out of bed and heads toward the kitchen. As he comes around the front of the bed, he turns his head to examine ever so quickly his appearance in a mirror on the back of the opened closet door. Gould's particular skill for improvisation, his capacity for jazz riffing, is easily missed at this moment. The slight turn he makes, seemingly as if it were a reflex, is utterly natural and yet carries with it an essential component in the construction of Marlowe in the film. It marks one of the few moments in which Gould/Marlowe displays any serious degree of self-awareness. That this moment is at best fleeting, I would argue, speaks to just how vulnerable the gesture is, just how precarious is Marlowe's perception of himself. Although we will have to wait longer to hear Gould utter his improvised mantra, "It's okay with me," we feel it here as an unspoken commentary on himself. Gould reiterates this rendering of Marlowe a short while later in a non-gesture. Not once in the film does Marlowe look out from his loft at the Los Angeles that spreads before him. The view seems not to interest him. The audience awaits that moment when Marlowe pauses on the catwalk that separates his apartment from the one next door and reflects on the world and his place in it. We await the point-of-view shot of the city followed by his reaction in a medium close-up of his face. Has he lived there so long that the view has lost its appeal? Or does he lack the self-awareness, the imagination to contemplate, even brood over, his place in the world?

Improvisation and irony

On the set of *Ocean's Eleven* (2001), Steven Soderbergh questioned Gould about the scene in the interrogation room, wondering if it had been improvised. The episode begins when Marlowe is brought in by the police for questioning. They know that he had driven Terry Lennox (Jim Bouton) to the Mexican border and suspect him of knowing Terry's whereabouts. Gould delivers a sustained use of improvised irony from the minute he is photographed at the station until he leaves his cell three days later. He makes a childishly mocking face when his mug shot is taken. When he is thrown into the interrogation room, he smears onto the two-way mirror what is left of the fingerprint ink on his hand. As he is being questioned, he puts streaks of the same black ink under his eyes, claiming that he's getting ready for the big game. He then uses the ink to cover himself in blackface and sings a few lines from "Sewanee," as if he were Al Jolson. A uniformed officer and plainclothes detective watch Gould's performance from the other side of the one-way glass. The officer calls Marlowe a real "cutie-pie." The detective corrects him. Marlowe is a "smart ass." Once the detective takes over the questioning, the irony becomes more aggressive. The detective asks, was Sylvia Lennox cheating on Terry? Marlowe responds with another question: "Are you cheating on your wife?" After the detective answers, "Maybe," Marlowe raises the stakes and asks, "She cheating on you?" When Marlowe leaves his jail cell three days later, he tells his run-at-the-mouth pot-head cell mate that it's only his body not his mind that is locked up. Marlowe cannot pass up the chance to deliver a smart line.

Gould's use of irony is most pointed and most dangerous in his two encounters with the gambler Marty Augustine (Mark Rydell). Augustine read in the papers that Marlowe had driven Terry to the border and concluded that Marlowe knows the whereabouts of the money Terry took with him to Mexico. Augustine and a few of his men confront Marlowe on his way to do his laundry. Told that Augustine wants to see him, he responds, "I only see hoods by appointment." From the backseat of the car Augustine asks, was that "a smart remark"? Marlowe responds, "It's the only thing I could come up with." He then turns to one of Augustine's men and asks, "What about you, Mabel?" This is met with a blow to the stomach. Up in his apartment, Marlowe is undaunted. He tells Augustine and his thugs that the girls across the way are "rockettes" who haven't received their tap shoes. To one of the men going through his laundry: "I don't take too much starch." But then Augustine teaches Marlowe a lesson. The gangster's girlfriend (Jo Ann Eggenweiler, talked into the part after waitressing Altman and Gould during a long and stoney afternoon at a local restaurant), who was waiting down in the car, comes up and asks if she can have a Coke. Augustine takes a half-empty bottle from Marlowe's refrigerator, drains it, then smashes it across the girlfriend's face. An end to smart remarks.

But later in Augustine's office there is more of the same. Marlowe asks Augustine, "Where's your girlfriend, the one with a Coke bottle for a nose?" When Augustine orders everyone to strip naked (one of his bozos is the notably muscular Arnold Schwarzenegger, in an early screen appearance), Marlowe says Augustine must have looked like one of the three little pigs as an adolescent with his clothes off. A $5,000 bill falls from Marlowe's jacket and he says he found it in a box of Cracker Jacks. On his way out, Marlowe asks Augustine's girlfriend, whose heavily bandaged face makes it almost impossible for her to move her lips, if she wants a cigarette. Marlowe is called a smart ass, a smart guy, a cutie-pie who makes smart cracks and smart remarks. If there is any one characteristic that typifies Gould's performance, it is his snide and brilliant use of irony. As a jazz actor, he riffs on cracking wise throughout the film. He uses irony to goad, to attack, to defend, to undermine, to withdraw, and at times simply because he can. In his work on modernist aesthetics, Peter Nicholls points out that "irony is a necessary defense against modernity even as it seems to assume that to be distinctively modern the poet must also be ironic" (5). With its emphasis on the use of improvised irony, Gould's performance seems very poetic in this way. More than loyalty, more than curiosity, more than a code of morality, irony is Marlowe's shield and his weapon.

"I even lost my cat"

Altman revealed in an interview that his intention in making the film was to take a 1940s Marlowe, along with the social mores he represented, and set him down in the 1970s. But he also agreed with what is fairly obvious, that the ending of the film has strong ties to the ending of *The Third Man* (1949) (Thompson 75). We are dealing not only with Rip Van Marlowe but also Rip Van Martins as Altman lifts the Joseph Cotten character from postwar Vienna, with all of its moral ambiguity, and sets him down in Los Angeles in 1973. In the final scene of Carol Reed's *The Third Man*, the American, Holly Martins, is being driven to the airport following the burial of Harry Lime (Orson Welles), whom he had killed in the sewers of Vienna with a single shot. It is forever uncertain whether, regardless of how corrupt the man had become, he was sparing his old friend what would follow were he taken alive, or taking Lime's life in reparation for the lives Lime himself had taken. We do know that Martins, a second-rate Zane Gray, has taken on more than he bargained for when he came to Vienna at Harry's bequest. Little did he foresee the entanglements of love, friendship, political fragmentation, and—for lack of a better word—evil in which he would find himself enmeshed. As they pass Anna (Alida Valli), Lime's former lover, now betrayed (and with whom Martins has fallen in love), Martins asks his escort, Major Calloway (Trevor Howard), to stop the jeep and let him out. He tells the exasperated Calloway that "one has to do something." A remarkable statement, a kind of innocent, perhaps simplistic, gesture. I say gesture because he knows very well that Anna will never forgive him for betraying Harry. He leans against a wagon, smoking a cigarette, as Anna walks past him without any sign of recognition. The posture of Martins's lanky frame and the casual way he smokes silently suggest that he knew things would end this way. But this innocent abroad, the American who had somehow escaped the nightmare of Europe, did feel that the gesture was necessary to make.

The parallels between the two films are fairly obvious, as are the differences. Events are compressed by Altman. Once having determined that Terry had indeed killed his wife Sylvia, and that he had subsequently faked his own suicide in order to escape punishment, Marlowe tracks him down in Mexico where his old friend intends to meet Eileen, his current lover and accomplice. With premeditation Marlowe confronts Terry in his hidden bower and kills him with a single shot. Ostensibly this is the moment when Marlowe's 1940s moral values are acted upon. Preceding this ending, however, are a series of ironic exchanges. Leaving the hospital room (where he has been taken after being struck by a car while pursuing Eileen), he tells the nurse not to spill the contents of the bedpan. When he arrives at Eileen's house in Malibu, searching for answers, the real estate agents confuse him with a Mr. Katz—the pun should not go unnoticed. The ironic play continues when he arrives in Mexico on Terry's trail. He rides around town with the two local officials, who had aided the fugitive, in what Marlowe calls their "golden chariot," in reality a late-model Cadillac that has seen much better days. Even in his final exchange with Terry there is an ironic touch. Marlowe's last words to his friend, "I even lost my cat," are also the final spoken words of the film.

This is surely the most complicated scene in *The Long Goodbye*. Irony and morality are woven together to the extent that they cannot be easily separated. But let me try. Marlowe kills Terry for personal reasons: Terry has taken advantage of Marlowe's unconditional loyalty, since when Terry asked for a ride to Mexico Marlowe didn't hesitate for a breath, never suspecting that Terry had murdered his wife. But he also shoots Terry so that justice might be served. After all, Terry has gotten away with bludgeoning a woman to death. But Marlowe ironically and mockingly tells Terry that he has come to kill him because in all the turmoil, his cat has gone missing. Here, then, is the angel of death descending on target, an angel whose significant other is a fickle pet cat. The greatness, perhaps even unique quality of Gould's performance is in his ability to play off his whimsical, neurotic, and yes, ironic persona—so apt for the 1970s—against the iconic typology of Marlowe.

The differences in the two films are sharpened in the moments immediately after the shooting and during the final credits. Gould walks back along the tree-lined road, away from the camera, and Eileen Wade passes him in a jeep, heading in the opposite direction, toward the camera. She is on her way to meet Terry, her lover, with whom she has conspired all along. This reverses the movement in *The Third Man*: here it is the woman in the jeep, heading toward the camera, the man moving away on foot in the opposite direction. Gould's performance as Marlowe in its final manifestation in the film is extraordinarily nuanced. He drops the deliberate gait and body language he had assumed minutes earlier in killing Terry and walks with a spring in his step, even does a little dance-like shuffle with his feet, plays a tune on the miniature harmonica, and in a moment of improvisational glee takes hold of a peasant woman and swings her around in a dance motion. He does this to the sounds of the Benny Goodman Band joyfully reprising "Hooray for Hollywood." Unlike the beginning of the film, when Gould slept through this Hollywood anthem, he is now fully awake and moving with the music. He has become Johnnie Davis leading the band. The Marlowe whom Gould constructed during the course of the film dissolves, evaporates, is erased. Gould's Marlowe does not enter the pantheon of Marlowes that came before (Bogart, Powell, etc.). He has been absorbed into another film entirely, dancing to the rhythms of Benny Goodman, marching off with Dick Powell and Johnnie Davis.

Beneath the energy of the music and Gould's remarkable shuffling of feet, there lies something eerie and disquieting. His authenticity as the agent of irony collapses in on itself. On a rudimentary level his cavorting has been directed at Eileen in the jeep. As she passes him she knows by his manner—so imbued with the offscreen persona of Gould—that something terrible has happened to her world. In the final stages, the ironist has become a god, looking down on the animated objects beneath him. Gould does not literally gaze out from his high perch but, as an ironist, he objectifies the world and encloses himself in his own subjectivity. Here Altman and Gould take it one step further and have the ironist vanish all together. *The Long Goodbye* concludes with a rather profound statement concerning the relationship between self and other, between authenticity and fantasy. Joyce never allows Bloom to be absorbed into the larger pattern. The contrapuntal relationship between self-identity and myth is maintained throughout Joyce's novel. Dare I say that through Gould's performance and Altman's cunning, something darker is expressed in *The Long Goodbye*. In an instant, self-identity vanishes in a joyful celebration of the artifact we call Hollywood.

Works cited

Altman, Robert. "Interview with Michael Wilmington," in David Sterritt, ed., *Robert Altman: Interviews*, Oxford: University of Mississippi Press, 2000, 131–50.

Cavell, Stanley. *The World Viewed: Reflections on the Ontology of Film*. Cambridge, MA: Harvard University Press, 1979.

Chandler, Raymond. *The Long Goodbye*. New York: Ballantine Books, 1973.

Gould, Elliott. "Interview with James Mottram," *The Independent* (21 July 2012).

Holmes, John Clellon. "The Philosophy of the Beat Generation," in Ann Charters, ed., *Beat Down to Your Soul: What Was the Beat Generation?*, New York: Penguin, 2001, 222–28.

Joyce, James. *Ulysses*. New York: Vintage Press, 1986.

Nicholls, Peter. *Modernisms*. Berkeley: University of California Press, 1995.

Self, Robert T. "Resisting Reality: Acting by Design in Robert Altman's Nashville," in Cynthia Baron, Diane Carson, and Frank P. Tomasulo, eds., *More Than a Method*, Detroit: Wayne State University Press, 2004, 126–52.

Tomlinson, Doug. *Actors on Acting for the Screen*. New York: Garland Publishing, 1994.

Thompson, David, ed. *Altman on Altman*. London: Faber and Faber, 2006.

Chapter 21
Al Pacino in *Donnie Brasco*
Timotheus Vermeulen

At around the time I was invited to contribute to this anthology a chapter—indeed, this chapter—on Al Pacino's performance in *Donnie Brasco* (Mike Newell, 1997), I was reading a novel, Ben Lerner's *10:04*, in a passage from which—a few pages in—the novel's narrator, also called Ben Lerner, talks about Jules Bastien-Lepage's 1879 painting *Joan of Arc*. The painting, as the narrator Lerner explains, depicts Joan as she responds to her divine call, which is, to be sure, nothing less than to save France. He writes:

> Joan appears to stagger toward the viewer, reaching her left arm out, maybe for support, in the swoon of being called. Instead of grasping branches or leaves, her hand, which is carefully positioned on the sight line of one of the other angels, seems to dissolve. The museum placard says that Bastien-Lepage was attacked for his failure to reconcile the ethereality of the angels with the realism of the future saint's body, but that "failure" is what makes it one of my favorite paintings. It's as if the tension between the metaphysical and physical worlds, between two orders of temporality, produces a glitch in the pictorial matrix. (9)

Thinking about Al Pacino's performance in *Donnie Brasco*, I am reminded of Lerner's discussion of *Joan of Arc*. At first glance, this may seem surprising. Lerner's novel tells the story of a contemporary novelist, while *Donnie Brasco* depicts an undercover agent infiltrating the 1970s mob. As far as I can tell, moreover, Pacino's hit man Benjamin "Lefty" Ruggiero, a.k.a. Lefty Guns, a.k.a. Horse Cock, with his twenty-six kills, looks nothing like Bastien-Lepage's angelic heroine Joan. However, Lerner's account of Joan's hand disappearing in thin air, its designation as a sign of different temporalities colliding and dissolving into one another, resonates with Pacino's slippery performance of Lefty. Aptly characterized by Kathleen Murphy as the mafia's "Willy Loman" (Arthur Miller's [in]famous salesman, delusionally perceiving the world according to his needs to cope, in spite of better judgment), Ruggiero deferentially toes the New York mafia line in the hope (though not, it appears, the convicted belief) that he will one day arrive at the top. He follows orders and sidesteps doubts, stands his ground and holds back for The Family's sake, all the while being passed en route by others who are happy to cut corners. In stark contrast to the Pacino of *The Godfather II* (1974), whose clenched jaw and measured, angular movements suggest a man concerned with—even obsessive about—control, or to Pacino's Tony Montana in *Scarface* (1983), biting his lip in anger, Ruggiero's bodily composure is less decisive, less straightforward. He moves either too hastily or too sluggishly: his mouth moves at times he isn't speaking, he often rolls his shoulders as if to lift a weight that isn't there, cocks his chest forward without there being anyone to fight. His arms frequently sway forward involuntarily whilst his hands tighten, grindingly, and his knees steady themselves like it's their first day on shore after a long trip at sea. It is as if Lefty, like Joan, is in two places at once, no longer at sea but not yet landed, drifting between the present and a future invisible to anyone but himself. Or caught in a drift rather, less sailor than fish. He is *caught between* "two orders of temporality." Indeed, I would argue that it is because he is *caught* in between, because he is ensnared in two strings or nets of time at once, that Lefty tends to be seen as a Lomanesque figure, a victim rather than a perpetrator.

Here I look closely at some of these often overlapping instances of Pacino's performance of inbetweenness: two scenes in particular, the first of which allows me to look at one gesture individually, whilst the other displays a sequence of tics, each one leading into the other, intensifying, nuancing, undermining. My focus lies with Pacino's control of his body, but inevitably I discuss this performance in relation to, in the context of, the devices at the disposal of the director and the elements of the mise-en-scène, as well.

I doubt whether any performance can ever be reduced to a type, to a gestural gimmick, but Pacino's performance in *Donnie Brasco*—or indeed any of his performances, even his most recent role in Adam Sandler's critically panned *Jack and Jill* (2011)—certainly cannot. If I say, as I have above, that Michael Corleone clenches his jaw or Montana bites his lip, my point is not that these characters are defined by these gestures but rather that these gestures communicate, relate to the world (theirs and ours) certain of these characters' mindsets or inclinations, for instance control and anger. In a similar sense, Pacino's enactment of Ruggiero is by no means exhausted by, say, the shoulder roll; but the roll is a tic that tells us, that is supposed to tell us, a lot about how Ruggiero feels at specific moments in the film. Lefty rolls his shoulders often before or after a stressful event (a heist gone wrong, a surprise encounter with a lion stolen from an airport freight warehouse and gifted to him, an unexpected and unexplained call from the boss), looking back, with whoever is with him as well as with us, in frustration, it seems, or anxious anticipation—but rarely during an event or action itself. Tellingly, during the one killing we see Lefty engage in personally, of one of his friends no less, his shoulders are as still as his hands appear calm, as if to explicate that, whatever he may feel afterwards or before, the act itself is devoid of any emotion whatsoever. For Lefty, behavior is surgical, and unproblematically so; it's in the run up and aftermath that his body protests he has cut himself as well as his victims. What I am getting at here, I guess, is that Pacino's schizoism, his moving his body, or parts of his body, in another context than the one at hand, are as much character traits as they are (or are not dissimilar to) what Greg M. Smith has called "mood-cues": emotional hints, intimating the affective register of a shot, scene, or even entire film.

To be sure, I am not talking about point of view, and I am most certainly not talking about identification. What I mean, rather, is a point of orientation, an emotional resonance. For instance, if Lefty shows signs of sadness, that orients—affords and limits, or at least is likely to afford and limit, can be expected by the audience to afford and limit—the range of emotional responses available to others in his vicinity; even if his emotional state is not shared by the audience the extent to which it affects his environment is apparent. As Murray Pomerance has noted, performance is, cannot but be, intertwined with place; it is *affected* by place, but it also *affects* place. Or, in the words of Andrew Klevan, talking about Marlene Dietrich in *The Scarlett Empress* (1934): "An appreciation of the effectiveness of performance ... depends acutely on understanding its *synthesis* with location" (47, my emphasis).

There is a scene midway through the film which is, I would say, a case in point, the first of the two scenes I want to discuss. Lefty and Donnie Brasco (Johnny Depp), an undercover agent pretending to be a jeweller who has come to be Lefty's right-hand man (no pun intended), are standing outside a burger restaurant late at night. A pile of burgers is stacked on top of Donnie's car, and are being fed through the slightly unrolled window to a lion occupying the backseat (to date, I haven't figured out how the car was driven there, with the lion roaring in the back, but that is another question). Lefty is visibly reeling, his body shaking from more than only the cold. He has just returned from a short, eventful ride with Sonny Black (Michael Madsen), expecting to get killed, but instead finding out that he has been passed over for promotion—which, given his seniority, feels to Lefty like screaming murder. The circumstances and the feeling might be said to be symbolized by Sonny's gift, the lion as booby prize. The establishing shots excepted, the scene cuts, for the most part, between two-shots of Lefty and Brasco from behind the car, and medium close-ups. The two men are only ever visible from the chest up, in compositions that, especially given the localized depth of field, with the background in shallow focus, put the emphasis on their shoulders and faces. As Lefty shares his grievances about his ride with Sonny Black, his face is sawtoothed with anger, eyes flaming and cheeks blowing, his words spit out between gritted teeth:

> Sonny Black they make skipper. I ain't a mutt. Thirty years busting my hump. For what? A lion. I'm like the invisible fucking man in this thing ... Thirty years I'm earning. Any work to be done, call Lefty. I never complained. Twenty-six guys I clipped. Do I get upped? No, they pass me by. Sonny Black gets upped. I don't get fucking upped.

His shoulders, however, convey another shape, another emotion: tiptoeing, shifting his weight from one foot to another, as in a boxer's routine, Lefty's shoulders move up and down, a movement made all the more manifest by the stillness of the car top, like waves crashing onto shore. This undulation is interrupted only by sudden, repeated rolls of the shoulders that accompany realizations of his misfortune: "I never complain. Twenty-six guys I clipped. [*roll*] Do I get upped? [*roll*] No,

Sonny Black gets upped. [*roll*]"), each roll hunching high into the neck but hitting nothing but its own sensation, punching out at nothing but itself. There is no direction to either the undulation or the rolling; they both form vicious circles, aimlessly drifting around. It is as if for all his anger, Lefty, our Willy Loman, this self-proclaimed "invisible man," less sailor conquering the waves than fish swimming with the currents, has already acceded to toe the line once again, once again and always once again, looking to step back into formation. Rolling his shoulders he ceaselessly, perpetually, hopelessly tries to fit on that oversized, ill-fitting coat of his, the garish plaid one, with the fake plush collar.

Interestingly, later in the scene, as Lefty dreams out loud about leaving the mob, about shedding his coat, his face and shoulders do move in sync with one another. As he tells Brasco that he'd "get in my car, with Annette, I'd drive down to the pier, get on that boat, and I'd go, I'd go," he nods his head to the left, looking offscreen into the distance, pulling his shoulders and chest with it. In both instances, Pacino uses his shoulders to show the extent to which Lefty is engaged less in the present than in the past or the future—for he is moving not in relation to the now but in the context of another time, one invisible to both Brasco and the viewer. Indeed, what is most striking here, perhaps, is the difference between Pacino's performance and that of Depp. Where Pacino moves his face, shoulders, and chest constantly, Depp's upper body is mostly still. In fact, the only time Brasco moves markedly is to steer clear of the lion, which is to say, in response to the present. This difference, this distinction in temporality, in temporal experience, between Lefty and Brasco is a pattern throughout the film. Donnie is living moment to moment, surfing the now; Lefty is living in memory and in hope. Indeed, if Lefty's body extensively inhabiting the past or the future is a trope, Joe Pistone's attunement to the present is, too, Joe who is truly Joseph who will become Donnie. It is no coincidence that the film opens with an extreme close-up of Joe's eyes as he strains to listen in on a conversation between mobsters, the camera registering his focusing gaze as the discussion turns rowdy. Here and always he is alert to what is happening now.

As V. F. Perkins once noted, most films use their opening scenes to introduce the audience to the rules of their game—the genre, tone, narrative scope, and range, the nature of the fictional world, the inclinations of their characters. These scenes train the viewer's eyes, as it were, providing instructions on how to look, how to exercise the perceptive muscles. *Donnie Brasco* is no exception. Its first few scenes detail, respectively, the genre (as the opening shot, a close-up of a face tensing up as it strains to listen in on a conversation, suggests an undercover sting); tone (terse, uneven, rising with the anxiety of the undercover agent and falling with the joviality of the mobsters); milieu (a grey and grimy Brooklyn); and characters (agents and mobsters of varying status, though with an emphasis on the middle men). To my mind, the scene that functions as an introduction to Pacino's performance of Lefty, to the full range of his performance, encompassing nearly all his most frequented gestures, takes place about ten minutes in. On the back of a successful swindle, Lefty casually but cautiously asks Donnie Brasco to hang out. He's only just met Brasco, and knows little about him. He doesn't know, obviously—and vitally for our eponymous protagonist's health—that Brasco is an undercover agent with the FBI. He doesn't know, further, that Brasco is married and a father of three. That he lives in New Jersey. Or indeed, that Brasco isn't really his name. What he knows, at this point, all he knows at this point, is that Brasco is a jeweller with an expensive car and an impressive right hook.

The scene opens with a slow and subtle restrained pan from left to right, which in the process tilts laboriously upwards ever so slightly and zooms in: takes long to zoom in, in fact, a mere few inches. As the camera is dragged closer, like a net in the sea, it shifts focus from the shiny red car in the foreground to the two men standing behind it to, eventually, the dusty brick buildings in the background, putting story and world on a par, or world and story, traversing from one to the other and back. The effect of this leveling of plot and place is that the viewer is persuaded to see the dialogue between Lefty and Donnie, and indeed these characters and their performances themselves, in the context of the environs; and vice versa, to take in the setting as an extension of the conversation and its participants. Certainly, looking at Lefty's beige coat, one is compelled by the end of the scene, when the hitman disappears into the background, to appreciate its correspondence with the dusty brown bricks of the apartment buildings behind him, one of which may well be—must be, given that this is where Lefty is dropped off, where he is left by Donnie, where he leaves Donnie, so that there is no reason to assume otherwise—his home. Similarly, from the outset Donnie's Bordeaux red leather jacket manifestly matches the color and tone of his shiny red DeVille. What the film seems to do here by leveling story and world is to give, quite literally, weight to Lefty's invitation to Donnie to join his company. Lefty isn't just asking Donnie to hang out; he is asking him, almost like a father asks a son, to come home, to join The

Family. Lefty is obsessively cautious, it's like his second nature. He's a small fish scanning for sharks. Indeed, his experience of his milieu as oppressing and precarious is a recurrent trope in the film: at numerous instances he states a desire to leave it behind for happier, safer seas. But here his caution is particularly poignant. There's a correspondence between him and his turgid surrounding, between his frumpy, depressing beige coat and the brown bricks of the apartment block—anchors weighing him down—that suggests there is a lot at stake: his whole life, in fact. Donnie, by contrast, is linked to a vehicle, movement, the temporary presence. He moved into this situation; for a while, as the film reaches its climax, he's trapped in it; but then he'll move on.

Pacino here performs Lefty's caution as a restlessness, a constant trepidation of the feet, chest, shoulders, eyes, and head. Throughout the scene he shifts his weight back and forth between the left foot and the right, leaning in and tilting away, literally on his toes, bowing his knees, turning his torso into one direction only to turn his head the other, looking around, scanning the environment for one thing while he talks about another. Sometime during my early childhood, I don't remember how old I must have been exactly, my parents lived next door to a police officer. Once, during a dinner party, this man, who liked to talk about his work, explained to us kids that criminals tend to stand with their back to the wall so no one can come at them from behind. I don't remember the whole story, nor do I know whether it was true, but seeing Lefty skip around, scanning his surroundings, I had to think of someone standing with his back to a kind of wall, someone who wants to be able to see whatever is coming his way. The moment he asks Donnie to hang out, his eyes shift, nervously, from left to right, as if he is worried someone else might overhear, only connecting with the younger man's eyes momentarily, midway through, to gauge his response. Earlier, bragging about the mob, Lefty hoppingly rotated his entire body to see that they were alone. Lefty is caught adrift, it seems, between the present, between making a friend, and the future, the implications making that friend might turn out to have.

In terms of the subtlety of Pacino's performance, it is interesting to note how his confusion and his caution compare. What differentiates them from one another is not the precise selection of gestures but the gestural sequencing, the manner in which one brief bodily expression follows another and leads into the next. In the first scene I discussed above, Lefty's confusion was signified by the disjunction between face and shoulders, portraying a man unsure of his own disposition. In the above scene, caution is the result of the constant conversion of one gesture into the next, creating an image of a man always alert to his surroundings, always racing.

There is one further gesture I would like to briefly consider, a gesture which appears, though in differing disguises, in both of the above scenes: the cocked chest. In the above scene, Lefty, his feet planted wide, hands thrust deep into his pockets, momentarily anchors himself, pushes forward his chest very slightly, and ever so briefly, at the instant he invokes the rituals and rules of the mob. In the scene outside the burger restaurant, Lefty pulls up his chest a number of times, but never as noticeably as the moment he complains to Donnie in the lion-feeding scene about not getting "upped," about not being awarded a promotion. It's the third time in the scene he mentions not getting "upped." As I have noted above, the first two times he rolls his shoulders the moment he raises the subject, signaling a sense of deflation. Here, as he spits out "I don't get fucking upped," the roll of his shoulders is accompanied by a pumping of the chest, like a last gasp of the spirit. In the lion scene, I would argue, Pacino uses the movement of his chest to suggest pride; in the scene outside Lefty's home, in stark contrast, he breathes air into it so as to create an impression of dissatisfaction, and even violence. He inflates himself, sucking in dignity. Both moments are illusory, since the mob as we see it has nothing to do with nobility, and Lefty certainly never acts upon his violent urge. But here, too, Pacino's performance of Lefty should be understood less as a register of gestures than as a sequencing of gestures, an overlapping and undercutting, a developing and extracting. The cocked chest is made meaningful, and is made meaningful only, in relation to the other gestures, the mise-en-scène, and the narrative.

Writing about Bastien-Lepage's *Joan of Arc*, Lerner—or his narrator—notes that Joan reaches "her left arm out, maybe for support, in the swoon of being called," but that instead "of grasping branches or leaves, her hand ... seems to dissolve." Lefty at no point in *Donnie Brasco* loses his hand, not even to the lion, but Pacino does show the extent to which he is grasping for branches and leaves that aren't there, the extent to which Lefty's body is adrift between different orders of time. In the two scenes I have discussed here, Pacino continually recomposes his frame from a select repertoire of movements and gestures without necessarily answering to the immediate demands of his environment. Lefty becomes someone whose corporeality, wittingly and unconsciously, inhabits multiple temporalities at once—and consequently neither temporality in its entirety. He tiptoes in search of balance whilst everyone else has found firm footing. He rolls his shoulders to put on a coat he is already wearing. He cocks his chest for a fight he will never start. Lefty is always already out of sync, never there where he is, the sign of a man whose way of life is catching up with him, who realizes it but cannot change it. Lefty may not have lost a hand, yet, but whether he has found it, whether he has a hand on things, is another question. Pacino, aided of course by director Mike Newell's choices, impressively contextualizes a ruthless killer as a victim, as a classic tragic schmuck caught in a net of time and latching on to whatever last strand he can grasp, wafting beyond his control. What Pacino does here, what makes this performance so great, is to act not just a character or even a subject but a sensation, a sentiment lingering throughout the film to pull it together, contract it, close it in upon itself.

Works cited

Klevan, Andrew. *Film Performance: From Achievement to Appreciation*. London: Wallflower, 2005.
Lerner, Ben. *10:04*. London: Granta, 2015.
Murphy, Kathleen. "Dancing on the High Wire: Al Pacino," *Film Comment* 36: 2 (March/April 2000), 18–31.
Perkins, V. F. *Film as Film: Understanding and Judging Movies*. Penguin: London, 1972.
Pomerance, Murray. *Moment of Action: Riddles of Cinematic Performance*. New Brunswick, NJ: Rutgers University Press, 2016.

Chapter 22

Whoopi Goldberg in *The Color Purple*

Lester D. Friedman

In considering the screen performances of African American actors like Whoopi Goldberg, it seems logical to assume that cultural expectations and historical film conventions play a larger role in their craft than is necessarily the case with white performers. No African American actor can possibly be unaware of the racist style that has characterized Hollywood filmmaking's depiction of black characters from its silent days till the present time, yielding a litany of derogatory portrayals repeatedly punctuated by histrionic gestures and movements (see Bogle). Throughout much of American cinema's history, black performers' physical characteristics—including exaggerated gestures, postures, body movements, and speech patterns—constituted a virtual catalogue of racist caricatures that represented black culture for movie audiences.

Speaking particularly about the career of Whoopi Goldberg, Rebecca Wanzo contends that her performances, including that in *The Color Purple*

(1985), contain an essential paradox faced by other black entertainers as well: "It can be impossible to avoid evoking stereotypical histories as black bodies carry a history of hypervisible degradation" (145). Goldberg, continues Wanzo, "teaches us how difficult it is for a black subject to remove herself or transform racial scripts" (146). She is not only a performer but also a "cultural object," who negotiates her status in a very public venue but who cannot escape an inherent relationship to the black community and, perhaps unwittingly, must also serve as one of its representatives to the dominant white culture. "Black subjects," concludes Wanzo, "carry the burden of almost all-encompassing denigrating images which they are sometimes rewarded for embodying" (149). In essence, as Wanzo argues, black performers cannot evade the cinematic history that preceded them. Female black actors are especially often reduced to singular identities in their appearances onscreen. Goldberg notably defended *The Color Purple* arguing that "there was not a 'mammy' or a 'nigger' in this film. I resent the fact that people think we actors would be involved in something that shows stereotypical behavior. Do people think that neither I am capable of judging what's exploitative, nor Danny Glover nor Oprah Winfrey" (Collins 124).

When Steven Spielberg released his screen version of Alice Walker's popular novel *The Color Purple,* few in the audience had ever heard of Whoopi Goldberg, the performance artist/comedian who played Celie, the lead role in the director's first "grownup movie." (Nor did many recognize the local Chicago talk-show host who played Sofia and soon emerged as one of the most famous people in America.) But, it was another director who put Goldberg on the path to stardom. In 1983, Mike Nichols viewed Goldberg's transgressive, one-woman performance in *The Spook Show,* staged at the Dance Theater Workshop in New York City's Chelsea district, and recognized her raw and prodigious talents. Nichols, a former comedian himself, watched Goldberg physically transform herself into the dope fiend (Fontaine); a teenage surfer chick who had an abortion; a severely crippled character; and a black girl of about thirteen who tried to change her color, each incarnation accompanied by a satiric, emotive, and biting monologue. Moved by her performance, Nichols worked with Goldberg to prepare and then produce her show for a larger audience. *Whoopi Goldberg* opened on Broadway in October of 1984, ran for 156 performances, and was later filmed as an HBO special, *Whoopi Goldberg: Direct from Broadway* (1985).

Alice Walker saw Goldberg on Broadway and recommended her to Spielberg, who quickly interviewed her for the movie. "I knew by your fifteenth breath that you were Celie," he said in an interview with Goldberg taped for "The View" (2 March 2016), much to the surprise of the actress herself. Over time, Goldberg (née Caryn Elaine Johnson) became one of the few performers to achieve the coveted EGOT (winning an Emmy, Grammy, Oscar, and Tony), appeared in over 150 movies, often in roles originally written for white men, became one of the highest paid actresses in Hollywood, co-hosted Comic Relief (for the Homeless) with Robin Williams and Billy Crystal, was awarded the Mark Twain Prize for American Humor (2002), narrated HBO's *Unchained Memories: Readings for the Slave Narratives* (2003), co-hosted and moderated "The View," emerged as an activist for LGBT rights among other liberal causes, and recently launched a medical marijuana product line for menstrual cramps. As Chris Holmlund notes, Goldberg is "far and away the most successful and prolific African-American *female* star" in Hollywood history (127). Labelling her screen activities with men as "covert involvements," Holmlund observes that Goldberg consistently "modifies the Hollywood stereotypes of black women as tragic mulattos and comic mammies" (128). But all this happened after her stunning debut in *The Color Purple*.

Alice Walker's feminist novel, which won both the National Book Award and the Pulitzer Prize for Fiction, sparked heated disputes because of its frank presentation of incest, spousal abuse, female sexuality, and lesbianism within black society. The movie ignited a larger firestorm by bringing these incendiary issues to a wide audience. Outside the black community, critics castigated Spielberg for candy coating Walker's graphic narrative: typical of the hostile responses were David Ansen's (*Newsweek*), noting "the disorienting sensation that I was watching the first Disney movie about incest" (quoted in McBride 365), and Rita Kempley's (*The Washington Post*), calling the director's version of rural Georgia "a pastoral paradise that makes Dorothy Gale's Kansas farm look like a slum" (in McBride 373). But these objections were tame compared to those arising from inside the black community. Along with a number of other critics, Jacquelyn Bobo rebukes the filmmaker for creating a production "in line with Steven Spielberg's experiences, cultural background, and social and political worldview . . . He tapped into his consciousness and experiences and produced a work that was in keeping with his philosophy and knowledge of Hollywood films about black people" (76). These controversies spilled from the page into the streets, starting with boycotts from the Coalition Against Black Exploitation and the Hollywood branch of the NAACP and proceeding to protest meetings in black churches across the country. Although the film received eleven Academy Award nominations, Spielberg was not selected to compete in the Best Director category. (*The Color Purple* won no Oscars, while an intrinsically more racist film, *Out of Africa*, captured the statuette for Best Picture.)

The scene I have selected marks a poignant moment of contact between Celie and Shug (Margaret Avery), the jazz performer who is also her husband's lover, and forms the foundation for Celie's eventual liberation and transformation. Although seemingly quite different from each other, Celie and Shug are sisters under the skin: two women whose children have been taken away from them, two women whose fathers have either abandoned or raped them (as we believe at this point in the story), two women who have suffered irreparable emotional trauma inflicted by their fathers—and by other men as well. For the first time since her cruel husband Mister (Danny Glover) so brutally separated her from her sister Nettie (Akosua Busia), Celie feels something for someone else, the beginning of her efforts to escape the harshly enforced boundaries within the patriarchal culture that dominates her life. Eventually, Shug's appreciation of Celie's kindness and warmth evolves into a deeply reciprocal love. In this scene, Celie sees herself through Shug's eyes, a decisive perceptual transference that allows her to recognize herself as a person of worth and substance and, as a result, to attain the inner strength needed to escape the physical and emotional oppression represented by Mister. Thus, the path to her literal and psychological emancipation begins here.

The scene begins with a close up of a Victrola playing a jazz tune, with a cut to Shug's fingers flicking ashes from her cigarette into an ashtray. As the camera pans up her body, we see that she is stylishly coiffed, dressed in a muted red dress, and expressing slight frustration while waiting for Celie to appear. "Come on, Miss Celie," she says, adding, "I don't wanna have to come in there after you now." Shug's straight posture with head held high and kind expression exude composure and confidence, as will continue during the entire sequence. Celie, however, is something else. As the camera pans back, we witness her emerging from behind a dark curtain. She clumps forward, dressed in the same sparkling red dress that Shug wore earlier when she sang "Miss Celie's Blues" in the juke joint. The dress works as both a recognition of their sisterhood and an appreciation of their unlikely similarities. The lyrics echo in our mind: "Sister/You've been on my mind/Oh, sister/We're two of a kind/So, sister/I'm keeping my eyes on you/. . . I'm something/I hope you think that you're something, too."

But unlike the sexy, uninhibited Shug, who could shimmy and shake and make the dress swirl around her, Celie looks unkempt and uncomfortable; in her comic attempt to mimic Shug, the straps of her white slip hang down beneath her shoulders and a white boa droops precariously off her body. Goldberg's body language betrays her insecurities. Her mouth is clamped shut, as it has been throughout much of the movie, her hand protectively concealing her protruding teeth. The large traditional cheval mirror highlights their differences. Celie is on screen right, while Shug's image in the mirror is on screen left. The actors share the frame but are spatially separated from each other, an apt visual representation of how they both fit together but remain detached from each other at this point. Later in the scene, their reflections will share the same mirror, emphasizing their progressive closeness. Shug reels off a string of compliments ("You can catch a fish without a hook; "You can make a blind man see") as Celie lurches forward, trying to be elegant but failing to achieve Shug's gracefulness. Placing her hands on Celie's hips and making them gyrate as she moves effortlessly into a dance, Shug commands her to "Show me your stuff. Shake your Shimmy, girl"—lines that, as the scene develops, have a sexual meaning as well. Celie, her hand still covering her mouth, moves away from Shug, but she turns back to look at her with a sense of gentle admiration, her wedding band prominently filling the room with a reminder of her debasement at the brutal hands of Mister.

Then, the transformation begins. "Why are you always covering up your mouth?" Shug asks Celie, moving to join her in the frame. "Show me your teeth." She is embracing Celie. "Show me that pretty smile." They bend forward together, cheek to cheek, the images trapped in both a rectangular mirror and the smaller round mirror attached to it. Slowly, Celie begins to open her mouth, just a little, while Shug's beautiful smile acts as a model for her to emulate. Celie snickers and covers her mouth again, fearful of revealing herself. "You need a smiling lesson," Shug replies. Together, they dance over to the cheval glass on the other side of the room. Shug turns Celie around so that her back is to the mirror, then spins her forward. Again, Celie quickly moves her hand to cover her mouth, but behind it we can clearly see she is smiling—barely but perceivably. Finally, Shug drags Celie's hand away from her face and, for the first time, Celie sees herself laughing in the mirror. It is a glorious moment of self-revelation, but when she tries to cover up again, Shug forces Celie's hands down, refusing to let her hide her smile—and all the other hidden parts of her life it symbolizes. Although Celie attempts to shield her mouth one more time, Shug will not allow her to do so. Finally, finally, a full-throated laugh bursts forth from Celie, a natural, joyful response to her new sense of herself and the sheer pleasure of the liberation she feels, at last allowing herself to be fully seen in the company of a woman she has grown to love.

Shug releases her hands and, in a close two-shot, joins Celie in laugher, sharing this moment between two women who, under the most unlikely of circumstances, have become friends. Now, ironically, Shug covers her mouth. But this is not a gesture of hiding her imperfections or protecting her secrets, but rather one of Shug sharing a space with another person who has been kind to her and for whom she has deep affection. Shug backs away, allowing Celie to see her whole self, alone, in the mirror, to take advantage of her new-found freedom. "You see, Miss Celie," she says, "You gots a *beautiful* smile!" With the camera still on Celie, Shug divulges that she must leave, and Celie's smile fades into a sad expression. "He beat me when you aren't here," she reveals, "he beat me for not being you." She turns and looks at Shug across the space they share. The only sound that fills the room is the record ending and the needle relentlessly scratching back and forth, until Shug replaces it with a new record, a new tune for what will quickly become a change in the situation.

Shug takes Celie's hand and they sit down on her bed together. The conversation then turns to sex, with Shug asking Celie if she minds her sleeping with Albert and Celie's incredulous response to the revelation that Shug actually enjoys sex. "Most of the time I preteen like I ain't even there," she tells Shug, "He don't ever ask me how I feel. Just climb on top of me and do his business." To this admission, Shug responds, "Then you still a virgin." "Yeah" says Celie shyly, "don't nobody love me." Goldberg turns her eyes downward and shrugs her shoulders, refusing to meet Shug's eyes. When Shug replies that she thinks Celie is beautiful, Goldberg at first returns the compliment with a muted anger, reminding her that at their first meeting Shug told her, "You sure is ugly." But now Shug leans over and kisses Celie on the cheek, then on the forehead. Celie slowly turns her face so she can get kissed on the other check, then back to the forehead. They stare at each other for a moment before Shug cups Celie's chin, draws her face to hers, and kisses her on the lips. At first, Celie backs away, fearful of the passion this kiss has aroused in her. Then she covers her mouth and laughs. But this time she takes her own hands away, and the camera follows them downward towards her lap. Shug smiles. Celie smiles, a big wide open, confident grin. She leans forward and plants a small kiss on Shug's lips. A peck really. Proud of herself, she giggles at her new-found boldness, raising her eyebrow, even giving a snort. Shug draws her into a far more passionate kiss, one with the promise of sexual adventures to accompany it, and Celie keeps her eyes open as if she thinks Shug might disappear. But she accepts the invitation. The camera follows Shug's hand to Celie's shoulder, to Celie's hand on Shug's waist, then slowly upward to rest on Shug's shoulder, and finally to the small wind chime tinkling above them.

Throughout this crucial scene, the various gestures, movements, and facial expressions of Goldberg and Avery become far more important than dialogue. In fact, a good deal of the scene takes place either in silence or without dialogue. Although Shug offers Celie words of encouragement, her actions remain most important for Celie, who aches for love and tenderness to heal her raw wounds. These two characters enter the scene without any knowledge of how it will end, and neither does the viewer. What begins as charming playfulness between two friends ends with the release of powerful emotions, both physically and psychologically. Remember that a drunken Shug's first words to Celie made fun of her looks, and Celie has served a very subordinate position in helping to heal Shug. Both Shug and Celie are surprised as their emotions take hold of them, and the viewer is as well. Celie displays a shy reticence throughout the scene, a willingness to let Shug control the action, as she has up till this point in the film. Yet, in the last few moments, Celie not only responds to Shug's kisses but begins to direct the action, although in a gentle, rather than demanding, manner. Interestingly, Spielberg chooses to shift from the actors' faces to the movements of their hands, as they tenderly touch each other. For Celie, a woman who has been degraded and mistreated her entire life, the fact that a beautiful and worldly woman like Shug can desire her, can love her, allows her to experience a flash of self-discovery, to realize that she possesses the worth to begin the process of reclaiming her dignity and ultimately her agency. For Shug, the act of loving Celie, both physically and emotionally, speaks to a recognition of how her priorities have dramatically shifted: it is Celie who now wears the shiny red dress that captivated men in the juke box, while Shug is clothed in a more demure outfit with muted colors. Shug's recognition of Celie's worth is the first step in Celie's finding the emotional strength and courage to reach out to her preacher father, a man whose respect and love she desperately craves and whom she needs to accept her as his daughter once again. These two are, indeed, sisters who both require and support each other.

This scene between Shug and Celie also foregrounds how the lack of physical beauty can be a disability that dooms one's ambitions. Shug has been accepted in the world because of her looks, as well as her talents, and Celie has been denied the basic rights owed a human being, even within her own racial group, at least partially because she is deemed ugly. In many ways, this scene is prophetic of Goldberg's subsequent film career. Mia Mask observes that Goldberg has often been excluded from conventional romantic comedies and is "one of the few female stars whose entertainment persona is not predicated on traditional notions of femininity, nubile sexuality, and happy-ever-after endings of heterosexual union" (106). Celie's unwillingness to show her teeth is a symbol of the repression and discrimination she has suffered her entire life. It represents the way Goldberg's Celie has been excluded from the traditional "social construction of beauty (and) dismissed as physically unattractive or even ugly ... her physiognomy doesn't conform to the widely held standard of beauty operating within mainstream white America and in African American communities" (112). Mask goes on to detail how notions of femininity are "still predicated on bodily signifiers (fair skin complexion, straight hair texture, low weight, and youthful appearances) that communicate a mimetic relationship between gender and sex" (113). All that Mask says about Goldberg can, indeed, be equally applied to Celie, perhaps one reason why Spielberg said, "There was nobody else alive in the world, in 1984, that could have possibly been Celie. She was the only Celie" (quoted in Brevard 57).

Many of Spielberg's detractors indicted him for drastically attenuating Walker's sexually liberated stance by eliminating the overt lesbian scenes she so lovingly describes between Celie and Shug, filming the relationship with a discrete 1950s obliqueness rather than a 1980s frankness. Granted that this scene does not offer viewers the more overt sexuality that greeted readers of the novel. But the vast majority of those seeing this scene cannot miss the sexual overtures and have no doubt as to what occurs offscreen. Jan Whitt talks about the "encoding" present in this scene and suggested by gestures and looks rather than by the limited physical contact between Shug and Celie (52). "I don't think a full-out love scene would have said it any better," Spielberg contends on the DVD interview that accompanies *The Color Purple*. While Walker was initially "annoyed that there was not more cuddling and kissing and making love," she looks back (on the DVD interview) and concludes that this scene "was very, very well done because it captures the sweetness of their relationship." The decision not to show the physical relationship between Shug and

Celie in more graphic detail was clearly an artistic and marketing choice. "Ultimately," says Spielberg, the women experience "a love relationship of great need. No one had ever loved Celie other than God and her sister. And here Celie is being introduced to the human race by a person full of love" (Collins 124).

Whether Celie's feelings for Shug are initially sexual or not hardly seems the point here. The fact that Celie is finally able to take her hands away from her mouth, to no longer feel compelled to keep her teeth—and her words and emotions as well—hidden, that she can smile with pleasure and laugh with exhilaration, forms an unbreakable bond between these two resilient women, one as strong as any felt by biologically related siblings. The fact that Celie and Shug become lovers expresses physically what they are experiencing emotionally, as Celie's recognition of her need to assert herself becomes entwined with her initiation into sexual arousal. Both Celie and Shug emerge from this scene as different women. Throughout the rest of the movie, they will never again experience the same level of physical intimacy with each other, but this empathetic moment of warmth and compassion will forever change them. Celie will go on to become a successful entrepreneur, regain the love of her children, and finally possess a home of her own. Shug will be able to settle down and join the circle of women at the end of the movie. Both women will take away something significant from their sexual encounter, something more than physical pleasure: a sense of who they are and what they might become that will steer towards the path to overcome their pain and find peace within a company of men who have tried to defeat them but, in the final analysis, have been forced to witness their triumph.

Works cited

Baron, Cynthia, Diane Carson, and Frank P. Tomasulo, eds. *More than a Method: Trends and Traditions in Contemporary Film Performance*. Detroit: Wayne State Press, 2004.
Baron, Cynthia, and Sharon Marie Carnicke. *Reframing Screen Performance*. Ann Arbor: University of Michigan Press, 2011.
Bernardi, Daniel, ed. *Filming Difference: Actors, Directors, Producers, and Writers on Gender, Race, and Sexuality in Film*. Austin: University of Texas Press, 2009.
Bobo, Jacqueline. *Black Women as Culture Readers*. New York: Columbia University Press, 1995.
Bogle, Donald. *Toms, Coons, Mulattoes, Mammies and Bucks: An Interpretative History of Blacks in Films*. New York: Viking Books, 1973.
Brevard, Lisa Pertillar. *Whoopi Goldberg on Stage and Screen*. Jefferson, NC: McFarland and Company, 2013.

Collins, Glenn. "Spielberg's Films: The Color Purple," in Lester D. Friedman and Brent Notbohm, eds., *Steven Spielberg: Interviews*, Jackson, MS: University Press of Mississippi, 2000, 120–5.

Holmlund, Chris. *Impossible Bodies: Femininity and Masculinity at the Movies*. London: Routledge, 2002.

hooks, bell. "The Oppositional Gaze: Black Female Spectators," in *Black Looks: Race and Representation*, Boston: South End Press, 1992, 115–31.

Mask, Mia. *Divas on Screen: Black Women in American Film*. Urbana, IL: University of Illinois Press, 2009.

McBride, Joseph. *Steven Spielberg: A Biography*. New York: Simon and Schuster, 1997.

Springer, Claudia. "Introduction," in Claudia Springer and Julie Levinson, eds., *Acting*, New Brunswick, NJ: Rutgers University Press, 2015, 1–24.

Wanzo, Rebecca. "Beyond a 'Just' Syntax: Black Actresses, Hollywood and Complex Personhood," *Woman & Performance: A Journal of Feminist Theory* 1: 16 (March 2006), 135–52.

Whitt, Jane. "What Happened to Celie and Idgie?: 'Aspirational Lesbians' in American Film," *Studies in Popular Culture* 7: 3 (April 2005), 43–57.

Chapter 23
Cate Blanchett in *Blue Jasmine*
Shonni Enelow

The grammar of the performance is the narrowing and widening of her eyes. Half-mooned, they're self-satisfied; teasing, but protective. Rounded, they're glassy, stunned, close to spilling. When she narrows them, it's attached to a close-lipped smile, cheekbones lifted like a shield; widening them, she leans in and lowers her chin, tilting it just slightly off-center. You could trace the trajectory of the performance through the fate of her eye makeup: at first immaculate, it later blurs and cakes, the mascara bleeding in spidery black marks on her face, shrouding her eyes in a muddy mask. Finally it disappears completely, leaving them vague and pale.

"There was no one like Hal," Cate Blanchett's Jasmine confides to her first-class seatmate, assured and confident, in the first scene of Woody Allen's *Blue Jasmine* (2013). She's on a plane, well dressed and relaxed-looking, and her conversation is animated and warm, as she takes pleasure in her own expressiveness, her charm in full flower. "One more year and I would have graduated," she drawls in semi-Boston style, in a mid-Atlantic diction worthy of Katharine Hepburn (whom the actress, as we may know, once played). When she tells her interlocutor she met Hal, her husband, at a party while "Blue Moon" was playing, then asks, not quite innocently, if she's heard of it, it's our first clue that there's not just something affected about Jasmine's performance, but something contrived, unconvincing, and, like her accent, vaguely anachronistic: who hasn't heard of "Blue Moon"? The woman in the next seat assents politely but slightly ironically; then, as the scene cuts to the airport, the tone shifts. Out of first class and onto a crowded escalator, Jasmine has stopped smiling. She's still in command, but tense, anxious, slightly shaking her head as she chats about her nervous breakdown. By the time she's waiting for the baggage, she's scattered, out of focus, her eyes roving, her speech jumping from one topic to another. Now she's not quite addressing her former seatmate except to toss off an occasional surprising, irrelevant remark. Her behavior seems more and more incongruous. We're aware of the mismatch between the situation and what she's saying, as when she tells her obviously uninterested interlocutor that she's come to San Francisco to stay with her sister Ginger, and that they were "both adopted." This information, exposition framed as such, gives another clue to what the film's Allen is up to: in *Blue Jasmine*, Jasmine's attachments, such as they may be, are all tenuous and easily broken, and she's not only out of place but strangely out of time, unmoored from all positions, both geographic and familial.

There's in fact something tenuous about all of Jasmine's behavior, even in the memory scenes when we see her in her tony former existence as an Upper East Side wife. In our first trip into Jasmine's past, occasioned by her dismayed entrance into her sister's (supposedly shabby) San Francisco flat, we see Jasmine and her husband (Alec Baldwin) coming through the door of their 5th Avenue apartment. If in San Francisco Jasmine was jittery, tentative, and easily ruffled, in her supposedly golden memories we notice she's still slightly awkward on her feet. Her very high heels and bootcut jeans make her seem oddly coltish, a bit uncertain. And then there's her voice, which is a little too sing-song, its tones a little put-on—"You shouldn't spoil me *so!*"—and Hal's clunky, expositional dialogue, "Did I tell you my news?" Something is off; it feels staged, forced, strained. We hear and see that over-dramatization again, as she mimes to the serving staff at an elegant dinner party we cut to next, and in an ostentatious interruption of the conversation delivers a scripted-seeming line about recalling "Blue Moon," part of her performance just as is Hal's next line: "I fell in love with the name Jasmine." Dutiful cooing at the dinner table. We cut back to the present and find Jasmine sitting alone in Ginger's apartment, filmed from behind, so that only the corner of her face is visible. "I changed it," she says to no one, finishing the remembered conversation, "Yeah, Jeannette had no panache." The contrast (in tone as well as setting) between the memory and the present is striking, but so is the fact that her face is very similar in both, now just a bit muted: it's the world that has changed around her, and as a result—in a kind of Kuleshov effect—her narrowed eyes and affected smile suddenly look sneering, bitter. This is the first time we see her talking to herself, the sign of her encroaching madness, and it's telling that what Jasmine is talking about here is her own characterization. Jasmine is a role; Blanchett is playing an actress.

James Naremore wrote of Marlene Dietrich, "She inhabits a realm where visible artifice becomes the sign of authenticity" (131). Cate Blanchett, in contrast to many of her contemporaries, has always been a performer unafraid of overt artifice. Her theatrical flair and self-aware magnetism call to mind a different generation of star, someone who belongs in the pantheon with Dietrich and Katharine Hepburn. And among her peers she's also the most convincingly theatrical animal (to use Elia Kazan's delicious phrase, describing himself and Tennessee Williams), a full-bodied actress equally at home onstage as on camera. A flexible, quick-witted, and responsive scene partner, she also projects a command of her own presence and an unapologetic enjoyment of that command that some find unnerving, if not off-putting. This is why she can play icons: Elizabeth I (in *Elizabeth* (1998), her break-out role), Hepburn herself (in *The Aviator* (2004)), Bob Dylan (in *I'm Not There* (2007)). We are never afraid for Blanchett, as we watch her; even when she plays victims or dupes (in *The Talented Mister Ripley* (1999), for instance), her vulnerability is never total. Instead, as in the opening scene of *Blue Jasmine,* in which her blathering remains too snide to garner much pity, she teeters on the edge of our dislike, rarely tempering her fundamental coolness with direct appeals to our sympathy. If she remains, nonetheless, an emotionally resonant actress, it's tribute to the way she has thematized her own charisma as a star, often directly or indirectly making her power of command part of the dynamics of the role. However self-aware, though, her performance in *Blue Jasmine* is strikingly low in irony. The dashes of affectation (the theatrical line readings, the divaesque self-righteousness) remain just this side of camp, and they're injected with enough classic psychological realism to frame them as strategic characterization choices, rather than a total style. More than anything else, *Blue Jasmine* is a character study of a person ripped from her context, a "performer" whose "theater" has suddenly disappeared, mid-act.

Acting the actress

Early on in *Blue Jasmine*, Augie (Andrew Dice Clay), Ginger's ex-husband and one victim of Hal's (Bernie Madoff-style) fraud (Hal's wealth turns out to be criminal gains), admonishes Ginger about her sister: "You said it! You said to me: she's a phony and had to know." But the accusation rings somewhat hollow. Jasmine both is and is not a phony. She did and did not know what her husband was doing. Instead, it's her world that's revealed to be phony: the Ponzi scheme her husband constructed, his lying assurances of fidelity, the elaborate pyramid of her cosseted life—all are revealed to be "mere" theater, built on fiction and deception, patriarchal privilege and the aspirational dreams of the middle class (pathetically demonstrated as Hal convinces Augie to invest their lottery winnings with his fraudulent company). And Jasmine, who once invented a self (changing her name, joining the upper class) now has to reinvent it: not remove the mask so much as don a new one. Naremore famously notes "a fundamental trope of realist film acting: the player assumes a representational stance, her gaze turned slightly away from the lens, and then makes at least two faces, both clearly visible to the audience, one coded as 'suppressed' the other as 'ostensive'" (80). In *Blue Jasmine*, Blanchett does show us these two faces, but then repeatedly blurs them, calling into question realist acting's foundational claims about the difference between the persona and the person. She's almost always in motion—touching her hair, rocking forwards and backwards, fiddling with her jewellery or her martini glass—and when she breaks, it's not "down" but "apart": she doesn't collapse as much as vibrate, toppling onto the couch, skidding out of the car and spilling the contents of her purse. Even her mental unraveling is as a shift into another form of fantasy, not a revelation of truth or depth, a less glossy, less sure act but not a "true self." Blanchett the actress plays Jasmine the actress as a strategic fabrication for getting along in a world of artifice.

In her first scene with Ginger, for instance, she alternates between pleading and pretended casualness: "I need to stay here for a while. Na – I . . . I do. I'm out of cash. I couldn't pay my rent in Brooklyn. I mean do you believe I had to move out of my beautiful home and take a place in Brooklyn?" She's chattering but with intensity, her voice skipping from high to low range, and she peers intensely at Ginger, eyes widening. "But I'm dead broke. Really. I mean the government took everything. And the lawyers. No and I can't be alone, Ginger? I really get some bad thoughts when I'm alone." She leans in, eyes even rounder, pointing a slightly shaking finger at her head. The self-justification is still there, but it seems panicked: she quickens her speech as her voice becomes husky. Ginger responds weakly, "Well, all I can say is that you look great." "Ah – oh, now who's lying!" And Jasmine leans back and puts her face back on, smiling again, slightly cocking her head and narrowing her eyes, but also moving backwards, retreating, as she tries to be airy in her melodic, high-pitched voice. "You know I was up all last night"—she demurs, looks away and plays with her pearls, but still smiling narrow-eyed, ducking her head—"I was so anxious about"—almost making fun of herself—"moving here, I wasn't sure how . . . (*pause*) . . . angry you still were." On the last phrase, her smile is there but her big eyes are back: her two faces, glamorous and desperate, come together. Then she quickly turns her back on her sister, turning in all directions: "Should I have another drink?"

Blanchett's performance here is multiply self-referential. *Blue Jasmine* is an adaptation of Tennessee Williams's *A Streetcar Named Desire*— indeed, the film is more *Streetcar* than many critics have noted: several of Allen's scenes quote directly from the play—and Blanchett's performance clearly alludes to her previous interpretation of Blanche DuBois with the Sydney Theater Company, in a production directed by Liv Ullmann, which toured just a few years before Allen's film. It's a performance, in other words, that refers biographically to Blanchett's own experience as an actress as well as intertextually to another dramatic fiction. What's more, Blanche DuBois is not just any dramatic character, she is the archetypical American dramatic fiction of a woman as performer.

Blanche's theatricality—her feminine stylizations, her efforts to turn her setting into a stage, with lighting and costume and sound—and her elaborate performances (as a knowing flirt with her brother-in-law Stanley Kowalski, as an ingenue for her sometime suitor Mitch) Williams emphasized over and over in his play. Blanche/Blanchett: the character and actress overlap and interpenetrate in *Blue Jasmine*. But they ultimately diverge. Like Blanche, Jasmine is a performer; like Blanche, we see her performance fall apart over the course of the film. But unlike both, Blanchett's control over the performance stabilizes and anchors the character's dissolutions in a triumph of actorly virtuosity, as in her first scene with Ginger. What we are watching is a dramatization of the difference between two kinds of performance: one failed (the character's) and one a brilliant success.

With *Blue Jasmine* and *Carol* (2015), we might quip that Blanchett's career has entered its mannerist phase. Insofar as her Jasmine is a performance about Blanchett as an actress, it thematizes Blanchett's performance style, her steeliness and aristocratic bearing. It's a performance about command and control—what it means to command a scene, and what it feels like to lose control of one. All the spaces in the film are under male control: the tony Manhattan apartment, the Connecticut mansion, and the Hamptons beach house all belong to Hal, and all disappear when he does; her sister's apartment is controlled by Chili (Bobby Cannavale), the new boyfriend (in addition to Augie, the film's other Stanley Kowalski stand-in); the dentist's office where Jasmine works for a time is commanded, to repulsive effect, by the dentist (Michael Stuhlbarg) who sexually harasses and assaults her; and her potential new paradise, a bay-view house in Marin County dangled out to her by the Prince Charming she meets at a party, the former diplomat Dwight (Peter Sarsgaard), is swiftly retracted by him. In the film's diegetic climax, Jasmine's repeated cry is, "What am I doing here?" and it's a question that hangs over the performance as a whole. Where does she belong? What scene can she command?

There is a feminist subtext, whether or not Allen intended one, in the acknowledgment that however commanding in certain settings and under certain circumstances the female performance may be, it depends on the goodwill and even whim of the man who's really pulling the strings and, as such, is profoundly vulnerable. Even before the crumbling of her wealth and position, Jasmine's life proves to be precarious. After all, what caused her to turn her husband in to the FBI was his announcement that he was about to abandon her for a teenage au pair (in other words, it's possible to read Jasmine's fall as a punishment for aging). And Blanchett's performance highlights this inequality: even "on the top of the world" with Hal, as Chili puts it, Jasmine is insecure, needy, and dependent on her husband's approval. Neediness, rather than calculation, is what drives her. As Blanchett plays it, even her decision to turn her husband in is a desperate grasp at control, not a play for revenge.

Jasmine is smart—she was an anthropology major and a straight A student—but she can't figure out how to navigate her new world. She *does* try. Blanchett's choice to highlight Jasmine's intelligence and pride, rather than her snobbishness, is on clear display in a bar scene between Jasmine and her dentist employer, where she reluctantly agrees to get a drink with him after work. At first, she is cynical and sullen, her face tired and eyes lowered. However, her lack of effort to please also renders her unusually frank; she even seems to be enjoying her increasingly drunken world-weariness. When the smarmy dentist makes his move she stares at him, incredulous and dismayed, her wounded pride registering through the slight furrowing of her brow. What Blanchett could have played with flippancy or contempt, instead she plays with intense focus that channels not disdain but rage: Jasmine knows she's trapped, but she refuses to be flattered.

This is what makes the film's climax so genuinely heart-breaking. Discarded by the Marin prince Dwight, who finds out about her past, Jasmine stumbles for a last attempt at connection to the music shop where her ex-stepson Danny (Alden Ehrenreich) works. Her opening gambit is poorly pitched, but her slack face and eyes tell a different story. Danny is cold, however. He tells her he knows "the whole story," which we then watch unfold: Jasmine confronting Hal about his infidelities is gas-lighted by his cruel composure, and, in a panic, sobbing and gasping for air, she phones the FBI. "The moment I did what I did I regretted it," she begs Danny, who turns her away. How can our sympathy not be with Jasmine, whatever her selfishness? She's been rejected at every turn. When she gets back to Ginger's, sweating and disheveled, she's like a cornered tiger, growling miserably and impotently, but we can see in her pleading eyes and slightly opened mouth that she hears Ginger's critique that her cavalier selfishness and Hal's are the reason she failed. Jasmine swallows, and snaps back, narrowing her eyes and pursing her lips high-and-mightily. This final play at being Jasmine-in-command—the sing-song voice chattering knowingly with the high-cheeked half-smile, despite her wet eyes and face and tensed, diminished carriage—ends as she lies that she and Dwight will be spending "the next few years in Vienna," her haughtiness massively undercut by her shaky unbuttoning of her dress.

Williams, in the end, holds out hope for his Blanche: flirting with the doctor who comes to take her away, she ends the play in camp grandeur. *Blue Jasmine* does no such thing. Blanchett plays Jasmine, in the end, as confused and alone, truly pathetic. Once her failure to repair a semblance of a life feels complete, Jasmine is deflated: her hair wet, and wearing no makeup, she shuffles down the San Francisco street and sits on a bench, muttering to herself, distracted, her gaze far away. Unmoored from a filmic flashback, Jasmine's madness is complete: now she mutters lines that actually don't add up. The film gives her one final gift, however. The ubiquitous retro jazz on the soundtrack shifts into "Blue Moon," and for one last time, the film matches her fantasy. "Blue Moon," she mumbles, "I used to know the words. I don't know the words. Oh, they're all a jumble."

Playing madness

Without a theater, David Thomson writes, "the only thing an actor can do is play scenes alone in his room, or walk the streets talking the lines. We have all of us edged away from those talking people; you know the way we write them off as disturbed or troubled. As if anyone ever thought that successful actors had grown sane on the life of pretending" (87). Thomson's description of acting and its nearness to insanity, in both concept and appearance, provides a strikingly apt portrait of Blanchett's performance of Jasmine, whose sanity ebbs and flows throughout the film as she attempts to find what we call a world. It turns out that acting a woman who is always acting and acting madness aren't far apart. Playing a scene that isn't happening: isn't this what actors do? Framed slightly differently, it's what crazy people do, too. Jasmine first shows her mental disintegration by acting scenes without a scene partner: her dialogue with no one on the couch in her sister's house, on the street, at a party, where her conversation seems normal enough that someone nearby inquires whether she's talking to him. She could almost be an actress running lines.

There's another track on which her disintegration runs, however, one that provides a counterpoint to these scenes where she is out of joint with the temporal reality of the story. At several points, Jasmine flies into miniature arias of psychic dissolution. Naremore notes that performances of "drunkenness or addiction provide excellent opportunities to show a character losing expressive control" (76), and indeed, Jasmine's arias often appear when she's drinking, as her eyes dampen and her fidgeting becomes sloppy. In a scene adapted from *Streetcar* but tellingly transformed, Jasmine interrupts Chili's game-watching with his friends to ask if they can turn down the volume on the television set while she studies. In *Streetcar*, when Blanche and Stella come home to find Stanley and his friends still playing their poker game, Blanche's intrusions are flirtatious, provocative; in *Blue Jasmine*, they're anxious, overwhelmed. When Jasmine first appears in the doorway to the living room, she's already sweating and unkempt, and despite her attempts at holding it together—for the first part of the scene, she keeps her voice mostly steady, intoning in her melodic aristocratic cadence, with chin up—she loses it quickly when Ginger baits her with their mother's taunt that her, "she got the good genes." Shaking her hands in two impotent fists by her face, she growls, "Aw, who do I have to sleep with around here to get a Stoli martini with a twist of lemon!" A pause, and then, just as quickly, as the room stills with embarrassment, she snaps out of it, glancing back and forth as she realizes what she's said. The unseemliness of her outburst is telling: it's a sudden jolt of camp in an otherwise realist scene. And not just any camp, but movie star camp. For a second, she is channeling a deranged Norma Desmond, vengefully demanding her due. Even these displays of Blanchett's prowess as a realist actress—able to move in and out of psychic states and convincingly "lose expressive control"—refer to Jasmine the character as a kind of actress in an acting lineage. If Allen's script provided the raw material for this allusion, it's Blanchett who makes it sing, her own technical brilliance and virtuosity giving us permission to enjoy the spectacle of an actress falling apart.

Vivien Leigh, the most famous Blanche DuBois of all, was given electroshock treatment during the London run of *Streetcar*. Our Jasmine was given "Edison's Medicine," too, as she reveals in a darkly funny scene with Ginger's two children at Chuck E. Cheese's. Thomson recounts Leigh's breakdowns during her tenure as Blanche in brushstrokes Jasmine would know well: "On several occasions," he writes, "Mrs. [Irene Mayer] Selznick, her producer, had to take Vivien off for electroshock treatment, which even then was known to disturb the memory, and discombobulate the personality—as if an underground pressure was being put on the actress to speak the part from out of herself—to blurt it out, under stress—rather than trust the lines" (90). This hardly describes Blanchett, but it does describe Jasmine, who blurs her performance so completely that once the run is over, she's bereft of all coherence.

Works cited

Naremore, James. *Acting in the Cinema.* Berkeley: University of California Press, 1988.

Thomson, David. *Why Acting Matters.* New Haven, CT: Yale University Press, 2015.

Chapter 24

Oscar Isaac in *A Most Violent Year*

Charles Ramírez Berg

Oscar Isaac's leading role as Abel Morales, the beleaguered New York City businessman in J. C. Chandor's *A Most Violent Year* (2014), won him his first major acting prize, the Best Actor award from the National Board of Review. Coming on the heels of Isaac's breakthrough characterization of the forlorn title character in the Coen Brothers' *Inside Llewyn Davis* (2013), his part in Chandor's film was probably the most challenging of his early film career, because *A Most Violent Year* fits squarely in theme, tone, iconography, and visual style within the gangster genre, a familiar film formula with a storied history that stretches back more than a century. Isaac's job was to develop the character of Abel with the ghosts of innumerable movie gangsters—and the actors who played them—looking over his shoulder.

Isaac responded to this acting "anxiety of influence" by turning in an original, powerful, and nuanced performance, a remarkable, multilayered turn that succeeded at three levels: performance, genre, and ethnic representation. Isaac, collaborating with writer-director Chandor, contributed to the creation of the character of Abel Morales. He revised the gangster character template. And he countered the genre's generally patronizing and condescending treatment of immigrants, creating in the bargain a new kind of Latino character.

Like all gangster films, *A Most Violent Year* is a morality play about the price of success in America. Isaac's Abel is an ambitious but besieged New York City entrepreneur trying to expand his heating oil business during the winter of 1981, the most lawless time in the city's recorded history. And like many gangster film protagonists who work their way up from the bottom, Abel is pressured to adopt violence as the easiest way—maybe the only way—to achieve and maintain the American Dream. To tell his tale, writer-director Chandor employs all the trappings of a typical gangster picture: moody, coffee-colored, low-key lighting; cramped, claustrophobic mise-en-scène and production design; an ominously hushed soundscape where any sudden noise might signal a threat; and the pervasive menace of goons with guns. Chandor wasn't aiming to make yet another gangland saga, however. His goal was to revise the genre by making a pacifist gangster movie. Rather than resorting to crime, Abel, a Latin American immigrant, is determined to find an honest and honorable pathway to mainstream success. Because the film had to look like a gangster flick while cutting against the genre grain, Isaac faced a number of daunting hurdles.

First, to bring something original to a genre that has produced some of the most memorable performances in film history: James Cagney in *Public Enemy* (1931), Edward G. Robinson in *Little Caesar* (1932), Paul Muni in the original *Scarface* (1932), to say nothing of Marlon Brando, Robert De Niro, and Al Pacino in *The Godfather* trilogy, Pacino's Cuban immigrant mobster in the *Scarface* remake (1983), as well as the mobsters played by De Niro, Joe Pesci, Jack Nicholson, Ray Liotta, and others in Martin Scorsese's extensive gangster filmography. How could Isaac avoid imitating such celebrated portrayals and add something fresh to an established movie character?

Complicating the issue was Abel's radical, even antithetical departure from the movie gangster protagonist, as a law-abiding businessman who rejects criminality. In a genre where the spectacle of violence is a key element, could the internal journey of a stubbornly nonviolent man make for captivating drama? Only if Isaac could externalize Abel's internal ethical dilemma.

In a typical gangster movie, the morality-of-violence question quickly becomes moot once the hero opts for violence, thereby unleashing some of the genre's more spectacularly familiar tropes: machine-gun shootouts, drive-by killings, merciless assassinations, score-settling murders, tortures, and executions. But *A Most Violent Year*'s story is not the standard simmering-until-it-explodes tale of a gangland war erupting between competing families. Its central conflict is individual and existential: at a time when social mores all around him are unraveling, will Abel capitulate to temptation and choose lawlessness? Or will he find the strength to adhere to his personal moral code? The performer's acting challenge was how to depict a character's interior state and make it clear, comprehensible, and compelling.

Isaac found a way. He broke new ground, overcame these obstacles, and his performance and the film were praised. Besides Isaac's Best Actor award, his co-star, Jessica Chastain, who plays Abel's wife, won the National Board of Review's Best Supporting Actress prize; the film was named the NBR's Best Film of the Year, and *A Most Violent Year* landed on numerous critics' yearly top ten lists (Dietz). Moreover, Isaac's performance had a significant ripple effect. Beyond upending gangster genre conventions, it positively affected the history of ethnic representation in film by successfully countering the century-long stereotype of the vicious and impulsive Latino male.

Acting analysis: methodology and assumptions

Filmmaking is such a complex and collaborative artistic activity that we'll never have a complete accounting of all the creativity involved in producing a film. At the same time, there are ways to gather a partial sense of what formed a performance and the actor's participation in it. One important factor in the present case was writer-director Chandor's cooperative directorial style, which not only allowed for collaboration but counted on it. The script, he told his players, "is what the movie you're going to be in looks like. Now you have to come and be this piece in it . . . Are you prepared to do that? And do you have ideas to help me tell that?" (in David Poland, *DP/30: The Oral History of Hollywood: A Most Violent Year*, online at www.youtube.com/watch?v=Mzh3FsLyfnM). This accommodating attitude allowed Isaac to contribute meaningful aspects to Abel's backstory and characterization.

Isaac's most substantial contribution was elaborating Abel's immigrant experience. Soon after signing on (after Javier Bardem, initially contracted, had left the picture), Isaac raised the obvious biographical questions about Abel that were not indicated in the script. When did he emigrate to the US and from where exactly did he come? It turned out that Isaac's own history— born in Guatemala and brought to the US as a five-month-old infant—was similar to Chandor's invention for Abel. Where Abel came from specifically was left for Isaac to discover, a creative opportunity the actor appreciated. "J.C. didn't want to just lay it [Abel's character] all out," he recounted later. "He wanted me to arrive at it" (Poland interview 1181). After researching Latin American history of the 1950s and 1960s, he filled in Abel's biography with what was for him a vital piece of character-building information, that Abel and his family came from Colombia, fleeing the ferocious civil war called "La Violencia" during the 1950s (Poland interview 1168).

That piece of personal history was crucial to Isaac's development of Abel's character, providing the motivation for a dogged anti-violent stance; resisting violence as an adult was the natural result of Abel's experiencing and escaping from it as a young boy, the foundational core of his identity that he would carry into his business dealings as an adult. But will Abel abide by that code when robbers begin hijacking his company's delivery trucks, assaulting his drivers and sales staff, stealing his oil, and jeopardizing a land purchase for a planned expansion? Isaac understood how deeply personal Abel's moral dilemma was. Abel had fled "La Violencia" "to show up for a better opportunity in this country," Isaac said, "and then at the moment that he's deciding to risk everything, it's also the time when violence is . . . chasing after him. So it is . . . an existential crisis for him" (Poland interview 1168).

Rejecting violence makes rational sense, and Abel is nothing if not a rational man, so his public, business persona is that of a calm, self-assured company head. But "backstage," in his private interactions with Anna (Jessica Chastain), who is also his accountant and business partner in the Standard Heating Oil Company, Abel reveals the emotions he hides from public view. He is a tender and supportive husband, a loving and caring partner, and sometimes, as business pressures begin to mount unbearably, impatient, exasperated, and angry. Again, in Isaac's words, "Apart from the . . . cold, calculating businessman, this isn't someone who is guarded with his emotions throughout. He's actually someone who's highly emotional and highly passionate" (Poland interview 1168).

That duality attracted Isaac to the role. He was fascinated by the tension within Abel's character, the pull between "what he's trying to project . . . and what he can't help but project," the rationality and the emotion (Poland interview 1181). As the film begins, Abel has mastered this balancing act and runs a growing, profitable business, his success built on impulse control. When thugs begin attacking his company's trucks and physically assaulting his drivers, he is pressured by the teamster's representative to allow them to carry side arms: "Let' em protect themselves. These are dangerous times and we have to adapt." Abel rejects the idea. Even his wife, whose father has gangland ties, believes it's time to respond to violence in kind. "We're at war here," she pleads. "No we're not," he insists. "Really? Because they are." Still, he keeps his cool and remains adamant—no guns. "He doesn't want to play that game," Isaac said about Abel's anti-violent stance, "he wants to play his game" (Poland interview 1181). How Abel reacts when his company's future is on the line will be the film's central question. How to dramatize Abel's inner turmoil would be Isaac's.

Using a well-known gangster archetype (in this case, Al Pacino's Michael Corleone) is a clever acting strategy because one may employ it in order to reverse it. The whole point of *A Most Violent Year* is to linger on Abel's agony as he strains to remain nonviolent. But to do his character's inner torment justice, Isaac would need to find a way to make the strain dramatic. Luckily for him, the method was right there in Chandor's script, in an early scene where Abel instructs his new sales team during a training session.

The sales lesson as acting lesson

"Now, you do this and only this." Abel is teaching three newly hired salespeople how to get prospective customers to switch from a competing oil delivery service to Standard. He shows how to inspect the home heating unit, then wipe it with a cloth. Looking down, he continues, "You don't say a word. You just stare down at the cloth and v-e-r-y s-l-o-w-l-y you just start shaking your head." Abel shakes his head, demonstrating the move, "Then," he continues, "after sitting in silence way longer than is comfortable, you turn. And say, 'I'd love to run a few numbers for you. Is there somewhere more comfortable we could sit?'"

Abel is a director, orchestrating every detail of his team's performance in a carefully scripted and meticulously timed scene. Having gone over the cost estimate, they are to perform a move he now specifies: after a short pause, "You look up at them," says he, taking a longer pause.

"And stare," demonstrating the look with the longest pause of all. He stares at each one of the new sales reps in turn. "*Stare longer than you should,*" he says, and with another prolonged silence he stares at them yet again—a look so long that one of the novice salesmen can't prevent his smile from becoming a laugh. "This is not a joke!" Abel quickly snaps the meeting back to serious business. "These people work very hard for their money, and these other guys are ripping them off... So when you look them in the eye you have to believe that we are better. And we are." He concludes with the lesson's crucial principle, one that is at the heart of both good salesmanship and effective acting: "You will never do anything as hard as staring someone straight in the eye and telling the truth."

Isaac is playing the role of a man who's playing the role of the honest businessman he aspires to be. The sales lesson is both his and the character's "acting technique," identical for both. Abel never acts out of character, never loses control of himself—or the situation. And so, in every public encounter—with the District Attorney, or with a needling competitor at a barbershop, or with the boss of the teamsters' union, or with the elderly Hassidic Jew who owns a parcel of land he's put a down payment on to expand his business, Abel reacts slowly, calmly, and deliberately, taking the time to gather himself and make a respectful and measured response, never an angry, heated, or reckless one. To portray a man who presents himself as his notion of an ideal businessman, Isaac is doing exactly the same thing.

The best place to appreciate Isaac's multi-tiered performance is at the climactic meeting of the heads of the heating oil companies. Knowing that one if not several of his competitors are behind the attacks on his trucks and the robbery of his oil, Abel has requested a meeting. There he plays his part and delivers his lines in precisely the way he taught his sales reps to do.

The big meeting

Chandor's script doesn't indicate the degree of Abel's controlled, unemotional delivery, nor the volume of the evenly modulated speech Isaac produces. Furthermore, Abel's dramatic, drawn-out silent pauses are only roughly suggested in the text (Chandor 107–8). Exactly in Abel's style, Isaac stretches his silences out "way longer than is comfortable."

Those pauses are so protracted that the attendees become uncomfortable. Onscreen, the silences are so unusually and increasingly prolonged it's hard to think of a movie precedent.

As Abel and his lawyer (Albert Brooks) join the assembled group of heating oil company owners, he is greeted by the union boss, Bill O'Leary (Peter Gerety): "Abel, please, sit down." He sits, unbuttons his suit jacket, and scoots his chair closer to the table; pan-scans the attendees around the circular table, stopping and holding on O'Leary. For *seven long seconds*, he says absolutely nothing, merely taps a clenched fist on the table three times. Breaking the awkward silence, O'Leary says, "Abel,—" offering the floor. Abel turns to glance at his lawyer, then looks at the others and waits *ten seconds*. Then he turns, faces forward, and says one word: "Stop."

Uttered in a normal tone of voice, this is more a statement than a command or threat. He scans the assembly, and Chandor cuts back and forth between Abel's looking at the other men's attentive but blank reactions. They're waiting for him to continue, elaborate, say anything at all, any words to fill the aching vacuum. Abel lets silence engulf the room—this time for *seventeen seconds*.

Finally, Peter Forente (Alessandro Nivola), the group's dapper young spokesman, speaks up. We've just discussed your situation, says he, and we've determined that the "guys who are doing this . . . don't actually work for anyone in this room."

Cool and respectful, Abel nods. Courteously: "Peter, thank you. Thank you. That may be true." After a *five-second* pause, that he spends looking at Forente, he presents his case to the group. (Here I quote the dialogue, describing Isaac's added, unscripted contributions in italic):

> Over the last six months 110,000 gallons of fuel have been stolen from me and my *family*.
> *[He pauses for THREE SECONDS to let that last word sink in.]* Now the reason we asked Bill to get you all here is because the people at this table are the only people within two hundred miles of here who have the ability to purchase and store that kind of quantity. *[THREE-SECOND pause during which he doesn't move. He's letting this sink in too.]* So . . . *[Abel slowly leans forward during a FOUR-SECOND pause, with just the trace of a smile appearing on his face, a look that indicates he's not buying Forente's explanation.]* . . . no matter what bullshit you've been telling each other, one of you . . . or two . . . or three . . . have been allowing this to happen by buying it from these cowards, or worse yet hiring them to do it. So, what I am saying is:

stop. *[During a SIX-SECOND pause, he nods his head, with a stern look on his face.]* Now. *[Giving them a hard look, he slowly stands, and turns to leave. He stops himself, though, and after NINE SECONDS turns back to them and concludes with a scolding final point:]* Have some pride in what you do and stop.

He turns and walks off, buttoning his coat on his way out.

Here is an extended version of the act Abel taught his crew, in a peerless performance of the upright businessman character. Impressively, Isaac has used the same technique in *his* performance, pushing it nearly to the cinematic breaking point, stretching out looks, pauses, and silences. It's a masterful exhibition of composure, poise, patience, and musicality. Abel of course appears through this scene to be pausing and waiting to create dramatic tension, pausing and waiting, as it were, invisibly.

Given time to plan ahead, then, Abel is very good at playing a part. At other times in the film, faced with unexpected on-the-job hitches, he is still able to portray the sensible company head as long as he has a moment or two to collect himself. What will he do, though, when events unexpectedly overtake him, and he doesn't have time to take a deep breath, gather himself, and slip into character? What will his reflexive reaction be when he catches two thugs in the act of stealing one of his trucks?

The trembling hand

As Abel is driving his Mercedes the next day, he spots two hijackers race right in front of him in a company truck. He accelerates to follow, and during a high-speed chase the robbers lose control of the truck, flipping it on its side. The driver has been knocked unconscious or killed, we can't tell, and the second thief escapes on foot. Picking up a pistol the bandit left behind, Abel runs after him, catching up at a deserted subway stop. He tackles the man to the ground, beating him with the gun. "Who hired you? Who do you work for?" The man won't talk, so Abel slugs him with the pistol several more times, then cocks it and shoves the barrel into one of his eye sockets.

"Please!' the man pleads, begging for his life, "Please!"

Abel's gun hand trembles uncontrollably. Finally, dropping his head, he pulls the gun away and climbs off. "Go," he tells him, "get outta here."

The crook struggles to stand, mumbles where he sells the oil he's been stealing from Abel, and staggers off.

The script called for Abel to start "beating on him very, very badly with the pistol. All the rage comes out of him. He then aims the gun" (Chandor 112). But the specifics as Isaac acts them—the number of hits, the barrel to the eye, the quivering hand—are none of them indicated. Nor are the details of Abel's merciful decision to let the culprit go free: "ABEL looks right through him and then finally lowers the gun and releases his hands from around [the culprit's] jacket..." (113).

Isaac's addition of the shaking hand is the telling detail, a visible way to chart Abel's gradual transition from rage to reason. Faced with a personal, criminal threat, Abel's anger is understandable. And his ability to regain his composure, not fire the gun, and release the culprit is likely due to a combination of bedrock moral beliefs and years of rigorously practiced self-discipline. Isaac found an effective way to show that even when pushed to the limit Abel still reverts to the part of the sensible, steady company owner, not the brash, hot-tempered Latino.

New takes on the gangster protagonist and the Latino male

Recounting a mobster's rise and fall, the gangster genre's grim critique of American capitalism is succinct and disheartening: success = crime and, since the gangster usually dies, crime = death. Viewers, Robert Warshow has argued, are taught to lower their sights, content themselves with failure, and soldier on, frustrated but alive (103). The armature that drives the genre is a certain type of protagonist: a tragic scapegoat whose reflexive brutality doesn't require explanation: an Other. Usually this means someone from the underclass, an immigrant or person from immigrant stock, or a member of a racial or ethnic minority, someone from a group whose stereotypical movie profile tags them as possessing a low emotional flashpoint and poor planning and coping skills, who is prone to violence and unencumbered by socially accepted moral and legal codes of behavior. Paul Muni's Italian American Tony Camonte in the original *Scarface* and Al Pacino's Cuban immigrant Tony Montana in the 1983 remake are textbook examples. Even Pacino's cerebral Michael Corleone fits the bill once it becomes clear that behind his calculating, Ivy-League-educated façade lies a cold-blooded killer.

Isaac's work in *A Most Violent Year* counters these familiar ethnic stereotypes in gangster movies as well as Latino stereotypes in American films in general, in many ways that layer his performance. First, his Abel replaces the barbarous, short-fused ethnic gangster with a thoughtful and self-regulated businessman struggling for legitimate success, even while everyone around him says that's impossible. Second, Isaac's Abel revises the tempestuous, hot-blooded Latino stereotype rooted in the familiar *bandido* villain of countless westerns and his more recent stereotypical descendants, urban gang members and maniacal Mexican drug lords. With Abel, we have something new, an anti-*bandido*. Abel, Isaac told one interviewer, "was the very first time that you see a Latin American man portrayed this way. He's not a gangster; he's nonviolent, he's powerful, he's quintessentially American, and he's not a sidekick. We get to see a very un-clichéd look at the Latin American immigrant experience and really what the backbone of this country is" (Zayda Rivera, "Oscar Isaac Talks 'A Most Violent Year' and Why He Changed His Latino Last Name," *New York Daily News*, 27 January 2015, online at nydailynews.com).

Finally, Isaac's multilayered performance brings an unexpected depth to Abel Morales, and a character with depth is never a stereotype. Instead of the clichéd Latino, Isaac created an American Everyman. As such, he joined a long line of movie strivers who have tried to better themselves in America. Armed not with a gun but with a long-term strategy, he is intelligent, confident, and determined, *acting* like the successful man he wants to become, and refusing to allow anything to divert him. Isaac's Abel is a new Latino twist on Horatio Alger.

All of this film's central reversals—Abel as an ambitious but non-violent non-gangster, as anti-*bandido*, and as the Latino Everyman—owe their trailblazing screen life to Oscar Isaac. His disruption of a long history of gangster genre protagonists and his overturning of stereotypical Latino portrayals was achieved in the best way imaginable for an actor, by successfully creating a complex, fascinating, and multidimensional character. In the truest sense of the saying, Abel Morales was a role Oscar Isaac was born to play.

Works cited

Chandor, J. C. *A Most Violent Year*. Online at gointothestory.blcklst.com/wp-content/uploads/2014/12/A-Most-Violent-Year.pdf.

Dietz, Jason. "Best of 2014: Film Critic Top Ten Lists," *Metacritic* (6 December 2014), online at www.metacritic.com.

Feinberg, Scott, and Tatiana Siegel. "Oscar Isaac, J. C. Chandor Team Up for 'A Most Violent Year' (Exclusive)," *The Hollywood Reporter*, 3 December 2013, online at hollywoodreporter.com.

Poland, David. Interview with J. C. Chandor and Oscar Isaac. *DP/30: The Oral History of Hollywood*, A Most Violent Year, 14187-#1168, online at youtube.com/watch?v=Mzh3FsLyfnM.

Poland, David. Interview with Oscar Isaac. *DP/30: The Oral History of Hollywood*, A Most Violent Year, 14200-#1181, online at youtube.com/watch?v=0g0nmXZx2M0.

Warshow, Robert. "The Gangster as Tragic Hero," in *The Immediate Experience: Movies, Comics, Theatre, and Other Aspects of Popular Culture*, Enlarged edn., Cambridge, MA: Harvard University Press, 2002, 97–103.

Chapter 25
Kristen Stewart in *Clouds of Sils Maria*
Elliott Logan

> I mean, she's got great presence, but I don't see what's so daring about it. (Maria (Juliette Binoche) in *Clouds of Sils Maria*)

Many of the plaudits that flow towards a star performance for playing strongly "against type" are, by now, familiar. For the film star looking to refurbish her image, a well-worn strategy is to seek out roles that will allow her to demonstrate—and critics to recognize—a level of acting talent, skill, and dedication that may have seemingly laid dormant until this special role. Consider, for instance, some recent cases of spectacular (and award-winning) actorly transformation: Matthew McConaughey as AIDS patient Ron Woodroof in *Dallas Buyers Club* (2013), Nicole Kidman as Virginia Woolf in *The Hours* (2002), or, perhaps the epitome of the phenomenon, Charlize Theron as serial killer Aileen Wuornos in *Monster* (2003). The relation between the star's existence on and off the screen, in a set of films and outside of them, is a perennial issue in thinking about movie stars in particular and film acting more generally. See, for example,

Cavell (25–9, 35), and Pomerance (esp. 67–85). Pomerance notes our potential attraction to a split between the actor's actual self and his screen roles in his discussion of Peter O'Toole: "Is not the break between a man like this and the men he becomes in front of the camera something to shock us and provoke wonder? How many civilians are living inside that body?" (79).

In each of the above-mentioned performances we see a star escaping a familiar screen image, and the accolades that followed support and reflect what George Toles describes as "the well-entrenched view that impressive film acting is measured by a performer's capacity to separate himself or herself from the restrictions and worrisome facility of the type (or persona) that the viewer associates with that actor" (33). That is to say, transformational star performances appeal to a widely held criterion of good acting: that an actor should craft and exploit a clear split between his fictional role and the audience's sense of the actor's own self—who the actor "really is." As Toles goes on to note, this criterion has a negative corollary in our tendency to dismiss a performance that works comfortably within the bounds of a star's known and accepted type, on the basis that their familiar screen presence hardly counts as acting. The stars are just "playing themselves" (33).

The case of Kristen Stewart in Olivier Assayas' *Clouds of Sils Maria* (2014), like the performances cited above, presents another instance of a star's critical transformation. A common critical response to *Clouds* was to express some surprise at the depth of Stewart's acting talent revealed by her performance. Not only was her performance a fixture of the acclaim for the film, Stewart won a César, France's highest award for film performance. A good measure of Stewart's critical elevation in the years immediately following the release of *Clouds* can be found in the July-August 2016 issue of *Film Comment*. On the cover is an image of her from *Personal Shopper* (2016), caught in a characteristically ambiguous pose: her hands are loosely held at her chest, her eyes cast just down off-camera, her expression muted and difficult to read. The headline accompanying the image declares it is "The Age of Kristen Stewart."

The praise for Stewart's acting, both in *Clouds of Sils Maria* and since, is noteworthy in light of her history as a movie star. Stewart began acting as a child, and received modest appreciation for her performances in a handful of films during the mid-to-late 2000s, among them *Into the Wild* (2007), *Adventureland* (2009), and *The Runaways*

(2010). During these years, however, Stewart's image was dominated by her starring role in the hugely popular *Twilight* series (2008–12); and, consequently, celebrity, fandom, and commodity stardom largely framed popular and critical discussions of her onscreen work as an actor. As Nick Davis observes in his *Film Comment* profile, neither Stewart's *Twilight* fans nor those critics who had noted her promise in other roles would likely have predicted "her recent spike in critical cachet" (26).

At the same time, however, the rapid discovery of Stewart's acting talent in *Clouds* cannot be understood on the model of the star actor playing "against type." Unlike Charlize Theron in *Monster*, for example, Stewart doesn't undergo a radical transformation, nor does she play a character wildly at odds with our sense of who she might be. In the film, Stewart plays Valentine, a young, outwardly confident personal assistant to the older acting star Maria Enders (Juliette Binoche). Valentine is comfortable with the pressures and traps of the film publicity machine, and negotiates film festival appearance management, high-end fashion shoots, and the red carpet with familiar ease. She displays the host of absentminded mannerisms that are found across the characters Stewart has played. Her performance is a veritable catalogue of her distinctive acting tics: a rapidly tapping foot, a sharp intake of breath, distracted scratching at an elbow or a forearm, worried biting at her lower lip, and so on. It can seem, if only for brief moments, as though Stewart's characters feel unsure how to hold themselves in a way that would comfortably stand the attention of others. And yet they have easy grasp of a confident self-possession, appearing to treat almost any situation as though it simply called for them to be ordinary. These twinned aspects of Stewart's performing style have particular implications in the case of Valentine. In her professional role as Maria's assistant, she is required to stand alongside Maria with ease during moments of intense publicity, such as at film premieres and film festival opening galas, while also accompanying Maria in moments that afford closer, less consciously performed companionship between employer and assistant, such as during backstage preparation, or, as we see later in the film, the ordinary routines of domestic life. Where Valentine's professional role and her less public relationship with Maria overlap, we see her struck by an anxious struggle to settle into an appropriate comportment.

A useful way to think about Stewart's seemingly reflex set of gestural tics can be found in certain paintings made during the eighteenth century by the French artist Jean-Baptiste-Siméon Chardin—paintings of people who, in states of deep absorption, appear to neglect otherwise nagging details of their appearance and surroundings. Such details function, for art historian Michael Fried, as "signs of the [painted] figure's obliviousness" to all but the activity they are immersed in, to the extent that they are free from the pressures of being watched (47). Through her absentminded mannerisms, Stewart's characters can seem highly conscious of scrutiny from the gaze of others while also, at other moments, appearing to be largely unaffected by the pressures of being looked at. And so, across Stewart's roles, the consistent appearance of gestures like those described above have helped to define her screen presence in paradoxical terms of both self-consciousness and unselfconsciousness.

A useful handle on Stewart's minimalist approach can be found in the terms that George Toles provides to characterize a very different actor's way of "underplaying." In his essay on Gary Cooper, Toles notes how Cooper's "signature moments show him 'apart' from acting somehow," as he sustains our interest by "not 'doing' much of anything" (34). While Stewart and Cooper may otherwise not have much in common, the idea of a performer appearing to be "'apart' from acting somehow" by "not 'doing' much of anything" approaches something crucial to Stewart's compelling screen presence, one that might draw the backhanded compliment that her talent is simply to "play herself." As Davis observes, one plausible reason that Stewart's style may have gone unappreciated

> is her commitment to a low-fuss, conversational directness that is rare among modern film performers, particularly in roles that accommodate flashier approaches. Instead, she has persuaded film culture to meet her where she lives—in a laconic, minutely expressive, barely laminated register of acting that's confusable with "just being." (20)

Stewart's performance as Valentine shows little sign of any attempt to jettison her established screen presence, one that is "confusable with 'just being.'" So why is it with *Clouds of Sils Maria* that Stewart's acting is found to hold especially compelling power and depth? How does Stewart work firmly within her established screen type or persona, while at the same time revealing previously unappreciated qualities and skills as an actor?

A key to answering these two questions can be found during certain moments in one arresting scene from the second part of *Clouds of Sils*

Maria. In the film's first part, we are introduced to Valentine and Maria as they travel by train to Zurich, where Maria is to accept an award on behalf of the publicity-shy playwright and director Wilhelm Melchior. Twenty years earlier, Maria starred in the original cast of Melchior's play *Maloja Snake* and rose to fame for her definitive performance as Sigrid—a young personal assistant to a middle-aged businesswoman named Helena. In Melchior's play, Sigrid draws Helena into a love affair but then abandons her, and the play ends with Helena committing suicide. En route to Zurich, Valentine gets news that Melchior has died. The award ceremony thus takes on the character of a sudden wake and public memorial, and it is in this context that Maria agrees to act in a new production of *Maloja Snake*, this time playing not the young Sigrid but the older character of Helena. The mirroring of Sigrid and Helena in Valentine and Maria is only the broadest example of the film's sometimes dizzying self-reflexivity. Maria has difficulty playing Helena because she carries strong memories of her performance as Sigrid, residual feelings that color her sense of Valentine's assistantship, the younger woman gradually coming to echo for Maria that character she played onstage two decades before; is Maria, in turn, a preview of Valentine's own future (and, at another level, of Stewart's)? Sigrid is now to be played (in an echo of Stewart herself) by the eighteen-year-old phenomenon Jo-Ann Ellis (Chlöe Grace Moretz), an up-and-coming Hollywood ingenue famous for starring in science-fiction blockbusters and who is fodder for considerable online celebrity gossip.

Valentine accompanies Maria to Melchior's house in the Swiss countryside, as Maria, today a film actress of pronounced international reputation, prepares for her upcoming role. The key moments of Stewart's performance arrive during the first of several scenes where Maria rehearses the role of Helena while Valentine reads the part of Sigrid. As they rehearse, the relationship between Valentine and Maria seeps into the fictional drama between Sigrid and Helena. As we watch the rehearsal scenes, it at times becomes very difficult to tell whether Valentine and Maria are performing *Maloja Snake* "in character" as Sigrid and Helena or whether, in certain moments, they are hardly putting on these fictional characters at all. It sometimes feels as though they are instead reading and responding to one another's lines simply as "themselves"—addressing each other through the very fortuitously scripted dialogue of Melchior's play.

The rehearsal scenes thus stage a self-reflexive interplay between the deliberate performance of a fictional role (i.e. Valentine as Sigrid) and the more unselfconscious, seemingly natural inhabitation of one's "actual self" (i.e. Valentine or Maria as themselves). In this way, the scenes further reflect on the extent to which Stewart is herself putting on an act in order to play Valentine. The ambiguity of whether we are seeing a performance, or simply someone being herself, is especially heightened in the case of Valentine who, unlike Maria, is not an actor. So it is plausible that Valentine should fall short of a transformational performance as Sigrid— one consistent with, to again quote Toles, the belief that "impressive film acting" is "measured" by the performer's ability to "separate" herself from a familiar type or persona (33). The character of Sigrid might offer Valentine an opportunity for such separation, to display, by exploring a wider-than-usual expressive spectrum, aspects of herself that she might not ordinarily make visible. Valentine might take the chance to shed her typical sense of self in order to enjoy a brief holiday as a very different person, namely Sigrid. But this is not the route that the film takes. In Stewart's performance, Valentine's attempts to perform Sigrid are only weakly differentiated from Valentine's usual expressive manner. Stewart thus blurs the boundary between Valentine simply "being herself" (as Maria's personal assistant) and Valentine "putting on" the character whose lines she is reading (as Sigrid, Helena's personal assistant). That is, the role of Valentine allows Stewart to maintain a broadly consistent expressive register while keeping fine control over multiple layers of performance. In this way, the rehearsal scenes in *Clouds of Sils Maria* provide a fitting context for Stewart to work within her distinctively minimalist approach to film performance—what Davis described as a "laconic, minutely expressive, barely laminated register of acting that's confusable with 'just being'" (20)—while also revealing the intelligence and skill of her acting that may otherwise go overlooked or underappreciated.

The subtle precision of Stewart's performance is most concentrated during particular moments of expressive transition in the first of the rehearsal scenes. Here, Stewart's achievement is to somehow have Valentine slide from a lacklustre and seemingly uncommitted reading of Sigrid's part into an absorbing performance as Sigrid, while avoiding any clear sense that Valentine is "putting on" the character. We rather get the strange impression that the more convincingly Valentine reads Sigrid's lines, the less she appears to be performing the character of Sigrid at all. At certain points, we might feel that in response to Maria's performance as Helena Valentine is simply delivering Sigrid's lines as herself. We are thus drawn into a strange, paradoxical tension. As we sense that Valentine is increasingly absorbed by the role of Sigrid, the more the role absorbs her identity, the more personally exposed to Maria she seems to become.

This tension is valuable not simply because it would be difficult to achieve but more so because it is necessary to the interest and success of the scene itself. A central interest of the rehearsal scenes is the way that Valentine and Maria's reading of the play has them give voice to aspects of their relationship that might ordinarily have gone unspoken. In the *Maloja Snake* scene that Valentine and Maria rehearse, Helena invites Sigrid into her office and asks Sigrid to become her personal assistant. Complimenting Sigrid's successful internship, Helena also expresses her jealousy of Sigrid's popularity at the company, where Helena is keenly aware of being disrespected, seen by employees and board members as the beneficiary of her father's nepotism—the undeserving head of a firm whose profits are in decline. Helena says that she finds her employees' praise for Sigrid personally humiliating, and that she can only feign the youthful vitality and self-possession that Sigrid more naturally possesses. The dialogue conveys Helena's attraction to the aspects of Sigrid that she painfully lacks in herself, whether they have been lost to age, or whether they were never really hers at all. But Sigrid senses that Helena's attraction may run more deeply than mere admiration—she suggests that what truly troubles Helena is a desire for Sigrid that Helena cannot face or hide.

The harboring of obscure desires is raised between Valentine and Maria the night before the first rehearsal scene takes place. Over dinner, Valentine presses Maria as to whether there was any sexual attraction between her and Melchior during their production of *Maloja Snake* twenty years earlier. Maria dances around the issue, saying, "Maybe I only remember what it suits me to remember." Later in the evening, Maria reveals a need for Valentine's affections when she reacts to her admiration of Jo-Ann Ellis with a wounded jealousy shaded by a sense of emotional betrayal, albeit kept from full expression by a slight tone of cold irony. Against this background, the *Maloja Snake* scene speaks to an undercurrent in Valentine and Maria's relationship that both women appear to sense, but can acknowledge only indirectly.

But the rehearsal of the scene can only tease out hidden aspects of Valentine and Maria's relationship if both Maria *and* Valentine are drawn into the fictional roles they are reading. If Valentine were to read her lines in a way that was too far "outside" the role of Sigrid, as though

Valentine were oblivious to the implications of the lines being spoken, we would have only a distanced recognition that the dialogue echoes the relationship between her and Maria. We would not develop the different kind of understanding that the rehearsal scene, as played by Stewart and Binoche, seems meant to support: our more deeply felt sense that, in delivering their lines, both Valentine and Maria find themselves momentarily exposed to oblique truths about their relationship. And so it is important that Valentine give an increasingly convincing reading as Sigrid, but without her emotional credibility seeming the effect of acting technique, which might impose too clear a distance between Valentine's inner sense of self and the emotional states that, as Sigrid, she is outwardly projecting. Stewart must maintain our sense of Valentine as a novice performer without access to well-practiced tools of expressive transformation.

The first rehearsal scene is quite long, nearly seven minutes, and so a comprehensive account is beyond the scope of this essay. In what follows, then, my more modest aim is to briefly analyse some moments that highlight Stewart's successful handling of the tensions outlined above. I hope to show how such moments reveal Stewart's ability to make, within a restricted range, fine adjustments of expression that have thoughtful implications without feeling thought-out.

The key moments of Stewart's performance in the first rehearsal scene are those of Valentine's apparent absorption in the role of Sigrid, but it is not yet clear how such absorption is to be distinguished. In his discussion of performance in *Psycho* (1960), however, Alex Clayton provides a useful measure of an actor's absorption in his role. Contrasting one scene from Hitchcock's film with its counterpart in Gus Van Sant's 1998 remake, Clayton notes how the "general flatness of delivery in the reconstructed scene highlights the extent to which Janet Leigh and Anthony Perkins are fully 'inside' the film, grasping the multiple implications of particular lines and picking them out through intonation" (75). Stewart has Valentine appear to be "inside" her role as Sigrid by handling Valentine's absentminded gestures so that they express the "multiple implications" of Sigrid's lines, "picked out through intonation" that remains consistent with Valentine's own, typically unselfconscious manner.

Stewart prepares these moments of Valentine's absorption by the way she handles Valentine's initial gestures and lines at the rehearsal's beginning, which conveys a split between Valentine and the part that she is reading. That split is highlighted by the way Maria prepares to enter into the part of Helena. Before rehearsal commences, Maria declares which pieces of furniture and which architectural features of the room will be part of the makeshift stage setting. Maria anoints each touchstone with a firm, definitive gesture: two solid pats on an armchair, a sharp sweep of each arm to mark the threshold of Helena's office door, and a clap of her prop notebook onto the dining table that will serve as Helena's desk. Maria's neat placement of the notebook solidifies her move into a posture of seated containment as she assumes Helena's command over her imaginary office. Maria thus reinforces, both for the watching Valentine and for herself, a solid boundary that would separate the ordinary space of the living room from the theatrical setting of the drama between Sigrid and Helena.

Stewart, by contrast, has Valentine approach Sigrid's opening actions with a mix of reluctance towards committed performance and gestures of overt, theatrical play-acting. Valentine arrives on her mark at Helena's office door, for example, with a slack shuffle of her feet, her weight falling casually onto her cocked left hip, as though not stepping out of herself and into character but simply going through the motions. And when Helena instructs Sigrid to take a seat, Valentine mistakenly goes to sit at a dining chair Maria had briefly considered as a stage prop, but had ultimately left out of the play's bounds. Maria has to then break character to correct Valentine, who turns to instead sit in the armchair Maria had specially singled out. At the moment she is interrupted from taking a seat, Valentine has one hand on the back of the dining chair, which, echoing Maria's consideration of the chair as a prop, she has tilted on two legs. Stewart doesn't try to cover-up the mistake through a subtle recovery, but instead replaces the chair with a sullen flourish, snatching back her hand into a clenched fist and dropping the chair with a scraping clump. Striding to the armchair she clears her throat, as though swallowing an irritation.

Because we have not seen any expressive transition marking Valentine's move "into character" as Sigrid, and because the business with the chair briefly suspends the fiction of the play, Stewart's gestures might seem to express Valentine's own frustration at Maria's pedantic order. Our sense that Valentine is fully removed from any attempt to occupy the character of Sigrid dissolves, however, as she takes her seat in the armchair. Valentine moves to the armchair with a few sharply paced steps, echoing the snap of her hand from the dining chair. But as Stewart lowers herself into the armchair, her movements seem to slow, as though her momentum is now restrained and gathered. There is a more deliberate sense of self-containment, as when she neatly tucks her hair behind one ear and delicately folds her right leg over her left while turning in the same direction to face Binoche, her head tilted precisely so her gaze is cast out from just below the frame of her glasses. Stewart's expression retains its muted neutrality, but her eyes harden. They issue an invitation to the onlooker in the form of a quietly alluring challenge, pressing for a response to this little display. Stewart thus has Valentine appear increasingly composed, but also posed. And so we develop, for the first time in the scene, a sense of Valentine shedding her usual presentation of self and putting on a performance as Sigrid. The moment may even cast a light shadow back over our reading of her business with the chair, now emerging, in hindsight, as a theatrical expression of Sigrid's self-confident contempt for Helena's authority.

Much of the ensuing dialogue in the *Maloja Snake* scene belongs to Helena, which Maria delivers at a languid tempo while pacing the room around the seated Valentine, who watches, listens, and is occasionally called on to respond. But where Stewart had Valentine "put on" the part of Sigrid by occupying the armchair with a display of polished composure, she now gives Sigrid's dialogue in a flat ramble. Each line is more or less simply read out, as though the words hold no precise dramatic meaning to be discerned through careful inflection. This is especially felt in the somewhat chaotic pacing of her delivery. Stewart skips natural pauses, with the effect that Sigrid's questions of Helena come across as blunt and pre-fabricated, rather than spontaneously formed in the space of Sigrid's mind. This first, half-wooden attempt at a rehearsal of the scene suddenly collapses when Maria flubs a line and violently breaks out of character into a torrent of self-directed abuse. Soon after, Valentine and Maria try to run the scene again, this time while sitting opposite one another at the outdoor breakfast table, which still bears the remnants of their morning meal.

Maria picks up the scene where they had earlier broken off. Helena is explaining why she feels humiliated by her employees' admiration for Sigrid. "It's to remind me," Helena says, "how happy they are to grant you what they never granted me. They're using you to humiliate me. It's not just your youth, or your powers of seduction. No—it's your aplomb, your unshakeable self-confidence." It is while she listens to this catalogue of Sigrid's qualities that Stewart comes to most convincingly occupy both Valentine and Sigrid simultaneously. The way Stewart responds to the delivery of Helena's lines has both a weight and a spontaneity that contrasts with her manner during Valentine and Maria's first attempt to read the scene. There, Valentine's spontaneity seemed to work outside of the play's meaning (her release of frustration with the chair), and her weight "as Sigrid" felt imposed in the form of an underlined theatricality. Whereas here at the breakfast table, in the second attempt to run through the scene, Valentine sustains her typical, unadorned way of being even as the timing and tone of her most unassuming gestures show her to be drawn more deeply inside the exchange between Sigrid and Helena.

As Helena tells Sigrid of her "powers of seduction," for instance, Assayas cuts to a shot favoring Stewart in time to catch her push her glasses back up the bridge of her nose, with the knuckle of one finger, as she holds eye contact with Binoche, her head tilted just slightly to the left. The gesture never steps out of the ordinary but suggests a touch of toying play. And as Helena's dialogue continues, onto Sigrid's "aplomb" and "unshakeable self-confidence," Stewart's gesture with the glasses slides into a distracted scratch at her forearm. With just the hint of a sharp shake of her head, as though irritated by something she has heard before, Stewart flicks her eyes away from Binoche and says, simply, without hesitation or defensiveness, "You don't know me." On "me," the eyes dart back, to once again return Maria's stare to which Valentine finds herself subjected. But Helena insists: "Nothing gets to you. You radiate self-confidence." In response to the idea that nothing "gets to her," Stewart stops scratching at her arm and instead plants her hand between her crossed thighs, as though to hide a hint of agitation by covering it up in a posture of comfortable self-possession. Stilling her aimless hand and drawing herself together, she gains composure in response to attention. Here, within Valentine's reflex gestures of discomfort Stewart contains the proof of Helena's claim as to Sigrid's "radiant self-confidence."

By not making any outward attempt to "separate" from her typical sense of self, Valentine can be responsive to the dialogue's implications, as though she herself were affected by the words and spurred into a set of intuitive, emotionally driven reactions. In doing so, Valentine finds the quality of absorbed "innerness" that makes credible and compelling her performance as Sigrid. Reflecting what binds us to Kristen Stewart's distinctive screen presence, Valentine's act feels less like a performance, and closer to a privately thoughtful but unselfconscious inhabitation of another person within herself.

Works cited

Clayton, Alex. "The Texture of Performance in Psycho and Its Remake," *Movie: A Journal of Film Criticism* 3 (2011), 73–9.

Davis, Nick. "Hiding in Plain Sight: The Casual Complexity and Low-Key Intensity of Kristen Stewart," *Film Comment* 52: 4 (2016), 18–23.

Fried, Michael. *Absorption and Theatricality: Painting and Beholder in the Age of Diderot.* Berkeley: University of California Press, 1980.

Toles, George. "Believing in Gary Cooper," *Criticism* 45: 1 (2003), 31–52.

The cast

Ethel Waters (Chester, Pennsylvania, 31 October 1896–1 September 1977, Chatsworth, California). *The Member of the Wedding* was released 22 December 1952.
Irene Dunne (Louisville, Kentucky, 20 December 1898–4 September 1990, Los Angeles, California). *The Awful Truth* was released 21 October 1937.
Cary Grant [Archibald Alexander Leach] (Horfield, Bristol, UK, 18 January 1904–29 November 1986, Davenport, Iowa). *His Girl Friday* opened 11 January 1940.
Janet Gaynor [Laura Augusta Gainor] (Germantown, Pennsylvania, 6 October 1906–14 September 1984, Palm Springs, California). *Sunrise: A Song of Two Humans* was released 23 September 1927.
Katharine Hepburn [Katharine Houghton Hepburn] (Hartford, Connecticut, 12 May 1907–29 June 2003, Fenwick, Connecticut). *The Lion in Winter* was released 30 October 1968.
Bette Davis (Lowell, Massachusetts, 5 April 1908–6 October 1989, Neuilly-sur-Seine, Hauts-de-Seine, France). *Dangerous* was released 25 December 1935.
James Stewart [James Maitland ("Jimmy") Stewart] (Indiana, Pennsylvania, 20 May 1908–2 July 1997, Beverly Hills, California). *Vertigo* premiered 9 May 1958 in San Francisco.
Carole Lombard [Jane Alice Peters] (Fort Wayne, Indiana, 6 October 1908–16 January 1942, Mount Potosi, Nevada). *To Be or Not to Be* was released in Los Angeles, 15 February 1942.
James Mason (Huddersfield, Yorkshire, 15 May 1909–27 July 1984, Lausanne, Vaud, Switzerland). *Lolita* was released 13 June 1962 in New York City.
Montgomery Clift [Edward Montgomery Clift] (Omaha, Nebraska, 17 October 1920–23 July 1966, New York, New York). *A Place in the Sun* was released 15 August 1951.
Tony Curtis [Bernard Schwartz] (The Bronx, New York, 3 June 1925–29 September 2010, Henderson, Nevada). *Sweet Smell of Success* premiered 24 June 1957 in New York City.
Peter Sellers [Richard Henry Sellers] (Portsmouth, UK, 8 September 1925–24 July 1980, London). *The Pink Panther* premiered in West Germany, 19 December 1963. Sellers was a Commander of the British Empire.

Richard Burton (Pontrhydyfen, Wales, 10 November 1925–5 August 1984, Céligny, Switzerland). *The Spy Who Came In from the Cold* was released 16 December 1965. Burton was a Commander of the British Empire.

Jerry Lewis [Joseph Levitch] (Newark, New Jersey, 16 March 1926 –20 August 2017, Las Vegas, Nevada). *The King of Comedy* was released 18 February 1983.

Sidney Poitier (b. The Bahamas, 20 February 1927). *In the Heat of the Night* was released 2 August 1967. Sir Sidney Poitier is a Knight Commander of the British Empire.

Gene Hackman [Eugene Allen Hackman] (b. San Bernardino, California, 30 January 1930). *The Conversation* premiered 7 April 1974 in Los Angeles.

Gena Rowlands [Virginia Cathryn "Gena" Rowlands] (b. Madison, Wisconsin, 19 June 1930). *Gloria* was released 1 October 1980.

Jack Nicholson [John Joseph Nicholson] (b. Neptune City, New Jersey, 22 April 1937). *The Passenger* [*Professione: Reporter*] was released in the United States, 9 April 1975.

Dustin Hoffman [Dustin Lee Hoffman] (b. Los Angeles, California, 8 August 1937). *Rain Man* was released 16 December 1988.

Elliott Gould [Elliott Goldstein] (b. Brooklyn, New York, 29 August 1938). *The Long Goodbye* was released for a limited engagement 7 March 1973 and generally 28 October 1973.

Al Pacino [Alfredo James Pacino] (b. New York, New York, 25 April 1940). *Donnie Brasco* was released 28 February 1997.

Whoopi Goldberg (b. New York, New York, 13 November 1955). *The Color Purple* was released 18 December 1985.

Cate Blanchett [Catherine Elise "Cate" Blanchett] (b. Melbourne, Australia, 14 May 1969). *Blue Jasmine* premiered in New York, 26 July 2013.

Oscar Isaac [Óscar Isaac Hernández Estrada] (b. Guatemala, 9 March 1979). *A Most Violent Year* premiered at the AFI Festival, 6 November 2014.

Kristen Stewart (b. Los Angeles, California, 9 April 1990). *Clouds of Sils Maria* was released at Cannes, 23 May 2014.

The contributors

Brenda Austin-Smith is Associate Professor and Head of the Department of English, Film, and Theatre at the University of Manitoba, where she teaches courses on Film and the City, cult film, documentary, and cinephilia. She is co-editor, with George Melnyk, of *Canadian Women Filmmakers: The Gendered Screen*, and has published recent essays on the odd couple of Henry James and Alfred Hitchcock, on screen acting, on James's *The American Scene*, and on cultural publishing by the Canadian left.

Rebecca Bell-Metereau teaches film, English, and directs the Media Studies Minor at Texas State University. She wrote *Hollywood Androgyny* and *Simone Weil*, co-edited *Star Bodies and the Erotics of Suffering*, wrote chapters in *Acting for America; A Little Solitaire; Cinema and Modernity; American Cinema of the 1950s; Film and Television after 9/11; Bad: Infamy, Darkness, Evil, and Slime on Screen; Ladies and Gentlemen, Boys and Girls; Writing With Technological Imperatives; Women Worldwalkers*; and essays in *College English, Quarterly Review of Film and Video, Journal of Popular Film & Television*, and *Cinema Journal*.

Charles Ramírez Berg is University Distinguished Teaching Professor in the Department of Radio-TV-Film at the University of Texas at Austin. He is the author of *Latino Images in Film; Cinema of Solitude: A Critical Study of Mexican Film, 1967–1983; Posters from the Golden Age of Mexican Cinema*; and *The Classical Mexican Cinema: The Poetics of the Exceptional Golden Age Films*. In addition, he has written numerous articles on Latinos in US film, Mexican cinema, film history, and narratology that have appeared in journals such as *Jump Cut, Film Criticism*, and *CineACTION*, as well as anthologies like *Film Genre Reader IV, A Companion to Film Theory, The Latino Condition, John Ford Made Westerns*, and *A Little*

Solitaire: John Frankenheimer and American Film. He has also contributed entries to the *World Film Encyclopedia*, *The International Dictionary of Films and Filmmakers*, and *The Oxford Encyclopedia of Latinos and Latinas in the United States*.

Janet Bergstrom, Research Professor of Cinema & Media Studies, UCLA, specializes in archivally-based, cross-national studies of émigré directors such as F.W. Murnau, Jean Renoir, Josef von Sternberg, Alfred Hitchcock, and Fritz Lang as well as French/Francophone directors Chantal Akerman and Claire Denis. She has published five film historical documentaries on DVD, most recently *Josef von Sternberg—Salvation Hunter* (Edition Filmmuseum, Austrian Film Museum, Vienna) with Sternberg's *The Salvation Hunters* (1924).

John Bruns is Professor of English and Director of Film Studies at the College of Charleston. He is the author of *Loopholes: Reading Comically*. His film articles have appeared in *Hitchcock Annual*, *Film Criticism*, and *New Review of Film & Television Studies*.

Alex Clayton is Senior Lecturer in Film and Television at the University of Bristol. His research interests include film criticism, the aesthetics of comedy, and the body in performance. He is the author of *The Body in Hollywood Slapstick*, co-editor of *The Language and Style of Film Criticism*, and sits on the editorial board of *Movie*. He is currently preparing a book about sketch comedy.

Shonni Enelow is the author of *Method Acting and Its Discontents: On American Psycho-Drama*. She is an assistant professor of English at Fordham University.

Anna Everett is a Professor of Film, Television and New Media Studies at the University of California, Santa Barbara. Her many publications include the books *Returning the Gaze: A Genealogy of Black Film Criticism, 1909–1949*; *Learning Race and Ethnicity: Youth and Digital Media* (for the MacArthur Foundation's Digital Media, Youth, and Learning program); her 2009 award-winning book *Digital Diaspora: A Race for Cyberspace*; and the edited volume *Pretty People*, among others. She is completing a book on President Obama, social media and millennials.

Lucy Fischer is a Distinguished Professor of English and Film Studies at the University of Pittsburgh where she directed the Film Studies Program for thirty years. She is the author of twelve books: *Jacques Tati*; *Shot/Countershot: Film Tradition and Women's Cinema*; *Imitation of Life*;

Cinematernity: Film, Motherhood, Genre; Sunrise; Designing Women: Art Deco, Cinema and the Female Form; American Cinema of the 1920s: Themes and Variations; Body Double: The Author Incarnate in the Cinema; and *Cinema by Design: Art Nouveau, Modernism, and Film History* (forthcoming); and has edited *Stars: The Film Reader* (with Marcia Landy); *Teaching Film* (co-edited with Patrice Petro); and *Art Direction and Production Design*. She has held curatorial positions at the Museum of Modern Art (New York City) and the Carnegie Museum of Art (Pittsburgh), and has been the recipient of both a National Endowment for the Arts Art Critics Fellowship and a National Endowment for the Humanities Fellowship for University Professors. She has served as President of the Society for Cinema and Media Studies (2001–3) and in 2008 received its Distinguished Service Award. In 2016, she received the Chancellor's Research Award for Senior Scholars at the University of Pittsburgh.

Lester D. Friedman is emeritus professor in Media and Society Program at Hobart and William Smith Colleges. Author, co-author, or editor of over twenty books and numerous articles, his areas of academic specialties include: film genres, American cinema of the 1970s, American Jewish cinema, British film of the 1980s, Health and Humanities, and Multiculturalism in film. He has written books about Steven Spielberg, Arthur Penn, Peter Pan, Frankenstein, and Clint Eastwood. He has authored two screenplays, *Prisoners of Freedom* (2002) and *Thomas Szasz and the Myth of Mental Illness* (1989).

Frances Gateward teaches courses on film and popular culture in the Department of Cinema and Television Arts at California State University Northridge. Her research focuses on issues of culture, power, and privilege as constructed in media texts. She has published in numerous anthologies and film journals. Her books include The *Blacker the Ink: Constructions of Black Identity in Comics and Sequential Arts*, co-edited with John Jennings and winner of the Eisner Award, Pen Oakland Literary Award, and the 2016 Roy and Pat Browne Best Edited Collection Award from the Popular Culture Association/American Culture Association; *Seoul Searching: Culture and Identity in Contemporary Korean Cinema*, and *Where the Boys Are: Cinemas of Masculinity and Youth*, with Murray Pomerance. She is currently working on a book about black women filmmakers.

David Greven is Professor of English at the University of South Carolina. His most recent books are *Intimate Violence: Hitchcock, Sex, and Queer Theory; Queering the Terminator;* and *Ghost Faces: Hollywood and Post-Millennial Masculinity*.

Jason Jacobs is Professor of Film and Television Studies and Head of the School of Communication and Arts at the University of Queensland. He was a lecturer in the Department of Film and Television Studies at the University of Warwick (1994–2000), and Griffith University (2000–8). His books are *The Intimate Screen; Body Trauma TV*; and *Deadwood*. He co-edited the collection *Television: Aesthetics and Style*, and has published essays on issues of judgment and value in television studies.

Elliott Logan is a doctoral candidate at the University of Queensland, Brisbane. He is the author of *Breaking Bad and Dignity*.

Douglas McFarland is retired Professor of English and Classical Studies at Flagler College, Saint Augustine, Florida where he taught Renaissance literature, Latin, and Greek. He has published on sixteenth-century English and French literature, as well as numerous articles and chapters on film. He is the co-editor (with Wesley King) of *John Huston as Adaptor*.

Adrienne L. McLean is Professor of Film Studies at the University of Texas at Dallas, and the author of *Being Rita Hayworth: Labor, Identity, and Hollywood Stardom*; and *Dying Swans and Madmen: Ballet, the Body, and Narrative Cinema*. She is the editor of *Behind the Silver Screen: Costume, Makeup, and Hair*; and *Cinematic Canines: Dogs and Their Work in the Fiction Film*, and co-editor of *Headline Hollywood: A Century of Film Scandal* as well as a ten-volume book series, "Star Decades: American Culture/American Cinema", with Murray Pomerance. Her own entry in the series is *Glamour in a Golden Age: Movie Stars of the 1930s*. She has published numerous essays in film journals and anthologies, and is working on a monograph on makeup and hair in the studio era.

R. Barton Palmer is Calhoun Lemon Professor of Literature at Clemson University, where he also directs the World Cinema program. Palmer is the author or editor of more than forty volumes devoted to various film and literary subjects, and he serves as the general editor of book series at six academic publishers. He is also the editor of the *South Atlantic Review* and the *Tennessee Williams Annual Review*.

Homer B. Pettey is Professor of Film and Comparative Literature at the University of Arizona. He serves as Founding and General Editor for three scholarly book series on global film studies. He is co-editor (with R. Barton Palmer and Steven M. Sanders) of *Hitchcock's Moral Gaze*, and has co-edited a forthcoming volume on biopics and British national identity. He has two other collections in progress: *French Literature on Screen* and *Emerging Cold War Film Genres*.

Murray Pomerance is Professor in the Department of Sociology at Ryerson University and the author, editor, or co-editor of numerous volumes. His most recent books are *The Man Who Knew Too Much*; *A King of Infinite Space*; and *Moment of Action: Riddles of Cinematic Performance*. He edits the "Horizons of Cinema" series at SUNY Press and "Techniques of the Moving Image" series at Rutgers University Press.

William Rothman is Professor of Cinema and Interactive Media at the University of Miami. He was founding editor of the "Harvard Film Studies" and "Cambridge Studies in Film" series. His own books include *Hitchcock—The Murderous Gaze*, *The "I" of the Camera*, *Documentary Film Classics*, *Reading Cavell's* The World Viewed: *A Philosophical Perspective on Film*, and (as editor) *Cavell on Film*, *Jean Rouch*, *Three Documentary Filmmakers* and (as co-editor) *Looking with Robert Gardner*.

Steven Rybin is Assistant Professor of Film Studies in the English department at Minnesota State University, Mankato. He is the author of *Gestures of Love: Romancing Performance in Classical Hollywood Cinema*; and editor of *The Cinema of Hal Hartley: Flirting with Formalism*, among other books, book chapters, and articles.

Kyle Stevens is Assistant Professor of Film Studies at Appalachian State University. He is the author of *Mike Nichols: Sex, Language, and the Reinvention of Psychological Realism*, and his essays have appeared in *Cinema Journal*, *Critical Quarterly*, *Film Criticism*, and *World Picture*, as well as several edited collections. He is also editor-in-chief of *New Review of Film and Television Studies*.

George Toles is Distinguished Professor of Literature and Film at the University of Manitoba. He has recently published a study of Paul Thomas Anderson and is also the author of *A House Made of Light: Essays on the Art of Film*. For twenty-five years George was the screenwriting collaborator of Canadian filmmaker Guy Maddin. He has written the original story and co-authored the screenplay of *Edison and Leo*, Canada's first stop-motion animated feature. His work on acting includes forty years of directing professional and University theatre productions.

Daniel Varndell is an interdisciplinary film scholar who lectures in English Literature at the University of Winchester. He is the author of *Hollywood Remakes, Deleuze and the Grandfather Paradox*, and his most recent publications include book chapters on Hal Hartley and John Barrymore. He is currently working on a new monograph on torture and etiquette in film performance.

Timotheus Vermeulen is Associate Professor in Media, Culture and Society at the University of Oslo. His current research interests are metamodernism, contemporary film and television aesthetics (in particular, space) and the philosophy of the "as-if". He is joint editor with Alison Gibbons and Robin van den Akker of *Metamodernism: History, Affect and Depth after Postmodernism*, and together with Martin Dines edited *New Suburban Stories*. In 2014 he published the monograph *Scenes from the Suburbs*.

Rick Warner is Assistant Professor of Film and Kenan Fellow in the Department of English and Comparative Literature at the University of North Carolina at Chapel Hill. He is co-editor of *True to the Spirit: Film Adaptation and the Question of Fidelity*, with Colin MacCabe and Kathleen Murray; and *The Film-Philosophy Reader*, a forthcoming three-volume anthology, with Gregory Flaxman and Elena Oxman. He guest edited a special issue of *Critical Quarterly* on Jean-Luc Godard's late films and videos (October 2009). He is the author of numerous chapters and journal articles on film aesthetics, technology, and history, and is currently finishing a book titled *A Form that Thinks: Godard and the Cinematic Essay*.

Index

39 Steps, The (Alfred Hitchcock, 1935), 147
4 Devils (F. W. Murnau, 1928), 54
7th Heaven (Frank Borzage, 1927), 47–8

Abrams, Nathan, 142
Actors Studio, the, 6
Adam's Rib (George Cukor, 1949), 61
Adorno, Theodor, 142
Affron, Charles, 5, 68–9
African Queen, The (John Huston, 1951), 61
Alice Adams (George Stevens, 1935), 60
All About Eve (Joseph L. Mankiewicz, 1950), 77
Althusserian Marxism, 3
Austin, J. L., 1
Awful Truth, The (Leo McCarey, 1937), 25–35, 39

Balázs, Béla, 7
Baldwin, James, 170–1
Barnes, Peter, 91, 94
Baron, Cynthia, 5, 200
Barthes, Roland, 77

Baudrillard, Jean, 163
Beavers, Louise, 18
Benjamin, Walter, 6–7
Benny, Jack, 91
Bergan, Ronald, 213, 218
Bergson, Henri, 142
Beyond the Forest (King Vidor, 1949), 76
Birth of a Nation, The (D. W. Griffith, 1915), 18
Black Power, 170
Blanchett, Cate, 253–62
Blue Jasmine (Woody Allen, 2013), 253–62
Bob & Carol & Ted & Alice (Paul Mazursky, 1969), 224
Bogart, Humphrey, 223
Bragg, Melvyn, 150, 154
Brando, Marlin, 101, 264
Brecht, Bertolt, 4
Bringing Up Baby (Howard Hawks, 1938), 29, 39, 42, 61
Britton, Andrew, 40

Brunette, Peter, 204–5
Burton, Richard, 147–56
Butler, Judith, 1

Cagney, James, 264
Camus, Albert, 116
capitalism, 271
Caps, John, 137
Carnicke, Sharon Marie, 5, 200
Carol (Todd Haynes, 2015), 258
Cavell, Stanley, 1, 26, 33, 37, 94, 148–9, 214, 226
Chatman, Seymour, 203, 206
Civil Rights Movement, the, 14, 19, 21, 169–71, 173
Clayton, Alex, 138, 281
Clift, Montgomery, 111–23
Clouds of Sils Maria (Olivier Assayas, 2014), 274–84
Color Purple, The (Steven Spielberg, 1985), 243–51
Conversation, The (Francis Ford Coppola, 1974), 178–87
Cooper, Gary, 277
Curtis, Tony, 124–34

Dangerous, 67–77
Davenport, Guy, 165
Davis, Bette, 67–77, 191
Davis, Brenda, 60
Davis, Nick, 276
Dawson, Kellie, 102
De Niro, Robert, 264
Depp, Johnny, 237–8

Desk Set (Walter Lang, 1957), 61
DiBattista, Maria, 26–7
Dietrich, Marlene, 254
Donen, Stanley, 39–40
Donnie Brasco (Mike Newell, 1997), 234–42
Dufrenne, Mikel, 141, 144
Dunne, Irene, 25–35
Dyer, Richard, 5, 174

Edelstein, David, 180
Eliot, Marc, 43
Epstein, Jean, 7

Farber, Manny, 214
feminism, 196, 258
Five Easy Pieces (Bob Rafelson, 1970), 201
Fried, Michael, 277

gangster films, 263–5, 267, 271–2
Garland, Judy, 4
Garner, James, 223
Gaynor, Janet, 47–54
Geduld, Harry M., 66
Gehring, Wes D., 25–6
Giant (George Stevens 1956), 123
Gledhill, Christine, 174
Gloria (John Cassavetes, 1980), 188–98
Godfather II, The (Francis Ford Coppola, 1974), 235

Goffman, Erving, 1, 126, 129, 133, 138, 154
Goldberg, Whoopi, 243–51
Gould, Elliott, 223–32
Graduate, The (Mike Nichols, 1967), 130, 214
Graham, Martha, 75
Grant, Cary, 27–31, 34, 36–45, 79
Guerrero, Ed, 170
Gunga Din (George Stevens, 1939), 39

Hackman, Gene, 178–87
Harlem Renaissance, the, 15
Harris, Mark, 172
Harvey, James, 26
Hepburn, Katherine, 29, 56–66, 254
Him (Candice Breitz, 2008), 201
His Girl Friday (Howard Hawks, 1940), 36–45
Hoffman, Dustin, 130, 212–22
Holiday (George Cukor, 1938), 39
Holmes, Phillips, 118
Holmlund, Chris, 245
Horkheimer, Max, 142
Hud (Martin Ritt, 1963), 149
Hyden, Steven, 185–6

improvisation, 34, 106–7, 159, 164, 176, 225, 228–9

In the Heat of the Night (Norman Jewison, 1967), 169–76
Isaac, Oscar, 263–72

Jackson, Cartlon, 149
jazz, 225
Jim Crow, 22, 24
Johnny Guitar (Nicholas Ray, 1954), 93
Johnstown Flood, The (Irving Cummings, 1926), 48
Julius Caesar (Joseph L. Mankiewicz, 1953), 101

Kael, Pauline, 38–9, 42–5, 214
Kaufman, Sarah, 38–9
Kelly, Amy, 59
Kerouac, Jack, 116, 225
Kidman, Nicole, 274
King of Comedy, The (Martin Scorsese, 1982), 158–68
Klaprat, Kathy, 70
Klevan, Andrew, 5, 148–9, 209n2, 237
Knight, Arthur, 65
Kolker, Robert, 167
Kouvaros, George, 5, 8
Kuleshov, Lev, 7, 127, 150, 202

Laing, R. D., 219
Langer, Susanne, 7

Lanzoni, Rémi, Fournier, 150
late-night television, 158–61, 167
Lavater, Johann Caspar, 129–30
Lerner, Ben, 234–5, 241
Letner, Kenneth J., 136
Lewis, Jerry, 158–68
Lewis, Roger, 135–6
Life and Death of Peter Sellers, The (Stephen Hopkins, 2004), 137
Lion in Winter, The (Anthony Harvey, 1968), 56–66
Lolita (Stanley Kubrick, 1962), 100–10
Lombard, Carole, 29, 91–9
Long Day's Journey into Night (Sidney Lumet, 1962), 57
Long Goodbye, The (Robert Altman, 1973), 223–32
Lyon, Sue, 103

Mandelbaum, Howard, 70, 72, 76
Mask, Mia, 250
Mason, Clifford, 170
Mason, James, 100–10
McConaughey, Matthew, 274
McDaniel, Hattie, 18
McQueen, Butterfly, 18
melodrama, 5, 18, 20, 148, 220
Member of the Wedding, The (Fred Zinnemann, 1952), 13–24

Merleau-Ponty, Maurice, 221
Meryman, Richard, 180
Method acting, 5–7, 23, 77, 107, 151, 174, 176, 204
Miller, Gabriel, 155
Mitchum, Robert, 131–2, 223
modernism, 152, 200, 208, 229
Monroe, Marilyn, 10
Montaigne, Michel, 174
Montgomery, George, 223
Montgomery, Robert, 223
Morning Glory (Lowell Sherman, 1933), 60
Moser, Laura, 68
Most Violent Year, A (J. C. Chandor, 2014), 263–72
Muni, Paul, 264, 271
Munn, Michael, 150, 152–3
Murphy, Kathleen, 235
My Favorite Wife (Garson Kanin, 1940), 39
My Man Godfrey (Gregory La Cava, 1936), 29

Naremore, James, 2–3, 5, 11, 40, 73, 254
Newman, Paul, 149
Nicholson, Jack, 199–210, 264
North by Northwest (Alfred Hitchcock, 1959), 103
Notorious (Alfred Hitchcock, 1946), 42
Novack, Kim, 81–2

O'Brien, George, 48–9, 52, 54
Ocean's Eleven (Steven Soderbergh, 2001), 228
Of Human Bondage (John Cromwell, 1934), 68
Only Angels Have Wings (Howard Hawks, 1939), 39
O'Toole, Peter, 56, 58, 61

Paar, Jack, 158–60
Pacino, Al, 234–42, 264, 271
Paglia, Camille, 217
Parsons, Louella, 125
Passenger, The (Michelangelo, Antonioni, 1975), 199–210
Pat and Mike (George Cukor, 1952), 61
Peacock, Steven, 183
Pearson, Roberta, 5
performance studies, 5, 199
Perkins, Anthony, 130
Perkins, V. F., 99, 238
Philadelphia Story, The (George Cukor, 1940), 39
Pink Panther, The (Blake Edwards, 1963), 135–45
Pinky (Elia Kazan, 1949), 14, 22
Place in the Sun, A (George Stevens, 1951), 111–23
Poitier, Sidney, 169–77
Pomerance, Murray, 5, 9, 26, 129, 142–4, 236, 274–5
poststructuralism, 4

Powell, Dick, 223
Psycho (Alfred Hitchcock, 1960), 81, 130, 213, 281
psychoanalysis, 3
psychological realism, 10–11, 256
Pudovkin, V. I., 197

Rain Man (Barry Levinson, 1988), 212–22
Rear Window (Alfred Hitchcock, 1954), 86
River of No Return (Otto Preminger, 1954), 131–2
Robinson, Edward G., 264
Rowlands, Gena, 188–98
Russworm, TreaAndrea, 170
Ryan, Robert, 111

Salinger, J. D., 116
Sandpiper, The (Vincente Minnelli, 1965), 152
Sansom, Ian, 1
Santayana, George, 135, 139–40, 144
Sarris, Andrew, 79
Sartre, Jean-Paul, 11
Scarface (Brian de Palma, 1983), 235
Schatz, Thomas, 67, 70
Schickel, Richard, 41, 70, 72
screwball comedy, 25–6, 29–30, 36–7, 39

Sellers, Peter, 101–3, 107–8, 135–45, 221
semiotics, 3
Shakespeare, William, 1
Shambu, Girish, 8
Shamrock Handicap, The (John Ford, 1926), 48
Shingler, Martin, 72
slow cinema, 209
Smith, Daniel, 214
Smith, Greg M., 236
Sojourner Truth, 20
Spicer, Andrew, 137, 142
Spy Who Came in from the Cold, The (Martin Ritt, 1965), 147–56
Stanislavski, Konstantin, 100, 204
Stanwyck, Barbara, 148
stardom, 6, 68, 111
stereotypy, 6, 14–15, 17–18, 27, 104, 170, 191, 244–5, 265, 271–2
Stern, Lesley, 5, 8
Stevens, Kyle, 5, 11
Stewart, James, 79–90
Stewart, Kristen, 274–84
Strasberg, Lee, 204
Street Angel (Frank Borzage, 1928), 47–8
Streetcar Named Desire, A, 257, 261
studio system, the, 5, 67

Sunrise: A Song of Two Humans (F. W. Murnau, 1927), 47–54
Suspicion (Alfred Hitchcock, 1941), 38
Sweet Smell of Success (Alexander Mackendrick, 1957), 124–34
Swift, Jonathan, 142

Taylor, Elizabeth, 112, 121–3
theatricality, 1, 74, 203, 258, 284
Theron, Charlize, 274
Third Man, The (Carol Reed, 1949), 230–1
Thomson, David, 45, 102, 189, 215, 260
To Be or Not to Be (Ernst Lubitsch, 1942), 91–9
Toles, George, 33, 275, 277, 279
Topper (Norman Z. McLeod, 1937), 39
Twilight series (2008–12), 276
Tynan, Kenneth, 167–8

Ulysses, 223, 232

Verrill, Addison, 65
Vertigo (Alfred Hitchcock, 1958), 79–90

Wanzo, Rebecca, 243–4
Wasson, Sam, 139
Waters, Ethel, 13–24
Weiler, A. H., 125–6
Whitt, Jan, 250
Willis, Sharon, 170
Winters, Shelley, 103
Wittgenstein, Ludwig, 1
Wojcik, Pamela Robertson, 5
Woman Under the Influence, A (John Cassavetes, 1974), 193, 197
Wood, Robin, 40–1
Woodroof, Ron, 274
World of Peter Sellers, The (Tony Palmer, 1969), 135